Using
BASIC

Phil Feldman

Tom Rugg

PROGRAMMING
S E R I E S

CORPORATION
LEADING COMPUTER KNOWLEDGE

Using
BASIC

© 1990 by Que® Corporation

Library of Congress Catalog No.: 89-64230

ISBN 0-88022-537-8

94 93 92 91   8 7 6 5 4

Interpretation of the printing code: the rightmost double-digit number is the year of the book's printing; the rightmost single-digit number, the number of the book's printing. For example, a printing code of 90-1 shows that the first printing of the book occurred in 1990.

Using BASIC is based on versions 2.0 through 3.3 of both Microsoft GW-BASIC and IBM BASICA.

Screen reproductions in *Using BASIC* were produced with InSet, a graphics and text-integrator program from INSET Systems Inc., Danbury, Connecticut.

D EDICATION ▼

For Rosie and Danny

Publishing Manager

Allen L. Wyatt, Sr.

Illustrations

Susan Moore

Cover Design

Dan Armstrong

Production

Bill Basham
Claudia Bell
Brad Chinn
Don Clemons
Sally Copenhaver
Tom Emrick
Denny Hager
Corinne Harmon
Tami Hughes
Bill Hurley
Becky Imel
Jodi Jensen
David Kline
Larry Lynch
Lori Lyons
Jennifer Matthews
Cindy L. Phipps
Joe Ramon
Dennis Sheehan
Mae Louise Shinault
Bruce Steed
Mary Beth Wakefield
Jenny Watson
Nora Westlake

Editors

Rebecca Whitney
Andy Saff

Editorial Assistant

Ann K. Taylor

Technical Editor

Gordon N. Arbuthnot

Indexer

Joelynn Gifford

Composed in Garamond and Universal Monospace
by Que Corporation

Phil Feldman

Mr. Feldman received his B.A. degree in physics from the University of California in 1968 and did graduate work in computer science at UCLA. For 15 years, he worked at TRW Systems, Inc., where he was a manager of software development on numerous aerospace engineering projects. He has written or coauthored many articles in engineering technical journals and personal computer magazines; he has coauthored with Tom Rugg more than a dozen books, including *Using QuickBASIC 4* and *QuickBASIC Programmer's Toolkit*. Mr. Feldman is chairman of 32 Plus, Inc., a software development and consulting firm.

Tom Rugg

Mr. Rugg received his B.S. degree in quantitative methods from California State University in 1969. His 20 years of experience in computer programming and systems analysis include positions with GTE Data Services, Inc., the U.S. Army (Pentagon), and Jet Propulsion Laboratory. He has authored or coauthored many articles in personal computer magazines; he has coauthored with Phil Feldman more than a dozen books, including *Using QuickBASIC 4* and *Turbo Pascal Programmer's Toolkit*. Mr. Rugg is president of 32 Plus, Inc., a software development and consulting firm.

CONTENT OVERVIEW

TABLE OF CONTENTS ▼

I   Fundamentals of BASIC ▼

II   Beginning Programming

4   Language Building Blocks **75**

III   **Intermediate Programming**

IV   Odds and Ends

V   Instant Reference

ACKNOWLEDGMENTS ▼

Hats off to the top-notch staff at Que Corporation—especially Allen Wyatt, who planted the seed and watered the garden, and Becky Whitney, who pruned and landscaped magnificently.

*T*RADEMARK
*A*CKNOWLEDGMENTS

Que Corporation has made every reasonable effort to supply trademark information about company names, products, and services mentioned in this book. Trademarks indicated below were derived from various sources. Que Corporation cannot attest to the accuracy of this information.

CONVENTIONS USED
IN THIS BOOK

A number of conventions are used to increase the readability of this book. All BASIC programs, program excerpts, and DOS commands appear in a monospace font, called `Universal Monospace` so that the type replicates the spacing that appears on the computer screen. Characters that you must type appear in bold.

When we introduce a new term, the term usually appears in *italic* type at its first reference.

Reserved words are in uppercase. These are BASIC's keywords such as `PRINT`, `FOR`, and `DATE%`. Similarly, variable names are also in uppercase. When you type keywords and variable names, you can use upper- and lowercase interchangeably. The book contains uppercase exclusively because, regardless of your typing, the BASIC editor converts lowercase to uppercase when BASIC lists a program.

Keys are referred to as they appear on the keyboard of an IBM PC. A keystroke combination such as Ctrl-F5 means to press the Ctrl key and hold it down while you press the F5 function key.

Writing a book puts pressure on a coding style. For purposes of reproduction in this book, code-line lengths are limited to 72 characters horizontally. Occasionally, we artificially compress program lines by using shorter-than-normal variable names or removing blank spaces that ordinarily appear next to operators. Recognize, however, that BASIC permits lines up to 255 characters and our infrequent style compromises are motivated by production considerations.

As each BASIC statement or function is introduced, we present a box containing the syntax associated with that keyword. Each parameter of the keyword appears in *italic* font, and descriptions of the parameters appear inside the box.

Introduction

More people program in BASIC than in any other computer language. That statement was true 20 years ago, and it is still true today. Why is BASIC so popular? Here are three main reasons:

❏ BASIC is easy to learn. Commands are descriptive and English-like.

❏ BASIC is flexible. Most programming tasks are suitable.

❏ BASIC is readily available. Most personal computers come with a version of BASIC.

BASIC remains popular with beginners and hobbyists. The language is ideal for those learning programming for the first time.

You probably have some questions about this book. Maybe we can anticipate your most likely questions...

Do I Need Any Previous Programming Experience?

None.

We wrote *Using BASIC* with the novice programmer in mind. We don't expect you to know any programming terminology or have previous experience writing programs.

Perhaps you have had some exposure to BASIC or you dabbled with the language some time ago. That's fine. You can build on your previous experience as you work your way through the book.

Why Should I Learn Programming?

Different people have different reasons. Perhaps one (or more) of the following motives applies to you:

❏ You have a specific application (for home or business) for which you cannot find commercially available software. Programmers can write programs that do *exactly* what they want.

❏ You want to learn more about your computer. Programming puts you in control of your machine.

❏ You want to explore the possibility of a career in computers or programming. Many job opportunities exist for qualified programmers.

❏ Programming seems intriguing and you would like to dabble with a new skill. Programming is satisfying and provides a real sense of accomplishment.

❏ You *have* to learn programming, perhaps in school or at your job. Some people in this situation feel apprehensive. Relax. Programming is easier than you think and can be a lot of fun.

What Can I Get from This Book?

Whether you have had some experience or are taking your first programming plunge, you will be able to write sophisticated programs by the time you finish this book.

Exactly what this book offers you depends on your background.

If you have little or no programming experience,

❑ Your biggest concern is becoming productive and comfortable as soon as possible. BASIC may seem a little bewildering at first. Don't worry. Rest assured that BASIC is an excellent tool with which to learn programming. This book should make a trusted teacher and companion.

❑ In some ways you have an advantage over those with previous BASIC experience. After all, you don't have any bad programming habits to overcome. Throughout this book, we try to teach sound programming principles and present well-constructed program examples.

❑ Most importantly, use this book with your computer on. Nothing beats "learning by doing."

If you have some previous experience with BASIC,

❑ You want to hone your skills and expand your knowledge. In the index and the table of contents, you can quickly locate information about any problem or subject as the need arises. Cross-references in the text point to related material in the book.

❑ Take time regularly to browse. In addition to increasing your BASIC knowledge, you will be in a better position to later use the book for reference.

An Overview of the Contents

Chapter 1, "An Overview of BASIC," answers your most likely questions about the BASIC language.

Chapter 2, "Up and Running," presents a short tutorial on installing BASIC, understanding the working environment, and interacting with BASIC through direct commands.

In Chapter 3, "A Hands-On Introduction to Programming," you become a programmer. We present many short programs that illustrate the main features of BASIC. Our approach is action-oriented—lots of things to try, no long discourses. We want you to become familiar with entering and running programs, and to get a hands-on feeling for the diverse things BASIC can do.

Chapters 4 through 12 introduce individual BASIC topics. Again, our approach is experiential, but we now discuss each concept thoroughly. These chapters cover such subjects as program structure, logic flow, data types, text output, subroutines, graphics, disk files, and using a printer. Many short program examples demonstrate the ideas.

Chapter 13, "Editing Techniques," explains the finer points of the BASIC editor. You will learn many shortcuts and tricks to make editing fast and easy.

Chapter 14, "Debugging and Testing," is a survival guide for the times when things go wrong. We discuss many programming traps and errors, and show you how to recognize and correct common problems. The emphasis is on practical techniques for debugging, tracing, and validating your programs.

Chapter 15, "Toward Advanced Programming," is an eclectic mix of more advanced programming subjects, including event and error traps, user-defined functions, direct memory referencing, and animated graphics. Here, you can browse and supplement your BASIC knowledge.

The "Keyword Reference" is a succinct survey of the BASIC language that presents each keyword along with a one-sentence description and a single-line program example.

The appendixes contain reference tables.

Finally, the book has an index that we tried to make detailed and thorough.

Part I

Fundamentals of BASIC

Although BASIC is easy to learn, it is a sophisticated software product. Before you can program successfully, you should feel comfortable with the programming environment. Our goal in Part I is to give you that comfortable feeling.

In order to feel at ease, you must be confident and adept with the fundamentals. You must know which techniques are the most important, practice those techniques, and have a solid foundation in the general workings of the BASIC environment.

By the time you finish Part I, you will have experience in the following areas:

- ❏ Understanding the history, philosophy, and outstanding features of BASIC
- ❏ Installing BASIC
- ❏ Gaining familiarity with the BASIC environment—issuing commands in direct mode and editing programs
- ❏ Practicing simple programming and file manipulation
- ❏ Learning the rudiments of BASIC programming

With this expertise, you will be suitably prepared to learn the BASIC programming language details, which follow in Parts II, III, and IV.

So now forge ahead into learning BASIC. We will try to make your experience enjoyable and rewarding.

1

An Overview of BASIC

Programmers have power—the power to make a computer do exactly what they want.

This book gives you that power. By learning BASIC, you can write programs that perform an amazing variety of tasks, useful for business or in your home. For example, here are just a few programming ideas that you might tackle:

- ❏ Keep track of a hobby collection, such as a coin collection.

- ❏ Analyze sales for a business, and plot graphs showing the sales trends.

- ❏ Play a computer game that you have designed. The game might include music and color graphics.

- ❏ Compute solutions to mathematical and scientific problems.

- ❏ Teach others a skill or subject that you know well.

Programming is creative, fun (most of the time), and challenging—a unique blend of art and skill. When your programs run successfully, you get that satisfying feeling of accomplishment. You will have successfully communicated with a computer *on the computer's terms.*

This chapter provides a short overview of BASIC. We discuss what a computer language is, provide a historical perspective on BASIC, and briefly discuss hardware and software. This material is for background, and you can skim if you want. In the next chapter, we plunge right into using BASIC.

The BASIC Essentials (Pun Intended)

This book teaches you programming with a computer *language* called BASIC. To use BASIC, you write *programs* that conform to the rules of the language. BASIC then *translates* your instructions into *machine-level* instructions that the computer understands. The computer *executes* these translated instructions in order to *run* your program.

That last paragraph is a mouthful! We introduced new terms that probably raised many questions. We devote the rest of this chapter to anticipating your questions and providing answers. We hope that you will get an idea of what BASIC is all about.

What Is a Computer Language?

At the heart of your computer is a hardware chip known as the *central processor*. This chip controls everything going on inside your computer—from the calculation of numbers to storing data in memory to sending signals to your video screen.

To make computers respond to our wishes, we must communicate with the central processor. We need a way to tell it what we want the computer to do and a way to have the computer report the results.

Unfortunately, we can't just talk to the central processor in English. Imagine sitting down in front of your computer and saying, "Computer, add the outstanding checks in my account and display my bank balance on the screen. And please hurry, I'm late for lunch!"

Don't laugh too hard. With the advances in computer technology, you *might* be able to do just that sometime in the 21st century.

But this is the 1990s. To get a computer to obey our commands today, we must "talk" to the computer in a language it understands.

What Language Does a Computer Understand?

The central processor understands instructions in its native tongue, known as *machine language* (or *assembly language*). Machine language is primitive in that machine-level commands work only at the most fundamental levels of the computer. For example, a machine-level instruction might move a data bit from one internal machine register to another or store a data byte at a particular memory location.

But "primitive" does not mean ineffective. With nothing but machine-level commands, you can get a computer to do anything of which it is capable. Furthermore, the computer executes machine-language instructions very quickly.

The problem is that something as simple as adding two numbers and displaying the result may require more than 25 machine-language instructions. Any mistake in one of these instructions could cause disastrous results. Also, machine language is not at all English-like. The instructions consist of many shorthand abbreviations and odd-looking terms.

We need a compromise. We want to communicate with the computer in English or at least a language close to English. But the computer accepts commands only in machine language.

A *high-level computer language* is just such a compromise.

Is BASIC a High-Level Language?

Yes.

How Does a High-Level Language Work?

Essentially, a high-level computer language such as BASIC is a *translator*. You, the programmer, write instructions using the high-level language. The high-level language then *translates* these instructions into machine-level instructions that the computer understands (see fig. 1.1).

Fig. 1.1. Running a BASIC program.

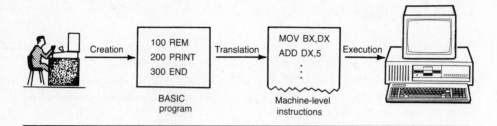

Are There Other High-Level Languages?

Yes, there are many high-level languages other than BASIC. Some others are Pascal, FORTRAN, COBOL, and C. Perhaps you have heard of one or more of these languages. Each language has its own strengths and weaknesses.

What Is Special about BASIC?

BASIC is an ideal language for beginning programmers, for three primary reasons:

❏ BASIC instructions are descriptive and English-like. As a result, BASIC programs tend to be understandable and easy to read.

❏ BASIC provides immediate feedback. When you run a program, the computer immediately translates the instructions and produces results.

❏ BASIC is interactive. When an error occurs, BASIC immediately reports the error with an informative message. In most cases, you can quickly correct the problem and resume execution of your program.

What Exactly Is a Program, Especially a BASIC Program?

A *program* is simply a series of instructions written according to the rules of the programming language. A BASIC program is a series of instructions written in the BASIC language.

In some ways, a program is like a recipe for baking a cake. A recipe is a series of instructions, written for a person to perform. You execute the instructions and, if all goes OK, you end up with a delicious dessert.

A program is also a series of instructions, written for a computer to perform. The computer executes the instructions and, if all goes OK, you end up with, well, a successful program.

How Do I Get a BASIC Program into My Computer?

You get a BASIC program into your computer in one of two fundamental ways:

1. Type the program directly into your computer. Whenever you create a brand-new program, you use this straightforward method.

2. Load a previously saved program from disk. As you work with BASIC, you probably will accumulate many programs on floppy disks (or on your hard disk if your machine is so equipped). These programs can be programs you wrote originally, programs written by friends, or perhaps programs you bought commercially.

What Happens When I Run a BASIC Program?

We say that you *run a program* when you have BASIC execute the instructions of a program. To run your program, BASIC works incrementally. To start, BASIC translates the first line of your program into machine-language instructions. The computer then executes these instructions.

Another Source for Programs

If you have a modem, you may have experience using a computer bulletin board or other on-line information service. (A modem lets your computer "call" other computers using regular phone, lines.) Many on-line services, such as CompuServe, provide BASIC programs that you can "download" and save as a disk file. Throughout the country, numerous "electronic bulletin boards" are operated by computer hobbyists. Often, BASIC programmers share their programs on such bulletin boards. You can download programs that you find interesting. And you can "upload" your programs so that others can benefit from your best efforts. Everyone benefits from this arrangement.

BASIC then translates the next line of your program, and the computer executes the resultant machine-language instructions. This translating-and-executing process continues throughout your program.

How Does the Computer Translate the BASIC Instructions?

You may be wondering, "If the computer responds only to machine language, how does the computer translate instructions written in BASIC?"

Simple. BASIC is itself a program *written in machine language*. BASIC is a complex program containing thousands of machine-language instructions. BASIC lets you write your own programs using the rules of BASIC.

What Is the Origin of BASIC?

BASIC was developed in the mid-1960s at Dartmouth College by professors John Kemeny and Thomas Kurtz. The name BASIC is an acronym for *Beginner's All-purpose Symbolic Instruction Code*.

Kemeny and Kurtz designed BASIC to be a vehicle with which to teach programming. BASIC, therefore, has English-like commands, is easy to use, and requires no specialized hardware knowledge.

Was BASIC Successful Immediately?

Yes. BASIC was an immediate success because of several favorable circumstances:

- ☐ Computer literacy was in vogue. Faculty members were eager to teach programming, and students were eager to learn.

- ☐ Time-sharing became available. On time-sharing systems, many programmers could use centralized computer facilities easily and economically. Such computing environments in a college setting were tailor-made for BASIC.

- ☐ The BASIC design goals were achieved superbly. The new language was much easier to use and to teach than existing languages such as ALGOL and FORTRAN.

When and How Did Personal Computers Enter the Picture?

In 1975, in Boston, a young Honeywell employee named Paul Allen got wind of the first personal computer being developed. This computer, called the Altair, was built by MITS corporation, of Albuquerque, New Mexico.

Paul conveyed his excitement to Bill Gates, a student at Harvard University. Paul and Bill were grade-school chums from the West Coast who shared a passionate interest in computers. Paul convinced Bill that they should develop a version of BASIC for the Altair.

Legend has it that the two men called MITS to see whether the company would be interested in a BASIC implementation for their new computer. When the answer was "yes," Paul and Bill licensed their BASIC to MITS. Paul moved to Albuquerque, and became, in effect, the MITS software department.

Their first BASIC ran entirely in 4 kilobytes of memory, including the user's program and the variable storage. (Four kilobytes, or 4K, is 4,096 bytes of memory, a piddling sum by today's standards. By comparison, most IBM PCs or compatibles have *at least* 512 kilobytes of main memory!) Gates, the primary developer, supposedly wrote this BASIC before he saw the new computer. The program worked almost immediately.

Within a few years, Gates and Allen developed BASIC for other emerging microcomputers. They moved back to their hometown of Seattle, Washington. Their company, Microsoft Corporation, remains at the leading edge of software development. Today, Bill Gates is a billionaire. At a recent computer gathering, we personally heard the venerable Microsoft chairman reminisce "that 4K BASIC is the best program I ever wrote."

What About BASIC on the IBM Personal Computer?

By the late 1970s, Microsoft was developing a version of BASIC for virtually every new personal computer, including offerings from Apple, Commodore, and Radio Shack.

IBM was no exception. When "Big Blue" entered the fray in 1981 with the IBM PC, the computer came with a language called BASICA. This language, developed by Microsoft and leased to IBM, sold under the IBM nameplate. BASICA was a far cry from its 4K BASIC ancestor.

Featuring numerous enhancements, and improved over the years, BASICA now has approximately 200 commands and requires more than 40 kilobytes of memory. In addition to BASICA, IBM originally provided a less-capable version, called simply "BASIC," that used less memory. BASICA means "BASIC, Advanced version." BASIC and BASICA now are identical.

What About BASIC for IBM-Compatible Computers?

As the IBM PC became a runaway success, several computer manufacturers began competing by making IBM-compatibles (often called "clones"). As part of their agreement with IBM, Microsoft was free to distribute BASIC for these compatibles.

For compatibles, Microsoft developed a version of BASIC called GW-BASIC. Most compatible manufacturers license GW-BASIC from Microsoft and include the language with their computers. If you have a compatible but do not have BASIC, you can buy GW-BASIC as a stand-alone product.

Are BASICA and GW-BASIC Equivalent?

Almost. BASICA runs only on IBM computers because part of the language is contained in IBM-proprietary ROM (read-only memory) chips. These chips are installed at the factory, and only true IBM machines have them.

GW-BASIC, on the other hand, runs on any IBM computer or compatible. GW-BASIC requires only the regular RAM (random access memory). No special hardware chips are necessary.

The features and functionality of BASICA and GW-BASIC are essentially identical. (There are a few trivial differences.) If you know one language, you know the other. A program running successfully under BASICA runs successfully 99.9 percent of the time under GW-BASIC, and vice versa.

From now on, we use the term "BASIC" to mean GW-BASIC *or* BASICA. If you have an IBM computer, think of BASIC as meaning BASICA. If you have a compatible, think of BASIC as meaning GW-BASIC (see fig. 1.2).

What Hardware Do I Need To Run BASIC?

You need an IBM computer (PC, XT, AT, or PS/2) or an IBM-compatible computer running DOS 2.1 or later. Your computer may have the following equipment:

❑ *A monitor.* This is the video screen. Many different types of monitors exist. You can run BASIC with any type of monitor, but, as they say in the airline business, some restrictions apply. Your monitor (and video hardware) determines what graphics you can produce. You obviously need a color monitor to get color graphics. And, if you have a monochrome monitor and monochrome video adapter, you cannot produce graphics at all. We discuss monitors and BASIC graphics in Chapter 11, "Creating Graphics."

Fig. 1.2. *BASIC on IBM and compatible computers.*

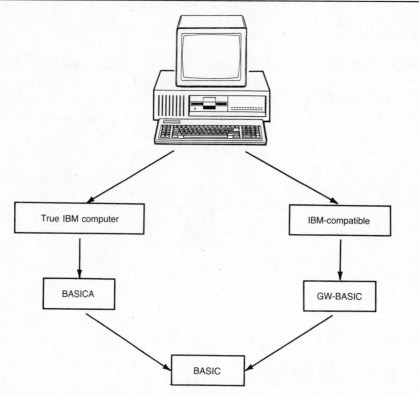

❏ *A disk drive or drives.* Your computer has one or more floppy disk drives. These are the devices into which you insert diskettes. If your system has one floppy drive, that drive is designated the A: drive. A second floppy drive is designated the B: drive. Your computer may also have one or more hard (or fixed) disk drives built into the machine. Hard disk drives are designated with the letters C: and up. You do not need a hard disk drive to run BASIC. For more information about disk drives, see Chapter 2, "Up and Running," and Chapter 10, "Using Disk Files."

❏ *A printer.* You don't need a printer to run BASIC, but having one is helpful. With a printer, you can list your programs and view the output at leisure. Most of the programs in this book are short and easily viewed on your monitor. A printer is useful, but not essential.

Do I Need To Know Much about DOS?

DOS is the operating system under which your computer runs. DOS provides the `A>` or `C>` prompt with which you are undoubtedly familiar. DOS, like BASIC, was developed by Microsoft Corporation. On IBM computers, DOS is called PC DOS. On compatibles, DOS is known as MS-DOS. In this book, we use the term "DOS" to refer to either PC DOS or MS-DOS.

We assume that you know how to do the simplest tasks in DOS, such as formatting a new floppy disk and copying a file from one disk to another. Rudimentary knowledge of disk directories is desirable. However, you certainly don't need to be a whiz at DOS.

In this book, we try to provide detailed instructions whenever a DOS subject arises. Chapter 10, "Using Disk Files," contains a brief tutorial on DOS directories and file naming. If you feel uncomfortable with even simple DOS commands, consult one of the excellent tutorial books such as *Using PC DOS*, 3rd Edition, published by Que Corporation.

Does This Book Explain Everything about BASIC?

Just about. Because our primary audience is beginners, we omit some advanced, complex features of BASIC that require detailed explanations (features such as networking and multilanguage programming, for instance).

We cover most of BASIC (maybe 95 percent) and certainly include every essential subject. Rest assured, when you finish this book, you will be able to tackle most any programming project and write quite sophisticated programs.

What Is Your Teaching Style?

We believe in learning by example. Programming is like bicycling, kissing, or driving a car: you can fully learn only by doing, not just by reading a book.

We provide numerous short programs (and program fragments) that are to the point. (As a learning tool, long programs tend to be confusing and distracting.) We hope that you will read this book with your computer on. Try the examples. Better yet, experiment on your own. The more you *do*, the faster you will learn.

What Is Your Main Goal for This Book?

Our main goal in this book is to make you a successful and confident BASIC programmer.

2

Up and Running

It's time for action. You probably are eager to get going with BASIC, and that is exactly what we will do in this chapter.

BASIC has two fundamental modes of operation:

❏ *Direct mode*. You enter a single command, and BASIC immediately performs your requested action.

❏ *Program mode* (also called *indirect mode*). You create a *program*, which is a series of instructions collected into a single unit. You then *run* your program. In rapid succession, BASIC executes program instructions one after another.

In this chapter, you will start BASIC and try a few commands in direct mode. The next chapter introduces program mode.

Here are the main topics covered in this chapter:

❏ Making a BASIC work disk (or work directory if you have a hard disk).

❏ Copying BASIC onto your work disk (or directory).

❏ Starting BASIC.

❏ Understanding the BASIC screen and working environment.

❏ Trying some commands in direct mode.

21

Installing BASIC

Before you can *use* BASIC for the first time, you must *install* it on your computer. The installation process is straightforward, but the details vary slightly depending on your computer system.

Answer the following two questions about your computer:

1. Do you have a true IBM machine (PC, XT, AT, PS/2) or an IBM compatible manufactured by an IBM competitor? (IBM compatibles are often called "clones.")

2. Which of the following disk drive configurations best describes your situation?
   a. Your computer has one floppy disk drive.
   b. Your computer has two floppy disk drives.
   c. Your computer has a hard (fixed) disk drive in addition to one or more floppy disk drives.

If you can answer these two questions, we provide specific installation directions for your computer system. Follow the directions that apply to your particular case. (If you need help answering the questions, please ask a knowledgeable friend or your computer dealer, or consult your system documentation.)

For any computer system, installing BASIC requires the following three steps:

1. Making a work diskette (or work directory).

2. Copying BASIC to your work diskette (or directory).

3. Starting BASIC.

Making a BASIC Work Diskette (or Work Directory on a Hard Disk System)

We suggest that you create a BASIC work diskette in conjunction with using this book. On this diskette, you will save a copy of the BASIC language and various BASIC programs.

A work diskette aids experimentation. We encourage you to experiment with our program examples and with programs of your own. With a work diskette, you can save programs for later experimentation and modification.

If your computer has a hard disk drive, you may create a BASIC work directory on your hard disk rather than using a work diskette. Skip ahead to the section titled "Creating a Work Directory on a Hard Drive System."

Creating a Work Diskette on a Floppy Drive System

First, you format a blank floppy diskette. We advise you to make a "system diskette" so that you can boot your machine directly from this diskette.

To do so, use the FORMAT command from DOS. The /S option creates a system diskette (with the necessary file COMMAND.COM). We now give instructions for a single- or dual-floppy drive system. (If you need additional help with the FORMAT command, consult your DOS documentation.)

If your system has two floppy drives, place a DOS diskette in the A: drive and a blank diskette in the B: drive. At the A> prompt from DOS, type

```
A>FORMAT B:/S
```

Your computer now formats the blank diskette in the B: drive. This diskette will become your BASIC work diskette.

If your computer has only a single floppy drive, place your DOS diskette in the A: drive and type

```
A>FORMAT A:/S
```

When you are prompted, place the blank diskette in your drive to create the work diskette.

You can now skip ahead to the section titled, "Locating Your Version of BASIC."

Creating a Work Directory on a Hard Drive System

On a hard drive system, you create a new subdirectory to hold your BASIC files. You may want to give this subdirectory a descriptive name such as USEBASIC, or perhaps just BASIC. We use the name USEBASIC in the directions that follow.

We assume that your hard disk is the C: drive. (You may have a hard disk with a higher letter, such as the D: drive. If you want to use such a hard disk, substitute D: or the higher letter for C: in the following directions.)

To create a new subdirectory, use the `MKDIR` command from DOS. At your `C>` prompt, type the following DOS command:

```
C>MKDIR \USEBASIC
```

This command creates a new subdirectory named `USEBASIC` off the root directory of your hard disk. If you don't understand DOS directories or the `MKDIR` command, Chapter 10, "Using Disk Files," contains a brief tutorial on directories and subdirectories. If you need additional help, consult your DOS documentation.

Locating Your Version of BASIC

For all computer systems, you must now locate BASIC among your system files. The name of your BASIC file depends on whether you have a true IBM computer or a compatible.

❏ If you have a true IBM computer:

You have BASIC on a file named `BASICA.COM`. You should find `BASICA.COM` on a diskette supplied by IBM, either the diskette containing DOS or perhaps a supplementary diskette. (If your computer has a hard disk, `BASICA.COM` may already reside in a directory on your hard disk.)

❏ If you have an IBM-compatible computer:

You have BASIC on a file named `GWBASIC.EXE`. You should find `GWBASIC.EXE` on a system diskette or, if your computer has a hard disk, perhaps already copied into a directory of your hard disk.

Copying BASIC to Your Work Diskette

Use the `COPY` command from DOS to copy BASIC to your work diskette (or to the `USEBASIC` directory on your hard disk). This section gives directions for a dual-floppy system, a single-floppy system, and a hard disk system. (If you need more help with the `COPY` command, consult your DOS documentation.)

Copying BASIC on a Dual-Floppy Computer System

1. Place the system diskette containing BASICA.COM or GWBASIC.EXE into your A: drive.

2. Place your work diskette in the B: drive.

3. If you have an IBM computer, type the following DOS command at the A> prompt:

   ```
   A>COPY A:BASICA.* B:
   ```

   If you have an IBM-compatible computer, type the following DOS command instead:

   ```
   A>COPY A:GWBASIC.* B:
   ```

Your work diskette now contains a copy of the BASIC language on the file BASICA.COM or GWBASIC.EXE.

Why the Asterisk in the COPY Command?

Our instructions for the COPY command specify the file extension with an asterisk (BASICA.* or GWBASIC.*). Why?

The asterisk instructs DOS to copy all files with the given root name (BASICA or GWBASIC) and *any* file extension.

Your version of DOS *may* have a secondary BASIC support file with an extension name other than .COM or .EXE. For example, PC DOS 3.3 contains a file named BASICA.PIF as well as BASICA.COM. By using the asterisk in the COPY command, you copy both files at once.

Copying BASIC on a Single-Floppy Computer System

1. Place the system diskette containing BASICA.COM or GWBASIC.EXE into your disk drive.

2. If you have an IBM computer, type the following DOS command at the A> prompt:

```
A>COPY A:BASICA.*  B:
```

If you have an IBM-compatible computer, type the following DOS command instead:

```
A>COPY A:GWBASIC.*  B:
```

3. When you are prompted by DOS to insert a diskette for drive B:, remove the system diskette from your disk drive and insert your work diskette.

4. Press any key to resume the copying.

5. When the copying is completed, turn your computer off and then on again. This step verifies that you can boot your system from the work diskette and also restores A: as the default disk drive.

Copying BASIC on a Hard Disk System

1. Place the system diskette containing BASICA.COM or GWBASIC.EXE into your A: drive.

2. If you have an IBM computer, type the following DOS command at the A> prompt:

```
A>COPY A:BASICA.* C:\USEBASIC
```

If you have a compatible system, type the following DOS command instead:

```
A>COPY A:GWBASIC.* C:\USEBASIC
```

The USEBASIC subdirectory on your C: drive now contains a copy of the BASIC language on the file BASICA.COM or GWBASIC.EXE.

Starting BASIC

Now you are ready to start BASIC. Again, we separately consider a floppy disk computer system and a hard disk system.

Starting BASIC on a Floppy Disk System

Place your work diskette in the A: drive. (If your computer is turned off, you can boot your system directly from this diskette.)

If you have an IBM computer, type the following command at the A> prompt:

```
A>BASICA
```

If you have a compatible, type the following command instead:

```
A>GWBASIC
```

Starting BASIC on a Hard Disk System

First, make USEBASIC the default directory. To do so, type the following DOS command at the C> prompt:

```
C>CHDIR \USEBASIC
```

If you have an IBM system, start BASIC with the following command:

```
C>BASICA
```

On a compatible, start BASIC with this command instead:

```
C>GWBASIC
```

Understanding the Initial BASIC Screen

Congratulations. You have started BASIC, and your screen should look something like figure 2.1. We say "something like" because your exact screen depends on whether you have BASICA or GW-BASIC, your version number of BASICA or GW-BASIC, and the amount of memory in your computer system.

Figure 2.1 shows our computer screen when we first start BASIC. As you can see, we have version 3.22 of GW-BASIC.

Compare your screen with figure 2.1. The first few lines on your screen identify your version of BASIC and specify various copyrights and licenses. Your screen may have more such lines than ours.

The line containing Bytes free indicates the amount of memory available for BASIC programs and data. (A *byte* is a fundamental unit of memory equivalent to approximately one letter or digit.) The number of free bytes shown on your screen will likely be different than the 60300 free bytes available on our system.

...

Fig. 2.1. *The initial BASIC screen on a typical computer.*

```
GW-BASIC 3.22
(C) Copyright Microsoft 1983,1984,1985,1986,1987
60300 Bytes free
Ok
_
```

```
1LIST  2RUN◄  3LOAD"  4SAVE"  5CONT◄  6,"LPT1 7TRON◄  8TROFF◄ 9KEY   0SCREEN
```

The BASIC Prompt—Ok

The next line says simply Ok. "Ok" is the BASIC prompt. This prompt means that BASIC is waiting for you to enter your next command. When you enter a BASIC command, BASIC does it (or tries to do it), and then displays the prompt Ok. "Ok" is BASIC's way of saying, "I did what you asked, and I'm ready for what you want to do next."

The BASIC Cursor—a Blinking Line

A blinking line appears below the Ok prompt. This line is the *cursor*. The cursor indicates where the next character you type will appear on the screen.

The Bottom Line— the Function Key Display

The bottom line of your screen contains a list of numbers and strange abbreviations. This line is known as the *Function Key Display*. The abbreviations designate meanings for the function keys (F1 through F10). As you will see in

Chapter 13, "Editing Techniques," you can use the function keys to quickly type frequently used commands.

For now, the function keys and the Function Key Display line are not important. Don't be distracted or concerned by the Display line. The line won't disturb anything you do. In the next chapter, you learn how to turn the line on or off at will.

Issuing BASIC Commands

The Ok prompt means that BASIC is waiting, and the blinking cursor invites you to type something, so let's put BASIC into action. Type a command and see what happens.

See whether you can greet the computer successfully. Try typing "hello." Just type the word **hello** and don't press any other key. Watch what happens on your screen as you type.

```
Ok
hello_
```

Boldface Represents Something You Type

When we present examples in this book, we show what *you* type in a boldfaced font and show *BASIC's* messages in monospace font. So, in the previous example, Ok appears in monospace font and **hello** appears in boldfaced font.

Did you watch the cursor as you typed "hello"? Each time you typed a letter, that letter replaced the previous cursor, and a new cursor appeared one space to the right. Remember, the cursor indicates where the next character you type will appear.

You typed "hello" but BASIC hasn't replied. Is this unfriendly? No. BASIC just hasn't "read" your command yet.

To actually send a command to BASIC and get BASIC's response, you must type the command *and* then press the Enter key. The Enter key is the oversized key located near the right side of your keyboard. (On some keyboards, the key is marked "Return" rather than "Enter." Also, some keyboards have two Enter keys. Press either one.)

Throughout this book, the phrase "press Enter" means to press the oversized key. Remember, you must press Enter before BASIC reads and processes any command you type.

Now press Enter and see what happens.

```
Ok
hello
Syntax error
Ok
_
```

Well, the Syntax error message is a little foreboding, but at least BASIC did do something. The message implies that BASIC didn't like or recognize your hello greeting.

In fact, the Syntax error response indicates that BASIC simply doesn't understand the hello command. *Syntax* refers to the components of a command and the way the components are put together. The message Syntax error is BASIC's way of saying, "I know you want me to do something, but I just don't understand what it is you want me to do."

One consequence of working with BASIC, or with any other computer language, is that you must specify commands and instructions within the vocabulary of the language. "Hello" is just not a word that BASIC understands. The words that BASIC does understand are called *reserved words*. BASIC has a vocabulary of approximately 200 reserved words, which are listed in Appendix A, "Reserved Words." Throughout this book, we discuss how to use most of BASIC's reserved words.

After the Syntax error message, BASIC reissued the Ok prompt and the cursor. That's reassuring because the prompt means that BASIC is waiting for you to try something new. Although you got an error message, you haven't done anything seriously wrong, and BASIC is ready for your next command.

Some Simple BASIC Commands

If you look at the list of reserved words in Appendix A, you see the word BEEP. BEEP is a BASIC command that causes the computer to do just what the command suggests: sound a beep from the speaker. Try it.

```
Ok
beep
Ok
```

> ### Experiment with BASIC, Please!
>
> Some beginning programmers are concerned about seriously damaging their computers should they type a BASIC command incorrectly or in some unusual way.
>
> If you have this concern, don't worry!
>
> Nothing you do from BASIC can have serious consequences to your computer system. You will never damage your computer hardware.
>
> Indeed, we encourage you to experiment. As you try some of our examples, you may be curious about what happens if you vary the examples somewhat. Perhaps one of our experiments may suggest another experiment to you.
>
> By all means, try any experiment that occurs to you. Sometimes you will get expected results and other times surprising results. Either way, you satisfy your curiosity and have a little fun. The more you experiment and do things with BASIC, the faster you learn the language and become a confident programmer.

Your computer beeps, and BASIC reissues the OK prompt. No Syntax error or any other error message appears. Evidently, everything worked all right. Indeed, you have just issued your first successful BASIC command. (As we discuss in Chapter 12, "Programming Hardware Devices," you use BEEP to get the attention of the person running your program.)

BEEP is a simple command that consists of just the single reserved word BEEP. Most BASIC commands, however, require a reserved word *and* additional information.

Capitalization

One thing you might have noticed is that Appendix A, "Reserved Words," lists BEEP in all uppercase letters. In the example command, however, you typed beep with all lowercase letters.

When it comes to reserved words, BASIC is not picky about capitalization. You can use upper- or lowercase letters equivalently. In the present example, you could type beep, BEEP, or even bEeP, and the command works fine. To convince yourself, try entering the BEEP command with some different capitalizations.

> ## You Can Type BASIC Commands In Upper- or Lowercase
>
> From now on, we show BASIC reserved words in uppercase. Be aware, however, that you can type the commands with upper- or lowercase letters. Use whatever is most comfortable.

Scrolling

By now, your video screen is probably becoming full. Each BASIC command you type and each response from the computer takes at least one new line on your video screen. What happens when you reach the bottom line, which now contains the Function Key Display?

When the cursor reaches the bottom line, the video screen *scrolls*. Scrolling means that everything on the screen moves up one line. The cursor remains on the now-blank bottom line to accommodate your next command or BASIC's next response. When the screen scrolls, the former top line "moves up" and simply disappears.

When we say the "bottom line" of the screen, we mean the line above the Function Key Display. The Function Key Display is not affected by scrolling. The Display line remains visible and is immune to the upward scrolling movement of other screen lines.

If you haven't yet seen the scrolling effect, try one of these experiments:

❏ Continually type BEEP (followed by pressing Enter) until the screen scrolls.

or

❏ Just press Enter repeatedly until scrolling occurs.

Clearing the Screen

A full screen sometimes appears cluttered, and you may want to work with a fresh slate. The CLS command wipes the screen clear and returns the cursor to the upper left corner. The letters CLS stand for *Clear Screen*. The CLS command does not erase anything in the computer's memory, but simply wipes the screen clear (except for the Function Key Display).

Try clearing your screen. Just type:

```
CLS
```

Your screen blanks, and the Ok prompt appears in the upper left corner. The cursor reappears just below the prompt. BASIC waits for you to type your next command. We examine CLS in detail in Chapter 9, "Writing Text on the Video Screen", and Chapter 11, "Creating Graphics."

> **No More Cursor**
>
> For simplicity, we will no longer show the cursor in our examples. However, whenever you see the Ok prompt, you know that the next line contains the blinking cursor.

Correcting Typing Mistakes

If you are at all like us, you make typing errors from time to time. Before going any further, we should tell you what to do if you realize that you have made a typing error while entering a command.

Suppose that you mean to type BEEP but you inadvertently type BEET. You realize your mistake just before you press Enter. What can you do to correct this mistake?

You have two choices:

1. Do nothing special. Just press Enter. A Syntax error message will appear, of course, followed by the Ok prompt. Now you can type BEEP as you intended.

2. Use the Backspace key. This is the key marked with a left-facing arrow. On most keyboards, the Backspace key is near the upper right.

Think of Backspace as your "Oops" key. Each time you press Backspace, you erase the last character you typed, and the cursor moves one space to the left.

Try Backspace now. First type BEET but don't press Enter. Now press Backspace. Watch how the "T" in BEET disappears. You can now type **P** and, sure enough, you see BEEP on the screen. Press Enter and you issue the BEEP command as usual.

You can press Backspace as many times as necessary on a single line. For example, suppose that you type BBEP rather than BEEP. Press Backspace three times. Only the first B remains. Now type **EEP** to complete the BEEP keyword.

The *PRINT* Command— Displaying Text on Your Screen

We have introduced two BASIC reserved words: BEEP and CLS. Each word created a valid BASIC command all by itself.

Most BASIC commands, however, require more than a single reserved word. Some commands contain two or more reserved words. And many commands consist of one or more reserved words *and* additional information that you supply.

Earlier in this chapter, you tried to "greet" the computer by typing hello. All you got was a Syntax error message for your efforts. Try typing this command instead (and press Enter):

```
PRINT "Hello"
```

BASIC responds by displaying Hello right back! Your screen looks like this:

```
Ok
PRINT "Hello"
Hello
Ok
```

No syntax error message occurs. PRINT "Hello" is evidently a valid BASIC command. In reply, the computer responds with Hello on the next line. Does this mean that the computer understands your greeting and "decides" to respond with Hello?

Not quite. As you probably realize, the computer is simply following your orders to display the word Hello. PRINT "Hello" commands the computer to display Hello.

PRINT is a reserved word. When a PRINT command is followed by text between quotation marks, the command prints on-screen whatever you type between the quotation marks.

Try making BASIC display the message Your wish is my command:

```
Ok
PRINT "Your wish is my command"
Your wish is my command
Ok
```

Experiment with various PRINT commands of your own. Type whatever you want between the quotation marks.

A PRINT command is an example of a command that consists of a reserved word *and* additional information. In our example case, PRINT is the reserved word and "Your wish is my command" is the additional information.

Note that, although capitalization is not important when you type PRINT, capitalization *is* important in the text between the quotation marks. In a PRINT command, BASIC prints literally whatever you type between the quotation marks. (Remember that you can type reserved words, such as PRINT, with upper- or lowercase letters.)

The following experiment demonstrates capitalization with various PRINT commands:

```
Ok
PRINT "HELLO"
HELLO
Ok
print "hello"
hello
OK
pRiNt "hElLo"
hElLo
Ok
```

As you will see throughout the course of this book, PRINT is a versatile command that takes many different forms. You will encounter PRINT often and explore it in detail in Chapter 9, "Writing Text on the Video Screen."

Quitting BASIC

The SYSTEM command ends BASIC and returns your computer to DOS. When you are finished with a BASIC session, you just type

```
SYSTEM
```

Summary

In this chapter, you installed BASIC and created a work diskette (or directory) appropriate for your particular computer system. You then started BASIC and began experimenting with direct mode.

In direct mode, you type a command and press Enter. BASIC responds immediately. BASIC displays the Ok prompt when it is ready for your next command. Typing mistakes are corrected easily with the Backspace key.

You learned four reserved words: BEEP, CLS, PRINT, and SYSTEM. BEEP, CLS, and SYSTEM form valid commands all by themselves. BEEP sounds the speaker, CLS clears the screen, and SYSTEM returns the computer to DOS. You can display text on your screen with PRINT. Use a PRINT command consisting of PRINT followed by the text in quotation marks. When you type any reserved word, upper- or lowercase letters are interchangeable.

A Hands-On Introduction to Programming

By the time you finish this chapter, you will be a full-fledged BASIC programmer. You will know what a program is, how to type a program into BASIC, and how to have BASIC run your program.

You learned about direct mode in Chapter 2, "Up and Running." In direct mode, you type a command, press Enter, and BASIC executes your command. That's fine, but direct mode has the obvious limitation that you can do only one thing at a time.

A program, on the other hand, collects several instructions into a single unit. When you run a program, BASIC executes the first instruction and then immediately proceeds to the next. With the ability to put numerous instructions together, you can write programs that accomplish anything (well, anything a computer can do, anyway).

This chapter introduces program mode. We discuss many important features and principles of BASIC programming using "hands-on" examples. Please turn on your computer, load BASIC, and follow along.

You will get the most from this chapter—and the entire book, for that matter—if you actually try the example programs. Type in the programs (they're short) and run them. Even if the ideas seem simple and you are confident that you understand everything, you will gain the necessary experience only by doing.

37

This chapter surveys several BASIC fundamentals (sorry if that sounds redundant). The groundwork is laid for the more thorough material in later chapters. Here are some of the topics covered in this chapter:

❏ Typing, running, and editing a program.

❏ Saving and loading programs on disk.

❏ Using line numbers.

❏ Introducing variables and assigning values to them.

❏ Doing simple arithmetic.

❏ Altering logic flow.

❏ Manipulating strings.

❏ Looping.

❏ Graphing shapes and figures.

BASIC Is for Beginners

Some people are convinced that they will never understand how to program a computer—that they can't learn to write simple BASIC programs. If this is you, don't be afraid!

Remember that the *B* in BASIC stands for "Beginner's." You will see that you don't need to be a technical genius, or even mathematically inclined, to use BASIC.

Introducing Program Mode

We are members of the "learn by doing" programming school. We cover the finer points of programming style as we go. Let's plunge right into the act of programming.

Here's a simple BASIC program:

```
100 PRINT "Hello"
200 PRINT "Goodbye"
300 END
```

We bet that you can make a good guess what the program does. Sure, the program displays the word `Hello` and then the word `Goodbye`.

Look at the first line of the program. The line looks very much like a `PRINT` command from the preceding chapter. Now, however, the number `100` appears at the beginning of the line. The other lines of the program also begin with numbers.

What do these numbers mean?

The numbers are called *line numbers*. A line number identifies the line as being part of a program. Without the line number, the line is a command suitable for BASIC's direct mode. We discuss more about line numbers throughout this chapter.

The program's third line ends the program. We experiment with `END` later in this chapter.

To see how program mode works, let's try running the program.

Typing a Program

First, you have to enter the program into BASIC. Begin by typing the first line of the program. Be sure that you include the line number. Type the first line but don't press Enter. Your screen should look like the following lines:

```
Ok
100 PRINT "Hello"
```

Now press Enter. What happens?

The cursor moves down the screen as usual, but you don't see the familiar `Ok` prompt. The number at the beginning of the line (100 in this case) "tells" BASIC that this line is part of a program and not a direct mode command. You get an `Ok` prompt only after BASIC performs a direct mode command. Here, you are entering a program (rather than issuing a command).

Type the remaining two lines of the program. Your screen should look like the following lines:

```
Ok
100 PRINT "Hello"
200 PRINT "Goodbye"
300 END
```

Does BASIC "memorize" the entire program?

Yes. Each time you press Enter, BASIC stores a copy of that line in the computer's memory. As you type a program line-by-line, BASIC retains the entire program in memory.

Running a Program

To run the program, type RUN. Don't include a line number! RUN is a direct mode command that tells BASIC to run the program stored in memory.

So, here goes. Type RUN and watch what happens:

```
Ok
100 PRINT "Hello"
200 PRINT "Goodbye"
300 END
RUN
Hello
Goodbye
Ok
```

Your RUN command makes BASIC run your program. As you no doubt expected, the program displayed Hello and Goodbye. But did you anticipate that last Ok prompt?

The Ok prompt simply indicates that BASIC performed your requested command (RUN, in this case) and now awaits your next command. At this point, you can do one of two things:

❑ Enter any direct mode command. You won't affect the program in memory. Try typing CLS or a direct mode PRINT command such as PRINT "I did it". To verify that the program is unaffected, rerun your program with a RUN command.

❑ Edit the program in memory. You can type new lines into your program or edit existing lines. We experiment with program editing next.

Editing a Program

Modifying a program is easy. You can add new lines, modify existing lines, or delete lines you no longer want. Let's try all three.

Adding a New Line

To add a new line, just type the new line. Be sure to include an appropriate line number. BASIC inserts the new line so that *all* program lines are kept in numerical order.

Our program has three lines, numbered 100, 200, and 300. You could give the program a new first line by typing a line with a line number of, say, 50; or a new last line with a line number greater than 300; or a new second line with a line number between 100 and 200.

Try inserting the following line and running the program:

```
150 PRINT "Still here"
```

Just type the line, followed by RUN:

```
Ok
150 PRINT "Still here"
RUN
Hello
Still here
Goodbye
Ok
```

Inside the computer's memory, the program now looks like this:

```
100 PRINT "Hello"
150 PRINT "Still here"
200 PRINT "Goodbye"
300 END
```

Allow for New Program Lines

When you write programs, avoid consecutive line numbers such as 10, 11, and 12. Why? You want to leave room for expansion in case you later need to add new lines between the existing lines.

A line number can be any whole number from 0 to 65529. BASIC arranges your program lines from the smallest line number to the largest.

We recommend that you leave a gap of at least 10 between successive line numbers. Many programmers use line numbers of 100, 110, 120, and so on. That way, they have room for nine new program lines between any two existing lines.

Occasionally, you may box yourself into a corner. For example you may want to insert 15 new lines between lines 120 and 130. There *is* a way out. You can renumber program lines with the RENUM command. We discuss RENUM and other advanced editing topics in Chapter 13, "Editing Techniques."

Modifying an Existing Line

To alter a program line, just type the new line using the existing line number. For example, you can change line 100 by typing in a new line 100. BASIC replaces the old line 100 with the new line 100.

Let's modify the program by adding sound. Remember BEEP from the last chapter? Change line 100 to BEEP, and rerun the program.

```
Ok
100 BEEP
RUN
Still here
Goodbye
Ok
```

Did you hear the beep when you ran the program?

Notice that the new line 100 replaces the old line 100. The program no longer displays Hello, which was the effect of the old line 100. The old line 100 is erased from the computer's memory. The program now looks like this:

```
100 BEEP
150 PRINT "Still here"
200 PRINT "Goodbye"
300 END
```

Deleting a Line

To delete a line, just type the line number (followed by pressing Enter). This removes the line permanently from the program.

For example, delete line 200 and run the program:

```
Ok
200
RUN
Still here
Ok
```

The program beeps and displays the message Still here. Line 200 is gone. Here is the program now:

```
100 BEEP
150 PRINT "Still here"
300 END
```

Now, let's see how to verify that the current program consists of these three lines.

Listing a Program

When you type a program or make program modifications, you may lose track of exactly what your program looks like.

At any time, you can view the current program with the LIST command. Just type LIST and press Enter. Try it now:

```
Ok
LIST
100 BEEP
150 PRINT "Still here"
300 END
Ok
```

Notice that line 200 is indeed gone.

Soon you will see how LIST can display only selected lines of a program.

Using END

Throughout these experiments, we haven't said much about line 300, the END instruction. END does just what the name suggests—ends the program. When BASIC encounters END, the program concludes and BASIC displays the Ok prompt.

Actually, you don't need an END instruction as the last line of a program. BASIC is "smart" enough to realize that your program ends after the last line. You could delete line 300 and the program would still run fine.

END does *not* indicate the physical end of the program, but rather the end of program execution. You can have more than one END instruction in a program. (Some programs contain END in the middle of the program. You learn why later in the book.) Remember, whenever BASIC encounters an END instruction, your program immediately terminates.

Add an END instruction in the middle of the program. Try this experiment:

```
Ok
125 END
RUN
Ok
```

When you run the program, you hear a beep but no message displays on-screen. The END instruction in line 125 terminates the program even though line 150 is still present.

Listing Parts of a Program

List the current program:

```
Ok
LIST
100 BEEP
125 END
150 PRINT "Still here"
300 END
Ok
```

You will frequently use LIST immediately after making a program change. For example:

```
Ok
125
LIST
100 BEEP
150 PRINT "Still here"
300 END
Ok
```

Here, you typed 125 to erase line 125. Next, you typed LIST to see the current program. Note that line 125 is now gone.

As you have seen, LIST displays all the lines of your program. LIST works quickly; sometimes *too* quickly. Suppose that your program has more than 20 lines. The early lines swiftly scroll off the screen as the listing completes. You may never get a chance to examine those early lines.

Fortunately, BASIC permits you to list a specific range of lines; just specify a line number range as part of the LIST command. Use a hyphen to separate the beginning and ending range of line numbers. For example, the following instruction lists only lines 150 through 300:

```
LIST 150-300
```

If you leave off the beginning or ending line number, BASIC substitutes the first or last line, respectively. Table 3.1 shows sample LIST commands.

Table 3.1. *Sample* LIST *commands.*

Command	Effect
LIST	Lists all lines of a program
LIST 100–400	Lists lines numbered from 100 to 400
LIST 200–	Lists lines numbered 200 and higher
LIST –300	Lists lines numbered from 0 to 300

When you list your program, LIST displays all reserved words in uppercase, regardless of whether you originally typed them with upper- or lowercase letters.

Remember from the last chapter that, when you enter direct mode commands, you can type reserved words with either upper- or lowercase letters. The same goes for reserved words in program instructions.

When you are entering a program, you can type reserved words with lowercase letters if you want. Many programmers do just that to avoid the hassle of unnecessarily holding down the Shift key.

To see how LIST converts lowercase to uppercase, try adding the following lines to your program. Type the lines as shown, with cls and print in lowercase.

```
Ok
50 cls
120 print "Hello again"
LIST
50 CLS
100 BEEP
120 PRINT "Hello again"
150 PRINT "Still here"
300 END
Ok
```

Note that LIST displays CLS and PRINT in uppercase (in lines 50 and 120). Do you remember CLS from the last chapter? CLS works the same as a program instruction or as a direct mode command: the screen clears.

Try running the program. Your screen clears, you hear a beep, and the following output is produced in the upper left part of your screen:

```
Hello again
Still here
Ok
```

No More Ok, Okay?

As you have seen, BASIC displays Ok after finishing a direct mode command such as CLS or RUN. When you type a line of a program, however, BASIC does not display Ok.

From now on, we do not always show Ok in our examples. Rest assured though, that your screen will always show Ok after a direct mode command. When the context is important, we show Ok for clarity or to emphasize a particular point.

Removing the Function Key Display

As explained in the previous chapter, the bottom line of your screen contains the Function Key Display. This line indicates special meanings attached to the function keys F1 through F10. We explain how to use the function keys and the display line in Chapter 12, "Programming Hardware Devices," and Chapter 13, "Editing Techniques."

For now, you may find the Display line distracting. You can easily remove it, by just typing the following command:

```
KEY OFF
```

The Display line disappears. You now have extra screen space for your program listings and other work. The line remains turned off for the rest of your BASIC session but reappears when you start BASIC the next time.

You can restore the Display line with the following companion command:

```
KEY ON
```

Saving and Loading Programs on Disk

As you create or modify a program, BASIC retains the program in memory. If you turn off your machine or leave BASIC, however, your program vanishes from your computer's memory.

You can save worthwhile programs on a diskette (or hard disk). After you save a program, you can later load it from the diskette back into the computer's memory. After loading, you can run the program or make additional modifications.

In this section, we discuss the following topics:

❏ Choosing a file name for the program.
❏ Saving a program on disk.
❏ Erasing a program from memory.
❏ Loading a program from a disk.

Choosing a File Name

Each program you save becomes a separate disk file. Before you save any program, you must choose a name for the disk file.

DOS file names are one to eight characters long. Optionally, you can include an extension with the main name. The extension, if present, consists of a period followed by one to three characters. You can use any combination of letters and numerical digits (and even some special characters such as & and #) in your file name. Table 3.2 provides some examples of DOS file names.

Table 3.2. *Some example file names.*

File Name	Comment
MYPROG.BAS	The extension .BAS is conventional for BASIC program files.
MYFILE	File names do not have to contain an extension.
ROSTER.1	Extensions can be numbers (and less than three characters).
BEEP.BAS	Try to make your file names descriptive.

If you need additional help with DOS file names, see Chapter 10, "Using Disk Files," or your DOS documentation.

DOS does not distinguish between upper- and lowercase letters in file names. For example, MYPROG.BAS and MyProg.BAS both refer to the same file.

By convention, BASIC program files have the extension .BAS. However, that extension is not mandatory. You can give your files any extension you choose (or no extension at all). The .BAS extension quickly identifies the file as being a BASIC program.

As much as possible, you want to choose meaningful file names. That way, you can readily associate the file name with the program contained in the file.

Saving a File on Disk—*SAVE*

Now, let's save your program on disk. If you followed our directions from the preceding chapter, you created a BASIC work diskette that is now in the A: drive of your computer. (Alternately, if your machine has a hard disk, you may be running BASIC from a hard disk directory.) If you have not yet created a work diskette, refer to the directions in Chapter 2, "Up and Running."

The SAVE command saves a program on disk. Just type SAVE followed by a file name in quotation marks. BASIC saves the current program to a disk file using the file name you specify.

Let's choose a file name of BEEP.BAS. Type the following line:

```
SAVE "BEEP.BAS"
```

When you press Enter, you should hear your disk drive whir. BASIC saves your program on diskette with the file name BEEP.BAS. (Of course, if you are running from a hard disk, the file is saved on the hard disk instead.)

You don't have to use uppercase letters when you type the file name. Remember, in file names, DOS treats lowercase and uppercase letters equivalently. And, as with all BASIC reserved words, you can type SAVE in lowercase also. Therefore, the following command works just as well (and doesn't require so many shifted keystrokes):

```
save "beep.bas"
```

SAVE provides a convenient feature. If you don't specify a file extension, SAVE automatically adds the .BAS extension. The idea is that the .BAS extension is normally used for BASIC program files. (However, you can override this default by specifying any extension you choose.)

One word of caution about SAVE. When you save a file, make sure that you don't already have a file with the same name on your diskette. If you do, BASIC replaces the old disk file with the new file. You won't get any warning that your old file is about to be replaced.

Of course, sometimes you *want* the new saved file to replace the old one. That's common when you modify an old program. In such a case, you often make changes that render the old program obsolete. So you just let the new disk file replace the old file.

Table 3.3 shows some sample SAVE commands.

Table 3.3. *Sample* SAVE *commands.*

Command	Comment
SAVE "BEEP.BAS"	Saves file on default disk drive.
SAVE "BEEP"	Saves file as BEEP.BAS. (Same effect as previous command.)
SAVE "MYPROG.1"	Saves file with name and extension as shown.

You can get a listing of the files on your diskette with the FILES command. We discuss FILES shortly.

Saving Files on Other Disk Drives (or Directories)

How does BASIC "know" on which disk drive (or disk directory) to save a file?

By default, SAVE writes files onto the drive (or directory) from which you started BASIC. If you followed our directions in the previous chapter, you created a work diskette (or directory) from which you start BASIC. As a result, BASIC saves files on that diskette (or directory).

You can override this default by using a drive and/or path designation as part of your file name. For example, the following command saves a file to the B: drive:

```
SAVE "B:BEEP.BAS"
```

As another example, the following command saves a file in a particular directory of a hard disk:

```
SAVE "C:\PROGRAMS\QUE\BEEP.BAS"
```

We provide more information about DOS file paths in Chapter 10, "Using Disk Files."

Throughout this chapter, we assume that all file input and output occurs on your default drive (and/or directory). As a result, we specify only file names (and neither drives nor paths) in our examples.

Erasing a Program from Memory—*NEW*

The NEW command erases the current program from memory. Simply type **NEW**. Use NEW when you are finished with one program and want to begin work on another. Of course, if your current program is important, you should save the program before you type NEW.

Try the following experiment. You erase the current program from memory, type in a new one-line program, and save the new program to disk. (Before you try this experiment, make sure that you already have saved the current program as BEEP.BAS.)

```
NEW
Ok
LIST
Ok
200 PRINT "Testing, one, two, three"
RUN
Testing, one, two, three
Ok
LIST
200 PRINT "Testing, one, two, three"
SAVE "TEST"
Ok
```

Note what happened after the first **LIST**. BASIC simply responded with **Ok** because there was no program left in memory. The **NEW** command erased the old program.

You then typed line 200, which created a one-line program consisting of a single PRINT instruction. You ran the program and listed it. (Note that the listing contains no remnants of the old program). Finally, you saved the new program. BASIC saves the file as TEST.BAS (automatically adding the .BAS extension to the file name).

Listing File Names—*FILES*

To see a listing of files saved on your work diskette, type FILES. BASIC shows you all files in your default drive (and/or directory).

Type FILES now and compare your output with ours:

```
FILES
A:\
COMMAND  .COM     GWBASIC  .EXE     BEEP  .BAS
  TEST  .BAS
 200704 Bytes free
```

The first line, A:\ in our case, indicates that the upcoming file list is for the root directory of the A: drive (the backslash, \, indicates the root directory).

Next, BASIC displays the file names. Four files are listed per line. The file list spreads to multiple lines if necessary. Our work diskette contains the following four files:

- ☐ COMMAND.COM   (The DOS system file)
- ☐ GWBASIC.EXE   (Our version of BASIC)
- ☐ BEEP.BAS   (The BEEP program we saved)
- ☐ TEST.BAS   (The TEST program we saved)

The last line indicates the number of free bytes on your work diskette (or directory). This number indicates how much room you have available for saving additional files.

Your FILES listing should be similar. (If you have an IBM computer, you see the file BASICA.COM rather than GWBASIC.EXE.) In any case, the main point is that FILES provides proof that you have successfully saved the program files BEEP.BAS and TEST.BAS.

Loading a File from Disk—*LOAD*

LOAD is the complementary command to SAVE. Whereas SAVE stores a program from memory to a disk file, LOAD transfers a program from a disk file back into the computer's memory. LOAD erases any old program from memory before loading the new program.

After loading a program, you can run the program, list it, make modifications, or whatever, just as though you had typed the program into your computer.

As with SAVE, a LOAD command includes the desired file name in quotation marks. Also similar, if you leave off the extension name, BASIC assumes the extension .BAS.

The following experiment shows LOAD in action:

```
NEW
Ok
LOAD "BEEP.BAS"
Ok
RUN
Hello again
Still here
Ok
LOAD "TEST"
Ok
RUN
Testing, one, two, three
Ok
LIST
200 PRINT "Testing, one, two, three"
Ok
```

Explaining Some Terminology

Before going on, we should clarify some terminology. We have been using terms such as *command*, *instruction*, and *reserved word* in proper context. Perhaps, however, some meanings are a bit unclear to you. If so, table 3.4 should resolve any ambiguities.

Table 3.4. *Definitions of some BASIC terms.*

Term	Example	Meaning
Reserved word	END	A reserved word is a word with a special meaning to BASIC. Most reserved words are integral parts of direct mode commands or program instructions. Appendix A lists all of BASIC's reserved words.
Keyword	CLS	Synonymous with *reserved word*.

Term	Example	Meaning
Command	SAVE "MYPROG"	Anything typed in direct mode. A command always contains a reserved word. Some commands (such as CLS and BEEP), are nothing more than a single keyword. Other commands consist of a keyword and additional information, such as the SAVE example shown here.
Instruction	200 BEEP	A program component for BASIC to execute. Each program *line* contains a line number and one or more instructions. Like commands, instructions consist of a reserved word and, in most cases, additional information. The primary difference between a command and an instruction is context: you type a command in direct mode; you place an instruction inside a program. (A few commands are not legal inside programs, and a few instructions cannot be typed as commands.)
Statement	PRINT	Any keyword (or combination of keywords) that forms the action verb of a command or instruction. Not all keywords are statements. For example, BEEP, CLS, and SAVE are keywords that also happen to be statements. OFF and ON, however, are keywords but not statements.
Text literal	"Hello"	Any group of characters enclosed in quotation marks.
String literal	"Same thing"	Synonymous with *text literal*.

Understanding Common Programming Techniques

In the rest of this chapter, we present some simple programs that illustrate important programming principles. Our primary purpose is to give you an understanding of commonly used BASIC programming techniques. We want you to develop an intuitive feel for what BASIC programming is all about.

The programs introduce various BASIC topics and several keywords. We are brief in this chapter, but later in the book we discuss in-depth most of these topics and keywords.

So don't let yourself get bogged down. If you don't understand something in this chapter, just move ahead to the next topic. Wait till we cover your troublesome subject in a later chapter.

Please try the programs as we present them. If you get the urge to deviate a little, by all means, go right ahead. We take that as a compliment.

Ready? Here we go. Take a look at this program:

```
100 PRINT "Please enter your name"
110 INPUT YOURNAME$
120 PRINT "Hello, "; YOURNAME$
```

A new keyword in this program is `INPUT`, which requests that the user provide input while the program is running. (If you run the program yourself, you are the user; if you give the program to someone else, that person is the user.)

Introducing Variables

The `INPUT` instruction (line 110) contains a *variable* called `YOURNAME$`. A variable is really nothing more than a name you give to a memory location or locations where data is stored. The value of the data can (and usually does) change while the program is running. By referencing a variable, you are really saying to the computer, "Use whatever value I currently have stored in the memory location reserved for that variable." Some BASIC instructions change the value of a variable; other instructions just use the value.

A variable permits a program to do different things each time the program is run, depending on what value is assigned to the variable. This particular program asks for the user's name, which might be almost anything.

Why does YOURNAME$ end with a dollar sign? Couldn't we just call the variable YOURNAME, and forget about that dollar sign?

No. The dollar sign *is* important. BASIC separates data into two fundamental categories: numeric data and *string* (or text) data. Accordingly, BASIC variables also fall into two fundamental categories (depending upon which kind of data the variable can store):

❏ *Numeric variables*. These variables store numeric values, such as 14, 33.8, and so on. You can change the value stored in a numeric variable, but the value must always be a numeric quantity.

❏ *String variables*. These variables store text information such as "Hello", "Indiana Jones", or "76 trombones". You can change the value stored in a string variable, but the value must always be text information.

Every variable is either a numeric variable or a string variable. The dollar sign at the end of a variable name indicates that the variable is a string variable. String data is alphanumeric data (letters, digits, and other characters) that are "strung" together in any desired length. YOURNAME$ is a string variable.

BASIC Ignores Case Distinctions in Variable Names

Variable names must follow certain rules, which have evolved over the years. Early versions of the BASIC language restricted variable names to one or two characters, but modern BASIC allows much longer, descriptive names.

BASIC permits variable names of as much as 40 characters. As with reserved words, BASIC treats upper- and lowercase letters of variable names as identical. Also like reserved words, BASIC converts all letters of variable names to uppercase when you list a program.

For example, you might type a variable as YOURNAME$, YourName$, or yourname$. BASIC treats each of these forms as the same variable, not as three different variables. All three forms appear as YOURNAME$ when you view the program with a LIST command.

In this book, for conformity with LIST, we show variables with all uppercase letters. But you can type them with lowercase letters if you want.

For further discussion of BASIC's rules for variable naming, see Chapter 4, "Language Building Blocks."

A variable name that doesn't end with a dollar sign is a numeric variable. YOURNAME would be a numeric variable that stored numeric quantities. YOURNAME$ and YOURNAME could coexist in the same program, but they would be two distinct variables, each of which stored different information.

Using *INPUT*

Again, here's the program we have been considering:

```
100 PRINT "Please enter your name"
110 INPUT YOURNAME$
120 PRINT "Hello, "; YOURNAME$
```

The contents of YOURNAME$ depend on what you type when you are prompted by the INPUT instruction. When you run this program and type your name as a response, the output might look like this (at least if your name is Whitney!):

```
Please enter your name
? Whitney
Hello, Whitney
```

The question mark at the beginning of the second line is a prompt character produced by the INPUT instruction in line 110. (Don't confuse the ? prompt with the Ok prompt from direct mode. The question mark comes when BASIC executes your INPUT instruction.)

The program is prompting you for input, much like a drama coach prompts an actor to speak lines. You do not need to respond promptly to the prompt, by the way; computers are very patient.

In this case, you responded by typing Whitney and pressing Enter. The INPUT instruction then stores the text string Whitney into the string variable YOURNAME$.

Printing the Value of Variables

The last line of the output comes from the PRINT instruction in line 120. That instruction prints both the text literal ("Hello,") *and* the value of the variable YOURNAME$—namely, Whitney.

Using Blank Spaces and Semicolon Separators

In line 120, did you notice the blank space after the comma that follows the word Hello? If you don't include that blank space, there will be no blank space in the output between the comma and the user's name.

In the PRINT instruction, a semicolon separates the items to be printed. A semicolon says to leave no additional spaces in the output. Try changing the number of spaces after the comma to see how the output's spacing changes.

And you might try rerunning the program and typing *your* name or maybe a friend's name.

Assigning Values to Variables

BASIC provides many ways of assigning a value to a variable. The last program demonstrates one way: line 110 is an INPUT instruction that assigns a string value to the variable YOURNAME$.

The most straightforward assignment method, however, involves assigning a value to a variable with the equal sign. You place the variable name on the left of the equal sign and the value to be assigned on the right.

For example, try the following program. (Before you type the new program, erase the existing program with NEW. If you want, you can save the old program on disk first.)

```
100 MYNAME$ = "Phil Feldman"
200 MYAGE = 42
300 PRINT MYNAME$
400 PRINT "is"
500 PRINT MYAGE
RUN
Phil Feldman
is
 42
```

Note how lines 100 and 200 assign values to the variables MYNAME$ and MYAGE, respectively. Instructions that directly assign values to variables are called, naturally enough, *assignment* instructions. As you can see, assignment instructions work equally well for both string and numeric variables.

However, you must be careful that you assign only numeric values to numeric variables, and only string values to string variables. The following two instructions are improper:

```
200 MYNAME$ = 25

300 MYAGE = "Teenager"
```

Do you see why neither instruction is legal? Line 200 attempts to assign a numeric value to a string variable, and line 300 does the reverse.

Well, what happens if you *do* try one of these illegal instructions? If you are curious, go ahead and find out. Type one of the instructions and run your program. You will find that BASIC catches the mistake. Your program stops and displays an informative error message. Later in this chapter, we discuss errors and what to do about them.

The right side of assignment instructions can be simple (as in our examples) or more involved. Sometimes the right side contains expressions involving several terms.

Assignment instructions are among the most frequently used BASIC instructions. We discuss assignment in the next chapter and throughout this book.

Performing Simple Arithmetic

Let's try a program that makes simple calculations. Suppose that you want a program which asks for entry of two numbers and then calculates the sum and product of the two numbers. The preceding program has a PRINT instruction to tell the user what to enter, followed by an INPUT instruction for the data entry. This next program uses another form of the INPUT instruction that accomplishes both tasks.

```
100 PRINT "This program makes calculations
   using two numbers"
110 INPUT "First number"; NUM1
120 INPUT "Second number"; NUM2
130 PRINT "The sum is"; NUM1 + NUM2
140 PRINT "The product is"; NUM1 * NUM2
```

If you run this program and enter the numbers 7 and 5, the output looks like this:

```
This program makes calculations using two numbers
First number? 7
Second number? 5
The sum is 12
The product is 35
```

Notice that the variables in this program, NUM1 and NUM2, do not end with dollar signs. As you have seen, that makes NUM1 and NUM2 numeric variables. Within BASIC's rules, you could name the variables almost anything—FRED, THEFIRSTNUMBER, or XB47JQX35R, for example. Needless to say, choosing simple but descriptive variable names is an important part of writing understandable programs.

Also notice that BASIC uses the asterisk (*) to indicate multiplication. The plus and minus signs indicate addition and subtraction, respectively. The slash (/) denotes division.

Do you see how the INPUT instructions in lines 110 and 120 work? Look again at the output and at lines 110 and 120.

Each INPUT instruction contains a text literal separated from the variable name by a semicolon. When BASIC prompts a user on-screen, it prints the text literal followed by a question mark. In this way, one INPUT instruction replaces the PRINT and INPUT combination used in the previous program.

Altering Logic Flow with *GOTO*

Suppose that you want to make the same calculations shown in the last program, but for many pairs of numbers. Do you have to run the program from the beginning each time?

No. You can insert program instructions that alter the logic flow. Instead of allowing the program to end after the last instruction, you can add a new instruction that tells BASIC to go back to the beginning of the program, or to any other point in the program, for that matter. By returning to earlier lines, you cause some instructions to repeat.

How do you specify which line the program should jump to? This is where line numbers come into play. Modify the program by adding the following new line (150):

```
150 GOTO 110
LIST
100 PRINT "This program makes calculations
    using two numbers"
110 INPUT "First number"; NUM1
120 INPUT "Second number"; NUM2
130 PRINT "The sum is"; NUM1 + NUM2
140 PRINT "The product is"; NUM1 * NUM2
150 GOTO 110
```

Look at line 150. That GOTO instruction transfers program flow directly back to line 110. Therefore, after line 140 executes, line 150 makes BASIC go back and reexecute line 110. From there, BASIC continues with line 120, 130, and so on. When line 150 comes up again, program control returns once more to line 110.

GOTO can jump logic flow anywhere within a program. You can "go to" an earlier line, to a later line, even to the line that contains the GOTO instruction! Note that GOTO is a single word (no space between GO and TO).

Looping

You may have detected a problem. How will our last program ever end? Line 150 always goes back to get two more numbers, creating an *endless loop* or *infinite loop*.

In general, a *loop* is a group of instructions that execute repeatedly. Endless loops, as the name suggests, repeat *endlessly*. (Well, until you take drastic action, anyway. If you are "stuck" in the program, press Ctrl-Break instead of entering a number, and you will interrupt the endless loop. We talk more about Ctrl-Break shortly.)

The program has an endless loop in lines 110 through 150. These lines repeat continuously.

What the program needs is a *conditional loop*. Such a loop repeats *until* a certain condition occurs. The following program revision solves the problem:

```
100 PRINT "This program makes calculations
    using two numbers"
110 INPUT "First number"; NUM1
120 INPUT "Second number"; NUM2
125 IF NUM1 = 0 AND NUM2 = 0 THEN PRINT
      "All Done": END
130 PRINT "The sum is"; NUM1 + NUM2
140 PRINT "The product is"; NUM1 * NUM2
150 GOTO 110
```

In the middle of the loop, at line 125, we added an IF instruction that, under certain conditions, causes the program to end. The conditions are that both NUM1 and NUM2 must equal zero. When these conditions are met, the program displays a message and ends.

Looping is a powerful programming technique. Many kinds of loops exist. We explore loops often throughout this book.

Placing Multiple Instructions on One Line

Note the use of the colon (:) in line 125. The colon is a way to combine two or more instructions on one program line. Don't confuse the colon with the semicolon; their uses are entirely different in spite of their similar appearance.

Punctuation Is Important

Punctuation characters are critical to BASIC programs. Simple (but hard to notice) typing errors can cause annoying error messages or incorrect program results.

Using Indentation and Spacing

Here's our current program with a modified, stylized look. Each instruction is identical to the old version, and the program operates exactly like before:

```
100 PRINT "This program makes calculations
    using two numbers"
110    INPUT "First number"; NUM1
120    INPUT "Second number"; NUM2
125    IF NUM1 = 0 AND NUM2 = 0 THEN PRINT
       "All Done": END
130    PRINT "The sum is"; NUM1 + NUM2
140    PRINT "The product is"; NUM1 * NUM2
150 GOTO 110
```

The only difference is that now the program has five lines indented from the others. Lines 110 through 140 are spaced further to the right than lines 100 and 150.

Indentation is entirely optional. You can put as many spaces as you want after a line number. Indentation provides a useful way to visually set off a block of related instructions. Here we used indentation to set off the program loop in lines 110 to 140.

Speaking of spaces, we should also mention that BASIC ignores blank spaces between reserved words, variables, and other pieces of an instruction. You may use one space, two spaces, or multiple spaces between instruction components. For example, here are just a few alternative ways you can write line 130:

```
130 PRINT    "The sum is"  ;   NUM1+NUM2

130 PRINT "The sum is";   NUM1  +   NUM2

130    PRINT "The sum is"; NUM1+NUM2
```

Spacing, however, *is* important within a reserved word, variable name, or string literal. You cannot write PRINT as P R I N T; neither can you write the variable NUM1 as NUM 1. When you print a string literal (text enclosed between quotation marks), any blank spaces are printed exactly as you typed them.

Interrupting a Program with Ctrl-Break

You may find, when you test a new program, that your program goes into an endless loop. As you have seen, this happens when a section of your program executes over and over continuously. You may realize your programming error but, meanwhile, your program keeps running with no end in sight. Help!

The way out is Ctrl-Break. (While pressing the Ctrl key, you simultaneously press the Break key.) BASIC terminates your program and comes back with an Ok prompt. You might think of Ctrl-Break as "Help, let me out of here!"

Try the following simple program to acquaint yourself with Ctrl-Break:

```
100 BEEP
110 GOTO 100
```

As you can see, this program is an endless loop. The BEEP in line 100 executes continuously. The result is a constant drone from your speaker. (The individual beeps blend into one continuous sound.) The noise is pretty annoying, so you probably will press Ctrl-Break right away.

Dealing with Program Errors

Errors are a fact of programming life. All programmers make mistakes, so don't feel bad when the inevitable errors occur. Recognize that errors are bound to happen, learn from them, and forge ahead.

Errors that are not discovered until you run a program are called *run-time* errors. There are three fundamental types of run-time errors:

1. *Syntax errors.* A syntax error occurs when an instruction does not follow the rules of BASIC. For example, you might spell a keyword incorrectly, use improper punctuation, or combine keywords in an illegal way. In such a case, the instruction is meaningless. As a result, BASIC cannot even *attempt* to execute the instruction.

2. *Execution errors.* An execution error occurs when an instruction requests an action that BASIC cannot perform. For example, you might divide a number by zero or GOTO a line number that doesn't exist. In such a case, no syntax error is present. However, an instruction attempts something illegal in the context of the whole program. BASIC understands what the instruction means, but cannot perform the requested action.

3. *Logic errors.* A logic error occurs when a program runs to completion but the results are incorrect. Somehow the program does not work correctly. In programming jargon, the program contains a *bug*. The programmer must *debug* the program, which means finding and correcting the error.

Correcting Syntax Errors

When a syntax error occurs, BASIC stops running your program and informs you of the guilty line.

Try the following experiment. Type line 110 exactly as shown with PRINT incorrectly spelled as PRNT.

```
NEW
Ok
100 PRINT "Hello"
110 PRNT "Goodbye"
RUN
Hello
Syntax error in 110
Ok
110 PRNT "Goodbye"
```

Nothing special happened when you typed line 110 incorrectly. BASIC does not catch syntax errors in program instructions until you actually run the program.

When you run this program, line 100 executes correctly and displays Hello. Next, BASIC moves to line 110, which contains the misspelled keyword PRNT. BASIC just can't make any sense out of PRNT.

Remember, BASIC insists that you follow its rules. You might think that PRNT is close enough to PRINT that BASIC should be able to "figure out" what you mean. No such luck. PRNT is indecipherable to BASIC, and a syntax error results.

When a syntax error is discovered, BASIC displays a message showing you the relevant line number. Then, after Ok, BASIC displays the guilty line in its entirety and puts the cursor at the spot in the line where the syntax error occurs.

In our example, the cursor is under the first quotation mark because that is the first character after the indecipherable `PRNT`. You can now edit the offending line. Use the left and right arrow keys to move the cursor anywhere along the line. You can delete characters with Backspace and type new characters as necessary. When the line is correct, just press Enter. The cursor can be anywhere on the line. You might then want to list your program to make sure that your editing is accurate. See Chapter 13, "Editing Techniques," for more details about editing.

Correcting Execution Errors

When an execution error occurs, BASIC stops your program and displays an explanatory error message. Try the following experiment:

```
NEW
Ok
100 PRINT "What's gonna happen?"
110 GOTO 105
RUN
What's gonna happen?
Undefined line number in 110
Ok
```

When you run this program, BASIC first executes line 100 and dutifully displays the question contained in the text literal. However, line 110 is a different story.

Line 110 attempts to "go to" line 105, but the program doesn't have any line 105. Note that the syntax of line 110 is fine. The instruction is constructed legally and follows BASIC's syntax rules. You don't get a syntax error.

Instead, line 110 results in an execution error. BASIC displays an explanatory message. In this case, the message indicates that line 110 references an undefined line number. Such a message makes it a snap to look at line 100 and discover the cause of the error. See Appendix D, "Error Messages," for a complete list of BASIC's error messages and their probable causes.

Debugging a Program

We have just touched on how to find and correct program errors. Chapter 14, "Debugging and Testing," examines this unavoidable subject in-depth.

Manipulating Strings

Many BASIC programs manipulate text data. In BASIC terminology, text data is stored in *strings*, and BASIC has an entire group of string-manipulation statements that operate on text data. As we have mentioned, string variables are recognizable by the dollar-sign character at the end of the variable name.

Let's look at a program that does some string manipulation:

```
100 REM - STRING1 - This program
    manipulates strings
110 INPUT "What is your name"; YOURNAME$
120 FOR POINTER = 1 TO LEN(YOURNAME$)
130    PRINT POINTER, MID$(YOURNAME$, POINTER, 1)
140 NEXT POINTER
```

This program introduces several new BASIC instructions, but first let's see what happens when "John" is supplied as the answer to "What is your name?"

```
RUN
What is your name? John
 1            J
 2            o
 3            h
 4            n
```

Commenting a Program

The first program line, line 100, is something new—a REM instruction. REM stands for *remark* and causes the remainder of the line to be treated as a non-executable comment rather than as a BASIC program instruction. When REM occurs, BASIC just ignores the remainder of the line and proceeds to the next line.

With REM instructions, programmers "self-document" their programs with comments and explanations. When someone looks at the program in the future, these remarks tell the person (including the original programmer) what the program is all about and how it works.

Notice that we have arbitrarily decided to show the program name in line 100, along with a short description of what the program does. The hyphens around the program name are not required by REM; we simply like to use some such way to separate the name from the description.

> ### A Comment on Comments
>
> Using numerous comments is a good habit. You will be amazed how much help a few comments can provide when you resume working with a program after a few months.

Introducing the *FOR...NEXT* Loop

The second program line (line 110) is nothing new—just an INPUT instruction that prompts the user for his or her name. But lines 120 through 140 contain a bunch of new material.

The three lines constitute a FOR...NEXT loop. The reserved words FOR (on line 120) and NEXT (on line 140) tell BASIC to repeat all the in-between instructions for a specified number of times.

And how many times is that? Well, the answer is a little tricky in this program, because the answer is based on something we have not covered yet—the LEN function.

Functions

A *function* operates on one or more arguments and produces, or returns, a single value. The arguments can be numeric or string. Also, the value returned can be numeric or string, depending on the particular function. BASIC provides a number of built-in functions, with each function specified by a reserved keyword.

LEN is a string function that calculates the length of whatever string is given in parentheses. For our program, the string in parentheses is the variable YOURNAME$. The length does not refer to the length of the variable name itself, but rather to the length of the string contained in that variable. If you type the name John, then LEN(YOURNAME$) is 4. So in this particular case, line 120 is the same as saying

```
120 FOR POINTER = 1 to 4
```

Well, then, why didn't we just *say* that to begin with? Why did we complicate the program with this funny LEN function?

The answer, of course, is that we didn't know how long a name would be entered. LEN enables the program to work correctly for any name, not just a four-character name.

Let's move on to the PRINT instruction in line 130. You can see from the output that this PRINT instruction displays two things on each line: a number and a single character. You have seen many PRINT instructions, but this one is different.

How does line 130 work, and why are there so many spaces between the two output items?

The first value on each output line is the number contained in the variable named POINTER. The FOR...NEXT loop causes this number to increase from one to four—one the first time, two the second, and so on. This is a fundamental, counting type of loop. The program is written this way in order to scan through the entered name one character at a time. POINTER identifies, or *points*, to the character being processed in each repetition of the loop.

The second PRINT argument uses the MID$ function to extract only the single character being pointed to. MID$ can have three parameters: the string to operate on, the extraction starting position, and the length of the extracted string. The first time the PRINT instruction executes, POINTER points at the first character, and MID$ extracts only that one character (the J in John). The second time, POINTER points to the second character (the o in John), and MID$ again extracts only that one character, and so on.

If you are having trouble understanding how MID$ works, don't worry. MID$ is a relatively fancy string function. We examine MID$ and working with strings in Chapter 6, "Manipulating Data."

Print Zones

Line 130 displays two items: the value of POINTER, and the value returned by the MID$ argument. But why so many spaces between the two items in each output line?

By separating the two items with a comma, BASIC displays each item at a predefined column position. These column positions, or *print zones*, as they are called, are set automatically by BASIC. Using print zones, you can conveniently produce table-like output with PRINT instructions. We examine PRINT and print zones in considerable detail in Chapter 9, "Writing Text on the Video Screen."

Try an experiment. In line 130, change the 1 at the end of the PRINT instruction to 2 or even omit the third MID$ parameter (and the preceding comma) entirely. What happens, and why? Look at the detailed description of MID$ in Chapter 6, "Manipulating Data," for an explanation.

Programming Graphics

So far, our programs have worked with numbers and text. Now let's venture into the stimulating world of another kind of data—graphics.

The following program gives you a "sneak preview" of how BASIC can create many interesting visual pictures. Be aware that graphics output is possible only if your video hardware supports graphics; the IBM Monochrome Display Adapter (MDA) does not support graphics, but the Color Graphics Adapter (CGA), Enhanced Graphics Adapter (EGA), and Video Graphics Array (VGA) do.

```
100 REM Program: GRTEST (Draw circle and
    two overlapping boxes)
110 CLS
120 SCREEN 2
130 XCENT = 300: YCENT = 100
140 LINE (XCENT - 150, YCENT - 50) -
    (XCENT + 150, YCENT + 50), 3, B
150 LINE (XCENT - 100, YCENT - 70) -
    (XCENT + 100, YCENT + 70), 3, B
160 CIRCLE (XCENT, YCENT), 60
170 LOCATE 21, 32
180 PRINT "Graphics Test"
```

Run the program. You should see two rectangles and a circle (see fig. 3.1).

Fig. 3.1. Output from the GRTEST *program.*

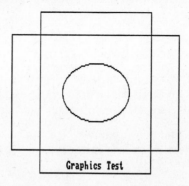

Graphics Test

When the program finishes, your screen will be in graphics mode. Note that the cursor is now a small rectangle rather than the familiar blinking line. Try listing the program. The listing went slower than usual, didn't it? Graphics mode displays output slower than the normal text mode.

To return your screen to text mode, type the following command:

`SCREEN 0`

Your screen will clear and things will be back to normal.

For now, we only briefly explain this program. We hope that the program whets your appetite for Chapter 11, "Creating Graphics," in which graphics is explained in detail.

BASIC has a variety of graphics instructions that simplify drawing certain shapes. In particular, the `LINE` instruction draws either lines or rectangles (boxes), and the `CIRCLE` instruction draws circles.

A `SCREEN` instruction initializes one of BASIC's graphics modes. Depending on your hardware, you have many different screen modes available. `SCREEN 2` is a graphics mode composed of 640 dots horizontally and 200 dots vertically.

Note that you can mix text with graphics. `LOCATE` moves the cursor to any spot on the screen (see Chapter 9, "Writing Text on the Video Screen). `PRINT` instructions work in graphics mode just as in normal text mode.

If you feel adventurous, make a few modifications to the program. You can't hurt your computer, even if you attempt to draw "outside" the normal screen boundaries. Change the value of the circle's radius (the `60` at the end of line 160). Or change the values of the X and Y center locations in line 130. Changes in lines 140 and 150 will draw different rectangles.

Summary

A program collects a group of instructions together in a single unit. In program mode, you work with a program stored in the computer's memory. When you run a program, BASIC executes the program instructions one after another.

It is easy to type, run, and edit programs. You can save worthwhile programs on disk and later load them back into memory.

All programmers make mistakes. Three kinds of programming errors are most common: syntax, execution, and logic errors. BASIC catches syntax and execution errors for you. Logic errors are more subtle because programs can run to completion even though the results are wrong. Programmers have the responsibility of debugging their programs.

This chapter provided a whirlwind tour of several programming topics. You learned about variables, assignment, loops, strings, graphics, comments, and altering the logic flow.

The following direct mode commands were explained: RUN, LIST, KEY OFF, SAVE, LOAD, NEW, and FILES.

BASIC has many statements and keywords for use in programs. We introduced the following keywords: END, INPUT, GOTO, IF, THEN, FOR, NEXT, REM, LEN, MID$, SCREEN, LINE, and CIRCLE.

Part II

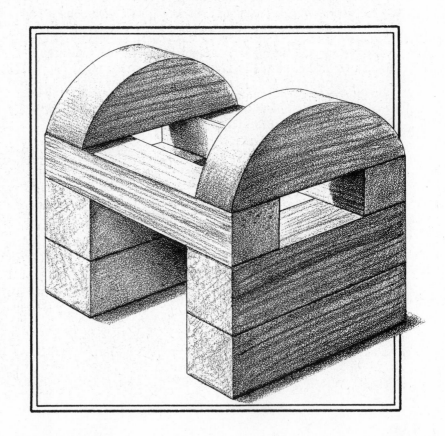

Beginning Programming

B ASIC is a flexible language suitable for both simple and complex programs. Our presentation of the language is from the ground up. We introduce the fundamentals, build a solid foundation, and then advance to the finer points.

Most of the sample programs and program fragments are intentionally short. Simple examples provide succinct, uncluttered illustrations. As we move on to intermediate programming in Part III, we will develop more detailed, full programs.

Please, please, please—like any skill or craft, programming is something you must *do* to understand. Books are fine, but reading can take you only so far. Your experience is the ultimate teacher.

At times, you may wonder what would happen if you change an example slightly or if you use an alternative method. Try it. If this book inspires you to put BASIC through its paces, we will have accomplished a major goal.

4

Language Building Blocks

```
LET, REM
```

Maybe as a child you played with a set of building blocks or some other construction kit to create a myriad of fancy structures. BASIC, like any programming language, is also a kind of construction kit. With BASIC, just as with your childhood blocks, you have many pieces you can arrange together to form finished products.

When you played with your blocks, you made all kinds of edifices. With BASIC, you make all kinds of programs. Using your BASIC "kit," you can construct programs ranging from simple "1-liners" to complex "20-pagers."

This chapter examines BASIC's fundamental building blocks—the various pieces that you join together to form a program and just how the pieces fit together. The following key concepts are presented:

❏ Program structure
❏ Data types (numbers, strings, and constants)
❏ Data holders (variables and arrays)
❏ Expressions and operators
❏ Comments

An Overview of a Program

Suppose that someone asked you, "What is a human being composed of?" You might say, "Two legs, two arms, a head, and so on." This is the large-scale (macroscopic) view. A chemist, however, might say, "Carbon, hydrogen, oxygen, and other atoms." This is the small-scale (microscopic) view. A doctor would probably adopt a middle position: "Water, blood, muscle, and fat." The point is that you look at something as complex as a person in many different ways.

Now, consider this question: What do you see when you look at a program? What is a program composed of?

Just as you can analyze a person, you can view the composition of BASIC programs in many different ways. Each view reveals different information. That is why it is useful to examine programs on both the larger and smaller scales. Figure 4.1 depicts the different "views" of BASIC programs.

Fig. 4.1. The structure of a BASIC program.

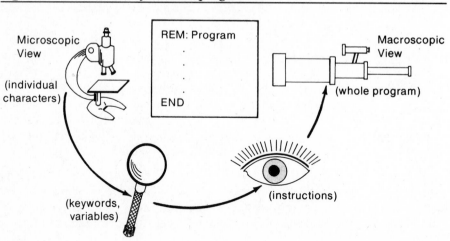

The smallest, most fundamental components of a BASIC program are the individual characters that you type. These individual characters are BASIC's "atoms."

The characters combine to form BASIC's "molecules." Variable names, expressions, and reserved words such as PRINT and 14 + MYAGE are typical examples.

"Molecules" combine to form "compounds." At this level in BASIC are individual instructions such as the following:

```
200 PRINT "The total cost is"; SUMTOTAL
```

Finally, the instructions combine to form the finished product: a working program.

The Macroscopic View

Let's begin by stepping back and looking at a BASIC program from the large-scale, *macroscopic* view. As the chapter progresses, we "zoom in" to look at program components on a progressively smaller scale until, finally, we take the microscopic view.

When you look at a BASIC program, the first thing you might notice is that the program consists of a series of lines. Each line begins with a line number and contains either of the following:

❑ A single instruction
❑ Two or more instructions separated by colons

Line length is limited to 255 characters

BASIC Instructions

An instruction is like a BASIC "sentence." Each instruction orders the computer to perform a particular task, such as calculating an arithmetic quantity, reading from or writing to a disk file, assigning a value to a variable, printing a result, or drawing graphics.

Here are two examples of BASIC instructions that you should already understand:

```
100 PRINT "A stitch in time saves nine."
400 INPUT "What is your name"; YOURNAME$
```

After the line number, every BASIC instruction begins with a *statement*. A statement is a reserved word (occasionally two or three reserved words) that specifies the particular action which that instruction performs. The statement in an instruction is similar to the verb in a sentence. The statements in the two sample instructions are `PRINT` and `INPUT`.

Some statements, such as END and CLS, are instructions all by themselves. However, most instructions contain a statement *and* additional (required or optional) information. The extra information might be expressions, parameters, or other keywords. The PRINT and INPUT instructions in the preceding paragraph are examples of instructions that contain additional information.

Every BASIC instruction must follow the syntax rules associated with the relevant statement. If not, a syntax error occurs.

The LET "Exception"

There is one exception to the rule that all instructions begin with a statement. Look at the following typical assignment instruction (which assigns a value to the variable SCORE):

```
300 SCORE = 21
```

Isn't this a perfectly valid instruction that doesn't begin with a statement?

Yes and no. The same instruction could be written as follows with the optional statement LET:

```
300 LET SCORE = 21
```

Both instructions do exactly the same thing. The first form simply has an implied LET after the line number. When this "exception" is viewed in this manner (the LET is implied), it really conforms to the general rule after all.

BASIC is a rich language that incorporates many different statements (more than 100, in fact). We examine most of them in this book.

Placing Multiple Instructions on a Line

You can place more than one instruction on a line. To do so, just place a colon between instructions. Here is an example of a multiple-instruction line:

```
100 XVALUE% = 18: YVALUE% = 31: ZVALUE% = -5
```

This one line contains three individual instructions. Rather than this one line, you could write three individual lines with one instruction per line:

```
100 XVALUE% = 18
110 YVALUE% = 31
120 ZVALUE% = -5
```

Understanding Line Numbers

You learned about line numbers in the previous chapter. Now we examine line numbers in a little more detail.

A *line number* must be a whole number from 0 to 65529 placed at the beginning of a line. Line numbers serve two important roles:

❏ They define the order of the program lines.

❏ They provide a place "name"—that is, a way you can refer to a particular line.

As you have seen, BASIC arranges all program lines into numerical order. When you LIST a program, you see the program lines placed in numerical order, regardless of the order in which you typed the lines.

The first line of a program can begin with any valid line number. The next line can have any larger line number. To allow for program expansion, consider numbering your program lines in standard increments such as 10, 20, 30, 40, or 100, 150, 200, 250. If you later find that you need to insert a new line, you can simply give the line a line number between the existing line numbers. In Chapter 13, "Editing Techniques," you will see how to renumber existing program lines with the RENUM command.

An Introduction to Data Types

Most programs manipulate data in one way or another. As you have seen, all program data reduces to the following two primary types:

❏ Numbers—arithmetic data

❏ Strings—text (character) data

The simplest way to specify a data value is just to write the value explicitly. For example, in the following instruction, the value 21 is explicitly specified in the PRINT instruction:

```
100 PRINT 21
```

Instead of specifying data values explicitly, you can store and manipulate the values with variables. For example, in the following instructions, the data value for the PRINT instruction in line 110 is stored in the variable MYAGE:

```
100 MYAGE = 21
110 PRINT MYAGE
```

When you write a data value explicitly, we say that the data value is specified by a *literal*. In the instruction PRINT 21, the 21 is a literal. Why? Because the value is specified with explicit numbers, not with a variable name such as MYAGE.

Some reference sources, such as your BASIC manual, use the term *constant* rather than the term *literal*. However, this book uses the term "literal" to refer to data values specified explicitly.

Numeric Literals

Numeric literals look quite natural—just the way most people write numbers. You need a decimal point only if the number has a fractional part (that is, the number is not a whole integer). Negative numbers must begin with a minus sign. For positive numbers, the leading plus sign usually is omitted, but you can include the plus sign if you want.

Consider the following program:

```
100 PRINT 458
110 PRINT -23.499
120 PRINT 0
130 PRINT .000012
```

The output is simply an echo of the values in the original instructions:

```
 458
-23.499
 0
 .000012
```

One thing you cannot do is place commas inside large numbers. For example, this is a no-no: MYNUMBER = 25,128.14. Also, you cannot embed a blank space anywhere in a numeric literal.

> ## Exponential Notation
>
> When numbers become extremely large or extremely small, you need a specialized notation. To say the least, literals such as .0000000000000389 and 4589100000 are awkward.
>
> To express such numbers, BASIC uses exponential notation, also called scientific notation. The literals 3.89E-14 and 4.5891E+09 specify the two numbers given in the previous paragraph. This notation is computer shorthand for the more common mathematical notations $3.89*10^{-14}$ and $4.5891*10^{9}$.
>
> To interpret exponential notation, just move the decimal point the number of places indicated by the exponent after the E. Move the decimal point to the right for positive exponents, left for negative exponents. (You may have to pad the number with zeroes to complete the alignment.)
>
> For example, 2.89E+05 is 289,000; -1.67E-06 is -0.00000167.

String Literals

You worked with strings in the previous chapter. A *string* is simply a sequence of text characters treated as a single value. To express a string literal, place a double quotation mark (not an apostrophe, sometimes called the single quotation) at each end of the text. These paired double quotation marks are called *delimiters* because they mark the beginning and end of the string.

For example, you already understand the following one-line program:

```
250 PRINT "Everything is gonna be OK."
```

The resulting output is just an echo of the string literal with the quotation marks removed:

```
Everything is gonna be OK.
```

Why do you need quotation marks around a string literal? Without them, BASIC interprets the text as variable names rather than as a string. To illustrate, let's try the preceding PRINT instruction again but this time without the quotation marks.

```
250 PRINT Everything is gonna be OK.
RUN
 0   0   0   0   0
```

What are all these zeroes? BASIC thinks that the words `Everything`, `is`, `gonna`, `be`, and `OK` are five variable names and not one long string literal. In this case, each variable has a value of zero. Because BASIC thinks that you want to display the values of the five variables, out come the five zeroes.

Remember, you need quotation marks to specify a string literal.

Data Holders: Variables and Arrays

Data holders store data values for subsequent use. BASIC has two kinds of data holders: variables and arrays. Each is appropriate for the following specific sorts of tasks:

❏ Variables hold a single value that can change.

❏ Arrays hold multiple values (of the same data type) that can change.

Understanding Variables

A variable is really just a name you give to an area of memory where a data value is stored. When you need to retrieve that data or modify its value, you simply refer to the memory location by the variable's name. For example, in a financial program, the variable `BALANCE` may hold the value of the current balance in your checking account. As the program runs, the value stored in `BALANCE` may change several times.

Think of a variable as a box. The box has a name, which you create, printed on the outside. The inside of the box has room for one data value (see fig. 4.2).

In a single program, you may use many such boxes, each box with a different name. To retrieve the data inside a box, or to change the value of the data, you simply refer to the name of the box.

You do not need any special instruction to create a variable. The first time your program uses a new variable name, you automatically create the variable.

Naming Variables

You are free to give variables meaningful, descriptive names. As you design your programs, think about what each variable represents, and choose an appropriately informative name.

Fig. 4.2. Picturing a variable as a box.

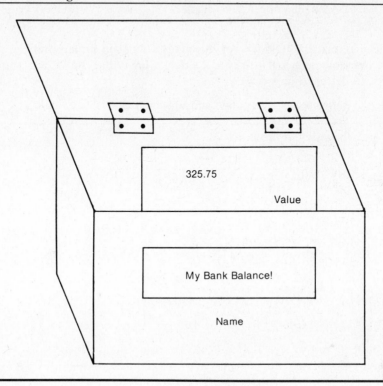

325.75

Value

My Bank Balance!

Name

BASIC does insist that you adhere to the following rules when you choose a variable name:

1. The first character must be a letter.

2. Succeeding characters can be letters, digits, or periods. (No other characters, including blank spaces, hyphens, or underscores, are permissible.)

3. The final character may optionally be one of the type-declaration characters (%, !, #, and $).

4. The name can be any length, but only the first 40 characters are meaningful.

5. A variable name cannot be a reserved word, although embedded reserved words are okay. (See Appendix A, "Reserved Words," for a list of reserved words.)

6. A variable name must not begin with the letters `FN`, which signal a call to a `DEF FN` function. (See Chapter 15, "Toward Advanced Programming.")

Remember that BASIC does not distinguish between upper- and lowercase letters in variable names. If you type a letter in lowercase, BASIC automatically converts the letter to uppercase.

Table 4.1 shows some acceptable and unacceptable variable names.

Table 4.1. Example variable names.

Name	Status	Comment
`MYAGE`	OK	
`X`	OK	
`INDEX%`	OK	Uses type suffix (see following section)
`123GRAPH`	Error	Names must begin with a letter
`FIG7.4`	OK	Embedded periods are okay
`BOB&RAY`	Error	An ampersand is not a valid character
`COLOR`	Error	`COLOR` is a reserved word
`MYCOLOR`	OK	`COLOR` is okay if embedded

The Four Fundamental Data Types

Besides choosing a name, you must make another important decision for each variable: what type of data can that variable store?

As we mentioned, the two primary data types are numbers and strings. But BASIC is even more specific. There are actually four fundamental data types: three different numeric types and the string type (see fig. 4.3).

Each variable you create will have one of these four data types. You will soon see just how you assign your desired data type to each variable. The process of associating a data type with a variable is known as *variable typing* (assigning a data "type," not "typing" on the keyboard).

An individual variable can store data of only its assigned data type. An integer variable, for example, can store only an integer number, not a string or a single-precision number.

Tips for Naming Variables

As you begin to write more and larger programs, you begin to appreciate just how much well-chosen variable names enhance your programs. When variable names are meaningful, you have a much easier time understanding what is going on in a particular program. After all, the more understandable your programs are, the easier it will be for you to make modifications and track down any errors.

Be creative with your variable naming. Some examples of good, clear variable names are `SALARY`, `LASTNAME$`, and `ROOMLENGTH`.

All of us try shortcuts in our lives, and programming is no exception. Sometimes, in the rush to get a program working or in the hope of saving some typing time, you might use short, nondescriptive variable names such as `X`, `A5`, or `JJ`. You can often rationalize these names by thinking, "Hey, my memory is good; I can remember what these variables mean." Six months later, you are apt to look at your previous work with a quizzical stare and throw up your hands in disgust.

Avoid short (and shortsighted), nondescriptive names. After you get in the habit of using descriptive variable names, you will actually be able to program faster with meaningful variable names than without them.

Don't go overboard, however, and make your variable names ridiculously long. Any good thing can be overdone. In your quest for meaningful variable names, you might get carried away with some multisyllabic tongue twisters. Such variable names are counterproductive. They make your programs cumbersome and awkward to read. You should never need such monstrosities as

```
NEXTCHARACTERINTHEUSERSINPUTSTRING$
```

or

```
TEAMSCOREATTHEENDOFREGULATION
```

To stretch our box analogy, for each variable you have four different kinds of boxes from which to choose. Each kind of box stores data of only one particular type. You can change the value stored in the box but only if the new value has the proper data type.

***Fig. 4.3.** The four fundamental data types.*

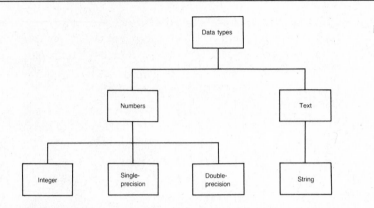

Numeric Data Types

Let's examine the three numeric data types a little more closely:

1. *Integer*. Integers are whole numbers—that is, numbers without fractional components. As such, integer values specify things that can be counted discretely. For example, an integer variable can designate the number of runs scored in a baseball game, the number of times through a programming loop, or the number of orders processed by a shipping department. Integers can be negative, zero, or positive. The range of the integer data type is from $-32,768$ to $+32,767$.

2. *Single-precision*. Many numbers do not lend themselves to the integer data type. For example, a number may have a fractional part, such as 89.22, or may be too large, such as 100,000. The single-precision data type handles such numbers. The range of single-precision is from (approximately) $-1.7E+38$ to $+1.7E+38$.

   The price you pay for using single-precision is that, in general, the computer cannot represent most such numbers exactly, only approximately. For most purposes, the approximation is close enough. Single-precision numbers are accurate to the first six digits. With PRINT, BASIC displays single-precision numbers with seven digits (however, only the first six are guaranteed to be accurate). For example, the fraction one-third is actually .3333333333333 (with an endless string of threes). In single-precision, BASIC displays one-third as .3333334 (you see seven digits, but only the first six are accurate). In practice, you normally do not need to be concerned with possible inaccuracies resulting from single-precision calculations. Only the heaviest number-crunching programs are susceptible to significant errors.

3. *Double-precision.* What do you do when you need more than single-precision accuracy? Double-precision comes to the rescue. Double-precision numbers stretch the accuracy of single-precision to 16 digits. In BASIC, the fraction one-third is now accurate to .3333333333333333 (16 digits). Double-precision has the same range as single-precision, ranging from approximately $-1.7D+38$ to $+1.7D+38$.

The exponential indicator for double-precision literals is D rather than E. The D simply indicates that the number should be interpreted as double-precision rather than single-precision.

The String Data Type

Whereas BASIC provides three numeric data types, there is only one string data type. The key feature of a string variable is that the stored string can be any length. Well, almost any length. The range is from a null (zero-length) string ("") to a medium-length string such as

```
"Zippety doo-dah, zippety aaay"
```

to a string of the maximum length of 255 characters.

A string variable can store only one data string at a time, but the length of this string may change frequently as the program runs. For example, the following program reassigns the value of the variable MYSTRING$ from a short string to a much longer string.

```
100 MYSTRING$ = "I'm not long"
110 PRINT MYSTRING$
120 MYSTRING$ = "You made me considerably l-o-n-g-e-r now"
130 PRINT MYSTRING$
RUN
I'm not long
You made me considerably l-o-n-g-e-r now
Ok
```

Choosing Numeric Data Types

You probably are wondering, "How do I know what data type to choose for each numeric variable? What are the trade-offs? If double-precision variables are the most precise, why not make all my numeric variables double-precision and get maximum precision?"

For numeric variables, the following three trade-offs come into play:

❑ Use of computer memory

❑ Speed of program execution

❑ Accuracy of calculation

When BASIC stores numeric data memory, it converts numbers into a special binary representation. (You do not need to be concerned about how your numbers are converted. BASIC handles the details "behind the scenes.")

The amount of computer memory needed to store each variable depends only on the data type of the variable, not on the actual value stored. Even when the value of the variable changes, the amount of memory needed for the variable remains constant. Table 4.2 shows how much memory BASIC uses for each variable type.

Table 4.2. *Memory required to store numeric values.*

Data Type	Memory Required
Integer	2 bytes (16 bits)
Single-precision	4 bytes (32 bits)
Double-precision	8 bytes (64 bits)

Integer variables take less memory than single- or double-precision. Significant memory savings occur if you use integer variables as much as possible.

Calculations are substantially faster with integer variables than with any other data type. Double-precision calculations consume the most time. The more you use integer variables rather than other data types, the faster your programs will run.

As we mentioned previously, integer variables also win in the accuracy contest. Double-precision, though still approximate, is more accurate than single-precision.

The conclusion is simple: use the simplest data type capable of expressing the numbers involved. Use integer if possible.

Tips for Choosing Numeric Data Types

As a beginning programmer, you do not really need to concern yourself about speed considerations or memory usage. Your programs will tend to be small with relatively few variables and without large arrays. The computer will have plenty of memory and run your programs as fast as you could want. For beginners, single-precision variables will probably suffice for all your numeric variables.

However, as you gain programming skill and your programs start to get larger and more sophisticated, you will need to address memory conservation and speed considerations more and more. Now the choice of numeric data types becomes more critical. You will find that experience will be your best guide.

Giving Variables a Data Type

You have learned about the four different data types, but how do you tell BASIC which data type any particular variable should have?

You can assign a data type to a variable in three different ways:

1. Use a type-declaration suffix character.

   By appending a type-declaration suffix to a variable name, you designate the data type for that variable. You are already familiar with this technique for string variables. When you place a dollar sign at the end of a variable name, you declare that variable to be a string variable. Table 4.3 lists the available suffixes.

Table 4.3. *Variable suffixes.*

Suffix	Variable Type	Example Variable Name
%	Integer	INDEX%
!	Single-precision	AREA!
#	Double-precision	MYDEBT#
$	String	FULLNAME$

2. Use a DEF*type* instruction.

   The statements DEFINT, DEFSNG, DEFDBL, and DEFSTR (integer, single-precision, double-precision, and string) declare that variables beginning with particular letters have a specified data type. These instructions are explained in Chapter 15, "Toward Advanced Programming."

3. Do nothing!

   That's easy. When a variable name has no special suffix (and no DEF*type* instruction is in use), the variable type automatically becomes single-precision. The effect is as though the variable had a ! suffix. If you name a variable COST, for example, COST is a numeric variable of type single-precision.

Variable Typing Conflicts

Variables with the same root name but different suffixes are distinct variables. For example, PRICE!, PRICE#, and PRICE$ are three independent variables that can coexist in the same program. Here's proof:

```
100 PRICE! = 349.62
110 PRICE# = 12345678.25
120 PRICE$ = "Too much"
130 PRINT PRICE!
140 PRINT PRICE#
150 PRINT PRICE$
RUN
 349.62
 12345678.25
Too much
```

Note that all three variables (PRICE!, PRICE#, and PRICE$) retain individual identities. Each variable stores a different value that the program displays with lines 130 through 150.

Now, suppose that you get cunning and introduce a variable named PRICE (with no suffix character). Add the following line to your program:

```
125 PRICE = 2.95
```

Remember, you just learned that BASIC treats a variable with no special suffix as a single-precision numeric variable. But your program already has the variable PRICE!, which is single-precision and clearly has the same root name as the variable PRICE. What do you think happens? Let's find out.

```
125 PRICE = 2.95
LIST
100 PRICE! = 349.62
110 PRICE# = 12345678.25#
120 PRICE$ = "Too much"
125 PRICE = 2.95
130 PRINT PRICE!
140 PRINT PRICE#
150 PRINT PRICE$
Ok
RUN
 2.95
 12345678.25
Too much
```

What's this? Line 130 displayed the value of PRICE! as 2.95, the value of the variable PRICE. Does line 125 reassign the value of the variable PRICE! as well as the value of the variable PRICE?

In fact, PRICE and PRICE! are simply one and the same variable. You can write single-precision variable names with or without the trailing exclamation point.

You might notice a subtle change between the way you typed line 110 and the way the line appears after LIST. BASIC adds a pound sign (#) to the numeric literal at the end of the line. This pound sign denotes that the literal is a double-precision number. We discuss such literals in Chapter 6, "Manipulating Data."

An Introduction to Arrays

Arrays are like "super variables." As you have seen, ordinary variables store only a single value. An ordinary variable may be of any data type, but it can store only a single data value (of the appropriate type).

An array, by contrast, houses multiple data values. A single array is a collection of values, with each individual value having the same data type. An array is like a set of ordinary variables.

Just like an ordinary variable, every array has a name you create. These names follow the same naming conventions as ordinary variables, including an optional suffix that identifies the data type of all the values in the array.

We call each individual array value an *element* of the array. Distinct elements of the array are referenced by an index number (sometimes called a *subscript*).

To see how arrays work, consider this example. Suppose that a company has 100 employees. The personnel department has assigned each worker an employee number. Because there are 100 employees, these numbers range from 1 to 100. The salary of each employee could be stored in an array called SALARY. To display the salary of employee number 73, for example, you use the following instruction:

```
300 PRINT SALARY(73)
```

Note that you enclose the index number in parentheses after the array name. The parentheses tell BASIC that this is an array rather than an ordinary variable.

Arrays can contain string values also. For example, you might create an array called WORKERNAME$ that contains the names of all the employees. Then you can store the name of good old employee number 73 with an instruction such as

```
400 WORKERNAME$(73) = "Joanna B. Nimble"
```

Arrays are a powerful tool for working with large groups of related data. Chapter 8, "Managing Large Amounts of Data," discusses the details of creating, managing, and utilizing arrays.

Another Look at Assignment Instructions

As we mentioned previously, you directly assign a value to a variable using the equal sign. Here are two typical assignment instructions:

```
230 LET MYTEMP = 98.6
340 TITLE$ = "Night in Casablanca"
```

The Optional *LET*

You can optionally begin any assignment instruction with the keyword LET. For example, the previous two instructions could be written as follows:

```
230 MYTEMP = 98.6
340 LET TITLE$ = "Night in Casablanca"
```

Both forms (with or without LET) do exactly the same thing. (LET is a vestige from early versions of the BASIC language, which required LET in assignment instructions.)

Righthand Sides of Assignment Instructions

The righthand side of an assignment instruction can consist of a general expression as well as a data literal. Here is a closer look at how assignment instructions work:

LET *varname* = *expr*

or simply

varname = *expr*

where *varname* is a variable whose value is to be assigned, and *expr* is an expression that provides the value to assign to *varname*.

Two things occur when an assignment instruction executes:

1. The value of *expr* is calculated.

2. This value is assigned to the variable *varname*.

The proper way to interpret an assignment instruction is "assign the value of *expr* to the variable named *varname*."

Think of the equal sign in an assignment instruction as meaning "is now assigned the value of." Therefore, the instruction

```
200 NUMITEMS% = 29
```

means "the variable NUMITEMS% is now assigned the value of 29."

Here are some examples of righthand sides containing general expressions.

```
270 TAX = COST * 0.06
380 YOURAGE% = 29 + 10
420 VOLUME = DEPTH * HEIGHT * LENGTH / 9
```

Now look at the following instruction:

```
250 X = X + 1
```

Does this make sense? Do we hear you saying, "How can this be? I'm no Einstein, but even I know that no value of X satisfies that equation."

When the instruction is viewed as a reassignment of the variable X, the instruction makes perfect sense. The instruction says "the new value of the variable X shall become the old value of the variable X plus 1."

In other words, first add 1 to the value of X. Then store this updated value back into the variable named X. The effect is that X now contains a value 1 greater than its previous value. This kind of instruction occurs frequently.

The general data type of *varname* and *expr* must correspond. That is, if the variable on the left side is numeric, the expression on the righthand side also must be numeric. Similarly, if the variable is a string, the expression also must be a string.

However, specific numeric data types do not have to correspond. If the variable is one of the three numeric data types (integer, single-precision, or double-precision), the expression on the righthand side can be any of the three data types. For example, the following instruction is okay:

```
200 MYAGE% = BIGNUM!
```

BASIC automatically converts the single-precision value in BIGNUM! to an integer value for MYAGE%. See Chapter 6, "Manipulating Data," for a further discussion of numeric data-type conversion.

Expressions and Operators

An *expression* specifies a single data value. Expressions occur frequently in BASIC instructions. You just saw that one place where expressions occur is on the righthand side of assignment instructions. As you examine more and more of BASIC, you will see expressions in many other contexts.

An expression can be a single literal (such as 38.66 or "Hello out there"), a variable (MYVALUE%), an array element (SALES(150)), a function (SQR(1.88)), or a combination of these elements formed with suitable operators (SQR(1.88 / MyValue%) + 38.66).

Every valid expression, whether simple or complex, evaluates to a single numeric or string value. For example, if the variable X has the value 2 and Y has the value 5, the expression X + Y has the value 7.

When an expression contains two or more parts, some sort of operator combines the parts to create the single value. We say that an *operator* manipulates one or more *operands* to create a value. Each operand is itself a data value or expression. In the present example, X and Y are operands and the plus sign (+) is an operator. Most BASIC operators are special symbols (such as + and >), but some operators are keywords (such as NOT and MOD).

In general, wherever BASIC requires a single value, you can substitute an expression. Already, you have used composite expressions on the righthand side of some assignment instructions.

Types of Operators

BASIC operators divide into four categories (see table 4.4).

Table 4.4. *Operator categories.*

Category	Description
Arithmetic	Manipulates numbers
String	Manipulates strings
Relational	Compares numbers or strings
Logical	Manipulates Boolean (true or false) values

Arithmetic Operators

Table 4.5 shows the arithmetic operators. The operand abbreviations I, S, and D stand for the three arithmetic data types:

❏ I   Integer

❏ S   Single-precision

❏ D   Double-precision

Table 4.5. *Arithmetic operators.*

Symbol	Name	Operand Types	Example	Result
+	Addition	I, S, D	1.5 + 4.9	6.4
−	Subtraction	I, S, D	3.4 − 1.2	2.2
*	Multiplication	I, S, D	1.5 * 2.2	3.3
/	Division	I, S, D	4.5 / 2.5	1.8
^	Exponentiation	I, S, D	3 ^ 2	9
−	Negation	I, S, D	−21	− 21
\	Integer division	I	6 \ 4	1
MOD	Remainder	I	6 MOD 4	2

You are probably familiar with most of the arithmetic operations and the operators involved. Addition and subtraction use the plus (+) and minus (−) signs just as you would expect:

```
Ok
PRINT 25.6 + 14
 39.6
Ok
PRINT 100 - 38
 62
Ok
```

Multiplication and division use the asterisk (∗) and "divide" sign (/) respectively:

```
Ok
PRINT 1.5 * 7
 10.5
Ok
PRINT 9 / 2
 4.5
Ok
```

Exponentiation is the process of raising one number to a power. For example, the math expression 2^3 means 2 raised to the power of 3. In BASIC this operation is written 2 ∧ 3. The exponential operator (^) is found on most keyboards as Shift-6. By the way, what is 2 ∧ 3? Let's find out.

```
Ok
PRINT 2 ^ 3
 8
Ok
```

In an exponential expression, the operands don't have to be integers. For example,

```
Ok
PRINT 3.4 ^ 1.29
 4.848503
Ok
```

Two arithmetic operations that may be new to you are integer division and remaindering. The integer division operator is the backslash (\), and the remaindering operator is the keyword MOD.

Integer division is the process of dividing one whole number by another. Only the whole number portion of the answer survives. Any remainder is discarded. If you attempt integer division with a single- or double-precision operand, the operand is first rounded to the nearest whole number.

The following program demonstrates the difference between regular division and integer division.

```
100 PRINT 14 / 5      'Regular division
110 PRINT 14 \ 5      'Integer division
RUN
 2.8
 2
```

Note that the result of the integer division is simply to "throw away" the fractional part (0.8) of the regular division answer, not to round the answer to the nearest whole number. If rounded, the answer would be 3 instead of 2. When one or both operands are single- or double-precision numbers, the operands are first rounded to the nearest whole number before the integer division proceeds.

Remaindering is a close cousin to integer division. The MOD operator extracts the remainder after dividing by a modulus or divisor. Another way to look at remaindering is that the MOD operator returns the part "thrown away" during integer division. If you are unfamiliar with modular arithmetic, think of the schoolhouse mnemonic "goes into." For example, 4 "goes into" 11 twice with 3 remaining. Or more properly, 11 modulo 4 is 3. Here is how this looks in BASIC:

```
100 PRINT 11 \ 4   'Integer division quotient
110 PRINT 11 MOD 4 'Integer division remainder
RUN
 2
 3
```

String Operators

The plus sign also works with string operands. Does this mean that you can add two strings together? Well, sort of.

Instead of adding the strings in an arithmetic sense, the plus sign merges the text of two strings into one composite string. This process is known as *concatenation*. The text of one string is simply juxtaposed with the text of a second string to form one new string. The following program demonstrates the technique:

```
100 FIRSTPART$ = "Coca"
110 LASTPART$ = "Cola"
120 FULLNAME$ = FIRSTPART$ + LASTPART$
130 PRINT FULLNAME$
140 PRINT "Pepsi" + LASTPART$
```

The output is

```
CocaCola
PepsiCola
```

The plus signs in lines 120 and 140 perform concatenation. Look at line 120. This instruction concatenates the value of FIRSTPART$ (namely "Coca") with the value of LASTPART$ (namely "Cola") to form the result ("CocaCola") and then assigns the result to the variable FULLNAME$.

Relational Operators

The relational operators compare two values to produce a "true" or "false" result. For now, we simply want to introduce the operators (see table 4.6). We explore the use of the operators in later chapters.

Table 4.6. Relational operators.

Symbol	Name	Operand Types	Example
=	Equals	All	4 = 4
<>	Not equal	All	"Dog" <> "Cat"
>	Greater than	All	8 > 5
<	Less than	All	3 < 6
>=	Greater than or equal to	All	9 >= 9
<=	Less than or equal to	All	"Hi" <= "Ho"

Each example in the last column of the table is true. Note that relational operators work on strings as well as on numbers.

The most common use of relational operators is to create testing expressions for decision instructions such as IF...THEN. Here is an example instruction:

```
225 IF OURSCORE% > THEIRSCORE% THEN PRINT "We won."
```

We discuss IF...THEN and relational operators in depth when we explore conditional testing in Chapter 5, "Program Flow and Decision Making."

Logical Operators

The last set of BASIC operators are the logical operators. Logical operators manipulate Boolean operands to produce Boolean results. (The term "Boolean" comes from George Boole, a prominent 19th-century British mathematician.)

What is a Boolean operand, you say? It is simply a true or false value.

Internally, BASIC represents true and false with arithmetic integers: 0 for false and −1 for true. You will see why when Chapter 5, "Program Flow and Decision Making," examines logical operations.

For now, we simply present the six logical operators and their official-sounding names in table 4.7. All the logical operators are keywords rather than symbols.

Table 4.7. Logical operators.

Name	Meaning
NOT	Complement (logical negation)
AND	Conjunction
OR	Disjunction (inclusive or)
XOR	Exclusive or
EQV	Equivalence
IMP	Implication

Operator Precedence

So far our sample expressions have had two operands and one operator. What happens when an expression contains more than one operator? How does BASIC resolve the value of such expressions?

For example, consider this instruction:

```
PRINT 4 + 3 * 2
```

What is the result: 14 or 10? Do you see the problem? The answer is 14 if you add 4 and 3 before multiplying by 2 (4 plus 3 is 7 and then 7 times 2 is 14). But the answer is 10 if you add 4 to the product of 3 times 2 (3 times 2 is 6 and then 4 plus 6 is 10). Let's find out what the answer is:

```
Ok
PRINT 4 + 3 * 2
 10
Ok
```

Well, BASIC returns 10. Why?

When multiple operators occur in an expression, certain operations are done before others. That is, some operators have *precedence* over others. The hierarchy of operations is shown in table 4.8. Each line in the table represents one level of precedence, from highest precedence at the top of the table to lowest precedence at the bottom.

Table 4.8. *Operator precedence.*

Level	Operator(s)	Name
1	^	Exponentiation
2	−	Negation
3	*, /	Multiplication and division
4	\	Integer division
5	MOD	Modulo arithmetic
6	+, −	Addition and subtraction
7	=, >, <, <>, >=, <=	Relational operators
8	NOT	Logical negation
9	AND	Conjunction
10	OR	Inclusive or
11	XOR	Exclusive or
12	EQV	Equivalence
13	IMP	Implication

When expressions contain two or more operators, higher precedence operations occur sooner. Our expression 4 + 3 * 2 resolves to 10 because multiplication has higher precedence than addition (in table 4.8 multiplication is at level 3, and addition is at level 6). In our expression, the multiplication is done before the addition. That is, 3 is first multiplied by 2 to yield 6. Then the 4 is added to 6 to finally produce 10.

When multiple operators occur at the same level of precedence, resolution proceeds from left to right. The expression 9 – 4 – 2 yields 3 because 4 is first subtracted from 9 to get 5 and then 2 is subtracted to produce the final answer of 3. (Note that the result is 7 if the second subtraction is done first.)

Using Parentheses in Expressions

Let's take another look at this command:

```
PRINT 4 + 3 * 2
```

You saw that the result is 10. That's fine and dandy if you want the multiplication to occur first.

But suppose that you want the addition to occur before the multiplication. Is there a way you can tell BASIC to do the addition first?

Yes, there is. Use parentheses to override the standard operator precedence. When an expression contains parentheses, BASIC evaluates terms inside parentheses before terms outside parentheses. So here is how you tell BASIC to do the addition first:

```
Ok
PRINT (4 + 3) * 2
 14
Ok
```

The parentheses force BASIC to evaluate 4 + 3 before multiplying this result by 2.

For more complicated expressions, parentheses can be nested inside each other. When an expression contains parentheses, BASIC evaluates terms inside parentheses before terms outside parentheses. Deeper-nested parentheses evaluate first.

For example:

```
Ok
PRINT (24 – (3 * 5)) / 2
 4.5
Ok
```

In this example, BASIC first evaluates the expression in the deepest-nested parentheses. So the first calculation is 3 times 5 to get 15. Then this value of 15 is subtracted from 24 to get 9. Finally 9 is divided by 2 to yield the answer 4.5.

Complicated expressions often require parentheses. For example:

```
200 ATOMICWEIGHT! = ENERGY!
    / (3 * ((SIZE! + 1.9) / (MASS! ^  3)))
```

Parentheses are not restricted to mathematical expressions. Relational, string, and logical expressions are also fair game.

```
500 IF (COST! > 99.95) OR ((FORM% = 39) AND
    (STATUS = "VIP")) ...
```

Even when operator precedence is not an issue, you should use parentheses liberally to clarify your expressions.

In a misguided effort to exhibit their programming sophistication, a few programmers go to great lengths to avoid parentheses. Often the result is instructions that are hard to read and difficult to troubleshoot. Consider this:

```
400 PROFIT! = 89.14 + 34.60 * 23.11 - 11.89 / 4.88 + 2.66
```

Here is a clearer rendition of the same instruction:

```
400 PROFIT! = (89.14) + (34.60 * 23.11) - (11.89 / 4.88) + 2.66
```

We wouldn't quibble if you wanted to leave out the first and last set of parentheses in this expression. Note that the two preceding instructions are equivalent. Each instruction assigns exactly the same value to PROFIT!. But the second instruction is much easier to read and understand.

Program Comments

In general, BASIC programs are quite readable. Most keywords, such as IF, BEEP, and PRINT, are English words with natural meanings or easy-to-decipher abbreviations. BASIC seldom requires obscure syntax compared to other languages such as C or assembler.

However, as you begin to write substantial programs, you soon realize that many subtleties occur in the final code. The cumulative effect of several instructions cannot be easily grasped by someone scanning your program for the first time—that is, unless you place comments in your programs.

In BASIC, a *comment* is a remark added to a program. Such remarks usually supply factual data (such as when the program was written), clarify fine points, or just explain what is happening inside the program.

The sole purpose of a comment is to provide explanation for you or another person who might need to see or modify your program. When running a program, BASIC simply ignores all the comments.

You have two ways to place comments in your programs: the REM statement and the single quotation mark (or apostrophe).

Using the *REM* Statement

The keyword REM identifies the rest of the line as a comment. (REM is short for REMark.)

REM *remark*

where *remark* is any sequence of characters.

For example, you might begin a loan amortization program like this:

```
100 REM Program: LOAN
110 REM Get the principal and interest rate.
120 REM Calculate the payment.
120 PRINT "Loan Calculator"
```

You can place a REM instruction on a line with other instructions. However, everything following the REM is part of the comment. Be wary of this sort of trap:

```
200 CLIENT$ = "ABC Plumbing":
    REM Get discount: RATE! = 23.14
```

This line *does* assign the string value "ABC Plumbing" to CLIENT$. However, the REM instruction makes the *remainder* of the line a remark. The value of RATE! does not change.

Using the Apostrophe

The single quotation mark (or apostrophe) is a substitute for the REM keyword. An apostrophe signals that the remainder of the line is a comment. You can place an apostrophe right after the line number (the whole line becomes a comment) or later in the line.

The apostrophe is often used to place a comment on the same line with other instructions. Unlike REM, you do not need a colon to separate the apostrophe from the other instructions on the same line. For example:

```
315 DEG.C! = ((DEG.F! - 32) * 5) / 9
      'Fahrenheit to Centigrade
```

There are two exceptions to the apostrophe initiating a comment. First, an apostrophe inside a string literal is simply part of the literal. For example:

```
450 PRINT "Randy's Donut Shop"
```

This instruction displays Randy's Donut Shop. The apostrophe in line 450 does not indicate a comment but is, instead, part of the string literal.

Second, an apostrophe inside a DATA instruction is part of the data and does not initiate a comment. See Chapter 8, "Managing Large Amounts of Data," for information on the DATA instruction.

Tips on Using Comments

Make frequent use of meaningful comments.

Obviously, meaningful comments go a long way toward making any program more readable. By peppering your programs with comments, you enhance the self-documentation of your programs. This practice facilitates the later chores of troubleshooting or modifying the programs—whether by you or by someone else. Experienced programmers know that well-placed comments help you "get into" a program.

In a work environment, you may find yourself under time pressure. Sometimes, it is tempting to forgo comments in the name of expediency. This is penny-wise and pound-foolish. Invariably, you will need that program (or part of it) later. You will spend some puzzling moments glaring at the enigmatic program that was so clear several months ago. One of programming's most sobering lessons comes the first time you have to rewrite a program because you can't decipher what you did before.

In fact, the following maxim is worth highlighting:

Every minute spent writing comments will be saved at least tenfold later on.

Consider the time you spend writing comments to be an investment. Your dividends come later in the form of time savings and avoided frustrations.

However, like ice cream and candy, any good thing can be overdone. In your zeal to provide comments, you can go overboard. Do not fall into the trap of commenting every line. Simple instructions with informative variable names require no comments.

```
400 NUMCHECKS% = NUMCHECKS% + 1    'increment NUMCHECKS% by 1
410 PRINT NUMCHECKS% 'display the number of checks
```

The comments on these two lines do nothing more than restate what's obvious from the instructions themselves. Such comments are frivolous and actually detract from the program's readability. Comments should add to your understanding. When each line is easily understood, you might write a comment every ten lines or so to explain what the following *group* of lines accomplishes.

The Microscopic View— the BASIC Character Set

Now let's zoom in all the way and quickly examine BASIC at the "atomic" level. Table 4.9 presents all the individual characters recognized by BASIC. Note that the third column, labeled *Primary Use*, lists only a single use for each character. Many characters have multiple uses in BASIC. For example, the uppercase letters are used to compose variable names as well as to compose keywords.

Table 4.9 lists those characters that, in the appropriate contexts, have special meaning in BASIC. Other characters can be displayed in textual output. For example, curly braces ({}) can be placed inside a string literal:

```
Ok
PRINT "{ This works OK }"
{ This works OK }
Ok
```

Table 4.9. *BASIC character set.*

Character(s)	Name	Primary Use
A - Z	Uppercase letters	Compose keyword
a - z	Lowercase letters	Compose identifiers
0 - 9	Digits	Compose number
	Blank space	Separator
!	Exclamation point	Single-precision suffix
#	Pound sign	Double-precision suffix
%	Percent sign	Integer suffix
$	Dollar sign	String suffix
&	Ampersand	PRINT formatting symbol
"	Quotation mark	Delimit string literals
'	Apostrophe (single quotation)	Initiate comments
.	Period	Compose numbers
,	Comma	Separate parameters
;	Semicolon	Separator
:	Colon	Separate instructions
+	Plus sign	Addition symbol
−	Minus sign	Subtraction symbol
*	Asterisk	Multiplication symbol
/	Slash	Division symbol
\	Backslash	Integer division symbol
^	Caret	Exponentiation symbol
=	Equal sign	Assignment symbol
<	Less than sign	Relational expressions
>	Greater than sign	Relational expressions
( )	Left and right parentheses	General delimiter
?	Question mark	Shorthand for PRINT
_	Underscore	Line continuation character
ENTER	Enter (carriage return)	Line terminator

Summary

This chapter examined the structure of BASIC programs and the building blocks (or components) that mold together to form programs. You saw that a program is a series of instructions, with successive instructions having increasing line numbers. The chapter briefly examined all the characters in the BASIC character set.

BASIC manipulates data of two fundamental types—numbers and text (strings). Numbers are further divided into the integer, single-precision, and double-precision data types.

Variables, which can have any data type, store a single data value. You can modify the value of a variable with an assignment instruction. Arrays are like composite variables, storing multiple data items.

BASIC has four different kinds of operators: arithmetic, string, relational, and logical. With the operators, you can form expressions to represent most any quantity. In an expression, operands can consist of literals, variables, and parenthetical subexpressions. However, all expressions resolve to a single value.

Comments help improve any program's readability. Appropriate comments make a program easier to understand and help when you track down errors.

CHAPTER 5

Program Flow and Decision Making

```
GOTO, ON GOTO, END, IF...THEN...ELSE, FOR...NEXT,
WHILE...WEND
```

Program flow refers to the order in which your program instructions execute. Generally, this flow proceeds line-by-line from the top of your program down to the bottom.

When you type RUN, BASIC first executes the line having the smallest line number. Line by line, the computer proceeds from the smallest line number to the largest. Eventually (if no error or other termination occurs), BASIC executes the bottom line of your program. With nothing left to do, the computer ends your program and displays the reassuring Ok prompt.

This sequential, "top-down" program order is straightforward and easy to understand. Many practical programs proceed entirely in this systematic sequence.

However, there is a limit to what you can accomplish with such linear sequencing. Frequently, you will need to redirect program flow. From one point in your program, you may want to transfer execution to a location a few lines away or perhaps many lines away. Usually, this redirection involves some sort of decision making, or testing.

When you get in your car for a drive, you probably look at the gas gauge and stop for gas if necessary. You *test* the value of the gas gauge and make a decision about where to go as a result.

Programs, just like people, often need to test a condition and then make a decision depending on the result. For example, a program might examine the value of a variable and then transfer execution to one of several lines depending on the result.

This chapter examines the following ways that program flow can be altered from the normal sequential execution order:

❏ Unconditional branching (GOTO).

❏ Conditional branching (ON GOTO).

❏ Ending execution (END).

❏ Conditional testing (IF...THEN).

❏ Looping (FOR...NEXT, WHILE...WEND).

Branching

Branching is the direct transfer from one line in your program to another line. In this chapter, you learn different ways you can make your program "jump" from one line to any other line.

For the sake of illustration, suppose that line 230 of a program contains an instruction which causes BASIC to immediately jump down to line 485. Then we say that line 230 *branches* to line 485.

Branching comes in two forms:

❏ *Unconditional branching* (program control transfers to a specific line in all cases).

❏ *Conditional branching* (program control transfers to one of several lines depending on the value of a testing expression).

Unconditional Branching with *GOTO*

As we mentioned in Chapter 3, "A Hands-On Introduction to Programming," you use GOTO for unconditional branches.

GOTO *linenum*

where *linenum* is any line number in the program.

To get a feel for GOTO, try the following program:

```
10 PRINT "I am"
20 GOTO 40
30 PRINT "not"
40 PRINT "happy"
50 PRINT "today"
RUN
I am
happy
today
```

Poor line 30! It never got a chance to do its thing. Do you see what happened? The GOTO instruction in line 20 transfers control directly to line 40. After line 40 finishes, the program continues with line 50, the next sequential instruction.

You might be thinking, "That's great, but what's the big deal?" If you wanted to skip line 30, why not just leave it out of the program entirely? For the time being, the answer has to be "Just wait and see." Later, this chapter discusses how GOTO combines with testing instructions such as IF . . . THEN to create powerful decision-making structures.

Using GOTO, you can branch anywhere in your program: to a previous line, to a subsequent line, even to the same line. Of course, the line number you specify at the end of a GOTO instruction must exist somewhere in your program. If not, the program terminates with an error message: Undefined line number.

You cannot use a variable for the *linenum* parameter. That is, if TARGET% is an integer variable, the following instruction is *not* legal:

```
214 GOTO TARGET%
```

Line 214 results in a syntax error.

Conditional Branching with *ON... GOTO*

The ON GOTO instruction extends the GOTO concept. With ON GOTO, you branch to one of a specified set of lines according to the value of a numeric expression.

ON *numexpr* GOTO *linenumlist*

where *numexpr* is a numeric expression, and *linenumlist* is a list of one or more line numbers separated by commas.

The value of the numeric expression determines which line in *linenumlist* executes next. Branching occurs to the corresponding line in the list: the first listed line if *numexpr* is 1, the second listed line if *numexpr* is 2, and so on.

If *numexpr* is 0 or greater than the number of lines in the list, execution simply continues with the instruction immediately after the ON GOTO. If *numexpr* is negative, your program terminates with the error: Illegal function call.

An example should make ON GOTO clearer:

```
200 ON NUMUNITS% GOTO 310, 440, 490, 530
```

The value of NUMUNITS% determines which line executes next. If NUMUNITS% equals 1, the program branches to line 310 and continues from there. If NUMUNITS% equals 2, the program goes to line 440. If NUMUNITS% = 3, the program branches to line 490. If NUMUNITS% = 4, the branch is to line 530.

If NUMUNITS% is 0 or greater than 4, the program continues with whatever line immediately follows line 200. If NUMUNITS% is negative, the Illegal function call error occurs.

The same destination can appear more than once in your line number list. For example, the following instruction branches to line number 300 if MYVALUE% is 1, 3, or 5:

```
140 ON MYVALUE% GOTO 300, 200, 300, 400, 300, 500
```

As shown in our examples so far, the numeric expression is simply a variable. But you can use any general expression. Here is an example of a more complicated expression:

```
400 ON ((MYSCORE% - 23) = AVERAGE%) GOTO 600, 630, 530, 690
```

The numeric expression should resolve to an integer number. A fractional value is simply rounded to the nearest whole integer to determine the line branched to.

Note that after execution branches, there is no implied return back to any common point. Consider the following program fragment from a golf game:

```
200 ON STROKES% GOTO 300, 400, 500, 600
250 PRINT "You got a bogie."
300 PRINT "You got a hole in one!"
400 PRINT "You got an eagle."
500 PRINT "You got a birdie."
600 PRINT "You got par."
```

Suppose that the value of STROKES% is 2. The program displays the following undesired result:

```
You got an eagle.
You got a birdie.
You got par.
```

For this type of ON GOTO construction, additional branching instructions are needed after each PRINT instruction. Something similar to the following does the trick:

```
200 ON STROKES% GOTO 300, 400, 500, 600
250 PRINT "You got a bogie.": GOTO 700
300 PRINT "You got a hole in one!": GOTO 700
400 PRINT "You got an eagle.": GOTO 700
500 PRINT "You got a birdie.": GOTO 700
600 PRINT "You got par."
700 REM    The program continues here
```

Later in this chapter, you will see another way to accomplish this same programming task.

In practice, ON GOTO has limited use because the programming situation must be just right for ON GOTO to be practical. You do not often have a program decision point where you want to branch to different line numbers depending on a numeric expression with possible values of 1, 2, 3, and so on.

Furthermore, many `ON GOTO` constructions can be programmed more easily with a block of `IF` instructions instead. Nevertheless, `ON GOTO` is handy in the right situations.

Ending Program Execution

The most abrupt way to alter program flow is to terminate your program. As you have seen, an `END` instruction immediately ends execution.

You can have more than one `END` instruction in a program, but no `END` instruction is required. If BASIC runs out of instructions, your program simply terminates normally. The effect is just as though an `END` instruction was the last line of your program.

It is a good idea to place `END` in each nontrivial program, even if only one such instruction appears as the final line. This shows, at least, that you *expect* the program to end at such a point.

Conditional Testing with *IF . . . THEN*

Just as decision making is an important and frequent part of your life, decision making is a perpetual programming theme. Like a fork in the road, a "logic juncture" is a place in your program where the subsequent execution path can go different ways.

When you program a logic juncture, your thought process goes like this: "If such and such is true, I want this to happen. If not, then that should happen instead."

You choose the program path based on the evaluation of a test condition. Your primary tool is the `IF . . . THEN` statement, which tests whether a condition is true or false and then directs logic flow depending on the result.

The Basic Form of *IF . . . THEN*

An `IF . . . THEN` instruction can take many forms. Let's start with the following simple example:

```
10 INPUT "What is the temperature outside"; TEMP
20 IF TEMP > 100 THEN PRINT "It's hot"
30 PRINT "So long for now"
RUN
What is the temperature outside? 106
It's hot
So long for now
Ok
RUN
What is the temperature outside? 84
So long for now"
Ok
```

Line 10 displays the question

```
What is the temperature outside?
```

and waits for you to respond. When you type in a value, the program stores your reply in the variable `TEMP`. An `INPUT` instruction accomplishes all this. (`INPUT` was explained briefly in Chapter 3, "A Hands-On Introduction to Programming," and is discussed further in Chapter 12, "Programming Hardware Devices.")

Line 20 is an `IF...THEN` instruction. Do you see how it works? Sure. If the value of the variable `TEMP` is greater than 100, then the program prints the message `It's hot`. (Remember that the > character is a relational operator meaning "greater than." Relational operators were introduced in the previous chapter and are discussed again later in this chapter.)

The example shows two sample runs of the program. The first time, the temperature was given as 106. Because 106 is definitely greater than 100, the program dutifully displays the `It's hot` message.

But the second time the temperature was input as 84. What happened? Did the computer just ignore the part of line 20 following `THEN`?

That's exactly what happened. When the test condition of an `IF...THEN` instruction is false, the computer disregards the part of the instruction after `THEN`. The program simply moves immediately down to the next program line.

In the second run, the value of `TEMP` is 84. The test condition is false because 84 certainly is not greater than 100. As a result, the computer ignores the part of the instruction after `THEN` (that is, the `PRINT` clause) and moves down to the next program line. In this case, the next line is line 30, which prints the `So long for now` message.

Adding an *ELSE* Clause to *IF...THEN*

Suppose that you want to do one thing if the test condition is true but another thing if the test condition is false. No problem. A second form of the IF...THEN statement adds an ELSE clause just for this purpose.

To illustrate, change line 20 so that the new program looks like this:

```
10 INPUT "What is the temperature outside?"; TEMP
20 IF TEMP > 100 THEN PRINT "It's hot"
   ELSE PRINT "Not too bad"
30 PRINT "So long for now"
```

Now try those two runs again:

```
RUN
What is the temperature outside? 106
It's hot
So long for now
Ok
RUN
What is the temperature outside? 84
Not too bad
So long for now
```

When the temperature is given as 106, the result is the same as before. But, now, when you give the temperature as 84, the computer displays the Not too bad message.

By adding an ELSE clause to an IF . . . THEN instruction, you specify what to do when the testing condition is false—the ELSE part—as well as what to do when the testing condition is true—the THEN part (see fig. 5.1).

Fig. 5.1. The IF . . . THEN . . . ELSE *instruction.*

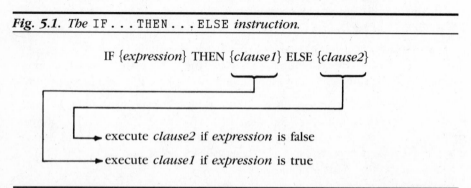

IF {*expression*} THEN {*clause1*} ELSE {*clause2*}

execute *clause2* if *expression* is false

execute *clause1* if *expression* is true

To summarize, here are the two fundamental forms of an IF...THEN instruction:

> IF *expression* THEN *thenclause*
>
> and
>
> IF *expression* THEN *thenclause* ELSE *elseclause*
>
> where *expression* is an expression that evaluates to true or false, *thenclause* is the action to perform if *expression* is true, and *elseclause* is the action to perform if *expression* is false.

THEN and *ELSE* Clauses

How fancy can the THEN and ELSE clauses get? For starters, each clause can be any single BASIC instruction. Here are a few sample instructions to give you the idea:

```
150 IF A = B THEN PRINT "Same" ELSE PRINT "Different"

200 IF A = B THEN GOTO 800 ELSE GOTO 900

250 IF A = B THEN BEEP

300 IF A = B THEN END

350 IF A = B THEN PROFIT = 20 ELSE PROFIT = COST * DISCOUNT
```

If an IF instruction does not have an ELSE clause, the THEN clause can contain multiple instructions. Simply separate each instruction with a colon. For example:

```
100 IF SCORE > 500 THEN RATE = 3.5: NUM% = 29:
    WINNER$ = "Debby"
```

Line 100 tests whether the value of the variable SCORE is greater than 500. If so, then the values of RATE, NUM%, and WINNER$ are assigned the values 3.5, 29, and "Debby", respectively. If the value of SCORE is not greater than 500, control passes directly to the next line without assigning values to any of the three variables.

GOTO is one of the most common statements to place in a THEN or ELSE clause. That way, you can branch to different lines depending on the result of a testing expression. For example:

```
100 IF AGE% > 20 THEN GOTO 500
```

If the value of AGE% is greater than 20, the program proceeds directly to line 500. Perhaps AGE% is the age of a person. When the person is an adult (at least 21 years old), the program branches directly to line 500 to begin the instructions found there. There may be several instructions between line 100 and line 500. Those instructions execute if the person is a minor—that is, under the age of 21.

GOTO is so common in THEN clauses that BASIC provides special shortened forms of the IF statement for such cases. When the THEN clause consists of GOTO, you can omit the GOTO keyword or the THEN keyword. For example, you can write the last instruction in either of the following ways:

```
100 IF AGE% > 20 THEN 500
```

```
100 IF AGE% > 20 GOTO 500
```

With ELSE clauses, you can omit the GOTO. For example, the following instruction is valid:

```
160 IF AGE% > 20 THEN 500 ELSE 700
```

Here's a summary of the special forms of the IF statement.

IF *expression* THEN *linenum1*

or

IF *expression* THEN *linenum1* ELSE *linenum2*

or

IF *expression* GOTO *linenum1*

or

IF *expression* GOTO *linenum1* ELSE *elseclause*

where *expression* is an expression that evaluates to true or false, *linenum1* is the line number to branch to if *expression* is true, *linenum2* is the line number to branch to if *expression* is false, and *elseclause* is the action to perform if *expression* is false.

Types of Testing Expressions

Now let's take a closer look at the testing expressions you can place in an IF statement.

The testing expression must be a Boolean expression, which simply means an expression that evaluates to true or false.

Most often, the expression is a *relational expression*. Such expressions use the equality and inequality operators to form natural conditional tests. Here are a few examples:

```
200 IF NUM% < 0 THEN PRINT "Number is negative"

300 IF NUM% <= 0 THEN PRINT "Number is not positive"

400 IF ANIMAL$ = "Dog" THEN PRINT "It's a pooch"

500 IF (MYSCORE + HERSCORE) > YOURSCORE THEN PRINT "You lose"
```

Line 200 uses the "less than" operator ($<$) to test the value of the variable NUM%. If NUM% has a value less than 0, the line displays the message Number is negative. If the value of NUM% is 0 or positive, line 200 displays no message at all.

Line 300 has a subtle difference from line 200. Line 300 uses the "less than or equal to" operator ($<=$). Here, the condition is true whenever NUM% is negative *or* 0. Note that lines 200 and 300 both display their messages when NUM% is negative. And neither line displays a message when NUM% is positive. When NUM% is exactly 0, line 300 displays its message but line 200 does not.

Line 400 demonstrates that testing expressions can be string as well as numeric. Here, the "equals" operator ($=$) tests whether the string stored in ANIMAL$ is Dog. If so, the line displays the message It's a pooch. In relational expressions, the equal sign really means "equals" (as opposed to the equal sign in assignment instructions that means "is assigned the value"). Also, note that the expression is "true" only when there is an exact match. If ANIMAL$ has the value DOG (all caps), the result is "false." "Dog" and "DOG" are *not* identical strings.

Line 500 shows an expression involving parentheses. Here the values of MYSCORE and HERSCORE are added together. This sum is then compared with the value in YOURSCORE to decide whether the expression is true or false.

Boolean Expressions Are Really Just Numbers

Internally, BASIC needs a way to represent Boolean values; that is, a way to represent "true" or "false." In fact, BASIC uses simple integer numbers: 0 for "false" and -1 for "true." As a result, Boolean expressions are really just special cases of numeric expressions.

When BASIC evaluates a Boolean expression, "false" becomes 0 and "true" becomes -1. (When you convert a number to a Boolean value, 0 becomes "false" and any nonzero number becomes "true.") You can demonstrate this conversion with the following short test:

```
100 NUMITEMS% = 0

200 IF NUMITEMS% THEN PRINT "Nonzero" ELSE PRINT "Zero"
```

In line 200, the variable `NUMITEMS%` is a Boolean expression all by itself. The output of this program is `Zero`, which demonstrates that 0 is treated as "false." Now change line 100 so that line `NUMITEMS%` has any nonzero value. For example:

```
100 NUMITEMS% = 22
```

The program now displays `Nonzero` because the Boolean expression has become "true."

The Relational Operators

BASIC provides six relational operators for your testing expressions. The operators were mentioned briefly in the previous chapter and are listed again in table 5.1.

***Table 5.1.** Relational operators.*

Symbol	Name	Example
=	Equals	4 = (3 + 1)
<>	Not equal	"Dog" <> "Cat"
>	Greater than	8 > 5
<	Less than	3 < 6
>=	Greater than or equals	9 >= 9
<=	Less than or equals	"Hi" <= "Ho"

Each example in the last column of the table is true. Note that some of the operators consist of two individual characters which together make one symbol. For example, the "less than or equals" operator is the "left-angle bracket" symbol (Shift-comma on most keyboards) followed by the equal sign.

Relational Operators Work on Strings

All the relational operators work on strings as well as on numbers. One string "equals" another string only if both strings contain exactly the same sequence of characters. That's easy enough to understand.

But how can one string be "greater than" or "less than" another string? How does the last example in table 5.1 work?

Every string character has an associated numeric value from 0 to 255. These values conform to an established code known as ASCII (American Standard Code for Information Interchange). For example, in ASCII, an *A* is 65, and an asterisk "*" is 42. (We discuss ASCII in Chapter 6, "Manipulating Data," and list all the ASCII values in Appendix B.)

Using ASCII, two strings can be compared character-by-character. The details are explained in Chapter 6, "Manipulating Data," but here's the essence of the method: characters at the same position in each string are compared (first character with first character, second with second, and so on). As soon as one pair of characters are different, the comparison stops. The ASCII values of the two characters (in the pair) are compared. One character must have a larger ASCII value than the other. The string containing the "larger" character is deemed the "larger" string.

Consider the last example in table 5.1 that compares "Hi" with "Ho". Both strings have *H* as their first character. The second characters, however, are different. The ASCII value of *i* is 105, and *o* has a value of 111. So *o* is larger than *i*, and "Ho" is larger than "Hi".

Compound Testing Expressions

Sometimes you need to test two or more conditions. For example, suppose that you want to assign the value "Perfect" to RESULT$ only if *both* of the following conditions are true:

❑ The value of SCORE% is 300.
❑ The value of GAME$ is "Bowling".

The following instruction does the trick:

```
225 IF (SCORE%=300) AND (GAME$="Bowling") THEN RESULT$="Perfect"
```

Here, you use a compound expression for the test. Note that the two conditions are combined with the logical operator AND. Both conditions must be true to assign Perfect to RESULT$. If only one condition is true (or neither condition), the test fails and program flow proceeds directly to the next line.

The parentheses in line 225 are not required. You can remove the parentheses, and BASIC will still interpret the line correctly. However, the parentheses make the line easy to read and understand. In similar instructions, we recommend that you use parentheses for clarity.

The Logical Operators

Line 225 uses AND to combine the two conditions. AND is one of BASIC's six logical operators. The logical operators combine Boolean expressions to create one large Boolean expression. (Remember that a Boolean expression is an expression that can be evaluated to "true" or "false.")

The most common logical operators are AND, OR, and NOT. They work as follows:

❑ AND combines two expressions. Each expression must be true for the entire expression to be true.

❑ OR combines two expressions. Either expression (or both expressions) must be true for the entire expression to be true.

❑ NOT negates a single expression.

Here's an example of NOT:

```
610 IF NOT (SCORE% = 300) THEN RESULT$ = "Could do better"
```

BASIC has three other logical operators: XOR, EQV, and IMP. Figure 5.2 shows the results returned by all the logical operators. In the figure, A and B represent Boolean operands that have a value of T ("true") or F ("false"). The table has four lines because there are four possible "truth configurations" for the two combined expressions:

❑ A and B are both true.
❑ A is true but B is false.
❑ A is false but B is true.
❑ A and B are both false.

Fig. 5.2. *Results of logical operators.*

OPERAND VALUE		VALUE OF LOGICAL OPERATION					
A	B	NOT A	A AND B	A OR B	A XOR B	A EQV B	A IMP B
T	T	F	T	T	F	T	T
T	F	F	F	T	T	F	F
F	T	T	F	T	T	F	T
F	F	T	F	F	F	T	T

Multiple *IF* Instructions

A single `IF` instruction is fine when your condition is nothing more than one true or false test. But suppose that you have a condition with several possible outcomes.

For example, reconsider the golf problem discussed earlier in this chapter. Recall that you wanted to examine the value of the variable `STROKES%` and display a different message depending on the value. Here's how that task was programmed using an `ON GOTO` instruction:

```
200 ON STROKES% GOTO 300, 400, 500, 600
250 PRINT "You got a bogie.": GOTO 700
300 PRINT "You got a hole in one!": GOTO 700
400 PRINT "You got an eagle.": GOTO 700
500 PRINT "You got a birdie.": GOTO 700
600 PRINT "You got par."
700 REM    The program continues here
```

Another way to program this problem is with consecutive IF instructions. For example:

```
200 IF STROKES% = 1 THEN PRINT "You got a hole in one!"
250 IF STROKES% = 2 THEN PRINT "You got an eagle."
300 IF STROKES% = 3 THEN PRINT "You got a birdie."
350 IF STROKES% = 4 THEN PRINT "You got par."
400 IF STROKES% > 4 THEN PRINT "You got a bogie."
700 REM    The program continues here
```

Note that any particular value of STROKES% can satisfy only one of the IF conditions. This guarantees that only one of the messages prints when you run this program fragment.

Sometimes you want to test a variable for different value ranges. For example, suppose that a program stores the age of a person in the variable AGE%. You want to print out whether the person is a child, teenager, or adult. Here's how you might program that with multiple IF instructions:

```
300 IF AGE% < 0 THEN PRINT "Error in age": GOTO 400
310 IF AGE% <= 12 THEN PRINT "Child": GOTO 400
320 IF AGE% < 20 THEN PRINT "Teenager": GOTO 400
330 PRINT "Adult"
400 REM    Program continues here
```

Do you see why the GOTO instructions are necessary in lines 300 through 320? Without the GOTOs, you get erroneous extra messages for some values of AGE%. For example, suppose that AGE% is 10 and the program has none of the GOTO instructions. Follow the logic and you see that the messages in lines 310, 320 and 330 will all print.

You can eliminate the GOTOs in these kinds of IF blocks by placing multiple tests in appropriate IF instructions. Here, for example, is another way to correctly program the last example:

```
300 IF  AGE% < 0                    THEN PRINT "Error in age"
310 IF (AGE% >= 0) AND (AGE% <=12) THEN PRINT "Child"
320 IF (AGE% > 12) AND (AGE% < 20) THEN PRINT "Teenager"
330 IF  AGE% >= 20                  THEN PRINT "Adult"
400 REM    Program continues here
```

Lines 310 and 320 contain multiple conditions. Note how the use of extra spacing in lines 300 and 330 makes the program easier to read.

Nested *IF* Instructions

You can nest IF instructions to two or more levels. The basic form looks like this:

IF *expr1* THEN IF *expr2* THEN *clause*

With ELSE clauses, the form looks like this:

IF *expr1* THEN IF *expr2* THEN *clause1* ELSE *clause2* ELSE *clause3*

Nested IFs provide another way to write compound tests. Once again, here's the previous line 225, which contains a compound testing expression:

```
225 IF (SCORE%=300) AND (GAME$="Bowling") THEN RESULT$="Perfect"
```

With nested IFs, the following instruction is equivalent:

```
225 IF SCORE%=300 THEN IF GAME$="Bowling" THEN RESULT$="Perfect"
```

We recommend against nested IF instructions. As you probably can gather, such instructions can get confusing quickly. Furthermore, things get even more muddled when nested IF instructions contain ELSE clauses.

Controlled Looping

A *loop* is any group of instructions that executes repeatedly. For example, this short program contains a loop:

```
10 PRINT "Begin beeping"
20 BEEP
30 PRINT "Still beeping"
40 GOTO 20
50 PRINT "How can I get here"
```

Lines 20 through 40 comprise the loop. In this case, we have an *endless loop*. Do you see why?

There's no way out. Line 40 always returns the program back to line 20. The loop and the beeping go on forever. Line 50 never gets a chance! You have to hit Ctrl-Break to interrupt this program, or turn off your computer, or stop paying your electric bills and wait until your power is disconnected!

A useful loop must have a way to end. When a loop has an ending mechanism, we call the loop a *controlled loop*. A controlled loop executes until a predetermined condition is satisfied. Some form of controlled loop occurs in most nontrivial programs.

BASIC provides two special structures for the programming of controlled loops: FOR...NEXT and WHILE...WEND. Though not identical, the characteristics of each structure are similar.

When you program a loop, you need to choose between FOR...NEXT and WHILE...WEND. As shown in figure 5.3, your choice generally depends on whether you know how many times you must go through the loop *before* the loop begins. As a rule, when you do know the number of repetitions beforehand, use a FOR...NEXT loop. When you don't know the number of repetitions, use a WHILE...WEND loop.

Fig. 5.3. *Selecting the appropriate loop structure.*

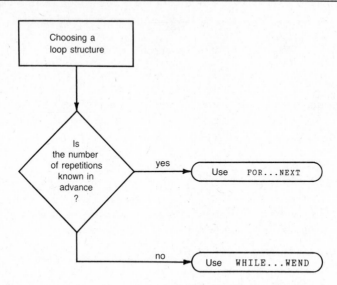

Using *FOR...NEXT* Loops

A FOR...NEXT loop uses a numeric variable to control the number of repetitions. This special variable is called a *counter variable* or *control variable*.

An Example of *FOR...NEXT*

Let's write a program that displays a table of the squares of the numbers from 0 to 6. (The square of a number is simply the number multiplied by itself.) This kind of task is perfect for a FOR...NEXT loop:

```
100 REM - Display Squares of Numbers
110 PRINT "Number", "Square"
120 FOR NUMBER% = 0 TO 6
130    SQUARE% = NUMBER% * NUMBER%
140    PRINT NUMBER%, SQUARE%
150 NEXT NUMBER%
160 PRINT "End of table"
```

Here's the output:

```
Number          Square
  0               0
  1               1
  2               4
  3               9
  4              16
  5              25
  6              36
End of table
```

Let's go over the program. Line 110 displays the title for the table. Note that the comma in the PRINT instruction forces the output (Number and Square) to align in predefined columns or "print zones." Print zones were discussed in Chapter 3, "A Hands-On Introduction to Programming," and are discussed in depth in Chapter 9, "Writing Text on the Video Screen."

The loop starts in line 120. NUMBER% is the counter variable. The value of NUMBER% changes each time through the loop. Line 120 sets the first value of NUMBER% to 0 and the final value to 6.

Line 150 marks the end of the loop. In a FOR...NEXT loop, all the instructions between the FOR and NEXT are called the *body* of the loop.

The body of a loop can have any number of instructions. Occasionally, a loop has more than 100 instructions. Here, the body of the more modest loop is the two instructions in lines 130 and 140.

Do you see how the loop works? The body of the loop executes repetitively. In succession, NUMBER% takes on the values 0, 1, 2, 3, 4, 5, and 6. The single PRINT instruction in line 140 displays every one of the numeric lines in the table. (Again, the comma aligns the output into columns.)

The first time through the loop, NUMBER% is zero. Line 130 computes the square of NUMBER%, so SQUARE% is also zero. Line 140 displays the first line of the table. Line 150 then effectively says, "Now it's time to increase the value of NUMBER%."

By default, the value of a counter variable increases by 1 each time through a FOR...NEXT loop. So the new value of NUMBER% becomes 1 (0 + 1 equals 1).

The program now returns to the beginning of the loop, at line 120. Here, the new value of NUMBER% (1) is compared against the final value of the loop (6 in this case). Because the final value is not yet exceeded, the body of the loop executes again. NUMBER% is 1 and SQUARE% becomes 1 also (1 times 1 is 1). Line 140 prints the second line of the table.

This looping process continues with NUMBER% continually increasing by 1. Eventually, NUMBER% reaches 6. The body of the loop still executes because NUMBER% has equaled—but not exceeded—the final value of the loop.

Line 150 then increases the value of NUMBER% to 7. Now, when control returns to line 120, the value of NUMBER% is finally greater than the maximum loop value of 6. This signals that the loop is over. The program then proceeds with the first line after the NEXT instruction. In our case, control passes to line 160, which prints the closing message.

The *STEP* Clause

By default, the counter variable increases by 1 each time through a FOR...NEXT loop. You can alter this increment by adding a STEP clause to the end of the FOR instruction. For example, in the following Squares program, line 120 is modified:

```
100 REM - Display Squares of Numbers
110 PRINT "Number", "Square"
120 FOR NUMBER% = 0 TO 6 STEP 2
130    SQUARE% = NUMBER% * NUMBER%
140     PRINT NUMBER%, SQUARE%
150 NEXT NUMBER%
160 PRINT "End of table"
```

The output becomes

```
Number          Square
  0               0
  2               4
  4              16
  6              36
End of table
```

The STEP clause specifies an increment of 2 each time through the loop. As a result, NUMBER% becomes successively 0, 2, 4, and 6.

With certain increments, you may not hit the final value of the loop exactly. For example, suppose that line 120 was written as follows:

```
120 FOR NUMBER% = 0 TO 6 STEP 4
```

The successive values of NUMBER% increase by 4 (0, 4, 8...). NUMBER% never becomes 6, the designated final value of the loop. In such a case, the loop terminates whenever the counter variable becomes greater than the final value. In this example, the body of the loop executes only for `NUMBER%` equal to 0 and 4. The loop terminates when `NUMBER%` becomes 8. The output is as follows:

```
Number          Square
  0               0
  4               16
End of table
```

You can specify negative increments. When the increment is negative, the counter variable decreases each time through the loop. For a proper "negative" loop, specify the final value of the counter variable to be smaller than the initial value.

For example, here's the program with line 120 specifying a negative `STEP` clause:

```
100 REM - Display Squares of Numbers
110 PRINT "Number", "Square"
120 FOR NUMBER% = 3 TO -2 STEP -1
130    SQUARE% = NUMBER% * NUMBER%
140    PRINT NUMBER%, SQUARE%
150 NEXT NUMBER%
160 PRINT "End of table"
```

The output becomes

```
Number          Square
  3               9
  2               4
  1               1
  0               0
 -1               1
 -2               4
End of table
```

Bypassing the Loop

BASIC bypasses a `FOR...NEXT` altogether if one of the following two conditions is met:

❏ The starting loop value is greater than the final loop value when the `STEP` increment is positive.

❏ The starting loop value is smaller than the final loop value when the `STEP` increment is negative.

Suppose that you change the FOR instruction as follows:

```
120 FOR NUMBER% = 5 TO 2
```

Here, the starting value of the loop (5) is greater than the final value (2). Because no STEP clause appears, the default increment is 1. BASIC "realizes" that you cannot count upward from 5 and reach 2! So the loop doesn't execute at all, not even once. The program output becomes

```
Number          Square
End of table
```

Using Variables in a *FOR* Instruction

You can specify the loop limits and/or the STEP increment with variables, or with entire expressions, for that matter. For example, all the following FOR instructions are acceptable:

```
600 FOR NUMBER% = 2 TO FINAL%

600 FOR NUMBER% = FIRST% TO LAST%

600 FOR NUMBER% = FIRST% TO LAST% STEP INCREMENT%

600 FOR NUMBER% = FIRST% TO LAST% STEP (LAST% - FIRST%) / 10

600 FOR NUMBER% = (VALUE1% - VALUE2%) TO 100
```

By using variables, a program may have different loop boundaries from run to run. For example, here's the Squares program modified to ask the user for the loop boundaries. When prompted, you type values for the first and last entries in the table.

```
100 REM - Display Squares of Numbers
    (Get Limits from user)
103 INPUT "Please input first value"; FIRST%
106 INPUT "Please input last value"; LAST%
110 PRINT "Number", "Square"
120 FOR NUMBER% = FIRST% TO LAST%
130    SQUARE% = NUMBER% * NUMBER%
140    PRINT NUMBER%, SQUARE%
150 NEXT NUMBER%
160 PRINT "End of table"
```

A typical run might look like this:

```
Please input first value? 4
Please input last value? 7
Number      Square
 4           16
 5           25
 6           36
 7           49
End of table
```

Note how line 120 now specifies the loop limits with the variables `FIRST%` and `LAST%`. The values for `FIRST%` and `LAST%` are supplied by the user with the aid of the `INPUT` instructions in lines 103 and 106.

What happens if you type a larger number for the first value than for the last value? Can you make a good guess? Try it and find out.

More about the Counter Variable

In a `NEXT` instruction, the counter variable is optional. That is, you can write line 150 as simply

```
NEXT
```

We recommend, however, that you always include the counter variable in `NEXT` instructions. That way, you make perfectly clear what the looping variables are.

We discuss nested loops a little later in this chapter. When two or more loops are active simultaneously, `NEXT` instructions are much easier to understand when the counter variables are included.

Syntax of *FOR...NEXT*

To summarize, here's the general syntax of a `FOR...NEXT` loop:

FOR *countervar* = *start* TO *end* STEP *increment*

.

.

   {*body of loop*}

.

.

NEXT *countervar*

where *countervar* is a numeric variable acting as the counter variable, *start* specifies the initial value of *countervar*, *end* specifies the final value of *countervar*, *increment* specifies how much to increase *countervar* each time through the loop, and *body of loop* is a block of BASIC instructions.

The STEP *increment* clause is optional. Also, *countervar* may be omitted in the NEXT instruction.

Placing a Loop in a Single Line

You can specify an entire FOR...NEXT loop in one program line. You don't have to isolate the loop components into separate physical lines. Simply use colons to separate the individual instructions. For example:

```
500 FOR ITEM% = 1 TO LASTITEM%: PRINT ITEM%: NEXT ITEM%
```

This single line has the same effect as the following three lines:

```
500 FOR ITEM% = 1 TO LASTITEM%
510    PRINT ITEM%
520 NEXT ITEM%
```

Of course, the body of the loop must be relatively small for a single-line loop to be feasible.

Using the Counter Variable

The counter variable can be any numeric type. So far, most of our counter variables have been of type integer (they're integer because of the percent sign at the end of the variable names).

The following loop works fine, however, with a single-precision counter variable named VALUE:

```
100 FOR VALUE = 1 TO 4
110    PRINT VALUE
120 NEXT VALUE
```

The output is just what you would expect:

```
1
2
3
4
```

Sometimes you *need* the counter variable to be single- or double-precision. For example, suppose that the loop increment has a fractional value:

```
100 FOR COUNTER = 0 TO 1 STEP 1/3
110    PRINT COUNTER
120 NEXT COUNTER
```

The output now contains fractional numbers:

```
0
.3333333
.6666667
1
```

If possible, use integer variables for your counter variables. Avoid single- or double-precision counter variables. Why?

First, loops with integer counter variables execute faster than loops with noninteger counter variables. Secondly, mathematical errors can occur when counter variables are single- or double-precision. Remember that BASIC cannot represent most single- and double-precision numbers exactly, only approximately. In certain situations, it is possible for what is known as *round-off errors* to occur in loops that contain fractional STEP increments.

An Example of a Round-Off Error

Try the following loop (which has a negative step):

```
100 FOR COUNTER = 1 TO 0 STEP -1/3
110    PRINT COUNTER
120 NEXT COUNTER
```

Here's the unexpected output:

```
1
.6666666
.3333333
```

What happened to the fourth line with a value of 0?

A round-off error, that's what. BASIC can only approximate the single-precision number one-third. Just before the fourth time through the loop, the value of COUNTER is less than 0—trivially less than 0 but still less than 0.

Any negative value of COUNTER, however, tells BASIC that the FOR...NEXT loop is complete. As a result, the loop executes only three times, and a programming error results.

We repeat the warning: use integer counter variables if at all possible.

Nesting *FOR* Loops

FOR...NEXT loops can be nested to any level. Many practical programs take advantage of nested loops. When you nest loops, be sure that each such loop uses a unique counter variable.

Innermost loops execute the fastest. This means that the NEXT instruction for an inner loop must occur before the NEXT instruction for an outer loop. Figure 5.4 shows the right and wrong way to nest loops. A NEXT without FOR error message occurs when nested loops are crossed incorrectly.

Fig. 5.4. *Nested* `FOR...NEXT` loops—the right way and the wrong way.

```
10 FOR A% = 1 TO 8
20    FOR B% = 3 TO 6
30       PRINT A%, B%
40    NEXT B%
50 NEXT A%
```

The right way

```
10 FOR A% = 1 TO 8
20    FOR B% = 3 TO 6
30       PRINT A%, B%
40    NEXT A%
50 NEXT B%
```

The wrong way

As an example of nested loops, here's a program that prints a multiplication table:

```
100 REM Program: MULTABLE (Demonstrate nested loops)
110 MAX% = 4              'Maximum value in table
120 PRINT "Value 1", "Value 2", "Product"
130 FOR A% = 1 TO MAX%
140    FOR B% = A% TO MAX%
150       PRODUCT% = A% * B%
160       PRINT A%, B%, PRODUCT%
170    NEXT B%
180    PRINT
190 NEXT A%
```

The output looks like this:

Value 1	Value 2	Product
1	1	1
1	2	2
1	3	3
1	4	4
2	2	4
2	3	6
2	4	8
3	3	9
3	4	12
4	4	16

Line 140 begins an inner loop while the outer loop is still active. The counter variables for the outer and inner loops are A% and B%, respectively. Note how line 140 uses A% (the counter variable from the outer loop) as the lower limit of the inner loop. The inner loop restarts each time that the outer loop increments. That's why "Value 1" in the output table increases each time the inner loop restarts.

You can edit line 110 to change the value of MAX%. By doing so, you can create larger (or smaller) multiplication tables.

Indenting Loops

Be liberal about indenting the body of the loop. This is not a requirement of BASIC but merely common sense. Consistent indentation makes programs easier to read. The result is programs that are easier to understand and easier to troubleshoot.

In our style, we place the FOR and NEXT keywords for each loop at the same indentation level. The body of the loop is indented three spaces. Nested loops are successively indented.

Common Traps in *FOR* Loops

Here are four "Don'ts" involving FOR...NEXT loops:

1. Don't redefine the control variable inside the loop.

Never explicitly change the value of the counter variable inside the body of the loop. Simply put, this is asking for problems. Beware of the common ways you might fall into this trap:

   a. Using the counter variable on the left side of an assignment instruction.

   b. Making the counter variable the object of an INPUT instruction.

   c. Reusing the same counter variable in a nested loop.

If you ever find yourself needing to program like this, throw some water on your face, then rethink your logic. There is bound to be a better way.

2. Don't depend on the value of the control variable outside the loop.

It is best to think of the counter variable as undefined once the loop terminates. You may reuse the counter variable for another purpose—often as a counter variable in a subsequent loop. But don't assume that the counter variable has any particular value after the loop terminates.

3. Don't branch into or out of loops.

You can use GOTO instructions that branch within the body of a loop, but don't branch into a loop from outside the loop. If you do, the limits of the loop are not properly defined. The loop may run indefinitely.

4. Don't use more than one NEXT for each control variable. That is, each FOR instruction must match with a single NEXT instruction. For example, the following loop (which contains two NEXT instructions) causes an error: NEXT without FOR in 150.

```
100 FOR NUM% = 5 TO 15
110    IF NUM% >= 10 THEN 140
120    PRINT " "; NUM%
130 NEXT NUM%
140    PRINT NUM%
150 NEXT NUM%
```

Instead, branch to a single NEXT at the end of the loop. The present loop should be written as follows (with line 130 modified):

```
100 FOR NUM% = 5 TO 15
110    IF NUM% >= 10 THEN 140
120    PRINT " "; NUM%
130    GOTO 150
140    PRINT NUM%
150 NEXT NUM%
```

Using *WHILE...WEND* Loops

WHILE...WEND loops are controlled by a *condition* rather than by a counter variable. Think of the condition as a true or false test placed at the top of the loop. The body of the loop continues to execute as long as the condition remains true.

Typically, the Boolean expression is a relational expression that BASIC automatically evaluates to true or false. Such relational expressions are just like the true or false expressions we used as tests in IF instructions.

Here are two examples of WHILE conditions:

```
400 WHILE TERMX% < 100                    'relational expression
500 WHILE (DAY$ = "Mon") OR (DAY$ = "Tue") 'compound logical
```

The WEND statement terminates the body of the loop.

```
WHILE boolexpr

   .

   .

   {body of loop}

   .

   .

WEND
```

where *boolexpr* specifies the condition as a Boolean (true or false) expression, and *body of loop* is any group of BASIC instructions.

Before BASIC enters the body of a `WHILE...WEND` loop for the first time, BASIC evaluates the condition in your `WHILE` instruction. If false, BASIC bypasses the loop entirely and execution continues on the line immediately following `WEND`.

If the condition is true, the body of the loop executes. Control then returns to the `WHILE` instruction, and the condition is reevaluated. As long as the condition remains true, the loop continues to execute.

Obviously, instructions inside the loop must do something to affect the testing condition, or the loop is in danger of executing forever. Usually, the body of the loop modifies one or more variables occurring in the testing expression.

As an example of `WHILE...WEND`, consider the following program that mimics a launching countdown:

```
100 REM Program: COUNTDWN.BAS (Demonstrate WHILE...WEND)
200 TIMELEFT% = 5
300 WHILE TIMELEFT% >= 1       'Boolean condition
400    PRINT TIMELEFT%
500    TIMELEFT% = TIMELEFT% - 1
600 WEND
700 PRINT "Blast off"
800 END
```

The output of `COUNTDWN.BAS` is

```
5
4
3
2
1
Blast off
```

Lines 400 and 500 contain the body of the loop. Note how line 500 decreases the value of `TIMELEFT%` with each pass through the loop. The condition in line 300 is true as long as `TIMELEFT%` has a value greater than or equal to 1.

Sometimes you can create a useful loop with an empty body of instructions. For example, the following `WHILE...WEND` loop pauses program execution until the user presses a key. (The function `INKEY$`, discussed in Chapter 12, "Programming Hardware Devices," detects characters typed at the keyboard.)

```
200 WHILE INKEY$ = ""
300 WEND
```

(Line 200 ends with two consecutive double quotation marks. The pair of quotation marks denotes an empty string—that is, a string containing no characters. The `INKEY$` function returns an empty string as long as no key is typed at the keyboard.)

To illustrate this loop, try the following program:

```
100 PRINT "I'm waiting for you to press a key"
200 WHILE INKEY$ = ""
300 WEND
400 PRINT "You finally pressed a key"
```

The program first displays the message in line 100. Next, the computer continuously executes the `WHILE...WEND` loop as long as you don't press a key. (The condition in line 200 remains true as long as you don't press a key.)

Effectively, the computer waits for you to press a key. When you do finally press a key, the condition in line 200 becomes false and the loop terminates. The program then continues with line 400, which displays the ending message.

As with `FOR...NEXT` loops, `WHILE...WEND` loops can be nested to any level and simple `WHILE...WEND` loops can be written on a single line (by separating the instructions with colons).

For example, the waiting loop could be written in a single line like this:

```
200 WHILE INKEY$ = "": WEND
```

Summary

Normal program flow progresses line-by-line down your program. Often, however, you need to alter this sequential order.

The most straightforward way to alter the program flow is with a *branch*. A branch is the direct transfer from one location in your program to another. With GOTO, you can make an *unconditional branch* to any instruction in your program. ON GOTO provides *conditional branching*: you branch to one of several instructions depending on the value of a particular expression.

An END instruction terminates your program completely. END instructions can be placed in the middle of a program as well as at the bottom.

Frequently, programs need to make decisions. Often, a condition is tested, and the program takes different actions depending on the result of the test. IF...THEN...ELSE instructions provide a versatile tool for conditional testing.

Loops are instruction blocks that execute repetitively. Loops are one of the most common and useful programming structures. Many programming tasks involve repetitive calculations for which a loop is ideally suited.

A *controlled loop* executes a limited number of times. BASIC has special statements for two kinds of controlled loops:

❑ FOR...NEXT when the loop should be executed a specified number of times.

❑ WHILE...WEND when the loop should be executed as long as a Boolean (logical) condition remains true.

CHAPTER 6

Manipulating Data

```
SIN, COS, TAN, ATN, EXP, LOG, CINT, CSNG, CDBL, FIX, INT,
RND, RANDOMIZE, ABS, SGN, SQR, LEN, LEFT%, RIGHT%, MID%,
ASC, CHR%, VAL, STR$, HEX$, OCT$, INSTR, STRING$, SPACE$
```

Most programs manipulate data. After all, when you program routine tasks (such as assigning values to variables, calculating numeric quantities, or printing results), you are manipulating data.

Indeed, the term *data manipulation* could be a title for the remainder of this book. In one way or another, nearly all programming topics relate to data manipulation.

In this chapter, we explore various ways of manipulating numbers and strings. Here are the main topics that we cover:

❏ Using BASIC's numerical functions.
❏ Using BASIC's string functions.
❏ Converting numbers from one data type to another.
❏ Forming string expressions.

141

Introduction to Functions

A *function* manipulates one or more arguments in a predetermined way to produce a single value. In programming terminology, we say that a function *returns* a single value. For example, the SQR function returns the square root of a single argument.

BASIC supports the following two kinds of functions:

❑ Built-in functions (these are automatically available to any program).

❑ User-defined functions.

A Word about User-Defined Functions

As the name implies, *you* create a user-defined function. You define such functions with DEF FN instructions. After a function is defined, your program may invoke your function over and over again. We discuss DEF FN and user-defined functions in Chapter 15, "Toward Advanced Programming." Until that chapter, the word *function* refers to built-in functions.

This chapter examines only the built-in functions. These functions are predefined in BASIC. You can use a function in any program at any time.

We have already introduced the SQR, LEN, and MID$ functions. These, however, are just the tip of the iceberg. As you will soon see, the wealth of BASIC functions provides an invaluable programming tool.

Each function call consists of a reserved word and, usually, one or more arguments (parameters) enclosed in parentheses (see fig. 6.1). Most functions use a single argument, but some functions require two or more arguments. (A special form of the random-number function RND actually has no arguments, but that is a unique case. We discuss RND later in this chapter.) When a function has multiple arguments inside the parentheses, the arguments are separated with commas.

Regardless of the number of arguments, every function returns a single value. The functions can be divided into the following two categories:

❑ *String functions.* These functions return a string value. The function name always ends with a dollar sign. Some string functions require a numeric argument or arguments; others require a string argument or arguments.

Fig. 6.1. A typical function call.

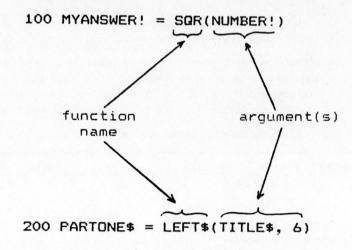

```
100 MYANSWER! = SQR(NUMBER!)
```

function name   argument(s)

```
200 PARTONE$ = LEFT$(TITLE$, 6)
```

☐ *Numeric functions.* These functions, naturally enough, return a numeric value. The function name never ends with a dollar sign. Most numeric functions require numeric arguments; some require string arguments.

Note that the argument (or arguments) of a function is not necessarily the same data type as the value returned by the function. For example, the LEN function returns a numeric value equal to the length of its string argument:

```
100 NUM! = LEN(MYSTRING$)
```

In general, you can call a function anywhere a single value is acceptable. For example, table 6.1 shows a few places where you might use an SQR function:

Table 6.1. Sample function calls.

Instruction	Comment
100 NUM = SQR(55)	Right side of assignment instruction
100 PRINT SQR(MYNUM)	In a PRINT instruction
100 A = SQR(SQR(24))	As an argument of another SQR function
100 IF SQR(A') < 5 THEN...	In an IF...THEN instruction

Using the Numeric Functions

When we discuss the numeric functions, we often use the term *general numeric expression*, or simply *numeric expression*.

A numeric expression is any expression that evaluates to a single numeric value. The expression may contain any combination of literals, variables, array elements, operators, and function calls. The final value can have any of the three numeric data types (integer, single-precision, or double-precision).

Table 6.2 shows a few examples of numeric expressions:

Table 6.2. *Sample numeric expressions.*

Numeric Expression	Comment
`435`	Simple numeric literal
`(COST! * NUMITEMS') / 12.2`	Expression with variables
`SALARY!(EMPLOYEE')`	Simple array reference
`SQR(SIDE!# - SIDE2#)`	Expression containing a function call

Obviously, the numeric functions are mathematical in nature. We recognize that many programmers are not math wizards and don't intend to write programs that do much mathematical manipulation. If this is you, feel free to skim the following material. Later, should the need arise, you can always come back for reference.

As table 6.3 shows, BASIC provides a host of numerical functions.

Table 6.3. *The mathematical functions.*

Name	Description
Trigonometric	
`SIN`	Sine of an angle
`COS`	Cosine of an angle
`TAN`	Tangent of an angle
`ATN`	Arctangent of a number
Logarithmic	
`EXP`	Exponential
`LOG`	Natural logarithm

Conversion

`CINT`	Convert a number to integer
`CSNG`	Convert a number to single-precision
`CDBL`	Convert a number to double-precision

Rounding

`FIX`	Truncate to integer
`INT`	Round to lower integer

Random Numbers

`RND`	Generate a random number

Arithmetic

`ABS`	Absolute value
`SGN`	Sign of a number
`SQR`	Square root

Unless otherwise stated, each mathematical function returns a single-precision result—even when the arguments are double-precision.

Using the Trigonometric Functions

The trigonometric functions `SIN`, `COS`, and `TAN` return, respectively, the sine, cosine, and tangent of an angle. BASIC also includes the `ATN` function, which returns the arctangent (or inverse tangent) of a number.

`SIN`(angle)

`COS`(*angle*)

`TAN`(*angle*)

`ATN`(*numexpr*)

where *angle* specifies an angle in radians, and *numexpr* is a general numeric expression.

Angles are specified in radians because radians are mathematically more convenient than degrees. One radian is approximately 57.3 degrees. There are 2π radians in a complete circle (that is, 2π radians equals 360 degrees, π is approximately 3.14). Figure 6.2 shows the mapping between radians and degrees.

Fig. 6.2. *Specifying angles in radians and degrees.*

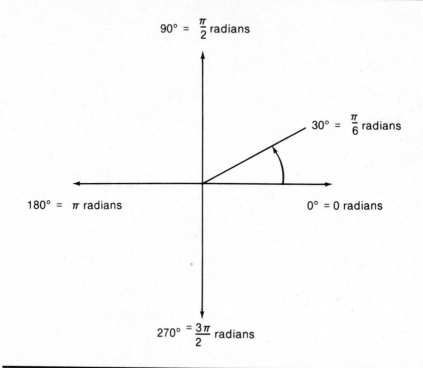

$$90° = \frac{\pi}{2} \text{ radians}$$

$$30° = \frac{\pi}{6} \text{ radians}$$

$$180° = \pi \text{ radians}$$

$$0° = 0 \text{ radians}$$

$$270° = \frac{3\pi}{2} \text{ radians}$$

The value of *angle* can be positive, negative, or zero. The SIN and COS functions always return a value from −1.0 to +1.0. TAN returns values ranging from large negative numbers to large positive numbers.

The arctangent of *numexpr* is the angle whose tangent has the value of *numexpr*. Thus ATN is the inverse function to TAN. The result of the ATN function is an angle expressed in radians. This angle is confined to the range from −π/2 to +π/2.

Using `ATN` To Find the Value of π

Many trigonometric programs need to work with the value of π. The `ATN` function provides a convenient way to store the value of π in a variable. Here's how.

The tangent of $(\pi/4)$ is exactly 1. This means that the arctangent of 1 is $\pi/4$. The following program fragment stores the value of π in a variable named `PI!` and then prints the value.

```
400 PI! = 4 * ATN(1)

410 PRINT PI!
```

Here is the output:

```
3.141593
```

Using the Logarithmic Functions

`LOG` returns the natural logarithm; the inverse function, `EXP`, returns the exponential.

`LOG(`*numexpr*`)`

`EXP(`*numexpr*`)`

where *numexpr* is a general numeric expression.

For the `LOG` function, *numexpr* must be positive, or an `Illegal function call` error occurs. (Mathematically, a logarithm is undefined for a negative argument.)

For the `EXP` function, *numexpr* can be positive, negative, or zero. The largest permissible value of *numexpr* is 88. (A value of *numexpr* above this limit creates numeric overflow because, mathematically, the exponential returns a value larger than the maximum single-precision number.)

`LOG` and `EXP` are based on the natural logarithms, also called logarithms to the base e. The mathematical constant e has a value of approximately 2.71828. You can see BASIC's value of e with the following experiment:

```
Ok
PRINT EXP(1)
 2.718282
Ok
```

You may need logarithms to the base 10, sometimes called common logarithms. The following instruction uses the LOG function to calculate the common logarithm of X!:

```
200 COMLOG! = LOG(X!) / LOG(10)
```

You can duplicate the exponential function with the exponential operator ^ (the caret, or up-arrow symbol—Shift-6 on most keyboards). Mathematically, EXP(X) is e^X (e raised to the power of X). Another way to express the same thing in BASIC is EXP(1) ^ X. For example, consider the following code fragment:

```
250 X! = 4.9
260 PRINT EXP(X!)
270 PRINT EXP(1) ^ X!
```

Here is the output:

```
 134.2898
 134.2897
```

(The values are slightly different due to internal rounding of calculated values.)

Use 10 ^ X to calculate the base 10 exponential of X (10 raised to the X power).

Using the Conversion Functions

BASIC has several functions that convert a number from one numeric type to another (such as from single-precision to integer). These are the conversion functions: CINT, CSNG, and CDBL.

CINT, CSNG, and CDBL convert a given numeric expression in any format into the equivalent number in a specified numeric format.

CINT converts to integer. The value of *numexpr* must be in the range from −32,768 to +32,767. If *numexpr* contains a fractional part, CINT rounds to the closest integer. (When *numexpr* has a fractional part of exactly .5, CINT rounds to the next higher integer.)

```
CINT(numexpr)

CSNG(numexpr)

CDBL(numexpr)
```

where *numexpr* is a general numeric expression.

CSNG converts to single-precision. The value of *numexpr* must be in the range from (approximately) $-3.37E + 38$ to $+3.37E + 38$.

CDBL converts to double-precision. The value of *numexpr* must be in the same range as for CSNG.

Table 6.4 shows the results of some direct-mode conversion commands.

Table 6.4. Sample commands using the conversion functions.

Direct-Mode Command	Result
PRINT CINT(-1.8)	-2
PRINT CINT(29.4)	29
PRINT CINT(29.8)	30
PRINT CSNG(1.23456789#)	1.234568
PRINT CSNG(1 / 7)	.1428572
PRINT CDBL(1 / 7)	.1428571492433548
PRINT CDBL(1# / 7)	.1428571428571429

In table 6.4, compare the results of the two CDBL examples with the last CSNG example. Although CDBL calculates to 16 digits of precision, only the first 6 digits are guaranteed to be accurate. The expression (1 / 7) produces only single-precision accuracy, and CDBL cannot convert a single-precision expression to double-precision accuracy. However, the expression (1# / 7) produces double-precision accuracy, and CDBL processes this expression to full accuracy.

The conversion functions are used primarily with subexpressions inside larger expressions to avoid loss of accuracy.

You *do not* need conversion functions when you assign a numeric expression to a variable. Consider the following instructions:

```
300 MYINT% = CINT(1234.5 * 4)
310 MYSNG! = CSNG(23.8# / 9)
320 MYDBL# = CDBL(38.23 * 14.7)
```

In each case, you get exactly the same result by omitting the conversion function. The assignment of a numeric expression to a numeric variable forces the appropriate type conversion. No conversion function is necessary.

Using the Rounding Functions

In addition to CINT, BASIC has two other functions that convert a general numeric expression into a whole number.

FIX(*numexpr*)

INT(*numexpr*)

where *numexpr* is a general numeric expression.

FIX simply strips off the fractional part of *numexpr*. This is called *truncation*. FIX(8.9) is 8, and FIX(-8.9) is -8.

INT returns the largest whole number that is less than or equal to the value of *numexpr*. This is called *rounding down* or *flooring*. INT(8.9) is 8 and INT(-8.9) is -9.

FIX and INT are similar functions. Each returns the same value when *numexpr* is zero or positive. However, when *numexpr* is negative, the functions produce different results.

Unlike CINT, FIX and INT can work with values outside the range of BASIC's integer numbers. Although FIX and INT return whole numbers, the results are single-precision. For example, PRINT FIX(123456.7) and PRINT INT(123456.7) each returns 123456.

Contrast that with PRINT CINT(123456.7), which causes an overflow error because 123456.7 is too large for BASIC's integer data type.

The following program, ROUND.BAS, demonstrates the difference between values returned by CINT, FIX, and INT.

```
100 REM Program: ROUND.BAS (Demonstrate rounding functions)
110 PRINT "X", "CINT(X)", "FIX(X)", "INT(X)"
120 FOR X! = -2.8 TO 2.8 STEP 1.4
130    PRINT X!, CINT(X!), FIX(X!), INT(X!)
140 NEXT X!
```

Here's the output from `ROUND.BAS`:

X	CINT(X)	FIX(X)	INT(X)
-2.8	-3	-2	-3
-1.4	-1	-1	-2
0	0	0	0
1.4	1	1	1
2.8	3	2	2

Using Random Numbers

The `RND` function returns a single-precision *random* number between 0 and 1.

`RND`

or

`RND(numexpr)`

where *numexpr* is a general numeric expression.

Note that the argument, *numexpr*, is optional.

How can a number be random? Just what does a "random" number mean?

A random number is simply an unpredictable number, a number that cannot be predetermined.

Many scientific simulations and game-playing programs use random numbers regularly. As a simple example, the following instruction tosses a simulated coin:

```
585 IF RND > 0.5 THEN PRINT "Heads" ELSE PRINT "Tails"
```

Values returned by `RND` are not truly random, but rather are computed by a numeric formula that creates *pseudorandom* numbers. This formula is kept internally by BASIC and you don't have to worry about it.

However, the formula does depend on an initial starting value, sometimes called a *seed*. By default, BASIC provides the same seed each time you run a program. Therefore, unless you reseed the random-number generator, `RND` produces the same sequence of random numbers each time the program is run.

So, how do you reseed the random-number formula? BASIC provides the RANDOMIZE statement just for that purpose.

RANDOMIZE *seed*

or simply

RANDOMIZE

where *seed* is a general numeric expression. The *seed* parameter is optional.

RANDOMIZE is not a function, but a full-fledged BASIC statement. Note that the seed parameter is not enclosed in parentheses.

Typically, you use a single RANDOMIZE instruction at the beginning of every program that uses RND. To change the random-number sequence each time a particular program is run, you must alter the value of *seed* with each run. BASIC's TIMER function provides a handy way to seed the random-number generator unpredictably. (TIMER is a special function that returns the number of elapsed seconds since midnight. We discuss more about TIMER in Chapter 12, "Programming Hardware Devices.") Use the following instruction:

```
120 RANDOMIZE TIMER
```

A RANDOMIZE instruction without the *seed* parameter causes BASIC to prompt you for a seed value by displaying the following message:

```
Random-number seed (-32768 to 32767)?
```

You must provide the seed before execution resumes.

RND operates differently depending on the value of the *numexpr* argument (see table 6.5).

The following program demonstrates the type of random numbers returned by RND:

```
100 RANDOMIZE TIMER
110 FOR J% = 1 TO 5
120    PRINT RND
130 NEXT J%
```

Table 6.5. *Operation of* RND function.

Value of Argument	Action Performed
numexpr > 0	Returns the next random number in the current sequence
numexpr omitted	Same effect as *numexpr* > 0
numexpr = 0	Returns the previous random number
numexpr < 0	Reseeds the random-number generator using *numexpr* and returns the first number of the new sequence

Here is the output from a typical run. (Your results will differ, of course. After all, these are random numbers.)

```
.5473383
.6511793
.9765581
.277216
.9823589
```

Note that RND always returns a decimal fraction between 0 and 1. What if you need a random integer, say from 10 to 35?

With the aid of RND and INT, the following formula produces a random integer in the range from *lowinteger* to *highinteger*:

INT((*highinteger* − *lowinteger* + 1) * RND + *lowinteger*)

For example, the command PRINT INT(26 * RND + 10) displays a random integer in the range from 10 to 35.

To illustrate this technique, here's a program that calculates and displays five random rolls of two dice.

```
100 REM Program: DICEROLL.BAS (Roll dice 5 times)
110 RANDOMIZE TIMER
120 FOR ROLL% = 1 TO 5
130    DIE1% = INT(6 * RND + 1)
140    DIE2% = INT(6 * RND + 1)
150    PRINT "Roll"; ROLL%; "is"; DIE1% + DIE2%
160 NEXT ROLL%
```

Here are some typical results of `DICEROLL.BAS`. (Again, your results will differ due to the use of the `RANDOMIZE` instruction.)

```
Roll 1 is 8
Roll 2 is 12
Roll 3 is 7
Roll 4 is 10
Roll 5 is 5
```

(The `PRINT` instruction in line 150 uses semicolons to separate displayed items. We mentioned this technique in Chapter 3, "A Hands-On Introduction to Programming," and discuss `PRINT` thoroughly in Chapter 9, "Writing Text on the Video Screen.")

Using the Arithmetic Functions

Three miscellaneous numeric functions remain—`ABS`, `SGN`, and `SQR`.

`ABS`(*numexpr*)

`SGN`(*numexpr*)

`SQR`(*numexpr*)

where *numexpr* is a general numeric expression.

The `ABS` function returns the absolute value of *numexpr*. The absolute value of a number is the magnitude of the number without regard to sign. For example, the absolute value of −21.7 and the absolute value of +21.7 are both 21.7.

Many calculations require you to find the difference between two numbers, regardless of which number is larger. For example, suppose that you have two variables named `A!` and `B!`. You want to set `DIFF!` to the positive difference between `A!` and `B!`. However, you don't know whether `A!` or `B!` has the larger value. You could use a messy `IF` instruction like this:

```
50 IF A! > B! THEN DIFF! = A! - B! ELSE DIFFERENCE! = B! - A!
```

There is a better way. Rather than fool around with cumbersome `IF` instructions, use `ABS` to calculate the positive difference as follows:

```
50 DIFF! = ABS(A! - B!)
```

The SGN function returns the sign of *numexpr*, not to be confused with the trigonometric SIN function discussed previously. As shown in table 6.6, the SGN function returns −1, 0, or +1 depending on the value of *numexpr*.

Table 6.6. *The* SGN *function.*

Value of numexpr	Result of SGN(numexpr)
Positive (> 0)	1
Zero (= 0)	0
Negative (< 0)	−1

The SQR function, which you have read about already, returns the square root of *numexpr*. Negative arguments are not allowed. The value of *numexpr* must be greater than or equal to 0.

Calculating Square Roots

Mathematically, the square root of a number is equivalent to raising the number to the one-half (.5) power. Therefore, the following two instructions return the same result:

```
800 MYROOT! = SQR(MYNUMBER!)

800 MYROOT! = MYNUMBER! ' 0.5
```

We think that the SQR form is easier to read when you glance at a program. Furthermore, BASIC executes the SQR form faster. For square roots, use SQR rather than the .5 exponent.

Manipulating Strings

We have discussed numbers for quite a while. Let's turn our attention to strings.

Length of a String

Every data string has a *length*. This length is simply the number of text characters (including blank spaces and punctuation characters) that comprise the string. For example, the string "Hello" has a length of five. The string

"Paris, Texas" has a length of 12 (including the comma and blank space). The maximum-length string is 255 characters.

A string variable also has a length. A variable length is just the length of the string currently stored in the variable.

The Null String

A string can have a length of zero! In BASIC jargon, a zero-length string is called a *null string*. You form a null string by placing two quotation marks together. For example:

```
400 MYTEXT$ = ""
```

MYTEXT$ has a length of 0 (the null string).

Don't confuse the null string with a string consisting of a single blank space. The latter string has a length of 1. When you "display" the null string with PRINT instruction, you don't get any characters at all (not even a blank space). Here's an example:

```
100 PART1$ = "check"
150 PART2$ = "book"
200 MIDDLE$ = ""              'null string
250 PRINT PART1$; MIDDLE%; PART2$
300 MIDDLE$ = " "             'one blank space
350 PRINT PART1$; MIDDLE%; PART2$
```

The result is

```
checkbook
check book
```

Joining Strings

As we discussed in Chapter 4, "Language Building Blocks," you use the plus (+) operator to join two strings together. This process, called *concatenation*, forms a new string composed of the first string immediately followed by the second string.

What's the length of the new string? Sure, just the sum of the lengths of the two operand strings.

Consider the following program fragment:

```
700 FIRSTPART$ = "Don't rock"
710 RESULT$ = FIRSTPART$ + "the boat."
720 PRINT RESULT$
```

The output is

```
Don't rockthe boat.
```

Concatenation does not do any formatting, trimming, or padding with blank characters. In the present example, to add a blank space between `rock` and `the`, you must change the program. Here is one solution (with line 710 changed):

```
700 FIRSTPART$ = "Don't rock"
710 RESULT$ = FIRSTPART$ + " the boat." 'blank space before the
720 PRINT RESULT$
```

Now, the output is more readable:

```
Don't rock the boat.
```

String Expressions

Just as you can form numeric expressions, you can also form string expressions. We use the term *string expression* to refer to any expression that evaluates to a single string value.

A string expression can be as simple as a single variable name or as complex as a combination of string literals, variables, functions, and the plus sign. Table 6.7 shows some examples of string expressions.

Table 6.7. *Some sample string expressions.*

Expression	Comment
`"Bob and Ray"`	Single literal
`TITLE$`	Single variable
`LEFT$(TITLE$, 3)`	String function
`"Mortimer" + LASTNAME$`	Combination expression

Using the String Functions

BASIC's functions are not all mathematical. Far from it. As shown in table 6.8, BASIC provides several built-in functions that manipulate strings.

Table 6.8. *String functions.*

Name	Description

Finding String Length

LEN	Return length of string

Returning a Substring

LEFT$	Return leftmost characters
RIGHT$	Return rightmost characters
MID$	Return substring

Converting to and from ASCII

ASC	Return ASCII value of a character
CHR$	Return character from ASCII value

Converting Strings to Numbers

VAL	Convert string to number
STR$	Convert number to string form
HEX$	Convert number to hex string
OCT$	Convert number to octal string

Searching for Substring

INSTR	Search for substring

Generating Strings

STRING$	Construct a string of identical characters
SPACE$	Construct a string of blank spaces

All of these functions operate on strings. Some of the functions return numeric values and some return string values. The functions that return string values have a dollar sign at the end of the function name. Functions that return numeric values do not end with a dollar sign. The functions that return numeric values take string arguments.

Finding String Length

Want to find the length of a string? Use LEN.

> LEN(*string*)
>
> where *string* is a string expression.

Consider the following program:

```
100 NULL$="" 'The double quotes form a null string
110 PRINT LEN(NULL$)
120 MYNAME$ = "Phil Feldman"
130 PRINT LEN(MYNAME$)
140 PRINT LEN("You had to be there")
```

The output is

```
0
12
19
```

Returning a Substring

The LEFT$, RIGHT$, and MID$ functions return a portion of a string. A portion of a larger string is called a *substring* of the larger string. For example, "water" is a substring of "Clearwater".

To use LEFT$, RIGHT$, or MID$, you must specify the length of the desired substring (the number of characters you want returned) and the position in the original string where the substring begins.

LEFT$ returns a substring copied from the leftmost characters in *string*. Similarly, RIGHT$ extracts the rightmost characters in *string*. The *stringlength* parameter must be in the range from 0 to 255. If *stringlength* is zero, a null string is returned. If *stringlength* is greater than the length of *string*, the whole *string* is returned.

Here is a simple example of LEFT$ and RIGHT$:

```
100 TEST$ = "Phil says hello to Tom"
110 PRINT LEFT$(TEST$, 15) 'leftmost 15 characters of TEST$
120 PRINT RIGHT$(TEST$, 12) 'rightmost 12 characters of TEST$
```

LEFT$(*string, stringlength*)

RIGHT$(*string, stringlength*)

MID$(*string, startposition*)

or

MID$(*string, startposition, stringlength*)

where *string* is a string expression, *stringlength* specifies the length of the substring to return, and *startposition* specifies the position in *string* where the substring starts.

The output looks like this:

```
Phil says hello
hello to Tom
```

The MID$ function extracts a substring from the interior of *string*. The *stringlength* and *startposition* parameters must be in the range from 1 to 255.

MID$ returns a substring that begins at *startposition* and has a length of *stringlength* characters. For example, if *startposition* is 6 and *stringlength* is 4, MID$ returns the sixth through ninth characters of *string*.

Another example should make clear just how MID$ works:

```
100 TEST$ = "Every good boy does fine"
110 PRINT MID$(TEST$, 7, 8) 'characters 7,8,9,10,11,12,13,14
120 PRINT MID$(TEST$, 12, 3) 'characters 12,13,14
130 PRINT MID$(TEST$, 12) 'characters 12 to end of string
```

The output is

```
good boy
boy
boy does fine
```

Note that MID$ has two forms: with and without the *stringlength* parameter. If you omit *stringlength*, MID$ returns all characters from *startposition* to the end of *string*. You get the same effect in the three-parameter form when *string* does not contain *stringlength* characters from *startposition* to the end of *string*. Lines 110 and 120 use the three-parameter form of MID$; line 130 uses the two-parameter form.

If *startposition* is greater than the length of *string*, MID$ simply returns a null string.

Here's a tricky example. Can you follow what happens?

```
100 FOR START% = 1 TO 6
110    PRINT MID$("BASIC", START%, 2)
120 NEXT START%
RUN
BA
AS
SI
IC
C
Ok
```

Note that there are six lines of output. The last line is blank because the start position (given by START% with a value of 6) is beyond the length of the five-character string "BASIC".

Converting Strings to ASCII

Every string character has an associated numeric value from 0 to 255. These values conform to a special code known as ASCII (American Standard Code for Information Interchange). For example, the uppercase letter "A" has an ASCII value of 65. The lowercase letter "a" is 97. A blank space is 32. Appendix B lists all the ASCII values and the associated characters.

The functions ASC and CHR$ convert between string characters and numeric ASCII values—ASC returns the ASCII code for a given string character and CHR$ returns the string character corresponding to a given ASCII value.

ASC(*strexpr*)

CHR$(*ASCIIcode*)

where *strexpr* is a string expression, and *ASCIIcode* is an ASCII code value in the range from 0 to 255.

Note that CHR$ ends with a dollar sign but ASC does not. CHR$ is a string function that takes a numeric argument but returns a string value. ASC, on the other hand, takes a string argument but returns a numerical value.

ASC returns the ASCII code of the first character in *strexpr*. If *strexpr* is a null string, a run-time error occurs (Illegal function call). Here's ASC in action.

```
200 PRINT ASC("A")
210 PRINT ASC("Apples")
220 PRINT ASC("2")
230 MOTTO$ = "23 Skidoo"
240 PRINT ASC(MOTTO$)
```

The result is

```
65
65
50
50
```

CHR$ complements ASC. CHR$ returns the single-character string corresponding to the value of *ASCIIcode*. For example, CHR$(65) returns A.

CHR$ enables you to easily display characters that have special meanings in BASIC. For example, suppose that you want to display a double quotation mark. PRINT """ doesn't work. You can't put a double quotation mark in a string literal because the quotation mark itself has a special meaning (as a string delimiter).

However, CHR$ comes to the rescue. The ASCII value for the double quote is 34. The following program uses CHR$(34) to display double quotation marks around a string:

```
200 PROVERB$ = "A rolling stone gathers no moss."
210 PRINT PROVERB$
220 PRINT CHR$(34); PROVERB$; CHR$(34)
```

The result is

```
A rolling stone gathers no moss.
"A rolling stone gathers no moss."
```

Converting Strings to Numbers

Sometimes you need to treat a numeric quantity (such as the value of a variable) as a string. That is, you want to convert a number into a string. At other times, you need the opposite capability—interpreting a string as a number. The STR$ and VAL functions do these conversions.

A Tour of the ASCII Character Set

If you browse through Appendix B, "ASCII Character Set," you will notice many special "characters" in addition to the normal letters, digits, and punctuation. For example, you will find graphic characters at the ASCII values from 128 to 255. You can beep the speaker or clear the screen with some of the "special effects" characters below ASCII 32. Try the following program for a little fun:

```
100 FOR J = 1 TO 255
200    PRINT CHR$(J); 'The semicolon is important
300 NEXT J
```

You just displayed the entire ASCII character set! What you see on your screen represents the character from 13 up. (You "printed" the lower characters, but character number 12 cleared the screen.)

Did you hear the speaker beep when you ran the program? The "bell" character is ASCII 7. You can actually beep your speaker with `PRINT CHR$(7)`.

Note how `CHR$` lets you easily get hard-to-type characters into your programs. For example, your keyboard doesn't have a key for the Greek letter alpha. But `CHR$(224)` is all you need.

For further discussion of `PRINT` with the special ASCII characters, see Chapter 9, "Writing Text on the Video Screen."

`STR$(`*numexpr*`)`

`VAL(`*stringexpr*`)`

where *numexpr* is a general numeric expression, and *stringexpr* is a string expression.

`STR$` converts *numexpr* into string form. If *numexpr* is positive, `STR$` adds a leading space. Here's an example:

```
100 NUMBER! = 1.8
110 NUM$ = STR$(NUMBER!)
120 PRINT "XXXXX"
130 PRINT NUM$
140 PRINT LEN(NUM$)
```

The output is

```
XXXXX
 1.8
 4
```

The `STR$` function in line 110 converts the number 1.8 into the string "` 1.8`" (with a blank space before the 1.) The output confirms the leading space and shows that the string length of `NUM$` is 4. (The four characters are the leading space and then the three characters in "1.8".)

Why would you want to convert a number into a string? In string form, you can manipulate numbers with the various string functions, and often you can format output easier. For example, the following code fragment prints the amount of a check surrounded by three dashes on each side:

```
100 AMOUNT = 458.62
110 AMOUNT$ = STR$(AMOUNT) 'Convert AMOUNT to string
120 NEWAMOUNT$ = RIGHT$(AMOUNT$,
    LEN(AMOUNT$) - 1)
130 ' --  Line 120 above strips leading blank from AMOUNT$
140 PRINT "Check amount is --"; NEWAMOUNT$; "--"
```

The output looks like this:

```
Check amount is --458.62--
```

Line 110 simply converts `AMOUNT` to string form. Remember, the string in `AMOUNT$` now contains " 458.62" (with a blank before the 4).

Line 120 is a bit tricky. The line strips off the leading blank in `AMOUNT$` and stores the new string in `NEWAMOUNT$`. Do you see how it works? The second argument of the `RIGHT$` function is the expression `LEN(AMOUNT$) - 1`. This expression has a numeric value 1 less than the length of `AMOUNT$`. So the `RIGHT$` function returns a string consisting of all but the first character in `AMOUNT$`. The result is that the leading blank is stripped from `AMOUNT$`.

The point of this exercise is that if line 140 uses `AMOUNT` or `AMOUNT$` rather than `NEWAMOUNT$`, the output contains an annoying blank just before the number:

```
Check amount is -- 458.62--
```

The `VAL` function complements `STR$`. `VAL` converts a string into a numeric value. `VAL` works by examining *stringexpr* from left to right until the first character occurs that cannot be interpreted as part of a number. (Blank spaces are ignored.) For example, `VAL("76 trombones")` returns 76.

If the first nonblank character of *stringexpr* is nonnumeric, `VAL` returns the value of 0. Table 6.9 shows examples of the `VAL` function.

Table 6.9. Results of the `VAL` *function.*

string	VAL(string)	Comment
`"43.21"`	43.21	`VAL` converts the string to the number.
`"28,631,409"`	28	`VAL` does not "understand" commas; conversion stops at the first comma.
`"    14"`	14	Leading blanks are ignored.
`"-19"`	−19	Negative numbers are fine.
`"-19"`	−19	Internal blanks are ignored.
`"Twelve"`	0	`VAL` returns 0 when string is nonnumeric.
`"Lotus123"`	0	`VAL` does not find embedded numbers. The `"L"` immediately signals a nonnumeric string.

Converting Numbers to Hexadecimal and Octal Strings

Like binary numbers, hexadecimal and octal numbers are specialized numbering systems appropriate for manipulating memory addresses and byte values. Two specialized functions, `HEX$` and `OCT$`, convert regular decimal numbers into hexadecimal and octal strings, respectively.

Such number systems are an advanced subject. We discuss binary and hexadecimal numbers in Chapter 15, "Toward Advanced Programming."

Searching for a Substring

Many string-processing programs need to search a large string (or several different strings) to see whether a particular substring is present. For example, a program that handles full names of employees might want to find all the last names of *Smith*.

The INSTR function searches a string for a specified substring and returns the position where the substring is found. BASIC has two forms of the INSTR function:

INSTR(*targetstr, substr*)

or

INSTR(*startposition, targetstr, substr*)

where *startposition* specifies at which character position to begin the search, *targetstr* is the string being searched, and *substr* is the string being searched for.

INSTR searches the target string left to right for the first occurrence of *substr*. In the two-parameter form of INSTR (without the *startposition* parameter), the search begins at the first character of the target string. In the three-parameter form (with *startposition*), you can specify at which character the search should begin.

Note that INSTR returns a numeric value. This value indicates whether a match is found and, if so, where. In general, a value of 0 means that no match was found. A positive value indicates the position in *targetstr* where the substring begins.

Table 6.10 shows how to interpret a value returned by INSTR.

Table 6.10. *The results of* INSTR.

Condition	Result of INSTR
Match is found	Position where the match occurs
No match is found	0
startposition greater than LEN(*targetstr*)	0
targetstr is null (" ")	0
substr is null	Value of *startposition* if given, otherwise 1

For example:

```
300 TARGET$ = "The one and only one"
310 PRINT INSTR(TARGET$, "one")
320 PRINT INSTR(7, TARGET$, "one")
```

The output is

```
5
18
```

Generating Strings of Repeated Characters

The `STRING$` function generates a specified number of identical characters.

STRING$(*strlength, ASCIIcode*)

or

STRING$(*strlength, strexpr*)

where *strlength* specifies the length of the string to return, *ASCIIcode* specifies the ASCII code (0 to 255) of the repeating character, and *strexpr* is a string expression whose first character specifies the repeating character.

For example, the ASCII code for the plus sign is 43. Thus `STRING$(8, 43)` creates a string of 8 plus signs. `STRING$` is often used to embellish output, as shown in the following example:

```
500 PLUS$ = STRING$(8, 43)
510 PRINT PLUS$; " Today's News "; PLUS$
```

The output looks like this:

```
++++++++ Today's News  ++++++++
```

Note that the repeating character can be specified with an explicit ASCII value or with a string expression. That is, the second argument for `STRING$` can be a numerical ASCII code or a string. Here is the previous program fragment using the latter form of `STRING$`:

```
500 PLUS$ = STRING$(8, "+")
510 PRINT PLUS$; " Today's News "; PLUS$
```

Both versions of STRING$ create the identical output.

When the repeating character is a blank space, a special function is available.

SPACE$(*numspaces*)

where *numspaces* specifies the number of spaces to return in the range from 0 to 255.

Because the ASCII code for a blank space is 32, the function SPACE$(*numspaces*) returns the same string as STRING$(*strlength*, 32) assuming that the values of *numspaces* and *strlength* are the same.

Comparing Strings

In the previous chapter, you saw that the relational operators in table 5.1 can compare two strings as well as two numbers. For example, you can write an IF instruction that compares strings, such as

```
200 IF MYNAME$ > "Joe" THEN . . .
```

just as you can write IFs that compare numbers, such as

```
200 IF MYAGE% > 32 THEN . . .
```

When BASIC compares two strings, it compares the ASCII values of corresponding characters. The ranking order of the two strings depends on the first character position in which the two strings differ. The higher ASCII value determines the "larger" string.

When a longer string begins with the identical characters of a shorter string, the longer string is "larger." Two strings are equal if each string is the same length and consists of the identical sequence of characters.

Each of the following expressions is "true":

```
"upper" > "Upper"
"Apples" <> "Oranges"
"Foot" < "Football"
```

```
"Chocolate cake" < "Chocolate ice cream"
("Big" + "Deal") = "BigDeal"
"3" >= "3"
"36" > "3245"
```

Type Conversion

Table 6.11 reviews BASIC's data types. Every variable has one of these four data types.

Table 6.11. *The four data types.*

Data Types	Sample Variable Name
String	MYNAME$
Integer	MYAGE%
Single-precision	PRICE!
Double-precision	MASS#

Mixing Data Types

When you assign a value to a variable, BASIC checks that the value matches the variable's type. What happens if there is a mismatch?

When it comes to numeric assignments, BASIC is quite forgiving. You can freely assign any numeric value to a variable of any numeric type. For example, the following instructions are perfectly legal:

```
200 MYAGE% = 39.9999
210 TAX! = 23456
```

BASIC converts the numeric value on the right side into the data type required by the variable. This process, whereby BASIC converts a value of one data type into another data type, is known as *numeric type conversion*, or simply *type conversion*. We explore several examples shortly.

However, strings and numbers are like water and oil: you just cannot mix them. You can't assign string data to a numeric variable or numeric data to a string variable. Each of the following instructions causes a run-time error (Type mismatch in 400):

```
400 MYAGE% = "Too much"
400 MYSIZE$ = YOURSIZE!
400 YOURSIZE$ = 38
```

Numeric Type Conversion

BASIC may convert a numeric value from one type to another in the following two situations:

❏ When you assign a value to a variable.

❏ When evaluating a numeric expression.

Type Conversion during Variable Assignment

If necessary, when you assign a value to a numeric variable, BASIC converts the value to the data type of the variable.

The following rules apply:

1. Rounding occurs when you assign a number with a fractional part to an integer variable. For example:

   ```
   200 MYNUM% = 34.84
   210 PRINT MYNUM%
   ```

   The result is

   ```
   35
   ```

   A fractional number is rounded (up or down) to the closest whole number. If the number ends in exactly .5, BASIC rounds up.

2. Rounding occurs when you assign a value of more than seven significant digits to a single-precision value. For example:

   ```
   100 POPULATION# = 132354861
   110 POPULATION! = POPULATION#
   120 TESTNUM# = 7.436921342D+20
   130 TESTNUM! = TESTNUM#
   140 PRINT POPULATION!, TESTNUM!
   ```

   The result is

   ```
   1.323549E+08      7.436921E+20
   ```

In line 120, the D is the exponential indicator for double-precision numbers. That is, the number on the right of the equal sign is double-precision. See Chapter 4, "Language Building Blocks," for more information.

3. An `Overflow` error occurs if you try to assign a value outside the allowable range of the variable. For example, the following instruction is illegal:

```
250 MYNUM% = 63111.5
```

The instruction is illegal, not because 63111.5 has a fractional part, but because the rounded value is too large for an integer variable (remember that an integer variable cannot be larger than 32,767).

4. Loss of precision may occur when you assign a single-precision value to a double-precision variable. Only the first six or seven digits (rounded) of the result are valid. For example:

```
700 MYNUM! = .11
710 MYNUM# = MYNUM!
720 PRINT MYNUM#
```

The result is

```
.1099999994039536
```

The digits after the sequence of nines are inaccurate.

Type Conversion during Expression Evaluation

During the evaluation of an arithmetic expression, as BASIC performs each operation, the operands must be at the same level of precision. If necessary, BASIC converts operands to achieve a consistent level of precision.

Here's a simple example:

```
300  TOTALCOST! = NUM% * UNITCOST!
```

The expression `NUM% * UNITCOST!` multiplies an integer value (`NUM%`) and a single-precision value (`UNITCOST!`). To do the multiplication, BASIC needs both operands at the same level of precision. So, before multiplying, BASIC automatically converts the value of `NUM%` to single-precision.

Why doesn't BASIC convert `UNITCOST!` to integer instead? What determines which operand gets converted?

BASIC converts the less precise operand to the precision of the more precise operand. Table 6.12 shows the precision order of numeric data types.

Table 6.12. *Precision of numeric data types.*

Data Type	Precision
Double-precision	Most precise
Single-precision	
Integer	Least precise

Losing Accuracy in Expressions

It is possible to lose accuracy during the evaluation of expressions. Consider the following program:

```
100 A% = 5
110 B! = 1.5
120 C# = 1000
130 PRINT (A% / B!) * C#
140 PRINT (A% * C#) / B!
```

The expressions in lines 130 and 140 are mathematically equivalent. The answers should be the same. However, here's the output:

```
3333.333253860474
3333.333333333333
```

Note that both results are displayed as double-precision numbers (due to the double-precision variable C#.) However, only the second number has double-precision accuracy.

To see why, consider line 130. The first operation (A% / B!) computes to single-precision accuracy. Then this temporary result is multiplied by the double-precision quantity C#. The net result is a double-precision value with only single-precision accuracy. That's why you see the nonsignificant digits (253860474) after the third decimal place. Note that an operation has double-precision accuracy only if each operand has double-precision accuracy.

Line 140 changes the operation order. First, A% is multiplied by C#. This temporary result has double-precision accuracy because each operand has double-precision accuracy. (A% is an exact number, not an approximation. That's why A% has full double-precision accuracy.) The final division by B! also involves two numbers with double-precision accuracy. (Again, B! is an exact number.)

Using Type-Declaration Characters on Numeric Literals

You can attach a type-declaration suffix to a numeric literal. This suffix specifies the data type of the literal. Table 6.13 shows some examples.

Table 6.13. *Examples of numeric literals.*

Literal	Precision
2	Integer
2!	Single-precision
2#	Double-precision
1.5	Single-precision
1.5#	Double-precision

When you list a program, BASIC sometimes converts a literal that you type into an alternate form containing a type-declaration suffix. For example, try the following code:

```
Ok
100 TWO! = 2.0
LIST
100 TWO! = 2!
Ok
```

Table 6.14 shows some more examples.

Table 6.14. *Examples of numeric literal conversion.*

You type this:	LIST shows you this:
2.	2!
123456%	123456!
1.23456789	1.23456789#
9876543210	9876543210#
1.3D+05	130000#

Summary

Data manipulation is a prevailing programming theme. Numeric and string data is often assigned to variables, combined into expressions, and displayed on-screen.

Numeric expressions can contain numbers of different data types. When BASIC evaluates expressions, if necessary, it converts parts of a numeric expression from one data type to another (for example, from single-precision to integer). Occasionally, your final results lose some accuracy during this process.

The length of a string is simply the number of characters in the string. Every string character has an associated numeric value from 0 to 255. These values comprise the ASCII character code. With ASCII, you can compare strings and determine which string is "larger." This lets you use strings, as well as numbers, in relational expressions.

BASIC provides an abundance of built-in functions. Each function takes one or more arguments and returns a single value (which can be numeric or string).

The numeric functions solve mathematical problems. BASIC has functions for arithmetic (SQR), trigonometry (SIN), logarithms (LOG), rounding (INT), and random numbers (RND).

The string functions make fancy manipulations a snap. BASIC includes functions that find a string length (LEN), convert ASCII values to strings (CHR$), find a substring (MID$), and convert a string to a number (VAL).

7

Modular Programming with Subroutines

GOSUB, RETURN, ON GOSUB

Imagine an isolated section of your program. At any time, you can *call* that isolated section from the main body of your program. After all the instructions in the isolated section execute, control passes back to the main program at the point where the original call was made.

A *subroutine* is just such a section of isolated lines. Without a doubt, the subroutine is one of the most important programming techniques. Subroutines enable you to break large tasks into more manageable subtasks and to program frequently needed program sections only once.

A subroutine is something like a miniprogram inside your main program. You call the subroutine from any point in your main program. The subroutine "does its thing" and then returns control to the main program. You can call the same subroutine from several different places in your main program. The subroutine acts as a kind of "righthand man"—ready to serve at your beck and call.

A Programming Example

Perhaps the best way to introduce subroutines is with a programming example. Consider the following programming task:

Task: Write a program that computes and displays the hypotenuses of three different right triangles. The first triangle has sides of 3 and 4. The second triangle has sides of 3.5 and 5.5. The third triangle's sides are 5 and 7.

Are you rusty on your trigonometry? A *right triangle* is any triangle that contains a 90-degree angle. The *hypotenuse* of a right triangle is the longest side — the side opposite the 90-degree angle (see fig. 7.1). If you specify the lengths of the other two sides, the length of the hypotenuse is given by a relatively simple formula. You first add together the squares of each side. The hypotenuse is the square root of this sum.

Fig. 7.1. *A right triangle.*

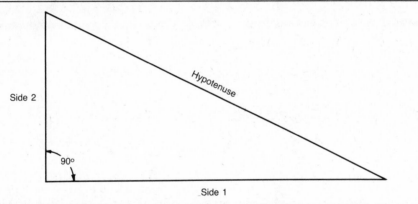

That is, if the two sides are called Side1 and Side2, the hypotenuse is the square root of the quantity (Side1² + Side2²). In BASIC, you might write the formula like this:

```
300 HYPOTENUSE = SQR(SIDE1 * SIDE1 + SIDE2 * SIDE2)
```

(Remember that multiplication has a higher precedence than addition. Inside the parentheses, the two multiplication operations take place before the addition.)

Now back to the programming problem. Here's a program that solves the task at hand:

```
100 REM Find Hypotenuse of three right triangles
150 PRINT "First side", "Second side", "Hypotenuse"
200 SIDE1 = 3: SIDE2 = 4
210 HYPOTENUSE = SQR(SIDE1 * SIDE1 + SIDE2 * SIDE2)
220 PRINT SIDE1, SIDE2, HYPOTENUSE
230 SIDE1 = 3.5: SIDE2 = 5.5
240 HYPOTENUSE = SQR(SIDE1 * SIDE1 + SIDE2 * SIDE2)
250 PRINT SIDE1, SIDE2, HYPOTENUSE
260 SIDE1 = 5: SIDE2 = 7
270 HYPOTENUSE = SQR(SIDE1 * SIDE1 + SIDE2 * SIDE2)
280 PRINT SIDE1, SIDE2, HYPOTENUSE
300 END
```

The output looks like this:

```
First side      Second side     Hypotenuse
 3               4               5
 3.5             5.5             6.519202
 5               7               8.602326
```

This program works fine, and the answers indeed are correct. Look at how much programming effort was duplicated, however. Three pairs of lines are exactly the same: lines 210 and 220 duplicate lines 240 and 250, which in turn duplicate lines 270 and 280.

Such equivalent lines are a prime candidate for a subroutine. You can write the pair of lines only once and make a subroutine out of them. The main program can then call your new subroutine three different times as needed. Let's see how to do that.

Introducing *GOSUB* and *RETURN*

The "main men" of subroutines are the GOSUB and RETURN statements. You call a subroutine with GOSUB and return from the subroutine with RETURN.

Let's see how GOSUB and RETURN work with a practical example.

Here's the hypotenuse-calculating program rewritten with subroutines. We call the program HYPOT.BAS.

```
100 REM Program: HYPOT.BAS (Calculate hypotenuses)
150 PRINT "Side 1", "Side 2", "Hypotenuse"
200 SIDE1 = 3: SIDE2 = 4
210 GOSUB 400
220 SIDE1 = 3.5: SIDE2 = 5.5
230 GOSUB 400
240 SIDE1 = 5: SIDE2 = 7
250 GOSUB 400
300 END
400 REM  Subroutine to compute and display hypotenuse
410    HYPOTENUSE = SQR(SIDE1 * SIDE1 + SIDE2 * SIDE2)
420    PRINT SIDE1, SIDE2, HYPOTENUSE
430 RETURN
```

The output of HYPOT.BAS is exactly the same as the previous program. The program flow is different, however. HYPOT.BAS has a subroutine in lines 400 through 430.

Lines 100 through 200 duplicate the lines in the previous program. But line 210 of HYPOT.BAS is something new. The GOSUB 400 instruction causes the program to jump down to line 400, which is the beginning of a subroutine. In other words, line 210 *calls* the subroutine, which begins at line 400.

The program transfers control to line 400 and begins the instructions found there. Note that lines 410 and 420 compute the hypotenuse and display the output using the same instructions found in the earlier program. But line 430 is a new animal—a RETURN instruction.

RETURN signals BASIC that the subroutine is finished and program flow should revert back to where the subroutine was called. The key feature of subroutines is that, when a GOSUB instruction occurs, BASIC keeps track of where the call occurred. That's why subroutines are so powerful. Effectively, the RETURN instruction tells BASIC to "go back where you came from."

Line 430 makes BASIC dutifully continue the program at line 220. Why line 220? Because line 220 contains the first instruction after the GOSUB instruction that called the subroutine.

RETURN always continues the program at the instruction immediately following the GOSUB instruction that called the subroutine in the first place.

Line 220 assigns the next pair of values to SIDE1 and SIDE2. Line 230 is another GOSUB that once again calls the subroutine beginning at line 400. When the subroutine finishes, the RETURN (line 430) now transfers the program back to line 240.

Line 240 once again reassigns SIDE1 and SIDE2. And line 250 calls the subroutine for the third and final time. The program terminates with the END instruction in line 300.

To summarize, you call a subroutine with GOSUB:

GOSUB *linenumber*

where *linenumber* is the line number on which the subroutine begins.

And you return from the subroutine with RETURN:

RETURN

Control passes to the first instruction after the GOSUB that called the subroutine.

Using *END* To Isolate Subroutines

Look again at line 300 of the program. The END instruction serves a very important purpose. Without that END, the program does not operate correctly. Do you see why?

Suppose that the END isn't there. After returning from the subroutine call in line 250, the program inadvertently "falls into" the subroutine. Lines 410 and 420 execute a fourth, unwanted time. Then the RETURN in line 430 has nowhere to go because no GOSUB call is active.

You can see the effect by changing line 300 to REM and rerunning the program. Here's what the output looks like:

```
300 REM
RUN
First side    Second side    Hypotenuse
 3             4              5
 3.5          5.5            6.519202
 5            7              8.602326
 5            7              8.602326
RETURN without GOSUB in 430
Ok
```

Note that the fourth line of the table duplicates the third line. The fourth line occurs when BASIC slips past line 300 and "accidentally" falls into the subroutine. (Because the variables SIDE1 and SIDE2 do not change values, the fourth output line is the same as the third output line.)

The RETURN instruction then causes an error. Because no GOSUB is active, the RETURN does not make sense. BASIC catches the error, prints a diagnostic-error message, and terminates the program.

The lesson is clear: be aware of erroneously falling into subroutines placed at the end of your program. Use an END instruction between your main program and your subroutines. That way, your program terminates appropriately.

Understanding Subroutines

Here are a few clarifications about subroutines:

❏ During a program, you may call a subroutine any number of times. These calls can come from the same GOSUB instruction (which might be in a loop) or from different GOSUB instructions.

❏ A subroutine can be any length. Some subroutines are only a single line, and others are well over a hundred lines.

❏ No special instruction indicates the beginning of a subroutine. A GOSUB instruction may branch to *any* line of your program (an earlier line, a later line, even the same line).

❏ GOSUB is similar to GOTO. The crucial difference between GOSUB and GOTO is that when GOSUB executes, BASIC keeps track of the program location where the call occurs. When a RETURN occurs, logic flow diverts to the instruction immediately following the GOSUB.

❏ A program can have any number of subroutines.

❏ Subroutines can be nested. You can call a subroutine from any point in a program, including from another subroutine. That is, you may execute a new GOSUB instruction before executing the RETURN for a previous GOSUB. BASIC keeps track of the nesting. Any RETURN instruction ends the most recently called subroutine. Subroutines can be nested to any level.

❏ Subroutines can be physically located anywhere in a program. As you will see shortly, we recommend placing subroutines at the end of your program. But that is not a requirement of BASIC.

A Programming Style for Subroutines

Over the years, we have developed a programming style for subroutines. We think that this style makes your programs easier to follow. Here are our tips for a good subroutine programming style:

❑ Place subroutines after the main body of your program. Use an END instruction at the end of your main program, just before the subroutines begin. This END serves the following two purposes:
  1. It terminates the main program so that execution doesn't inadvertently fall into the subroutines.
  2. It physically separates the main program from the subroutines. This enhances program clarity.

❑ Begin each subroutine with a REM instruction that explains what the subroutine does (line 400 of HYPOT.BAS, for example). This REM instruction is the actual line to which the GOSUB instruction or instructions branch when the main program calls the subroutine.

❑ Make the last line of a subroutine a RETURN instruction.

❑ Don't use any RETURN instructions inside the body of a subroutine. Instead, use GOTO instructions that branch to the single RETURN at the end of the subroutine.

❑ Indent all the lines in the body of the subroutine. That is, indent the lines between the REM (the first line of the subroutine) and the RETURN (the last line of the subroutine). Such indentation plainly sets off the physical limits of the subroutine.

Figure 7.2 shows our recommended design for programs containing subroutines. Note that the main body of the program terminates with an END instruction and that the subroutines are placed below the main program.

The line numbers shown in figure 7.2 are arbitrary. When you program subroutines, the actual line numbers depend on the lengths of the main program and the subroutines. It's a good idea, however, to start each subroutine with a nice round line number (that is, a line number ending with a few zeros).

Fig. 7.2. *Skeleton form of a program with subroutines.*

```
                        ┌   ┌──────────────────────────────┐
                        │   │  100  REM  My Program         │
                        │   │         ⋮                     │
                        │   │  300    GOSUB 800             │
Main program body includes│  │         ⋮                     │
GOSUB calls to the subroutines│ 400   GOSUB 900             │
                        │   │         ⋮                     │
                        │   │  600    END                   │
                        └   │ ─ ─ ─ ─ ─ ─ ─ ─ ─ ─ ─ ─ ─ ─ ─ │
                        ┌   │  800    REM  Subroutine A     │
                        │   │         ⋮                     │
                        │   │  890    RETURN                │
Subroutines are placed  │   │ ─ ─ ─ ─ ─ ─ ─ ─ ─ ─ ─ ─ ─ ─ ─ │
after the main program  │   │  900    REM  Subroutine B     │
                        │   │         ⋮                     │
                        └   │  990    RETURN                │
                            └──────────────────────────────┘
```

Modular Program Construction

As your proficiency with BASIC grows, you soon will want to tackle large programming projects. At first, a complex programming job can seem bewildering, almost impossible. You may hardly know where to start. Many beginners feel intimidated by the thought of writing a large program.

Experienced programmers, on the other hand, know the secret of writing a large program. And here's that secret: divide and conquer. The idea is simple. Tackle a large-scale task by partitioning the single task into a group of smaller subtasks. It's much easier to solve a collection of small tasks than one large task. Each subtask isn't so bad. The whole is merely the sum of its parts.

Guided by the maxim of divide and conquer, men and women have vanquished civilizations, traveled to the moon, and created epic movies. And, oh yes, they have written large programs too. The idea of breaking a large program into isolated chunks is the foundation behind modern *modular programming*.

However, it's one thing to philosophize and another to put the ideas into practice. The subroutine is your primary tool for modular programming in BASIC.

For example, suppose that you want to write a program which handles a weekly payroll. That's a big programming job.

Before you write a single line of the program, you should first isolate the individual tasks that the payroll program must accomplish. Your list might look like this:

PAYROLL PROGRAM:

1. Read last week's employee data (names, salaries, and so on) from an existing disk file.

2. Ask the user for any changes to the employee information (new hires, old employees who have left, salary changes, and so on).

3. Update employee information.

4. Print salary checks for each active employee.

5. Write a new disk file with the current salary information.

6. Print a report showing the weekly payroll (total paid to each employee).

After you list the subtasks in this manner, you are well on your way to writing the whole program. The key idea is to make each of these six tasks a module—that is, a subroutine.

You can then write each subroutine individually. (We realize that we haven't yet explained how to program things like reading or writing a disk file. We explain such subjects later in the book. Our purpose here is only to show you how to organize a large program into subroutines.)

In a fully modular program, the main program may consist of nothing more than GOSUB instructions. Each subroutine is called one at a time. Here's what the skeletal outline of this program might look like:

```
100 REM Program: PAYROLL.BAS (Weekly payroll Maroon Corp.)
200 GOSUB 1000    'Read last week's data from disk
300 GOSUB 2000    'Get changes from user
400 GOSUB 3000    'Update employee information
500 GOSUB 4000    'Print the checks
600 GOSUB 5000    'Write updated employee data on disk
700 GOSUB 6000    'Print a report for management
800 END
1000 REM  Read old data from disk file
1990 RETURN
2000 REM  Ask user for changes
2990 RETURN
3000 REM  Update employee information
```

Listing continues

Listing *continued*

```
3990 RETURN
4000 REM  Print the weekly payroll checks
4990 RETURN
5000 REM  Write disk file with updated employee information
5990 RETURN
6000 REM  Print the management report
6990 RETURN
```

Do you see the idea? The main program is trivial—nothing more than a series of subroutine calls. All the programming details are relegated to the subroutines. We arbitrarily numbered the last line of each subroutine (the RETURN instruction) with a line number 990 larger than the first line of the subroutine.

Each subroutine accomplishes one task and can be programmed individually. As shown here, the skeletal program leaves out the guts of each subroutine. By "guts," we mean all the lines between the REM at the beginning of each subroutine and the RETURN at the end.

Benefits of Subroutines

In case you think that we are on the subroutine bandwagon—you're right! Simply put, subroutines lead to well-written programs. Almost any large program (and many small programs) benefit from using subroutines. Here's a summary of the advantages:

❑ Repetitious sections of code can be written only once and called as often as necessary.

❑ The main body of the program can be short, resulting in an easy-to-understand overall logic flow.

❑ Future programming changes are simplified. You can easily isolate the area that needs modification.

❑ A big problem can be segmented into little ones. Complex programs can be broken down into separate modules, which can be individually tested and perfected.

These are all important benefits, but perhaps the most important is the last. The human mind cannot keep track of hundreds, or even dozens, of details at once. By using subroutines, you can think of a program in terms of logical modules rather than endless details.

Using *ON GOSUB*

ON GOSUB works analogously to ON GOTO. Recall, from Chapter 5, "Program Flow and Decision Making," that ON GOTO branches to one of several lines depending on the value of a numeric expression.

The difference between ON GOSUB and ON GOTO is that with ON GOSUB, each branch is to a subroutine. When a RETURN occurs in the subroutine, program flow continues with the instruction immediately following the ON GOSUB instruction.

ON *numexpr* GOSUB *linenumlist*

where *numexpr* is a numeric expression, and *linenumlist* is a list of one or more line numbers separated by commas.

---

linenumlist is a list of line numbers, each line number being the first line of a subroutine. The value of the numeric expression determines which subroutine is called.

The numeric expression acts as an index to the list of subroutines. If the value of *numexpr* is 1, BASIC calls the first subroutine in the list. If the value of *numexpr* is 2, BASIC calls the second subroutine in the list, and so on.

If *numexpr* is zero or greater than the number of lines in the list, execution simply continues with the instruction immediately after the ON GOSUB. If *numexpr* is negative, the program terminates with the error:

```
Illegal function call.
```

An example should make ON GOSUB clearer. Consider the following instruction:

```
500 ON INDEX% GOSUB 2000, 3000, 5000, 2000, 1000
```

BASIC checks the value of INDEX%. If the value is 1, BASIC calls the subroutine that begins with line 2000. If the value is 2, the subroutine at line 3000 gets the call. Similarly, if the value is 3, 4, or 5; the subroutines at lines 5000, 2000, and 1000 respectively get called.

If INDEX% is 0 or greater than 5, BASIC just continues with the line immediately after line 500. If INDEX% is negative, an error occurs.

Note that the line numbers in the list do not have to be in ascending order. Furthermore, you can repeat line numbers in the list. In our sample, the subroutine at line 2000 gets called if INDEX% is 1 or 4.

Also, as in our example, *numexpr* is usually just a single variable name. However, any numeric expression is acceptable. For example, the following instruction is perfectly okay:

```
600 ON (YOURAGE% - MYAGE%) GOSUB 200, 5000, 6000
```

A Sound-Effects Generator—a Sample Program Using *ON GOSUB*

You probably have used some menu-driven software programs. By "menu-driven," we mean a program that displays a list of choices and asks you to input the number of your choice. When you make your selection, the program does what you request and then either quits or shows you the menu again.

Let's have some fun. Here's a menu-driven program that produces a variety of crazy sound effects. You see a list of the possible sound effects and choose one. After "bending your ear" with the requested effect, the menu reappears and you can choose a new effect. One of the menu choices ends the program.

To create the noises, the program makes frequent use of the SOUND instruction. We are getting a little ahead of ourselves because we don't discuss SOUND until Chapter 12, "Programming Hardware Devices."

Our purpose now is twofold:

1. Demonstrate a program with several subroutines.

2. Show how ON GOSUB facilitates writing a menu-driven program.

Here's the program, which we call NOISES.BAS.

```
100 REM Program: NOISES.BAS (Generate sound effects)
110 REM --------------------------------------------------------------
120 CLS
130 PRINT "Pick a sound effect"
140 PRINT "    1) Alarm"
150 PRINT "    2) Spinning coin"
160 PRINT "    3) Crickets"
```

```
170 PRINT "     4) Zooming spaceship"
180 INPUT "Enter number (or 0 to end program)"; CHOICE%
190 IF CHOICE% = 0 THEN 500
200 ON CHOICE% GOSUB 1000, 2000, 3000, 4000
210 GOTO 120
500 END
1000 REM Subroutine to make alarm sound
1010    FOR J% = 1 TO 5
1020       SOUND 1000, 7
1030       SOUND 500, 7
1040    NEXT J%
1050 RETURN
2000 REM Subroutine to make the sound of a spinning coin
2010    FOR J% = 30 TO 1 STEP -1
2020       SOUND 500, 1
2030       SOUND 32000, J% / 15
2040    NEXT J%
2050 RETURN
3000 REM Subroutine to make the sound of crickets
3010    FOR J% = 1 TO 50
3020       FOR K% = 3 TO 10
3030          SOUND 2500 + RND * 1000, .1
3040       NEXT K%
3050    NEXT J%
3060 RETURN
4000 REM Subroutine to make the sound of zooming spaceship
4010    FOR J% = 40 TO 7000 STEP 5
4020       SOUND J%, .05
4030    NEXT J%
4040    FOR J% = 7000 TO 40 STEP -5
4050       SOUND J%, .05
4060    NEXT J%
4070 RETURN
```

When you run the program, your screen clears and you see the following menu:

```
Pick a sound effect
    1) Alarm
    2) Spinning coin
    3) Crickets
    4) Zooming spaceship
Enter number (or 0 to end program) ?
```

You can then enter a number from 0 to 5.

If you type 1 to 4 (and press Enter), you hear the requested sound effect. The menu then reappears for your next choice.

If you type 0, the program ends. If you type a number larger than 4, you are reprompted for another choice. If you type a negative number, the program ends with an error message.

Let's look at how NOISES.BAS works. Line 120 clears the screen. (We introduced CLS in Chapter 3, "A Hands-On Introduction to Programming.") The PRINT instructions in lines 130 through 170 display the menu on-screen. Line 180 is an INPUT instruction that gets the user's choice and stores it in the variable CHOICE%.

Line 190 then checks whether CHOICE% is 0. If so, the user has had enough and wants to quit. The program branches to line 500, where an END instruction terminates the program.

Line 200 is the focal point of the program—the ON GOSUB instruction. Depending on CHOICE%, the ON GOSUB instruction calls one of the four sub-routines that begin at lines 1000, 2000, 3000, or 4000. Each subroutine generates one of the four sound effects. When the called subroutine finishes, control returns to line 210. Line 210 branches back to line 120. The screen clears, the menu reappears, and the user gets another choice.

Suppose that you type a choice of 8, too big for the actual list. With CHOICE% equal to 8, line 200 doesn't call any subroutine. Execution simply continues with the next line, which, in this case, clears the screen and redisplays the menu. That's exactly what you want.

Try NOISES.BAS. We think that you will enjoy the program. You may be amazed at the sounds you can generate with a few simple BASIC instructions. (We especially like the crickets.)

Summary

A subroutine is like a program island. From anywhere in your program, you can "fly" to the island and then "fly" back. GOSUB and RETURN are your "airplanes." You call a subroutine with GOSUB. At the end of a subroutine, you use RETURN to branch back to where the call was made.

ON GOSUB is a more flexible version of GOSUB. With ON GOSUB, you can branch to one of several subroutines depending on the value of a variable (or numeric expression).

One advantage of subroutines is that you don't have to write a block of instructions over and over. You just write the instructions once, making a subroutine out of the instruction block. Then, you can call the subroutine whenever you need it throughout the program.

Perhaps the most significant advantage of subroutines is as a tool for tackling large programming projects. Major programming projects are best handled by modular programming. You divide the large task into several smaller tasks, or modules. To create the large program, you write several smaller modules that you piece together into the final program.

Subroutines are the backbone of modular programming. Each module becomes a subroutine. The main program can then call each module, one at a time.

CHAPTER 8

Managing Large
Amounts of Data

DATA, READ, RESTORE, DIM, OPTION BASE, ERASE

Ordinary variables store only a single value. Such variables are certainly quite useful, but ultimately limiting. Many programming projects require the storage and manipulation of large amounts of information.

For example, suppose that you want to write an inventory-control program for an automobile-parts company. You might have thousands of different parts to deal with. How are you going to manipulate such large amounts of data with ordinary variables? Well, the simple truth is, you're not.

To handle such sizable data requirements, you need *arrays*. Arrays are like super variables, storing multiple data values under a single name. We introduced arrays in Chapter 4, "Language Building Blocks," and will explore them in depth here.

The other main topic of this chapter concerns getting large amounts of data into your program. That's where READ and DATA statements play a major role.

Storing Data in Programs with *DATA* and *READ*

Of course, if your program is going to manipulate data, you must first, some-how, get the data into your program. There are three general techniques for crossing this fundamental bridge.

1. Request the data from the user at run-time.

   This is the backbone of interactive programs. The program usually prompts the user who types in the relevant data from the keyboard. (Refer to the `INPUT` statement in Chapter 12, "Programming Hardware Devices.")

2. Read the data from a disk file.
   Data can be saved on a disk file and then read using a program. This is common in business applications. Perhaps your program processes monthly sales figures that are stored on disk. (See Chapter 10, "Using Disk Files.")

3. Store the data as part of the program.
   This is the simplest technique. What's simpler than storing the data as part of the program? Assignment instructions are one way to store data in a program. After all, the instruction `200 MYDOS! = 3.2` stores the value 3.2 directly inside the program.

Another way to store data inside the program is with `DATA` instructions.

The Baseball Coach—a Case Study

Let's say that you are the coach of the "Mudville Nine"—a Little League Base-ball team. Like most baseball fans, you are infatuated with players' statistics. At the end of the season, you get a report from the league office that shows how each of your batters fared (see fig. 8.1).

You want to calculate each player's batting average. (For you nonbaseball fans, the "batting average" is the number of hits divided by the number of times at-bat. For example, if Babe Ruth has 2 hits in 8 at-bats, his batting average is 2 divided by 8, or 0.250).

You decide to write a program that displays each player's name along with his batting statistics. You want a four-column table. The first column is the player's name. Columns two through four are each player's hits, times at-bat, and batting average.

Fig. 8.1. *Mudville Nine batting.*

Team Name: Mudville Nine

Player	Hits	Times at Bat
Johnnie	21	82
Melanie	15	66
Slugger	34	95
Casey	16	88
Babe	31	79
Christine	29	74
Solly	21	74
Debbie	14	58
Rick	8	84

Computing the batting average for each player is easy. You just divide each player's hits by the number of times at-bat. The problem is getting the data into the program in the first place.

You *could* write a program that looks something like this:

```
200 PLAYER$ = "Johnny"
210 HITS% = 21
220 ATBATS% = 82
230 BATAVE! = HITS% / ATBATS%
```

Listing continues

Listing continued

```
240 PRINT PLAYER$, HITS%, ATBATS%, BATAVE!
250 PLAYER% = "Melanie"
260 HITS% = 15
270 ATBATS% = 66
280 BATAVE! = HITS% /ATBATS%
290 PRINT PLAYER$, HITS%, ATBATS%, BATAVE!
300 PLAYER% = "Slugger"
    .
    .
```

This works okay but makes for a needlessly long program containing too many repetitious instructions.

The following program, BASEBALL.BAS, places data in the program in a much better way—with DATA instructions.

```
100 REM Program: BASEBALL.BAS
105 REM (Print Batting Averages for Mudville Nine)
110 DATA Johnny, 21, 82
120 DATA Melanie, 15, 66
130 DATA Slugger, 34, 95
140 DATA Casey, 16, 88
150 DATA Babe, 31, 79
160 DATA Christine, 29, 74
170 DATA Solly, 21, 74
180 DATA Debbie, 14, 58
190 DATA Rick, 8, 84
200 REM
300 PRINT "Season Stats for Mudville Nine"
310 PRINT
320 PRINT "Player", "Hits", "At Bats", "Batting Average"
330 FOR J% = 1 TO 9
340    READ PLAYER$, HITS%, ATBATS%
350    BATAVE! = HITS% / ATBATS%
360    PRINT PLAYER$, HITS%, ATBATS%, BATAVE!
370 NEXT J%
400 END
```

Here's the output of BASEBALL.BAS:

Player	Hits	At Bats	Batting Average
Johnnie	21	82	.2560976
Melanie	15	66	.2272727
Slugger	34	95	.3578948
Casey	16	88	.1818182

```
Babe          31      79        .3924051
Christine     29      74        .3918919
Solly         21      74        .2837838
Debbie        14      58        .2413793
Rick           8      84        .0952381
```

Do you get the general idea of how DATA works? The DATA instructions in lines 110 through 190 contain the data values that the program will use. The READ instruction in line 340 "reads" the data and assigns appropriate values to the variables: PLAYER\$, HITS%, and ATBATS%. Line 340 is in a FOR...NEXT loop that eventually reads all the data from the DATA instructions. Let's take a closer look at DATA and READ.

Understanding *DATA* and *READ*

DATA instructions store numeric or string literals in a data list. READ instructions then assign the data values to variables.

DATA *literals*

where *literals* is a list of data values (numeric and/or string) separated by commas.

READ *varnames*

where *varnames* is a list of variable names separated by commas.

A DATA instruction can contain one or more values. Use a comma to separate multiple values. For example:

```
300 DATA 25
310 DATA 40, 23.677
320 DATA 510, 31.33, 1.67E-21, 92
```

As these examples show, numbers can be in any form: integers, numbers with decimal points, or scientific notation with the E symbol (but not expressions with operators such as 14 * 6).

> ### DATA Instructions Are Nonexecutable
>
> DATA instructions don't really *do* anything. In BASIC terminology, DATA instructions are *nonexecutable*. The sole purpose of DATA instructions is to specify values so that READ instructions can assign these values to variables. The READ instruction actually causes the assignment.

Each READ instruction contains one or more variable names. Again, separate multiple variable names with commas:

```
500 READ NUM!
510 READ A, B, C
```

You can have any number of DATA instructions in a program. Regardless of the number of DATA instructions, or the number of values in each DATA instruction, think of all the DATA instructions as creating one long list of values. The list begins with the values in the first DATA instruction. The list grows by adding the literals from each successive DATA instruction in the order the DATA instructions appear in your program.

BASIC maintains a pointer to the current item in the data list. Each READ instruction plucks as many data values from the list as necessary—one data value for each variable in the READ instruction. For example, even though the variable names are spread across two READ instructions, this program still assigns the numbers 1 through 5 to the five variables MON, TUE, WED, THU, and FRI.

```
600 DATA 1, 2, 3, 4, 5
610 READ MON, TUE, WED
620 READ THU, FRI
```

This works just as well also:

```
700 DATA 1, 2
710 DATA 3, 4
720 DATA 5
730 READ MON, TUE, WED, THU, FRI
```

Where To Place *DATA* Instructions

You can place DATA instructions before or after the associated READ instructions. When a READ instruction occurs, BASIC "finds" the DATA instructions, even if the DATA instructions are at a higher line number than the READ. Programmers usually place DATA instructions in one of the following three locations:

1. In a block near the beginning of the program.

2. In a block near the end of the program.

3. Near the READ instructions.

Your program doesn't have to read all the values in your DATA instructions:

```
200 DATA 4, 7, 9
210 READ D%, E%
```

D% and E% have the values 4 and 7, respectively. The data value of 9 never gets assigned to any variable. That's okay, no harm is done.

It's another story, however, if you try to read past the end of your data list:

```
200 DATA 4, 7
210 READ D%, E%, F%
```

This causes your program to terminate with the error message

```
Out of DATA in 210
```

That makes sense. You tried to read three data values in line 210 but only two values were available.

Storing Strings with *DATA*

As demonstrated by the BASEBALL.BAS program, DATA and READ work with strings as well as with numbers. You can freely mix string and numeric values in the same DATA instruction.

Separate string values with commas, just as you do with numeric values. For example:

```
200 READ CITY$, STATE$
210 DATA Dallas, Texas
220 PRINT CITY$
230 PRINT STATE$
```

The result is

```
Dallas
Texas
```

Notice that you don't have to enclose the string data values with quotation marks as you do in assignment instructions such as the following:

```
300 CITY% = "Dallas"
```

However, you *can* use the quotation marks. You could write line 210 as follows:

```
210 DATA "Dallas", "Texas"
```

The result is the same.

You *have* to use quotation marks with DATA in these cases:

1. Your string contains a comma or colon.

2. Your string contains leading or trailing blanks.

Consider this example:

```
100 READ WHO$, WHAT$, WHERE$
110 DATA "Elvis Presley", "      Concert", "Toledo, Ohio"
120 PRINT WHO$
130 PRINT WHAT$
140 PRINT WHERE$
```

The result is:

```
Elvis Presley
      Concert
Toledo, Ohio
```

Now, stay on your toes because this gets tricky. Suppose that you try the same program but change line 110 to remove the quotation marks (note the blank spaces before Concert):

```
110 DATA Elvis Presley,      Concert, Toledo, Ohio
```

The result is now

```
Elvis Presley
Concert
Toledo
```

The blank space between Elvis and Presley causes no problems. But the blank spaces before Concert are stripped away (DATA does that). And the comma between Toledo and Ohio just makes the city and the state two separate data values.

> ## Mixing Strings and Numbers
>
> When you mix strings and numbers in DATA instructions, be careful that each READ variable is assigned a data value of the proper type. If a variable has a numeric data type, the corresponding data value must be numeric. A string variable causes a run-time error (Syntax error).
>
> For a string variable, the corresponding data value should be string. However, a numeric value does not produce an error. Instead, BASIC just treats the numeric value as a string value (a simple sequence of text characters).

In a DATA instruction, you can't use the apostrophe (single quotation mark) to indicate a comment. Instead, the apostrophe is treated just like any other string character. To place a comment at the end of a DATA instruction, use :REM. For example:

```
600 DATA 7631.45, 5558.33, 6711.72    :REM Quarterly Sales
```

This line shows why you must use quotation marks around any string data value that contains a colon. In a line with a DATA instruction, just like any other program line, the colon separates multiple instructions.

Adjusting the Data List Pointer with *RESTORE*

Occasionally, you may want a program to read the same data list more than once. You can "manually" adjust the data list pointer with RESTORE.

RESTORE *linenum*

or

RESTORE

where *linenum* is the line number of a DATA instruction.

Without a line number parameter, RESTORE reinitializes the data pointer back to the top of the list. The next READ instruction gets the first data value of the first DATA instruction.

For example:

```
200 DATA 1, 2
210 DATA 3, 4
220 READ A%, B%, C%
230 RESTORE
240 READ D%
250 PRINT A%, B%, C%, D%
```

The result is

```
1              2              3              1
```

With a line number parameter, RESTORE moves the data pointer to the beginning of the designated line.

Using Arrays

In our program examples so far, all variables have been simple variables. We say "simple" because each variable stores a single value. In the following instructions, for example, the variables MONTH1$, MONTH2$, MONTH3$ are separate variables that store separate values.

```
200 MONTH1$ = "January"
210 MONTH2$ = "February"
220 MONTH3$ = "March"
```

Simple variables can be numeric or string. The value of a variable might change during a program. However, at all times, each simple variable "houses" a single data value.

Arrays change all that. *Arrays*, or more properly, *array variables* consist of several data values maintained under a common name. The beauty of arrays is that large amounts of related data can be easily manipulated. With only a few program lines, you can recalculate hundreds of data values or print a large table. You will see how shortly.

Just as with ordinary variables, every array has a name that you create. Array names follow the same conventions as ordinary variables, including the optional !, %, #, or $ suffix that identifies the data type of the array. When a data type is given, every element of an array conforms to that data type.

The distinguishing feature of an array is the *subscript* (or *index number*) that immediately follows the name (see fig. 8.2). The subscript is enclosed in parentheses.

Fig. 8.2. Array syntax.

```
300 VALUE! = COST!(38)
```

array
name

subscript

The parentheses tell BASIC that this is an array rather than an ordinary variable. The value of the subscript identifies a single element of the whole array. For example, the collection of month names can be written as an array like this:

```
200 MONTH$(1) = "January"
210 MONTH$(2) = "February"
220 MONTH$(3) = "March"
```

Here, we have an array called MONTH$. It is a string array because the name ends with a dollar sign. Each individual element of MONTH$ contains a string value. The first element of the array, MONTH$(1), has the value January. The second element, MONTH$(2) has the value February.

Arrays can be string or numeric. Just as with ordinary variables, numeric arrays can be integer (%), single-precision (!) or double-precision (#). For any array, every element of the array contains data of the same type (string, integer, single-precision, or double-precision).

In the baseball program, for instance, you might create an array called AVERAGE! that represents each player's batting average. You could consider each player to have a number from 1 to 9. The batting average of player number 6, for example, would be in element AVERAGE!(6) of the array.

An array subscript is always enclosed in parentheses immediately after the array name. The subscript can be an explicit number, a variable, or even an expression that evaluates to a number. See table 8.1 for some examples.

Table 8.1. Sample array subscripts.

Array Element	Type of Subscript
MONTH$(2)	Explicit number
SALARY!(Employee%)	Variable name
COST#(23 + J%)	Simple expression
COST#((J% - 1) * 3)	Expression containing parentheses

Subscript values must be whole numbers. If not, BASIC rounds the value to the nearest integer. For example, if SALARY! is an array containing the salaries of a company's employees, SALARY!(433.2) references employee number 433, and SALARY!(228.8) references employee 229.

A Sample Program with Arrays

Let's look at arrays in action. The following program demonstrates that a few simple FOR...NEXT loops can manipulate a great amount of data.

Suppose that you own Ace Accordion Supply. Your 1990 monthly sales figures have finally arrived. You want to write a program that lists the monthly sales and computes the yearly total.

The SALES.BAS program does the job:

```
100 REM Program: SALES.BAS
110 REM (Monthly sales for Ace Accordion Supply)
150 DIM MONTH$(12), NUMSOLD%(12)   'Set limits of each array
160 REM
200 DATA Jan, Feb, Mar, Apr, May, Jun
205 DATA Jul, Aug, Sep, Oct, Nov, Dec
210 DATA 28, 21, 14, 32, 25, 26, 20, 16, 23, 19, 29, 26
250 FOR J% = 1 TO 12
260    READ MONTH$(J%)          'Read string data for each month
270 NEXT J%
280 FOR J% = 1 TO 12
290    READ NUMSOLD%(J%)        'Read number sold each month
300 NEXT J%
400 PRINT "Ace Accordion Supply - 1990 Sales"
410 PRINT "MONTH", "NUMBER SOLD"
420 FOR J% = 1 TO 12
430    PRINT MONTH$(J%), NUMSOLD%(J%)
440 NEXT J%
450 PRINT
460 TOTAL% = 0
470 FOR J% = 1 TO 12              'Calculate yearly sales total
480    TOTAL% = TOTAL% + NUMSOLD%(J%)
490 NEXT J%
500 PRINT "YEARLY TOTAL", TOTAL%
600 END
```

The output looks like this:

```
Ace Accordion Supply - 1990 Sales
MONTH          NUMBER SOLD
Jan            28
Feb            21
Mar            14
Apr            32
May            25
Jun            26
Jul            20
Aug            16
Sep            23
Oct            19
Nov            29
Dec            26

YEARLY TOTAL   279
```

Let's examine this program. The first thing you might notice is the DIM instruction in line 150. "What's that?" you ask. DIM (short for DIMension) instructions tell BASIC the names and sizes of the arrays that will be used in a program. We discuss the details of DIM a little later in this chapter. But, for now, line 150 informs BASIC that this program uses two arrays:

1. A string array named MONTH$.

2. An integer array named NUMSOLD%.

Both arrays contain 12 elements. DIM only establishes the names and dimensions of the arrays. You still must get data values into the individual array elements.

Lines 200 through 210 contain the data values that will be stored in the array elements. Line 200 has 6 data strings, the abbreviations for each of the first 6 months. Line 205 also has 6 data strings, for the remaining 6 months. Line 210 contains the month-by-month Accordion sales (28 sold in January, 21 sold in February, and so on).

The FOR...NEXT loops in lines 250 through 300 read the data values into the arrays. Look at how these two simple loops read all the data values. That's the power of array subscripting. Now each array contains 12 data values in preparation for the rest of the program. In the NUMSOLD% array, for example, NUMSOLD%(1) is 28, NUMSOLD%(2) is 21, and so on).

> ### READ and DATA Work Well with Arrays
>
> Lines 200 through 300 of the `SALES.BAS` program demonstrate just how well `READ` and `DATA` work with arrays. By placing a `READ` instruction inside a loop, you can assign data to all elements of an array with a few simple program lines.

The program now displays the output. A two-column table is created. Line 410 displays the heading for each column.

The `FOR...NEXT` loop in lines 420 through 440 displays the monthly sales figures. These values are nothing more than the data values picked up from lines 200-210. But, again, notice how easily a simple loop can display an entire array full of data.

Line 460 begins the calculation of `TOTAL%`, the total sales over the whole year. First, line 460 initializes `TOTAL%` with a value of 0.

The ultimate value of `TOTAL%` is the sum of the monthly sales figures. That is, `TOTAL%` should be the sum of all the elements of the `NUMSOLD%` array: `NUMSOLD%(1) + NUMSOLD%(2) + ... + NUMSOLD%(12)`.

Again, a simple `FOR...NEXT` is the answer. Lines 470 through 490 calculate the value of `TOTAL%`. Note how line 480 adds one array element at a time to the current value of `TOTAL%`. When the loop finishes, `TOTAL%` contains the desired sum that is displayed by line 500.

SALES.BAS demonstrates the power of arrays. With a few simple loops, array elements are easily manipulated. Notice how the `FOR...NEXT` counter variable (`J%` in this program) is often used as an array subscript. That's commonplace in programs with arrays.

Loops and arrays naturally work well together. Loop counter variables increment sequentially, which is exactly how array elements are subscripted.

Dimensioning Arrays with *DIM*

As demonstrated by line 150 of `SALES.BAS`, you use `DIM` to declare the arrays that a program will use. A `DIM` instruction accomplishes the following four things:

1. Establishes the name of the array.

2. Establishes the data type of the array.

3. Specifies the number of elements.

4. Initializes the value of each element of the array: numeric array elements become zero, and string array elements become the null string.

DIM *arrayname*(*subscriptlimit*)

where *arrayname* is the name for the array, and *subscriptlimit* specifies the largest subscript for the array.

Array names follow the same conventions as variable names. In particular, a data type suffix (!, #, %, or $) establishes the data type for each element of the array (recall that every element of an array must be the same data type). If you don't use a suffix on the array name, the array is single-precision.

The lowest legal subscript value is 0, not 1. The highest legal subscript value is specified by the `subscriptlimit` parameter in the DIM instruction. For example, the following instruction establishes an integer array named NUMVOTES%, which has 11 elements: NUMVOTES%(0), NUMVOTES%(1), ... , NUMVOTES%(10).

```
200 DIM NUMVOTES%(10)
```

A DIM instruction can declare two or more arrays. In these cases, use a comma to separate the array names. Table 8.2 shows some sample DIM instructions:

Table 8.2. *Sample* DIM *instructions.*

DIM *Instruction*	Description
10 DIM CLIENT$(200)	String array with 201 elements: CLIENT$(0) to CLIENT$(200)
20 DIM PROFIT!(30), COST(30)	Two single-precision arrays, each with 31 elements

Table 8.2 continues

Table 8.2. continued

DIM *Instruction*	*Description*
30 DIM A%(45), B%(34), C$(21)	Three arrays; an integer array with 46 elements: A%(0) to A%(45), another integer array with 35 elements: B%(0) to B%(34), and a string array with 22 elements: C$(0) to C$(21)

Where To Put DIM Instructions

A DIM instruction can appear anywhere before the first use of the array. However, when possible, you should place all your DIM instructions together near the beginning of the program.

Changing the Base Subscript—*OPTION BASE*

An OPTION BASE instruction changes the default lower array subscript from zero to one.

OPTION BASE *basesub*

where *basesub* specifies the lowest array subscript for subsequent DIM instructions.

The only legal values for *basesub* are zero and one.

Consider the following program fragment:

```
100 OPTION BASE 1
110 DIM MYARRAY!(200)
```

Line 100 changes the default lower array bound from zero to one. As a result, line 110 creates an array with elements from `MYARRAY!(1)` to `MYARRAY!(200)`.

"What's the big deal?" you ask. Not much, really. Even if an array has a zero subscript, you don't have to use it. Changing the base from zero to one does conserve a small amount of memory storage. This isn't too important until you come to two-dimensional arrays (later in this chapter).

DIM with Small Arrays

You can use an array without making an "official" declaration in a `DIM` instruction. In such a case, BASIC assigns a default element range from 0 to 10. For example, suppose that the following lines are the first two lines of a program:

```
100 DATA 21, 45, 18, 32
110 READ LOTTO%(1), LOTTO%(2), LOTTO%(3), LOTTO%(4)
```

Notice that no `DIM` instruction appears even though `LOTTO%` is used as an integer array. This *does* work. BASIC treats `LOTTO%` as an integer array with elements from 0 to 10. It's just as though you dimensioned `LOTTO%` with an instruction such as the following:

```
80 DIM LOTTO%(10)
```

Although you can get away without `DIM` for small arrays, we recommend against such "nondeclarations." Good programmers `DIM` every array, small arrays included. You want to make your programs easy to read, verify, and modify. Take advantage of every opportunity to do so.

Array and Variables Naming Conflicts

You can give an array and an ordinary variable the same name. However, it is poor programming practice to do so. In such a case, the array and the variable are two distinct entities that can coexist in the same program. Consider this:

```
100 DIM CLIENT$(200)

110 CLIENT$ = "Donald Trump"
```

The ordinary variable named `CLIENT$` is totally distinct from the array of the same name. Throughout the program, BASIC can always distinguish the array from the variable because the array has a subscript and the variable does not.

Using Variables as Array Dimensions

So far, the example DIM instructions specify the number of array elements with numeric literals. But you can use variable names also.

Variables provide a convenient way to alter array boundaries between successive runs of a program. For example, suppose that you have a program which displays results of your track club's road races. The program dimensions arrays as follows:

```
200 DIM LASTNAME$(300), FIRSTNAME$(300)
210 DIM AGE%(300), WEIGHT!(300)
220 DIM RACETIME!(300)
```

A more flexible solution is to use a variable name like this:

```
190 MAXRUNNERS% = 300
200 DIM LASTNAME$(MAXRUNNERS%), FIRSTNAME$(MAXRUNNERS%)
210 DIM AGE%(MAXRUNNERS%), WEIGHT!(MAXRUNNERS%)
220 DIM RACETIME!(MAXRUNNERS%)
```

Not only is the name MAXRUNNERS% easier to understand than the literal 300, you need to change only the value in line 190 once (instead of all the DIM instructions) should the number 300 need changing between successive runs of the program.

Sometimes, you can ask the user to supply the array boundaries. For example, you might change line 190 to

```
190 INPUT "How many runners in the race"; MAXRUNNERS%
```

Remember, in DIM instructions, you can use variable names (as well as literals) for the subscript limits.

Table Lookup—a Sample Program with Arrays

Let's say that you want to write a program which asks the user for a telephone area code. After the user gives the code to the program, the program responds with the name of the state or province associated with that area code. For example, if the user enters the number 213, the program displays "California."

How would you tackle this task *without* a computer? Suppose that your job was to respond with a state name whenever you were given an area-code number? What would you do? Think for a minute before you continue reading.

Most likely, you would first find a list or table of all the area codes and the corresponding states. Then, whenever anyone asked about a particular area code, you would scan your list looking for that code. If you find a match, you respond with the corresponding state name. If you don't find a match, you reply that there is no such area code on your list.

This general technique is known as *table lookup*. You look through a table to find a specific entry. When you find it, you get the corresponding information from an adjacent "column" of the table.

Here's a program, named `AREACODE.BAS`, that does precisely the same table lookup. To keep the program relatively short, we have not included the entire area-code list.

```
100 REM Program: AREACODE.BAS (Show the state for any area code)
150 DIM CODE%(150), STATE$(150)
190 REM =======================================================
300 NUM% = 1
310 READ CODE%(NUM%), STATE$(NUM%)    'Read data into arrays
320    IF CODE%(NUM%) = 999 THEN 400  'All data is read
330    NUM% = NUM% + 1
340 GOTO 310
350 REM =======================================================
400 NUM% = NUM% - 1  'Make NUM% the number of table values
500 INPUT "Enter area code (use 0 to end program)"; ENTRY%
510    IF ENTRY% = 0 THEN 600         'User is all done
520    MESSAGE$ = "No such area code found"
530    FOR J% = 1 TO NUM%
540       IF ENTRY% = CODE%(J%) THEN MESSAGE$ = STATE%(J%)
550    NEXT J%
560    PRINT MESSAGE$
570 GOTO 500
590 REM =======================================================
600 PRINT "All done"
610 END
690 REM =======================================================
700 REM The area codes and state names follow:
710 DATA 201, New Jersey
712 DATA 202, D.C.
714 DATA 203, Connecticut
716 DATA 204, Manitoba
```

Listing continues

Listing *continued*

```
718 DATA 205, Alabama
720 DATA 206, Washington
722 DATA 207, Maine
724 DATA 208, Idaho
726 DATA 209, California
728 DATA 212, New York
730 DATA 213, California
732 DATA 214, Texas
900 DATA 999, XXX
```

Here is some sample output from the program:

```
Enter area code (use 0 to end program)? 201
New Jersey
Enter area code (use 0 to end program)? 212
New York
Enter area code (use 0 to end program)? 714
No such area code found
Enter area code (use 0 to end program)? 0
All done
```

The DATA instructions after line 700 provide the area-code list. The lines from 300 through 340 read the area codes and state names into arrays that the program can later search for matches. Lines 500 through 570 ask the user for an area code, search through the area-code array until a match is found, and then display the corresponding state name.

Table 8.3 shows how the area codes and state names are stored in the CODE% and STATE$ arrays.

Table 8.3. *Partial contents of the area code and state-name arrays.*

Element Number	Area Code—CODE%	State Name—STATE$
1	201	New Jersey
2	202	D.C.
3	203	Connecticut
4	204	Manitoba
5	205	Alabama

Let's examine AREACODE.BAS to see how the program works. Some of this explanation is review, but you should find the details helpful in understanding a typical application of arrays.

The `DIM` instruction in line 120 sets aside 150 elements for the `CODE%` and `STATE$` arrays. (Actually, the line reserves 151 elements for each array because BASIC gives the first array element an index of 0, not 1. Our program, however, uses only the elements from 1 upward.) Because fewer than 150 area codes exist, 150 elements provide ample space for every possible area code.

Line 300 sets the variable `NUM%` equal to one. This variable is destined for big things. `NUM%` will point to each array element while the data is read into the arrays; afterward `NUM%` will help count the number of area codes found in the `DATA` instructions. `NUM%` is set to one because the first area code should be placed into the first element position in the array.

Line 300 begins the array initialization phase of the program. By *initialization*, we mean the process of setting (in the beginning of a program) the program's variables to the values they will need during the main part of the program. The `DIM` instruction reserves memory space for the arrays but does not put the `DATA` instruction values into the arrays. Line 310 reads each pair of data items (area code and state) and stores that information in the two arrays. Line 320 checks whether the final pair of data items has been read. The program uses the nonexistent area code 999 to indicate that no more area codes are in the list. If the last line has been read (that is, `CODE%(NUM%)` equals 999), the program branches to line 400.

Line 330 adds one to `NUM%` in preparation for reading the next pair of data items into the subsequent pair of array-element slots. Line 340 branches back to line 310 to continue reading more data.

Line 400 receives control from line 320 when area code 999 is encountered. At this point, the arrays are filled with all the area-code and state-name data, and the program can continue with its processing. However, one necessary chore must be done first.

We need to subtract one from `NUM%` in order to have an accurate count of the number of area codes in the `CODE%` array. Do you see why? When line 400 gets control, the `NUM%` element of the `CODE%` array contains 999. This is a special "flag" value that is not part of the actual data. After subtracting one from `NUM%`, the `NUM%` element of `CODE%` contains the last real area-code value.

The `INPUT` instruction in line 500 begins the "user input" section of the program. The lines from here to line 570 ask the user for an area code, display the corresponding state name, and then repeat the process until the user says to stop—by entering 0 as an area code. Line 510 checks whether the entry is 0; if so, the program branches to line 600 to conclude the program. (*Note:* You can terminate the program by simply pressing enter when you are prompted for an area code. If you do so, line 500 assigns a value of 0 to `ENTRY%`.)

The variable MESSAGE$ stores the response that the user will eventually see. At first, in line 520, MESSAGE$ is set to report that a match is not found. If a match is subsequently found, MESSAGE$ is updated later.

The FOR...NEXT loop in lines 530 through 550 searches through the area codes in the CODE% array looking to match the entered area code. When a match is found (line 540), the counter variable J% contains the number of the matching element from the CODE% array. At this point, MESSAGE$ is assigned the proper state name from the STATE$ array. Note how the same index value of J% points to the proper corresponding value in the STATE$ array. That's table lookup in action.

When the loop finishes, line 560 prints the program's response. Note that MESSAGE$ contains the appropriate message whether or not a match was found. If a match was found, MESSAGE$ is the matching state name; if no match was found, MESSAGE$ is the "no match" message set back in line 520.

Line 570 branches back to line 500 to process the user's next request. Even if the previous request resulted in a match, line 520 reinitializes MESSAGE$ in anticipation of a possible failure this time around.

Line 600 prints the concluding message, and then line 610 terminates the program. Line 600 can be reached only from line 510 (when the user is done with the program).

The remainder of the program is the DATA instructions that list the area code and state-name information.

Now try making some changes to the program. First, consult your phone book and add DATA instructions for more area codes. Insert your new DATA instructions just before line 900. You might want to add more messages, perhaps a line between lines 400 and 500 that displays NUM%, the number of area codes in the array. If you feel really ambitious, change the program to ask for the state name, not the area code, and then have the program respond by displaying all the area codes for that state.

Using Multidimensional Arrays

So far, our sample arrays have been one-dimensional—a list of values. For example, the array SALARY!(EMPLOYEE%) contains salary information as a function of employee number. One-dimensional arrays use but a single subscript to span all the values of the array.

Suppose, however, that you have data in the form of a table (a spreadsheet, for example). Such data has a two-dimensional, row-and-column structure.

Two-Dimensional Arrays

BASIC supports two-dimensional arrays to represent such two-dimensional data. You need two subscripts to specify an element of a two-dimensional array—one subscript for the row number and one subscript for the column number. Use a comma to separate the two subscripts.

For example, a chessboard can be considered a two-dimensional array. Figure 8.3 shows a chess game in progress. The chessboard is eight squares wide by eight squares high. Each square of the 8-by-8 board has a row number from 1 to 8 and a column number from 1 to 8.

Fig. 8.3. *A chess game in progress.*

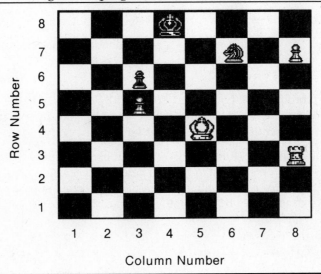

For the chessboard, a two-dimensional array named PIECE$ contains the name of the chess piece that currently occupies each square. The following instructions represent the board shown in figure 8.3.

```
200 DIM PIECE$(8, 8)
210 FOR ROW% = 1 TO 8
220    FOR COLUMN% = 1 TO 8
230        PIECE$ (COLUMN%, ROW%) = "None"
240    NEXT COLUMN%
250 NEXT ROW%
300 PIECE$(3, 5) = "White Pawn"
310 PIECE$(8, 7) = "White Pawn"
```

Listing continues

```
320 PIECE$(8, 3) = "White Rook"
330 PIECE$(5, 4) = "White King"
340 PIECE$(3, 6) = "Black Pawn"
350 PIECE$(6, 7) = "Black Knight"
360 PIECE$(4, 8) = "Black King"
```

Line 200 dimensions the PIECE$ array with a DIM instruction. The array is designated to be two-dimensional by the use of two subscripts. This DIM instruction tells BASIC the following information:

❑ PIECE$ is a two-dimensional string array.

❑ The first dimension has subscript values ranging from 0 to 8.

❑ The second dimension has subscript values ranging from 0 to 8.

Note that each dimension actually spans nine values (because the lowest value in each dimension is 0, not 1). So altogether, there are 81 (9 by 9) elements in the PIECE$ array.

In lines 210 through 250, two nested FOR...NEXT loops initialize the value of each array element with the string value "None". Note how nested loops quickly reference an entire two-dimensional array.

The remaining lines (300 through 360) assign specific string values to the array elements that represent squares which contain pieces. In each array reference, the first subscript is a column number and the second subscript is a row number. So, for example, PIECE$(3, 5) refers to the piece at column 3 and row 5.

Clothing Sales—a Case Study of 2-D Arrays

Suppose that you manage the clothing department of Bizarre's Department Store. You sell only three kinds of garments: raincoats, swimsuits, and underwear. (Now you see why the store is named Bizarre's).

At the end of the year, the sales figures look like figure 8.4. You want to write a program that displays this information and totals the seasonal sales.

Fig. 8.4. *Yearly clothing sales.*

		Bizarre's Department Store		
	Winter	Spring	Summer	Fall
Raincoats	522	309	101	486
Swimsuits	82	334	623	111
Underwear	362	295	384	244

Here's the program, named `GARMENT.BAS`.

```
100 REM Program: GARMENT.BAS (Demonstrate 2-D Arrays)
140 DIM GARMENT$(3)
150 DIM SALES%(3, 4)       '3 Items by 4 seasons
200 REM =====================================================
210 FOR ITEM% = 1 TO 3: READ GARMENT$(ITEM%): NEXT ITEM%
220 FOR ITEM% = 1 TO 3
230    FOR SEASON% = 1 TO 4
240       READ SALES%(ITEM%, SEASON%)
250    NEXT SEASON%
260 NEXT ITEM%            'Done reading data
270 REM =====================================================
300 PRINT , "WINTER", "SPRING", "SUMMER", "FALL"
310 FOR ITEM% = 1 TO 3
320 PRINT GARMENT%(ITEM%),
330    FOR SEASON% = 1 TO 4
340       PRINT SALES%(ITEM%, SEASON%),   'Print sales data
350    NEXT SEASON%
360 NEXT ITEM%
370 PRINT
380 REM =====================================================
400 FOR SEASON% = 1 TO 4   'Store total sales in 0 element
410    SALES%(0, SEASON%) = 0
420    FOR ITEM% = 1 TO 3
425       TEMP% = SALES%(ITEM%, SEASON%)
430       SALES%(0, SEASON%) = SALES%(0, SEASON) + TEMP%
440    NEXT ITEM%
450 NEXT SEASON%
460 PRINT "All Garments",
```

Listing continues

Listing continued

```
470 FOR SEASON% = 1 TO 4
480    PRINT SALES%(0, SEASON%),    'Total sales by season
490 NEXT SEASON%
500 END
510 REM ===================================================
600 DATA Raincoats, Swimsuits, Underwear
610 REM Winter, Spring, Summer, & Fall sales data follow
620 DATA 522, 309, 101, 486 :REM Raincoats (W, S, S, F)
630 DATA 82, 334, 623, 111 :REM Swimsuit sales by season
640 DATA 362, 295, 384, 244 :REM Underwear sales by season
```

The output looks like this:

```
              WINTER     SPRING     SUMMER     FALL
Raincoats      522        309        101        486
Swimsuits       82        334        623        111
Underwear      362        295        384        244

All Garments   966        938       1108        841
```

Let's examine GARMENT.BAS to see how the program works.

Lines 140 and 150 dimension the two arrays. GARMENT$ is a one-dimensional array containing the string names of the three garments.

The key array is SALES%, a two-dimensional array containing the seasonal sales for the three garments. This array represents the number of items sold as a function of the garment *and* the season. There are three garments (raincoats, swimsuits, and underwear) and four seasons (winter, spring, summer, and fall). So SALES% is dimensioned 3 by 4.

Lines 210 through 260 read the array. The data itself is in the DATA instructions from line 600 on. Note how the nested FOR...NEXT loops in lines 220 through 260 read all the data for the SALES% array.

Line 300 displays the column headings for the table. The first comma moves the column headings one extra print zone to the right. The commas at the end of lines 320 and 340 move the cursor to the next print zone but keep the cursor on the same line. For more information about PRINT and print zones, see Chapter 9, "Writing Text on the Video Screen."

Next, the program totals the garments sold in each season. Here, we take advantage of zero elements in the SALES% array. When referring to each garment, the first dimension of SALES% varies from 1 to 3 (1 = raincoats, 2 = swimsuits, 3 = underwear). The program uses the element number 0 to refer to total garment sales.

For example, SALES%(1, 2) refers to the spring sales of raincoats (1 = raincoats, 2 = spring). SALES%(0, 2) refers to the spring sales of all garments (0 = all garments, 2 = spring).

The loop in lines 400 through 450 computes the zero element for each season. Line 410 initializes the value to 0. (Strictly speaking, this line is not necessary because BASIC automatically initializes each numeric array element with a value of 0.) For each item, the inner loop (lines 420 through 440) increments the value of SALES%(0, SEASON%) by SALES%(ITEM%, SEASON%).

All that remains is displaying the bottom line of output—the total sales of each garment in each season. That's the job of lines 460 through 490.

SALES.BAS demonstrates the power of two-dimensional arrays with nested FOR...NEXT loops. Although the array bounds in this program were modest (three items, four seasons), you can see that managing a much larger array (for example, 1000 items by 14 stores) is no more complicated. With a few program lines, arrays can manipulate tremendous amounts of information.

By the way, SALES.BAS represents the beginning of a two-dimensional spreadsheet program. You may be familiar with commercially available spreadsheets such as 1-2-3 or Excel. Of course, SALES.BAS is much simpler than these products, but the same programming themes prevail.

Extending Arrays to Higher Dimensions

Arrays are not limited to two dimensions. BASIC permits arrays with as many as 255 dimensions! In practice, arrays higher than 3 dimensions are rare. To declare a multidimensional array, just specify the array bounds with a DIM instruction.

For example, the following instruction specifies a three-dimensional array.

```
200 DIM PROFIT!(6, 15, 12)
```

This array might represent the profits of a department-store chain as a function of the individual store, the department, and the month. For example, PROFIT!(2, 8, 11) refers to the profit from store #2 (let's say the Miami store), department #15 (maybe cosmetics), in November.

Reclaiming Array Memory

Of necessity, BASIC requires considerable memory resources to store large arrays, especially large multidimensional arrays. For example, BASIC needs more than 15,000 bytes of memory to store the following array:

```
200 DIM SALARY!(300, 12)
```

(Because of the 0 subscript, the SALARY! array is actually 301 elements by 13 elements. This is 3913 elements altogether. Each single-precision element requires 4 memory bytes. So the total memory requirement is 15,652 bytes—3913 times 4.)

With an ERASE instruction, you can "erase" an array from memory. The array elements become permanently lost. However, BASIC may now use the array's previous memory space for other purposes, such as dimensioning a new array.

ERASE *arraylist*

where *arraylist* is a list of array variables separated by commas.

For example, the following instruction erases the previously dimensioned arrays named SALARY! and CLIENT%.

```
800 ERASE SALARY!, CLIENT%
```

There are two primary reasons for erasing an array:

1. Your program no longer uses an array. By erasing the array, you free up memory for other purposes.

2. You want to redimension an array. Note that after an array is dimensioned, you get an error if you execute a second DIM instruction with the same array name. By first erasing the array, you can DIM the array again. Keep in mind, however, that the ERASE instruction permanently removes the old contents of the array.

Summary

The array is your primary tool for managing large amounts of related data. Arrays are like "super variables" that store multiple elements under a common array name. You refer to the individual array elements with a subscript or subscripts. Arrays can be single- or multidimensional.

Arrays and loops work well together. Inside a loop, the loop's counter variable is often used as a subscript in array references. A simple FOR...NEXT loop can manipulate all the data in a huge array.

With `DATA` instructions, you can conveniently store numerous data values as part of your program. `READ` instructions can then assign the data values to individual array elements. `DATA` and `READ` work with ordinary variables as well as with arrays.

Part III

Intermediate Programming

You now have a sound understanding of BASIC's fundamentals. It is time to dig deeper. Part III explores more of the language, especially subjects relating to input and output (that is, how BASIC interacts with the external environment).

Here are some of the topics explored in Part III:

❏ Writing text on the video screen, including format control and colors
❏ Storing and retrieving data from disk files
❏ Creating graphics
❏ Sending output to a printer
❏ Using the keyboard interactively
❏ Producing music and sound effects

CHAPTER 9

Writing Text on the Video Screen

```
PRINT, PRINT USING, TAB, SPC, CLS, LOCATE, COLOR,
SCREEN, WIDTH, VIEW PRINT, POS, CSRLIN
```

BASIC can take full advantage of your computer hardware to create dazzling video screens of text and graphics. This chapter focuses on text; the graphics discussion is deferred until Chapter 11, "Creating Graphics."

Maybe the word *text* doesn't conjure up the glamorous images associated with *graphics*, but BASIC has powerful text features. Text can be written in specialized formats, placed anywhere on the screen, "colorized," and even animated.

Regardless of the video adapter and monitor attached to your computer, you can display text. In fact, by default, BASIC programs put your video screen in text mode.

In text mode, PRINT instructions produce white characters on a black background. Your screen can display as many as 2,000 characters—80 characters per line and 25 total lines (EGA and VGA systems can display even more). As you will see later in this chapter, these defaults can be changed with COLOR and WIDTH instructions.

Understanding the Text Screen

To understand text mode, think of the screen as an imaginary 80-by-25 grid of cells (see fig. 9.1). The lines or rows are numbered from 1 to 25 from the top of the screen to the bottom. The horizontal positions or columns are numbered from 1 to 80 from left to right.

Fig. 9.1. *The default text screen.*

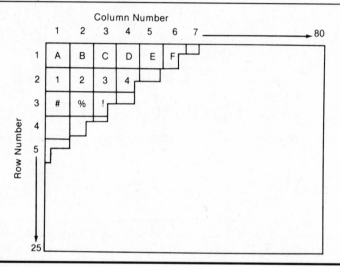

Each grid cell can be occupied by one text character. There are 256 different characters available, as shown in Appendix B, "ASCII Character Set."

The ASCII character set includes not only the standard numbers, letters, and punctuation symbols, but also some foreign letters, special symbols, cursor-movement "characters," and even some line-graphics characters.

In general, you can position the cursor at any cell in this imaginary grid and then use a PRINT instruction to write text beginning at that spot. If text is written in column 80, the cursor does an automatic "carriage return" and moves down to column 1 of the next line. When a carriage return occurs on the 25th line, all screen text scrolls up one line and subsequent text is written on the newly blank 25th line. Text formerly on the top line scrolls off the screen.

Using the 25th Line As a Status Line

Actually, the 25th line is a special case. By default, BASIC uses the bottom (25th) line of the screen as a status line that displays the keystroke sequences assigned to the function keys. You can turn off this Function Key Display by using the KEY statement discussed in Chapter 3, "A Hands-On Introduction to Programming," and Chapter 12, "Programming Hardware Devices."

When the Function Key Display is on, you can write only on lines 1 through 24, and scrolling occurs after line 24 rather than line 25. When the Function Key Display is off, the full 25 lines are available for text.

Using the *PRINT* Statement

The workhorse of text-mode displays is the PRINT statement. PRINT writes both string and numeric values to the video screen.

PRINT *exprlist*

where *exprlist* is an optional list of expressions. Individual items in *exprlist* are separated by a comma, a semicolon, or some number of blank spaces.

Optionally, the entire instruction may end with a comma or semicolon.

Each expression in *exprlist* must be in numeric or string form and can consist of a literal, variable, function, or a more general construct combining two or more individual components with appropriate operators. String literals must be enclosed by a pair of quotation marks. In all cases, each individual expression in *exprlist* must reduce to a single value, which BASIC then displays. Here are six simple PRINT instructions:

```
10 PRINT "Hello, my friend" ' String literal
20 PRINT X                  ' Numeric variable
30 PRINT Sales(Factory%)    ' Numeric array element
40 PRINT 4.6 * SQR(Area)    ' Mathematical expression
50 PRINT LEFT$(LastName$,10)' String function
60 PRINT                    ' No argument
```

Use PRINT by itself (no *exprlist*) to force a carriage return. This causes the cursor to reposition itself at column 1 of the next lower line (lower in the sense that it is toward the bottom of the screen). If the cursor was already in column 1, you get a blank line on the screen.

Using ? for PRINT

When you enter a program, you can type a question mark (?) as an abbreviation for the keyword PRINT. When you later list the program, BASIC converts the question mark to the full keyword PRINT. For example, suppose that you type the following one-line program:

```
100 ? "No kidding"
```

Now list the program with the LIST command. You find that BASIC displays

```
100 PRINT "No kidding"
```

Does the abbreviation save typing time? Some people say Yes and others No. You have to answer that question for yourself.

String *PRINT* Formats

PRINT displays a string value straightforwardly; each character from the string occupies one character position on your screen. For example:

```
10 MESSAGE$ = "There is no"
20 PRINT MESSAGE$              'PRINT contents of variable
30 PRINT "place like home."    'PRINT a string literal
```

The output is

```
There is no
place like home.
```

Note that, in a PRINT instruction, a string literal must be enclosed in quotation marks. Without the quotation marks, BASIC attempts to interpret the text after PRINT as a variable name or numeric quantity.

Numeric *PRINT* Formats

When you display numbers, PRINT uses the following special formats:

❏ Every number prints with a trailing space.

❏ Negative numbers have a leading minus sign (−).

❏ Positive numbers (and zero) have a leading space.

The printed degree of precision depends on the numeric format.

Integer

The following program shows how PRINT displays integer variables:

```
10 NEGNUM% = -123
20 POSNUM% = 12345
30 PRINT NEGNUM%
40 PRINT POSNUM%
```

The output demonstrates the leading space in front of the positive integer value:

```
-123
 12345
```

Single-Precision

PRINT displays single-precision values in fixed-point format, if possible, or exponential format otherwise. Fixed-point format uses only the digits and, if necessary, a decimal point and a minus sign. The first six digits of any number are guaranteed to be accurate. PRINT can display single-precision numbers in fixed-point format with as many as seven digits. Occasionally, the seventh digit is not accurate.

The following program demonstrates how PRINT formats some single-precision numbers using fixed-point representation:

```
100 EXAMPLE1! = 2.5 * 4
110 EXAMPLE2! = 1 / 1000
120 EXAMPLE3! = -1 / 3
130 EXAMPLE4! = 100000 / 3
140 EXAMPLE5! = 123 + .456
150 PRINT EXAMPLE1!
160 PRINT EXAMPLE2!
170 PRINT EXAMPLE3!
```

Listing continues

Listing continued

```
180 PRINT EXAMPLE4!
190 PRINT EXAMPLE5!
200 PRINT 1 / 7
```

The output looks like this:

```
 10
 .001
-.3333334
 33333.33
 123.456
 .1428572
```

If a single-precision number happens to have an exact integer value (no fractional part), BASIC displays the whole number without any decimal point. The variable `EXAMPLE1!` in the sample program is just such a case. Note that the program displays the value of `EXAMPLE1!` as 10 (not as 10. or 10.0).

Fixed-point display uses as many as seven digits of precision. As a result, the largest possible value is `9999999` and the smallest possible (positive) value is `.0000001`.

To display values outside these limits, `PRINT` resorts to exponential format. Again, the maximum degree of precision is seven digits. But the exponential indicator, E, can set the decimal point through the full range of single-precision numbers (approximately $-1.0E-38$ to $1.0E+38$).

The following program demonstrates exponential format:

```
10 EXAMPLE1! = 10 ' 8 '10 * 10 * 10 * 10 * 10 * 10 * 10 * 10
20 EXAMPLE2! = EXAMPLE1! / 3
30 EXAMPLE3! = 1 / EXAMPLE1!
40 EXAMPLE4! = -1.234 * EXAMPLE3! * EXAMPLE3!
50 PRINT EXAMPLE1!
60 PRINT EXAMPLE2!
70 PRINT EXAMPLE3!
80 PRINT EXAMPLE4!
```

Here is the output:

```
 1E+08
 3.333334E+07
 1E-08
-1.234E-16
```

Double-Precision

For double-precision values, PRINT extends the fixed-point format up to 16 digits. The exponential indicator for double-precision is D rather than E. Consider the following program:

```
200 A# = 1# / 3#
210 B# = 10000000# * 10000000# * 10000000#'7 zeroes each
220 C# = -A# /B#
230 D# = 1.23456789# * 1000000000#'9 zeroes in 2nd number
240 E# = D# * 1000000000#'9 zeroes in 2nd number
250 PRINT A#
260 PRINT B#
270 PRINT C#
280 PRINT D#
290 PRINT E#
300 PRINT 1# / 7#
```

The output is

```
 .3333333333333333
 1D+21
-3.333333333333333D-22
 1234567890
 1.23456789D+18
 .1428571428571429
```

In the program, note the use of the pound sign (#) on the numeric literals to retain full double-precision accuracy. For more information on this topic, refer to Chapter 6, "Manipulating Data."

Multiple Expressions

A single PRINT instruction can display two or more values on one screen line. All you need to do is place two or more elements in the expression list. Use either a semicolon or comma to separate individual items in the expression list. When BASIC displays the output, it inserts blank spaces between each displayed item. The number of separating blank spaces depends on the delimiter you choose.

The Semicolon Delimiter

If a semicolon separates the two items, no blank spaces are inserted and the items are simply juxtaposed. For example:

```
10 MYSTRING$ = "This is a note"
20 PRINT MYSTRING$; "worthy achievement"
```

The PRINT instruction causes the following output:

```
This is a noteworthy achievement
```

The PRINT instruction in line 20 displays both the value of MYSTRING$ and the string literal worthy achievement. All the text displays on the same screen line with no blank spaces between the text. The result is a meaningful sentence.

You must be careful with numeric output. Recall that numbers automatically are printed with a trailing blank. Positive numbers and zero are displayed with a leading blank; negative numbers have a leading minus sign but no automatic space before the minus sign.

The following program demonstrates how this automatic formatting of numbers can be either helpful or annoying when you display multiple expressions with one PRINT instruction:

```
10 REM Demonstrate numeric formatting
20 HIGHTEMP% = 47
30 LOWTEMP%  = -12
40 PRINT "The high today was";HIGHTEMP%; "degrees"
50 PRINT "and the low was"; LOWTEMP%; "degrees."
```

The output is

```
The high today was 47 degrees
and the low was-12 degrees.
```

Note that the first line of output looks good. A blank space appears both before and after the 47. The second line is annoying, however, because no blank space appears before the -12.

You could force a blank by explicitly placing a blank in the string literal between the "s" in "was" and the quotation mark. If the value of LOWTEMP% is positive, however, the resulting output contains two blank spaces (one from your explicit blank and one from the automatic blank that BASIC adds in front of each positive number).

The Space Delimiter

You can separate multiple items in your expression list with one or more blank spaces. BASIC treats this situation as though a semicolon separated the items. The result is simply that the displayed items appear juxtaposed. For example:

```
10 PRINT "I see"  76  "trombones"
```

The output is

```
I see 76 trombones
```

The result is the same as though the original program line were

```
10 PRINT "I see"; 76; "trombones"
```

The Comma Delimiter and *PRINT* Zones

By separating items in your expression list with commas, a PRINT instruction aligns output into predefined fields or zones.

To understand this zoning, picture each potential 80-character line of screen output divided into five zones. Each zone, except the last, is 14 characters wide. The zones begin at column positions 1, 15, 29, 43, and 57.

When you use a comma between items in your expression list, you request tabbing to successive zones. Consider the following one-line program:

```
10 PRINT "Zone1", "Zone2", "Zone3"
```

The result is zoned output as follows:

```
Zone1         Zone2         Zone3
```

Numbers still are displayed inside the print zones with the usual leading and trailing spaces. One convenient use of comma separators is to display simple tables neatly. For example:

```
10
REM Program: SHOWZONE.BAS (Demonstrate PRINT zones)
20 PRINT , "Position", "Batting Avg"
30 PRINT
40 PRINT "Rose", "First Base", .347
50 PRINT "DiMaggio", "Center", .287
60 PRINT "Ruth", "Right Field", .301
70 PRINT "Uecker", "Catcher", .106
```

This results in the following aligned table:

```
                Position        Batting Avg

Rose            First Base      .347
DiMaggio        Center          .287
Ruth            Right Field     .301
Uecker          Catcher         .106
```

Note how the beginning comma in the first PRINT instruction forces Position to be printed in the second print zone.

If a particular item needs more than 14 characters (and, as you have seen, some numbers display to 16 or more characters), a comma tabs the next item to the beginning of the subsequent print zone. You must be careful not to ruin your table's alignment. The PRINT USING statement, discussed in the next major section, can correct such problems.

Trailing Punctuation

You may have noticed that, so far, the example PRINT instructions produce a carriage return and line feed after the output is displayed. That is, after each PRINT instruction is executed, the cursor jumps down a line and returns to column 1. A subsequent PRINT instruction displays output on this new line.

Sometimes, you may want to suppress the carriage return and line feed at the end of a PRINT instruction. To do so, terminate the PRINT instruction with a semicolon or comma.

A trailing semicolon on a PRINT instruction retains the cursor immediately after the last printed item. A subsequent PRINT instruction simply resumes printing from that point. For example, the following program produces only one line of output:

```
10 PRINT "A stitch in time saves";
20 PRINT 9
```

The result is

```
A stitch in time saves 9
```

A trailing comma on a PRINT instruction tabs the cursor to the beginning of the next print zone. A subsequent PRINT instruction resumes printing from that point.

Why would you want to suppress the carriage return and line feed at the end of a PRINT instruction? The most common reason is that you must test some condition to determine how to finish a line of output. For example, look at the following program fragment:

```
200 REM The value of AGE% is set earlier in the program
210 PRINT "This person is ";
220 IF AGE% > 20 THEN PRINT "an adult" ELSE PRINT "a minor"
```

Note that line 210 ends with a semicolon. If the value of AGE% is greater than 20, this program fragment displays

```
This person is an adult
```

If the value of AGE% is 20 or less, the output is instead

```
This person is a minor
```

The *TAB* and *SPC* Functions

The TAB and SPC functions provide you with additional control over the horizontal cursor position. These two functions are valid only as part of the expression list in a PRINT (PRINT#, or LPRINT) instruction.

TAB(*column*)

where *column* is an integer expression in the range from 1 to 255.

TAB advances the cursor to the specified *column* position on the same line. If the cursor is already positioned beyond *column*, the cursor drops down to the next line at position *column*.

TAB makes it a snap to display aligned, columnar output at tab positions of your choosing. For example, suppose that you keep track of clients' names in an array called CLIENT$, and billable hours in an array called BILLHOURS. The following program fragment displays a summary table:

```
300 PRINT "#"; TAB(6);  "Client"; TAB(35); "Billable Hours"
310 PRINT
320 FOR J = 1 TO NUMCLIENTS
330    PRINT J; TAB(6); CLIENT$(J); TAB(35); BILLHOURS(J)
340 NEXT J%
```

The SPC function displays a given number of blank spaces.

SPC(*numspaces*)

where *numspaces* is an integer expression in the range from 1 to 255.

For example, `PRINT "Heave"; SPC(20); "Ho"` displays the following output (with 20 embedded blank spaces):

```
Heave                    Ho
```

If you place either `TAB` or `SPC` at the end of the expression list in a `PRINT` instruction, the cursor remains at the end of the line (that is, no carriage return is issued). In essence, there is an implied semicolon after each `SPC` or `TAB` function, whether or not you explicitly include the semicolon. For example:

```
200 FOR NUM = 1 TO 7
210    PRINT NUM; SPC(NUM)
220 NEXT NUM
230 PRINT "Done"
```

The result is the following single line of screen output:

```
 1   2    3     4      5       6        7         Done
```

Note that the number of blank spaces between each successive digit increases by one.

Controlling Formats
with *PRINT USING*

For many programs, especially programs without complicated demands on visual output, `PRINT` instructions are all you need to display results. But for special demands, such as printing reports, BASIC extends the capabilities of the simple `PRINT` statement with the `PRINT USING` statement.

With `PRINT USING`, you can specify customized formatting strings that enhance your control over the appearance of the output. Here are some of the things you can do with `PRINT USING`:

❑ Align columns of numbers on the decimal point.

❑ Display part of a string.

❑ Place a dollar sign immediately before a number.

❑ Display any number in scientific notation.

❑ Restrict the number of decimal digits in an output number.

A `PRINT USING` instruction has the following form:

PRINT USING *formatstr*; *exprlist*

where *formatstr* is a string containing formatting instructions, and *exprlist* is a list of expressions separated by semicolons or commas.

Optionally, you can end the instruction with a comma or semicolon.

The expression list is the list of items to be displayed, just as in the regular `PRINT` instruction. `PRINT USING`, however, does not distinguish between the different punctuation delimiters contained inside the expression list. Commas are treated just like semicolons in the sense that no tabbing to specific columns occurs.

Just as with `PRINT`, a trailing comma or a trailing semicolon suppresses the final carriage return and line feed. The cursor remains just after the last displayed item.

The special feature of `PRINT USING` is the format string. With the format string, you describe your intended format for the strings and numbers contained in the expression list. The format string may be specified by a string literal enclosed in double quotation marks. Alternatively, you can store the format string in a string variable and then use the variable name in the `PRINT USING` instruction.

Various special characters in the format string cause special printing effects, as shown in table 9.1.

This table may be a bit overwhelming at first. Don't worry. Like most programming topics, `PRINT USING` is easier to fathom after you have seen some examples. Try some of the following examples and experiment with a few of your own.

Displaying Numbers with *PRINT USING*

The format string sets up a numeric field, which specifies exactly how the number will look. Each # in the format string indicates a digit position. Such a

Table 9.1. PRINT USING *format characters.*

Character	Effect
Numbers	
#	Holds place for a single digit
.	Prints a decimal point
,	Places a comma every three digits
+	Prints the sign of the number
—	Prints negative numbers with a trailing minus sign
**	Places leading asterisks before the number
$$	Places a dollar sign before the number
**$	Places leading asterisks and a dollar sign
⌃⌃⌃	Specifies exponential notation
Strings	
&	Displays the entire string
!	Displays the first character of the string
\ \	Displays a specified number of characters from the beginning of the string
_ (underscore)	Displays the next character of the format string
<Any>	Displays any other character not in this table

position is always filled by a digit, a leading minus sign, or, if necessary, a blank space. A period in the format string indicates where the decimal point should go.

For example,

```
Ok
PRINT USING "#.##"; 6.5218
6.52
Ok
```

Note that the output contains only two digits to the right of the decimal point because the format string contains only two digits to the right of the decimal point. To display the number, the computer first rounds the number to two decimal places.

We specified one digit before the decimal point. The computer obliges by displaying only the 6 to the left of the decimal point. Note that the 6 was printed in column 1 of the output. In this case, the computer suppressed the single blank space that normally precedes all positive numbers.

Suppose that we display the same number but this time specify five digits before the decimal point. Here is what happens:

```
Ok
PRINT USING "#####.##"; 6.5218
    6.52
Ok
```

BASIC adds leading blank spaces to accommodate the extra specified digits. This has the effect of right-justifying the number in the specified field.

The following program demonstrates more features of numerical formatting with PRINT USING. The program displays the same number using several different format strings.

```
100 REM Demonstrate PRINT USING with numbers
110 MYNUMBER = 39.82
120 PRINT USING "######"; MYNUMBER
130 PRINT USING "####.#"; MYNUMBER
140 PRINT USING "###.####"; MYNUMBER
150 PRINT USING "+###.###"; MYNUMBER
160 PRINT USING "###.###-"; MYNUMBER
170 PRINT USING "###.###-"; -MYNUMBER
```

Here is the output:

```
   40
 39.8
 39.8200
+39.820
 39.820
 39.820-
```

Note that the format string in line 120 does not specify a decimal point. As a result, the number is rounded to the nearest whole number and displayed without a decimal point. Lines 140 through 170 demonstrate that extra # characters after the decimal point cause zeroes to fill the field.

A plus sign in a format string means that the sign (plus or minus) will always be displayed with the number. The sign prints before the number if the plus sign is at the beginning of the format string, or after the number if the plus sign is at the end of the format string. A minus sign at the end of the format string means that negative numbers will be printed when a trailing minus appears. Lines 150 through 170 demonstrate these effects.

One of the most common uses of PRINT USING is to align columnar numbers on the decimal point. Look at the following program, which uses a simple PRINT instruction on line 40:

```
10 NUM = 5.5
20 FOR J = 1 TO 5
30    NUM = NUM
40 PRINT NUM
50 NEXT NUM
```

The result is

```
30.25
166.375
915.0625
5032.844
27680.64
```

Now try PRINT USING instead. Change line 40 as follows:

```
40 PRINT USING "######.##"; NUM
```

Here's what you get:

```
   30.25
  166.38
  915.06
 5032.84
27680.64
```

The decimal points align neatly, and the output has a much cleaner appearance.

Suppose that you specify a format which does not allow the necessary number of digits to the left of the decimal point. In such a case, BASIC displays the full number but adds a percent sign (%) in front of the number to indicate insufficient formatting. For example:

```
Ok
PRINT USING "##.###"; 1234.5678
%1234.568
Ok
```

Place four carets (^) in a format string to specify exponential notation. You can have any number of decimal positions before the decimal point. However, significant digits are left-justified, and the exponent is adjusted accordingly. For example:

```
10 PRINT USING "##.###^^^^"; 4592.9
20 PRINT USING "####.###^^^^"; 4592.9
30 PRINT USING "##.###^^^^"; -0.00000148
```

The output is

```
4.593E+03
459.290E+01
-1.480E-06
```

The comma, if it appears anywhere before a decimal point, causes a comma to be printed between every three digits. This is great for displaying large numbers. For example:

```
Ok
PRINT USING "#####,####"; 1234567
 1,234,567
Ok
```

The * and $ formats are used to specify monetary values in financial programs, such as check-writing programs. Each * and $ character in the format string counts as one digit position in the numeric field. Thus, "$$###" specifies a five-character numeric field of which one character will be the dollar sign. Table 9.2 shows some monetary formats.

Table 9.2. *Examples of* PRINT USING *monetary formats.*

Format	Number	Displayed Result
"**######"	987.65	*****988
"**######.#	987.65	*****987.65
"$$######.##	987.65	$987.65
"$$#,####.##"	37823.19	$37,823.19
"**$#####.##	101	****$101.00
"**$#####.##	.478	******$0.48
"**$#####.##	−32.45	**** − $32.45

Displaying Text with *PRINT USING*

The !, &, and \ are special characters used in the format string to display text. When these characters are used, the text to be printed consists of a string literal (enclosed in quotation marks) or a string variable.

The exclamation point (!) indicates that only the first character of the data string should be displayed. The ampersand (&) specifies the entire string.

Two backslashes (\ \) indicate that you want to print only part of the data string. How big a part? That depends on how many blank spaces you place between the backslashes. The format \\ (no intervening spaces) tells BASIC to print only the first two characters of the data string. In this case, one character prints for each backslash. The format \ \ (three intervening spaces) means that five characters should be printed. BASIC prints one character for each backslash and one character for each blank space between the backslashes.

If the format field specifies more positions than occur in the string, the output string is padded with spaces to the right.

The following sample program demonstrates some string formatting:

```
10 REM Demonstrate PRINT USING with strings
20 MYSTRING$ = "BASIC"
30 PRINT USING "!"   ; MYSTRING$
40 PRINT USING "&"   ; MYSTRING$
50 PRINT USING "\\"  ; MYSTRING$    'No spaces between slashes
60 PRINT USING "\ \"; MYSTRING$    ' 2 spaces between slashes
```

The result is as follows:

```
B
BASIC
BA
BASI
```

Using Variables as Format Strings

So far, the PRINT USING examples specify the format string with a string literal enclosed in quotation marks. But you have an alternative. Rather than a string literal, you can specify the format string with a string variable that you create. You probably will want to use a variable whenever different PRINT USING instructions share the same format string.

In the following example,

```
100 MONEYFORM$ = "$$####.##"
110 NUMITEMS = 15
120 ITEMCOST = 127.43
130 TOTALCOST = NUMITEMS * ITEMCOST
140 PRINT "Number of items ="; NUMITEMS
150 PRINT
160 PRINT "Cost per item =";
170 PRINT USING MONEYFORM$; ITEMCOST
180 PRINT "Total cost    =";
190 PRINT USING MONEYFORM$; TOTALCOST
```

the resulting output is

```
Number of items = 15

Cost per item =  $127.43
Total cost    = $1911.45
```

Line 100 stores the format string in a string variable named MONEYFORM$. Later, both PRINT USING instructions (lines 170 and 190) use this format.

The program also demonstrates some of the other printing techniques we have been discussing. Look at the PRINT instructions in lines 160 and 180. Note how the equal signs in these two instructions align. We added blank spaces to the string in line 180 to force this alignment. Don't you think that the resulting output has a sleek appearance with the equal signs and decimal points aligned?

Also, did you notice that lines 160 and 180 each end with a semicolon? Remember that this temporarily freezes the cursor on the same output line. In each case, the subsequent PRINT USING instruction finishes off the line of output.

PRINT USING with Multiple Fields

Although we have discussed PRINT USING in some depth, you have really only begun to see what you can do with it. The true power of PRINT USING becomes apparent when your expression list contains more than one expression. Why? Because you can display multiple items under the control of a single format string.

Here's a program that neatly displays the sine, tangent, and square roots of some decimal numbers between 7 and 8:

```
100 PRINT USING "   &      "; " J ", "SIN", "TAN", "SQR"
110 MYFORMAT$ = "###.###     "
120 FOR J = 7 TO 8 STEP .1
130    PRINT USING MYFORMAT$; J, SIN(J), TAN(J), SQR(J)
140 NEXT J
```

Here's the output, neatly aligned:

```
     J            SIN           TAN           SQR
  7.000         0.657        0.871         2.646
  7.100         0.729        1.065         2.665
  7.200         0.794        1.305         2.683
  7.300         0.850        1.617         2.702
  7.400         0.899        2.049         2.720
  7.500         0.938        2.706         2.739
  7.600         0.968        3.852         2.757
  7.700         0.988        6.443         2.775
  7.800         0.999       18.507         2.793
  7.900         0.999      -21.716         2.811
  8.000         0.989       -6.800         2.828
```

Look at the PRINT USING instruction in line 130. A single format string (specified by MYFORMAT$) displays the four numbers J, SIN(J), TAN(J), and SQR(J) each time the instruction executes. BASIC simply reuses the format string to satisfy all the expressions in your expression list. Line 100 prints four text strings under the control of a single format string.

You may notice that the format strings in lines 100 and 110 contain blank spaces. For each such blank space, BASIC simply places a blank space in the final output. For example, the MYFORMAT$ format string in line 110 has four blank spaces between the last pound sign and the trailing quotation mark. As a result, BASIC adds four blank spaces after each output number in the table.

Format strings can even contain multiple formats merged together. This sets up a correspondence between successive formats and the various items in the expression list.

For example:

```
10 FORM$ ="& ### &"
20 PRINT USING FORM$; "Car", 54, "Where are you?"
30 PRINT USING FORM$; "Fahrenheit", 451
40 PRINT USING FORM$; "A", 1, "and", "a", 2, "and", "a", 3
```

The output looks like this:

```
Car  54 Where are you?
Fahrenheit 451
A    1 anda   2 anda   3
```

The format string in line 10 merges three formats together. The first format is the ampersand, which designates that an entire text string is to be printed. The second format is the three pound signs, which specify a three-digit number. And the third format is another ampersand.

Line 20 prints a text string followed by a number and then another text string. This matches the format string exactly and so the

```
Car 54 Where are you?
```

message prints appropriately. In line 30, however, we print only a text string followed by a number. If the number of formats in the format string is greater than the number of items in the expression list, BASIC simply ignores the extra formats.

Line 40 is a bit trickier. Now the number of expressions exceeds the number of formats. No problem. BASIC recycles the formats until all the items are displayed.

When nonspecial characters (that is, characters not listed in table 9.1) appear in your format string, BASIC displays those characters in the resulting output. This enables you to add any desired annotation to your format strings. For example:

```
10 FORM$ = "Check Number##### was for **$####.##"
20 PRINT USING FORM$; 1033, 544.67
```

The result is

```
Check Number 1033 was for ***$544.67
```

It is worth mentioning again that a blank space is treated just like any other nonspecial character. Each blank space in your format string creates a corresponding blank space in the final output.

Use the underscore to display one of the special formatting characters as part of your text output. Occasionally you will want to treat one of the special characters as just an ordinary nonspecial character. The underscore in a format string says to consider the next character as text you want displayed, not as a special formatting character. For example:

```
Ok
PRINT USING "I saw Romeo _& Juliet # times"; 5
I saw Romeo & Juliet 5 times
Ok
```

Without the underscore, the ampersand indicates that a string value, not a number, is expected. This causes an error: Type mismatch.

One additional warning: don't use any punctuation (such as commas, semicolons, or even blank spaces) to separate items in your format string. All punctuation has a special effect.

Recall that a comma is reserved for displaying commas in large numbers and thus has meaning only in numerical formats. A semicolon or blank is treated like any other general character and thus is displayed in your final output just as it appears in your format string.

Clearing the Screen

As you saw in Chapter 3, "A Hands-On Introduction to Programming," you can clear the screen of text with the CLS instruction (CLS is short for "*CL*ear *S*creen"). Try CLS in direct mode (simply type **CLS** and press Enter). Here's what happens:

❑ All text on the screen is erased.

❑ The cursor moves to the upper left corner.

❑ The computer prints Ok in anticipation of your next command.

CLS does not affect the Function Key Display on line 25. If the bottom line of your screen shows the Function Key Display, CLS does not remove it. (Use KEY OFF to turn off the Function Key Display.)

Also, CLS does *not* remove any program you might have in memory. (Type NEW to clear your current program.) If you have a program stored in memory, you can reassure yourself that the program is still there by typing LIST.

In the next section of this chapter, you place a CLS instruction directly inside a program.

Controlling the Cursor

As you have learned, PRINT and PRINT USING instructions display text at the current position of the cursor. In many programs, you may want to move the cursor before writing particular information. By gaining such cursor control, your programs design full-screen text displays with information printed exactly where you want.

Fortunately, BASIC provides you with extensive cursor control. You can do the following:

❑ Position the cursor at a specified row and column.

❑ Turn the cursor on or off.

❑ Change the shape of the cursor.

❑ Determine the current cursor position.

Positioning the Cursor

Use `LOCATE` to move the cursor around the screen. Here's the simple form of `LOCATE`:

`LOCATE` *row*, *column*

where *row* is the cursor's desired row number (1 to 25) and *column* is the column number (1 to 80).

With `LOCATE`, you can move the cursor to any screen location and then use `PRINT` to place text at that location. For example, the following program prints "Hello" messages in the upper left, middle central, and lower right parts of the screen:

```
10 REM Demonstrate LOCATE with PRINT
20 CLS                    'First clear the screen
30 LOCATE 3, 5
40 PRINT "Hello from up here"
50 LOCATE 13, 28
60 PRINT "Hello from the middle"
70 LOCATE 23, 50
80 PRINT "Hello from down here"
```

`LOCATE` is a great tool for creating text displays. Try your own experiments. You might begin by modifying this program. Change some of the row or column positions and print new, appropriate messages.

Using Advanced Cursor Features

This section is not essential for beginning programmers. You can skip ahead to the section on color text screens without losing continuity.

Using Optional *LOCATE* Parameters

The full form of the `LOCATE` instruction accepts five parameters.

> LOCATE *row, column, cursorflag, startline, stopline*
>
> where *row* is the cursor's row number, *column* is the column number, *cursorflag* makes the cursor visible or invisible, and *startline* and *stopline* specify the cursor's shape.
>
> Each of the five parameters is optional.

Normally, the cursor is invisible as your program executes (one common exception is during INPUT prompts). If you want the cursor to become visible, specify the *cursorflag* parameter. Use 1 to turn the cursor on, 0 to turn it off. For example, the following instruction causes the cursor to appear:

```
100 LOCATE , , 1
```

Note how LOCATE treats optional parameters. Two commas appear, but no values for the *row* and *column* are specified. If you omit a parameter specification, BASIC just uses the current value of that parameter. In this instruction, therefore, the values of *row* and *column* remain unchanged.

Also, the fourth and fifth parameters are not specified. Again, BASIC just uses current values for any parameters left off the end of the instruction. Here are some more examples of this technique:

```
200 LOCATE 14        'Move to row 14, keep current column
210 LOCATE , 56      'Move to column 56, keep current row
```

When you make the cursor visible, you can also change its shape. To do so, specify values for *startline* and *stopline*. The cursor occupies a rectangular cell consisting of horizontal scan lines numbered from 0 at the top to 7 at the bottom (monochrome systems go from 0 to 13). Try adjusting the values of *startline* and *stopline* to see the effect. If *stopline* is less than *startline*, a two-tiered cursor results.

The following program, which prints your name vertically on the screen, demonstrates various capabilities of the LOCATE instruction:

```
100 REM Demonstrate the LOCATE   statement
110 CLS
120 LOCATE , , 1, 3, 5  'Turn cursor on and change the shape
130 INPUT "What's your name (note cursor shape)"; YOURNAME$
140 CLS
150 COLUMN% = 25
160 FOR ROW% = 1 TO LEN(YOURNAME$)
170    LOCATE ROW%, COLUMN%
180    PRINT MID$(YOURNAME$, ROW%, 1)
190 NEXT ROW%
```

One thing to note from this program is that you can specify parameters in `LOCATE` with variables as well as with numeric constants.

Determining the Current Cursor Position

You can determine the cursor's current position with `CSRLIN` and `POS`.

`CSRLIN` returns the current row of the cursor as an integer from 1 to 25. `POS` returns the horizontal position of the cursor as an integer from 1 to 80. The `POS` function requires a dummy argument.

POS(*dummyargument*)

where *dummyargument* is a dummy argument that can have any value.

That `POS` requires a dummy argument and `CSRLIN` does not is simply an unfortunate quirk of BASIC. (Technically, `CSRLIN` is a system variable and `POS` is a function.)

You can use `CSRLIN` and `POS` in conjunction with `LOCATE` to move the cursor relative to its present location. For example, the following instruction moves the cursor from its current position to a new position 3 rows down and 10 positions to the left:

```
100 LOCATE CSRLIN + 3, POS(0) - 10
```

Adding Color to Text Screens

Now have a little fun and make your programs more colorful. So far, text displays have been drab—nothing but black and white. You can easily display text in color. Of course, your computer system must have a color monitor and one of the following video adapters: Color Graphics Adapter (CGA), Enhanced Graphics Adapter (EGA), or Video Graphics Array (VGA).

The `COLOR` statement enables you to work with colored text. For now, our discussion of `COLOR` is confined to text screens. In Chapter 11, we move on to graphics and discuss how to use the `COLOR` statement with graphics screens.

The *COLOR* Statement in Text Mode

Picture your text screen as an 80-by-25 grid of rectangular cells. Within each cell, you can place one character. The character is displayed with a foreground color and a background color. The foreground is the character itself; the background is the rest of the cell in which the character resides. In the normal default mode, the foreground color is white, the background color black.

With the COLOR statement, you can modify the values of the foreground and background colors, and also change the color of the border surrounding the entire screen.

COLOR *foreground*, *background*, *border*

where *foreground* is an integer expression (0 to 31) that specifies the color and attribute of the text character, *background* is an integer expression (0 to 15) that specifies the color of the character's background, and *border* is an integer expression (0 to 15) that specifies the color of the screen border.

Each of the three parameters is optional, but at least one parameter must appear.

A COLOR instruction does *not* change text already on the screen. COLOR defines only the characteristics of subsequent text that you display with PRINT instructions. After you change the foreground and/or background colors with a COLOR instruction, the new colors remain in effect until you change them with another COLOR instruction. In general, the procedure to write colored text involves the following three steps:

1. Choose text colors with a COLOR instruction.

2. If necessary, move the cursor with a LOCATE instruction.

3. Write the text with a PRINT instruction.

You select colors using the integer values in table 9.3.

Table 9.3. *Available colors.*

Code	Color	Code	Color
0	Black	8	Gray
1	Blue	9	Light blue
2	Green	10	Light green
3	Cyan	11	Light cyan
4	Red	12	Light red
5	Magenta	13	Light magenta
6	Brown	14	Yellow
7	White	15	High-intensity white

As a first experiment, run the following short program:

```
10 COLOR 1         'Change foreground color to blue
20 PRINT "I feel blue today."
```

How about that? Do you like the blue printing?

Now change the background color as well as the foreground color:

```
10 COLOR 4, 3      'Red foreground and cyan background
20 PRINT "This should be red on cyan"
```

Are you ready for a surprise? Try this:

```
10 COLOR 25, 0      'Surprising foreground, black background
20 PRINT "This makes me blink"
```

Are your eyes blinking?

The value of *foreground* controls the color of the character and whether the character blinks. A *foreground* color from 0 to 15 selects the color shown in table 9.3. By adding 16 to a color code value, a blinking character of the appropriate color appears. That's why the *foreground* value of 25 in the sample program produces light blue, blinking characters.

To stop your screen from blinking and return to normal white-on-black printing, do this:

```
Ok
COLOR 7, 0
Ok
```

The allowable range of *background* is actually from 0 to 15, but values from 8 to 15 produce the same colors selected by values from 0 to 7. The bottom line is that you have only eight choices for the background color.

The border value controls the perimeter of your screen (the region outside the normal text area). This border can be painted a solid color, but only on some CGA systems (the border parameter, if present, is ignored by most EGA and VGA systems). You can select any of 16 border colors according to the values in table 9.3. A border color changes immediately after execution of the COLOR instruction; you don't have to issue a PRINT instruction to complete the effect.

On EGA and VGA systems, you can modify the 16 available colors with the PALETTE statement. See the discussion of PALETTE in Chapter 15, "Toward Advanced Programming."

Each of the three parameters in a COLOR instruction is optional, but you must specify at least one of the parameters. Any parameter you don't specify simply retains its current value. By default, the initial parameter values correspond to the instruction COLOR 7, 0, 0 (white text on a black background with a black border).

Here are some examples of COLOR instructions:

```
10 COLOR 2, 8, 14      'Green text, gray, yellow border
10 COLOR , 1           'Change background to blue
10 COLOR HUE%, , 4     'Change text color toHue%, red border
10 COLOR 22            'Change text color to blinking brown
10 COLOR , , 9         'Change border to light blue
10 COLOR               'Illegal; no parameters are specified
10 COLOR 22, 23        'Illegal; value of (23) too large
```

One word of caution: Be wary of making your foreground and background colors the same, or your subsequent text will be invisible!

A Colorful Program

To whet your appetite for the range of possible color effects, run the following program on your color system. This program should literally "wow" you:

```
10 REM Try different text colors and attributes
20 FOR FORE% = 0 TO 31
30 FOR BACK% = 0 TO 7
40    COLOR FORE%, BACK%
50    PRINT "-Wow-"; 'Be sure to include that semicolon
60 NEXT BACK%
70 NEXT FORE%
```

Text "Colors" on Monochrome Systems

If your system has a Monochrome Display Adapter (MDA), the `COLOR` statement produces special character attributes rather than colors. The possible effects are normal text (white on black), underlining, reverse video (black on white), invisible text (black on black), high-intensity text, and blinking.

Many, but not all, of these effects can be combined. Table 9.4 shows the values of *foreground* and *background* that produce these attributes.

Table 9.4. *Character attributes on monochrome systems.*

Effect	Foreground	Background
Normal (white-on-black)	7	0
Reverse (black-on-white)	0	7
Invisible (black-on-black)	0	0
Underlining	1	0
High intensity	Add 8	No change
Blinking	Add 16	No change

Effects in the upper half of table 9.4 cannot be combined. For example, underlined reverse video is impossible. However, you can use high intensity or blinking (or both) with any of the four basic effects from the upper half of the table. Simply add the indicated amount to the value of the foreground parameter (add 8 for high intensity, 16 for blinking, or 24 for both).

The `border` parameter has no effect with MDA video cards.

Using Advanced Features of Text Screens

The remainder of this chapter describes features needed only by fairly sophisticated programs. If you are a beginner, you can skip ahead to the next chapter without any loss of continuity.

However, some of these subjects are fun to explore. Even beginners might enjoy trying some of the sample programs that perform text graphics and animation.

Determining the Character at a Specific Location

In some programs, you need to know what character is currently visible at a given screen location. This need frequently arises in interactive programs, such as games or text processors, where the user is entering information displayed on the screen.

The SCREEN function determines what character, if any, is at any given screen location and also determines the character's color attributes. (Note: Don't confuse the SCREEN function with the SCREEN statement. The SCREEN statement is discussed in Chapter 11, "Creating Graphics.")

SCREEN(*row, column*)

or

SCREEN(*row, column, optionflag*)

where *row* is the screen row from 1 to 25, *column* is the column position from 1 to 80, and *optionflag* is a numeric expression specifying which information to return.

The *optionflag* parameter is optional, and the *row* and *column* parameters are mandatory.

When you omit *optionflag*, the SCREEN function returns the ASCII value (an integer from 0 to 255) corresponding to the character at the specified screen row and column. If no character has been written to the specified location, SCREEN returns 32 (the ASCII value for a blank space). Appendix B contains a table of the ASCII codes and their corresponding characters.

The following program fragment counts the number of asterisks currently displayed on the screen; the result is stored in the variable NUM%:

```
200 NUM% = 0
210 CODE% = 42          'ASCII Code for an asterisk (*)
220 FOR ROW% = 1 TO 25
230 FOR COLUMN% = 1 TO 80
240   IF SCREEN(ROW%, COLUMN%) = CODE% THEN NUM% = NUM% + 1
250 NEXT COLUMN%
260 NEXT ROW%
```

If *optionflag* is present and evaluates to a nonzero value, SCREEN returns the attribute (color) of the referenced character rather than the ASCII value of the character itself.

The attribute is expressed as an integer number from 0 to 255. The number can be deciphered to reveal the following attributes of the character: foreground color, background color, and whether the character is blinking.

The following program shows how to use SCREEN to decipher the attribute information for a character at the location (ROW%, COLUMN%). The techniques used in this program are somewhat advanced, but we include the program for your reference.

```
300 REM Print attributes of character at (ROW%, COLUMN%)
310 ATTRIBUTE% = SCREEN(ROW%, COLUMN%, 1)
320 PRINT "Foreground color ="; ATTRIBUTE% MOD 16
330 PRINT "Background color ="; (ATTRIBUTE% AND &H70) \ 16
340 PRINT "Blinking         =";
350 BLINK% = (ATTRIBUTE% AND &H80) \ 128
360 IF BLINK% = 1 THEN PRINT " Yes" ELSE PRINT " No"
```

Switching the Text Width

To this point, the text screen has been 80 characters wide by 25 lines high. Unless you have a monochrome monitor, your computer is capable of a 40-by-25 text mode. In 40-column mode, each character is twice as wide (horizontally) as in the standard 80-by-25 mode. The wider characters create more dramatic screen displays.

To switch the text width, use the WIDTH statement.

WIDTH *numcolumns*

where *numcolumns* is the text width, either 40 or 80.

The only legal values for *numcolumns* are 40 and 80.

When the width changes, the screen clears and the cursor returns to the upper left corner.

All locating instructions adjust correctly to each text width mode. Consider, for example, a 40-column mode. LOCATE and POS refer to the horizontal location using a number from 1 to 40. PRINT still uses 14-column print zones for comma-delimited lists. There are effectively only two print zones: columns 1 through 14 and 15 through 28. The third zone would stretch to column 42—too far!

> **Other Uses of `WIDTH`**
>
> Chapter 11, "Creating Graphics," discusses the `WIDTH` statement with respect to graphics modes. The `WIDTH LPRINT` statement adjusts the printing width of your line printer. Refer to Chapter 12, "Programming Hardware Devices."

Creating a Text Viewport

You can restrict text to a rectangular slice of the screen by using the `VIEW PRINT` statement. This creates a text viewport. When a text viewport is active, you can display text and scroll only within the viewport. Note: some versions of BASIC do not support `VIEW PRINT`.

`VIEW PRINT` *toprow* TO *bottomrow*

or simply

`VIEW PRINT`

where *toprow* is an integer expression defining the top row of the viewport, and *bottomrow* is an integer expression defining the bottom row of the viewport.

The viewport extends from *toprow* to *bottomrow* across the entire width of the screen. The instruction `VIEW PRINT` (without a parameter) reinstates the entire screen as the viewport. The following program, `VIEWTEXT.BAS`, demonstrates the use of a text viewport:

```
100 REM Program: VIEWTEXT.BAS (Demonstrate text viewport)
110 REM
120 CLS
130 LOCATE  5, 1: PRINT "No scrolling above the viewport"
140 LOCATE  6, 1: PRINT STRING$(50, 205)  ' Line above viewport
150 LOCATE 16, 1: PRINT STRING$(50, 205)  ' Line below viewport
160 LOCATE 17, 1: PRINT "No scrolling below the viewport"
170 REM
180 VIEW PRINT 7 TO 15           'Set viewport from line 7 to 15
190 REM
200 FOR LINENUM% = 1 TO 100
210    PRINT "This is line number"; LINENUM%
220 NEXT LINENUM%
230 END
```

Before opening the viewport, the program draws a double line and prints messages above and below the upcoming viewport. Then the text viewport is opened. The `PRINT` instruction in line 210 causes text to scroll but only within the confines of the viewport. Figure 9.2 shows the screen after the program finishes.

Fig. 9.2. *The output of the* `VIEWTEXT.BAS` *program.*

```
No scrolling above the viewport
================================
This is line number 94
This is line number 95
This is line number 96
This is line number 97
This is line number 98
This is line number 99
This is line number 100
Ok

-
================================
No scrolling below the viewport
```

Clearing the Text Screen— *CLS* Revisited

As we saw earlier, you can wipe the screen clear of text with a `CLS` instruction. If you have a text viewport active, however, `CLS` erases only the text inside the viewport.

The `CLS` statement accepts an optional parameter that has meaning when a viewport is active. Two forms of the `CLS` statement are relevant (see table 9.5).

Table 9.5. *Using* `CLS` *with text screens.*

Instruction	Effect
CLS	Clears text only within the graphics viewport
CLS 0	Clears the entire screen

The default viewport is the entire screen. If you haven't issued a `VIEW PRINT` instruction, `CLS` and `CLS 0` both clear the entire screen. The screen clears to the background color, and the cursor returns to the upper left corner of the current viewport.

CLS also works with graphics screens. See the discussion of CLS in Chapter 11, "Creating Graphics."

Note that some versions of BASIC do not support CLS with parameters.

Creating Text Graphics

The phrase text graphics may seem like a contradiction in terms. After all, text is text and graphics is graphics, right? Well, almost.

By "text graphics," we mean special effects generated by the unusual characters found in the extended ASCII character set. To produce graphics-like effects in text mode, all you have to do is print these characters with PRINT instructions.

Appendix B contains a table of ASCII codes and characters. The ASCII character set is a treasure chest full of secrets and surprises. Besides the normal letters, numbers, and punctuation, here are some of the "characters" found in the extended ASCII set:

❏ Foreign-language letters and symbols

❏ Cursor-movement characters

❏ Math, technical, game, and music symbols

❏ Speaker-beeping codes

❏ Outlining and graphing symbols

To give you a taste, turn to Appendix B and look at the symbol with an ASCII value of 3. This is the heart symbol. To display a heart symbol, PRINT CHR$(3) does the trick. So, if you are a "chocoholic," you might try something like this:

```
Ok
PRINT "I "; CHR$(3); "  chocolate."
I ♥ chocolate
OK
```

Two-Dimensional Object Strings

The real power of text graphics comes from strings that describe two-dimensional objects. Because the ASCII character set includes cursor movement (see table 9.6), you can build complex strings that print as various shapes.

Table 9.6. *ASCII values of cursor-movement characters.*

ASCII Value	Effect
28	Cursor right
29	Cursor left
30	Cursor up
31	Cursor down

The general technique of using two-dimensional text strings is a three-step process:

1. Build a string variable using CHR$.

2. Move the cursor with LOCATE.

3. PRINT the string variable.

A fun, simple example of this method is shown in the following program, SHOWMAN.BAS, which displays three stick-figure men:

A fun, simple example of this method is shown in the following program, SHOWMAN.BAS, which displays three stick-figure men:

```
100 REM Program: SHOWMAN.BAS (Draw 2-D Text Strings)
110 REM
120 DATA 1, 29, 31, 197, 29, 31, 94:   'ASCII codes for man
130 MAN$ =""                           'Initialize MAN$
140 FOR J% = 1 TO 7
150    READ CODE%
160    MAN$ = MAN$ + CHR$(CODE%)        'Build MAN$ string
170 NEXT J%
180 REM
190 CLS
200 LOCATE  3,  9: PRINT MAN$           'Stick Figure 1
210 LOCATE 10, 50: PRINT MAN$           'Stick Figure 2
220 LOCATE 17, 25: PRINT MAN$           'Stick Figure 3
230 END
```

Figure 9.3 shows the output of SHOWMAN.BAS.

The key technique in SHOWMAN.BAS is the building of the MAN$ string. The seven data values in line 120 are the ASCII code values that make up MAN$. Codes 1, 197, and 94 correspond to the three graphic characters that embody each stick figure. The codes 29 and 31 move the cursor left and down, respectively, in position for the next graphics character.

Fig. 9.3. The output of `SHOWMAN.BAS`.

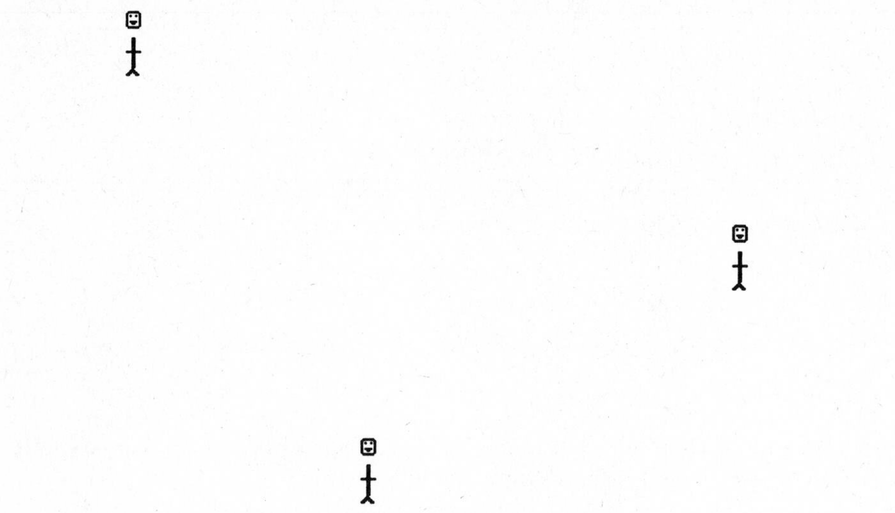

With the `MAN$` string constructed, it's easy to draw the graphics figure. Just position the cursor with `LOCATE` and use `PRINT MAN$`.

Text Animation

Even animation is possible with two-dimensional text strings. Now you're really getting fancy. Here's the basic technique:

1. Build string variables using `CHR$`.

2. Use `LOCATE` to position the cursor for drawing.

3. `PRINT` the string variable to display your shape.

4. Pause for a short time (approximately 1/10 second).

5. Erase the shape drawn in step 3.

6. Go back to step 2.

Text animation is just an extension of the ideas used to draw two-dimensional objects.

Step 5 requires the erasing of the previously drawn figure. There are many ways to do this. One method is to define an "erasing" string for each shape-drawing string. The erasing string contains a blank space, CHR"(∃근), everywhere the drawing string contains a printable character. Cursor-movement "characters" are retained in the erasing string at the same positions they occur in the drawing string.

A shape can be erased by PRINTing the erasing string at the same cursor position used to draw the original shape. Remember to use LOCATE if necessary to reposition the cursor at the same screen position where the original shape was drawn.

Step 4 requires a pause. The upcoming sample program, JUMPMAN.BAS, uses the TIMER function inside a WHILE...WEND loop to accomplish a delay. See Chapter 12, "Programming Hardware Devices," for more on the TIMER function.

To get the flavor of text animation, try the JUMPMAN.BAS program. The same stick figure used in SHOWMAN.BAS now shows off by jumping up and down on your screen.

The string variable MAN\$ displays the stick figure, and the corresponding variable WIPEOUT\$ erases the man.

```
100 REM Program: JUMPMAN.BAS (Text Animation of Jumping Man)
110 '
120 DATA 1, 29, 31, 197, 29, 31, 94:    'ASCII codes for man
130 MAN$ =""                            'Initialize MAN$
140 FOR J% = 1 TO 7
150    READ CODE%
160    MAN$ = MAN$ + CHR"(CODE%)        'Build MAN$ string
170 NEXT J%
180 '
190 DATA 32, 29, 31, 32, 29, 31, 32:    'ASCII codes to erase man
200 WIPEOUT$ = ""                       'Initialize WIPEOUT$
210 FOR J% = 1 TO 7
220    READ CODE%
230    WIPEOUT$ = WIPEOUT$ + CHR$(CODE%) 'Build WIPEOUT$ string
240 NEXT J%
250 '
260 CLS
270 FOR ROW% = 20 TO 1 STEP -1          'Jump up loop
280    LOCATE ROW%, 40: PRINT MAN$
290    NOW = TIMER
300       WHILE TIMER < NOW + .1         'WHILE-WEND delays
310       WEND                           'for 1/10 second
320    LOCATE ROW%, 40: PRINT WIPEOUT$
330 NEXT ROW%
340 '
```

Listing continues

Listing continued

```
350 FOR ROW% = 2 TO 20              'Jump down loop
360    LOCATE ROW%, 40: PRINT MAN$
370    NOW = TIMER
380       WHILE TIMER < NOW + .1     'WHILE-WEND delays
390       WEND                       'for 1/10 second
400    LOCATE ROW%, 40: PRINT WIPEOUT$
410 NEXT ROW%
420 END
```

You can extend this technique to create more sophisticated animation. One idea is to have your figure drawn in several different stances or postures. For example, a man waving might raise and lower his hand as he "walks." This requires two or more string variables, which are alternated as the man moves. (Of course, you will need a corresponding erasing variable for each such string variable.)

Summary

This chapter examined ways to display text information on the video screen. The primary tool was the PRINT statement. We saw how PRINT displays both numbers and text, and how to use PRINT's automatic tabbing. When you needed further control over output appearance, the PRINT USING statement provided customized formatting.

The location of the cursor indicates the current printing position. You saw how to move the cursor with LOCATE and also how to determine the current cursor location.

Finally, the chapter got fancy by exploring some advanced but fun techniques. You displayed text in color, and opened text viewports. Text graphics were introduced by creating, displaying, and even animating text strings and figures.

10

Using Disk Files

```
OPEN, CLOSE, WRITE #, INPUT #, PRINT #, PRINT # USING,
INPUT$, LINE INPUT$, EOF, LOF, LOC, PUT, GET, FIELD,
LSET, RSET, MKI$, MKS$, MKD$, CVI, CVS, CVD, MKDIR,
RMDIR, CHDIR, FILES, KILL, NAME
```

As programmers, you face a recurring challenge: getting data into your programs. Most programs manipulate data in one way or another. After all, you are manipulating data when you simply add two numbers or when you display text on the screen. Think for a moment about the ways you get data into your programs.

You are already familiar with the following two fundamental techniques for inputting data in your programs:

❑ *Store the data directly in the program*. This is the simplest method. An assignment instruction such as

```
300 CITY$ = "Phoenix"
```

stores the data ("Phoenix" in this case) as part of the program itself. Also, DATA and READ instructions (see Chapter 8, "Managing Large Amounts of Data"), store data directly in the program.

261

❑ *Ask the user for the data.* When the person running the program must supply data, your program can prompt him or her to type in the data from the keyboard. Your primary tool for this method is the `INPUT` statement (introduced in Chapter 3, "A Hands-On Introduction to Programming," and discussed in-depth in Chapter 12, "Programming Hardware Devices.")

These methods work fine, but they are appropriate only when the amount of data is relatively small. What if your data requirements become more demanding? Suppose that you want to write a program which manages a large database, such as your baseball-card collection or the inventory of a hardware store. It is just not feasible to store all the necessary data inside the program or to ask the user to supply the data when the program runs. Furthermore, the data changes with time and needs periodic updating.

The common solution to these problems is data files on disk. The data file can be on a floppy disk or, if your machine is so equipped, on a hard disk. After a data file exists, your program can read the data directly from the file, process the data, and then write a new (or updated) data file directly to the disk.

By storing data on disk files, independently from the programs, you derive many benefits, including the following:

❑ Data files can be maintained and updated.

❑ Large databases can be accessed conveniently.

❑ Programs are kept intact and relatively small.

❑ Files can be shared by several programs.

❑ Data files created from external sources (such as a word processor or spreadsheet) can be read.

BASIC supports two kinds of data files: *sequential* and *random-access*. In this chapter, we discuss how to use each file type and the advantages and disadvantages of each.

Of course, if you work with disk files, you become immediately involved with disk directories. This is normally the domain of DOS, but BASIC furnishes a number of file-maintenance tools.

Here are the major topics covered in this chapter:

❑ Maintaining disk directories from BASIC.

❑ Using sequential files.

❑ Using random-access files.

Files and Directories in DOS: a Brief Tutorial

As a user of BASIC, you are unavoidably involved with PC DOS or MS-DOS. DOS places certain demands on what you can and cannot do with disk files. Substantial discussion of DOS is beyond the scope of this book. However, in the interest of establishing some common ground and terminology, a brief tutorial on DOS file maintenance is included here. For more details, consult your DOS documentation or one of the many excellent books on PC DOS, such as *Using PC DOS*, published by Que Corporation.

Your computer has one or more disk *drives*. Each drive is designated with a letter followed by a colon. Floppy disk drives (into which you insert floppy diskettes) usually are designated A: and B:; fixed disk drives usually are designated C: and D:. For the purposes of this discussion, the term *drive* refers not only to the hardware drive but also to the medium currently in the drive. Thus, "storing a file on the A: drive" means storing a file on the diskette in drive A:.

Each drive is organized in a *directory* structure. The base directory is called the *root*. The root may spawn one or more *subdirectories*, each of which may also have one or more subdirectories, and so on. (The terms *directory* and *subdirectory* are used interchangeably in practice.)

A *file* is a collection of bytes given a name and stored in a directory. Two different directories may contain files with the same name. Such files, however, are independent and can contain completely different data.

To uniquely identify a file, you must specify not only the name of the file but also the *path* to the file. The path consists of the drive and the chain of directories from the root to the directory containing the file.

Directory names are one to eight characters long. In a path, the backslash character (\) separates directory names and also indicates the root directory at the front of the chain.

File names also have one to eight characters but optionally can include an extension of one to three characters. If the extension is included, it is separated with a period. Thus MYPROG, MYPROG.BAS, M.ME, and ABC123. all are valid file names. In a file or directory name, upper- and lowercase letters are not differentiated; MyProg.Bas and MYPROG.BAS are the same file.

A *filespec* is the complete specification of a file. As we mentioned, this includes the path to the file as well as the name of the file. Here are some examples:

```
A:\BASIC\MYPROG.BAS

B:\MYPROG.BAS

C:\LISTINGS\HOMES\3BEDRM\SALES.DTA
```

In each case, the file name appears after the last backslash. The path name is the portion up to but not including the file name. The path name consists of the drive designation and the directory chain.

At all times, DOS maintains a default drive and a default path on each drive. Filespecs can be given relative to these defaults. For example, A:BASEBALL\CARDS.DTA refers to a file named CARDS.DTA that resides on the A: drive in the subdirectory BASEBALL.

The key point is that BASEBALL is a subdirectory of the current (or default) directory on the A: drive. Note that no backslash appears immediately after the drive designator; this indicates a relative path. The simple filespec ROSTER.DTA means that the file resides in the default directory of the default drive.

When you first turn on your computer, the default directory on each drive is simply the root directory.

File and Directory Maintenance in BASIC

BASIC has six statements that perform DOS-like commands (see table 10.1). Use these statements to do file and directory manipulation from within your programs or in BASIC's direct mode.

Table 10.1. *BASIC's DOS-like statements.*

BASIC Statement	Equivalent DOS command	DOS Abbreviation	Effect
MKDIR	MKDIR	MD	Creates a directory
RMDIR	RMDIR	RD	Removes (deletes) a directory
CHDIR	CHDIR	CD	Changes current directory
FILES	DIR		Lists files in a directory
KILL	ERASE	DEL	Deletes a file
NAME	RENAME	REN	Renames a file

The syntax of these six statements is straightforward:

MKDIR *pathname*

RMDIR *pathname*

CHDIR *pathname*

FILES *filespec*

KILL *filespec*

NAME *oldfilespec* AS *newfilespec*

where *pathname* is a string expression specifying a path; *filespec*, *oldfilespec*, and *newfilespec* are string expressions that specify a file. For FILES, the *filespec* parameter is optional; for the other statements, the parameters are mandatory.

Using *MKDIR*, *RMDIR*, and *CHDIR*

In a MKDIR, RMDIR, or CHDIR instruction, the *pathname* parameter can optionally include a drive designator. If you omit the drive in *pathname*, BASIC assumes the default drive (from where you invoked GW-BASIC or BASICA). Standard DOS path-naming conventions apply.

Note that *pathname* must be a string—either a literal (in double quotation marks) or a string variable. For example, to create a directory called \CLIENTS on your B: drive, you could use

```
400 MKDIR "B:\CLIENTS"    'Note the quotation marks
```

or

```
400 NEWDIR$ = "B:\CLIENTS"
410 MKDIR NEWDIR$    'The path is stored in a string variable
```

but not

```
400 MKDIR B:\CLIENTS       'The path is not a string
```

pathname has a limit of 63 characters. If *pathname* is the null string, or if *pathname* does not designate a valid directory, a run-time error occurs (Path not found or Bad file name).

The statements MKDIR, RMDIR, and CHDIR operate just like their DOS counterparts. Refer to your DOS documentation for additional information. Note that if you change the directory (with CHDIR) on the drive from which you invoked BASIC, you will be in that default directory upon termination of your program.

Using *FILES*, *KILL*, and *NAME*

In a FILES, KILL, or NAME instruction, the *filespec* parameter can optionally include a drive and path specification. If omitted, the default (or current) path is selected. Again, standard DOS naming conventions apply. There is a 63-character limit on a *filespec*. Except with the NAME instruction, wild-card characters (* and ?) are permitted in a *filespec*. If you are not familiar with wild-card characters, see your DOS documentation for details.

Using the *FILES* Statement

FILES displays on-screen a list of files and subdirectories in a disk drive. The effect is similar to the DOS command DIR/W. Multiple files are shown on one line. Subdirectories are indicated with the notation <DIR>. The listing terminates with the number of free bytes on the drive referenced by the *filespec* parameter. If you omit the *filespec* parameter, all the files in the current directory are listed.

Here are some examples of FILES instructions:

```
250 FILES "B:\HOMES\*.*" 'Lists all files in subdirectory

250 FILES "VERSION?.TXT" 'Lists all 8-character files whose
                          'names start with "VERSION" and
                          'have a "TXT" extension

250 FILES                 'Lists all files on current directory

250 FILES "A:"            'Lists all files in the current
                          'directory of drive A:

250 FILES "A:\"           'Lists all files in root directory of
                          'A: drive
```

Using the *KILL* Statement

KILL deletes only files, not directories. Use a RMDIR instruction to delete directories.

Be careful when you use wild-card characters in a *filespec*. You may accidentally erase more than you bargained for. If you try to KILL a file that is open, a File not found error occurs. (Opening and closing files is discussed in this chapter.)

Using the *NAME* Statement

NAME renames a file. The *oldfilespec* parameter identifies the existing file; *newfilespec* is the new name for the file. When *oldfilespec* and *newfilespec* specify the same path, NAME simply renames the file on the same drive. After the NAME instruction, the file exists in the same location on the disk, but with a new name. The *oldfilespec* and *newfilespec* parameters can specify different paths, but each path must be on the same physical drive. That is, you cannot rename a file from your A: drive onto your B: drive.

Manipulating Directories in Direct Mode

Although you certainly can use MKDIR, RMDIR, CHDIR, FILES, KILL, and NAME inside your programs, these instructions are also quite useful directly from the Ok prompt.

For example, try this. Place a formatted diskette containing some files into your B: drive. (If your machine does not have a B: drive, you can use the A: drive or the C: drive if your machine has a hard disk. Simply replace the letter B: in the following instructions with A: or C: as appropriate.) Now from BASIC's Ok prompt, type the following command.

```
FILES "B:\"
```

BASIC responds by displaying a listing of the files (and subdirectories) on the root directory of your diskette.

For example, our test diskette contained two files: the BASIC program TEST.BAS and another file named OURSTUFF.DAT. Here's our output.

```
Ok
FILES "B:\"
B:\
TEST    .BAS     OURSTUFF.DAT
 360448 Bytes free

Ok
```

The notation 360448 Bytes free indicates the amount of unused disk space on the specified drive. This amount and the names of the actual files will vary on your test diskette.

Now create a subdirectory named QUE. You use MKDIR and then FILES to verify the directory's creation:

```
Ok
MKDIR "B:\QUE"
Ok
FILES "B:\"
B:\
TEST    .BAS       OURSTUFF.DAT       QUE          <DIR>
 359424 Bytes free

Ok
```

BASIC displays the annotation <DIR> to indicate that QUE is a subdirectory rather than a file name. The number of free bytes is less than before because some disk space was necessary to store the new subdirectory.

Last, remove the new subdirectory with RMDIR and return the diskette back to its original configuration.

```
Ok
RMDIR "B:\QUE"
Ok
FILES "B:\"
TEST    .BAS       OURSTUFF.DAT
 360448 Bytes free

Ok
```

Manipulating Data Files — General Techniques

Now that you have established a background of DOS file and directory maintenance, refocus your attention to data files on disk. As we mentioned, BASIC supports two types of data files.

Sequential files store data as ASCII text. Information is written to the file in much the same way as information is displayed on the video screen.

Random-access files store data in special BASIC internal formats. Such files require a rigid file structure.

Which file type is best? Well, as you might expect, each type is better in certain situations. In general, sequential files are easy to program and understand, but reading or writing the files is relatively slow. Random-access files require more programming complexity, but the I/O operations are relatively fast. This chapter has much more to say about the trade-offs.

Whether a program uses sequential or random-access files, some general techniques are common to both file types. To communicate with a disk file, a program must follow these essential steps:

1. Open the data file. With the OPEN statement, you inform BASIC of the file name, file type, and how the program expects to use the file.

2. Read data from and/or write data to the file. BASIC provides a variety of statements to perform I/O operations.

3. Close the data file. With the CLOSE statement, your program terminates I/O operations on the data file.

Using the *OPEN* Statement

Before using any disk file, you must establish a communication link. The OPEN instruction serves several purposes:

❏ It declares the name and path of the data file.

❏ It establishes the file type and the I/O mode.

❏ It opens a communications channel between the program and the file.

❏ It associates an integer number with the data file.

Throughout this chapter, we examine various forms of the OPEN instruction while we discuss each file type.

Using the *CLOSE* Statement

After your program concludes I/O activity on a data file, use the CLOSE instruction to cancel the communications link. CLOSE terminates the association between the data file on disk and the corresponding file number. We explore the CLOSE statement in detail throughout this chapter.

Using Files for Database Maintenance

The most common application for sequential files and random-access files is database maintenance. A *database* is simply a collection of related information. For our purposes, each database is stored on a disk file.

A database consists of a series of *records*. Each record is divided into one or more *fields*. For example, in a personnel list, each employee becomes a record in the file. The fields for each employee might be his or her name, department, salary, and service date.

Or consider a database of your stock investments. Each stock you own is a record. The fields might be the name of the stock, date of purchase, purchase price, and the current value.

A Coin Collection—a Sample Database

To provide a common thread for the rest of this chapter, we need a sample database. Let's use a coin collection. Suppose that, as a budding numismatist, you decide to maintain a list of your coin assets in a database file.

Each coin is a record. For every coin, you want to maintain four items of information:

❑ The year the coin was minted.

❑ The category of coin (penny, dime, quarter, and so on).

❑ The value of the coin.

❑ Any additional pertinent information about the coin.

Let's assume that your coin collection consists of three coins. (OK, you aren't Donald Trump yet, but you have to start somewhere!)

Your database file will have three records, one record for each coin. The three records in this database might be organized as in table 10.2.

Table 10.2. *A coin-collection database.*

Year	Category	Value	Comments
1910	Lincoln penny	$ 70.00	S mint mark, uncirculated
1916	Mercury dime	$ 47.25	
1935	Silver dollar	$200.00	Bought at auction for $75

As you examine sequential and random-access files, you will write programs that manipulate this database.

Sequential Files

Sequential files are written as ASCII text. This gives the files a degree of portability; many word-processing programs and other applications programs can read and write ASCII files. Also, you can use the TYPE command from DOS to display a sequential file on your screen.

Within a record, fields are separated by commas. Record boundaries are maintained automatically. BASIC provides several statements to read and write sequential files conveniently. As such, programming is relatively easy.

However, there are two main drawbacks to sequential files.

❏ Records must be read sequentially. If you want information in, say, the 50th record, you must read through the initial 49 records first. This process is relatively slow.

❏ You cannot read and write a sequential file simultaneously. You must open the file for either reading or writing and close the file before reopening it in the other mode.

You might think of a sequential file as something like a cassette music tape (see fig. 10.1). Individual songs on the tape are like records on the file. To listen to a song in the middle of the tape, you must first play through the previous songs. To read a record in the middle of the file, you must first read the previous records.

Fig. 10.1. *A sequential file.*

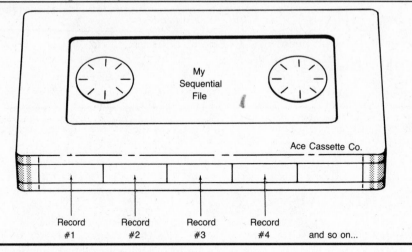

```
                        My
                     Sequential
                        File


                                           Ace Cassette Co.
```

Record   Record   Record   Record
  #1   #2   #3   #4   and so on...

Creating a Sequential File

When you create a sequential file, your program must follow these steps:

1. OPEN the file as a sequential file for writing.

2. Prepare your data for writing to the file.

3. Use the WRITE# instruction to write data to the file.

4. CLOSE the file.

Let's examine each step and then try a sample program.

Opening the File

The open statement has many forms. Here is the syntax you use when you create a new sequential file:

OPEN *filespec* FOR OUTPUT AS *#filenum*

where *filespec* is a string expression that specifies the name (and optionally the path) of the new sequential data file, and *filenum* is an integer expression from 1 to 255 that associates a numeric value with the opened file.

For example, the following instruction opens a file named `MYDATA.QUE` (in the root directory of the B: drive) as a sequential file that you are creating. A file number of 35 is assigned to this file.

```
600 OPEN "B:\MYDATA.QUE" FOR OUTPUT AS #35
```

The pound character (#) is optional before the *filenum* parameter. That is, the previous instruction could also have been written as follows:

```
600 OPEN "B:\MYDATA.QUE" FOR OUTPUT AS 35 "No # before"35
```

The phrase `"FOR OUTPUT"` tells BASIC that this file is a sequential file to which you are going to write output. (As you will see later, `OPEN` accepts other phrases with other meanings.)

When you open a file for `OUTPUT`, the file does not need to exist previously. In fact, the file should *not* previously exist. Why? Because if the file already exists, BASIC erases the old file contents completely. Don't open an existing file `FOR OUTPUT` unless you intend to create a brand-new file. Make sure that your `OPEN` instruction specifies the path and file correctly. You don't want to lose data inadvertently by specifying the wrong file. Of course, it is a good idea to have a backup version of your important files just for such emergencies.

The file number (35 in the current example) provides a convenient way to refer to the file in later instructions. As you will see, when you want to write data to the file, you simply say "write on file 35" instead of writing the full-blown file name. The `OPEN` instruction tells BASIC exactly what you mean by file number 35.

Preparing the Data

When you first create a database file, you must somehow get the data into your program. The trick here is to decide the best way to enter the data. You usually will use one or a combination of the following techniques:

❏ Enter data explicitly in `DATA` instructions, and use `READ` instructions.
❏ Prompt the user for data with `INPUT` instructions. (The sample program that follows uses this technique.)
❏ Read data from other data files or devices.
❏ Compute data values using various BASIC functions.

Writing the Data

When each record is ready to write, use the `WRITE#` statement to send the record to the disk file. `WRITE#` works with both strings and numbers.

WRITE#*filenum, expressionlist*

where *filenum* is the file number, and *expressionlist* is a list of expressions separated by commas.

Each WRITE# instruction writes one record to the file. Each expression in *expressionlist* is the data for one field of the record.

WRITE# does some special formatting, which we examine shortly in the sample program. WRITE# sends data to a file in the same form that WRITE sends output to the video screen. See the discussion of WRITE in Chapter 9, "Writing Text on the Video Screen," for more details.

Often, you place the WRITE# instruction inside a loop. This loop processes all the records in the data file.

Closing the File

After all the records are written to the file, close the file with a CLOSE instruction.

CLOSE #*filenum*

where *filenum* is an integer expression that specifies the file to close. As with OPEN instructions, the pound character (#) is optional.

For example, use the following instruction to close file number 35 (which was previously opened for output):

```
900 CLOSE #35
```

CLOSE terminates the association of the file number with the data file. As a result, the file number becomes available for a subsequent OPEN instruction. CLOSE also flushes the file buffer, which simply means that all information written to the file is properly processed.

The Sample Program *SFCREATE.BAS*

Now let's put these BASIC statements into action. Remember the coin collection? Here is a program called SFCREATE.BAS, which creates a new sequential data file called MYCOINS.SEQ. The user responds to various prompts to supply the data.

```
100 REM Program: SFCREATE.BAS (Create a sequential file)
110 REM
120 PRINT "Creating Sequential Data File: B:MYCOINS.SEQ"
130 PRINT
140 OPEN "B:MYCOINS.SEQ" FOR OUTPUT AS #1
150 REM
160 REM ---- Begin Input Loop at Line 200 ----
170 REM
200     INPUT "Year (or  <Enter> when all done)"; YEAR%
210     IF YEAR% = 0 THEN 300       'End input loop
220     INPUT "Category of Coin"; CATEGORY$
230     INPUT "Value"; VALUE
240     LINE INPUT "Comments (if any)? "; COMMENT$
250     WRITE #1, YEAR%, CATEGORY$, VALUE, COMMENT$
260     PRINT
270     GOTO 200                    'Get data for next coin
300 CLOSE #1
310 PRINT "All done - B:MYCOINS.SEQ is created"
320 END
```

The OPEN instruction in line 140 declares that the file will be written on drive B:. Because no more detailed path is specified, BASIC assumes that the file should appear in the current directory on drive B:. This directory is the root directory (unless you changed the default directory before you started BASIC). You can (and often do) specify in the OPEN instruction an explicit directory path such as B:\DATA\MYCOINS.SEQ or B:\MYCOINS.SEQ (root directory). The OPEN instruction assigns the file number 1 to the newly opened file.

Each data record corresponds to one coin in the collection. Each record contains four fields: the year the coin was minted, the category of the coin, the value of the coin, and any pertinent comments about the coin. Two of the fields (Year and Value) are numeric, and two fields (Category and Comment) are string.

The year is a whole number, such as 1976, suitable for an integer variable: YEAR%. The value is expressed in dollars and cents, such as 47.25, suitable for a single-precision variable: VALUE. The category and comment are stored in the string variables CATEGORY$ and COMMENT$, respectively.

The loop in lines 200 through 270 performs the main work of the program. For each coin, an INPUT or LINE INPUT instruction prompts you for each of the four pieces of information. The value must be input as a number in dollars. However, the dollar sign is not part of the input. Thus, if the value of the coin is $103.50, you must type 103.50, but not $103.50.

The Comment field requires a `LINE INPUT` prompt because commas might be used as part of the input string. A regular `INPUT` instruction would treat such commas as input delimiters.

For each coin, the program prompts you for the necessary information and stores the values in the variables `YEAR%`, `CATEGORY$`, `VALUE`, and `COMMENT$` Then the `WRITE #1` instruction in line 250 writes the record to the data file. Note that all four data fields are written with a single `WRITE#` instruction. The `#1` is the same file number you assigned to the file in the `OPEN` instruction.

When all the data is entered, you simply press the Enter key in response to the `Year` prompt. This step assigns a value of 0 to the variable `YEAR%`. Note how the `IF` instruction in line 210 tests for this condition and terminates the loop when `YEAR%` has the value 0.

Here is a sample run of `SFCREATE.BAS`. Boldface type indicates what you type.

```
RUN
Creating Sequential Data File: B:MYCOINS.SEQ

Year (or  <Enter> when all done)? 1910
Category of Coin? Lincoln Penny
Value? 70
Comments (if any)? S mint mark, uncirculated

Year (or  <Enter> when all done)? 1916
Category of Coin? Mercury Dime
Value? 47.25
Comments (if any)?

Year (or  <Enter> when all done)? 1935
Category of Coin? Silver Dollar
Value? 200
Comments (if any)? Bought at auction for $75

Year (or  <Enter> when all done)?
All done - B:MYCOINS.SEQ is created
Ok
```

Examining a Sequential Data File

You have created the sequential data file `MYCOINS.SEQ`. What does the file look like? Let's find out.

Examining the file is easy. Because sequential files are standard ASCII text files, you can use the `TYPE` command in DOS to view the file contents. Or you can view and modify the file with most word processors and text editors.

Try the DOS TYPE command. You must leave BASIC. To do so, type **SYSTEM** at BASIC's Ok prompt. You should now get your normal DOS prompt. Issue the DOS command **TYPE B:MYCOINS.SEQ**. You should see the following:

```
1910,"Lincoln Penny",70,"S mint mark, uncirculated"
1916,"Mercury Dime",47.25,""
1935,"Silver Dollar",200,"Bought at auction for $75"
```

The three records (lines) of this file were created with BASIC's WRITE# statement. Note how WRITE# formats the output. Within a record, WRITE# places a comma between adjacent fields.

String values are enclosed in double quotation marks. This avoids ambiguity if a string value contains an embedded comma. A null string is just two consecutive quotes—for example, the Comment field (last field) of the second record. Numbers do not contain any leading or trailing blanks. This saves disk space by minimizing the file size.

As you will soon see, you can read sequential files with INPUT# instructions. WRITE# creates records in the exact form that INPUT# expects.

Appending a Sequential File

Suppose that you acquire some new coins. To accommodate your growing collection, you want to write a program that adds new records to the end of your existing sequential file MYCOINS.SEQ. The process of adding new records is called *appending* the file.

Appending sequential files is easy with BASIC. You open the file in a special mode called APPEND. In your OPEN instruction, simply use the phrase FOR APPEND rather than FOR OUTPUT. For example, line 140 of SFCREATE.BAS would now look like

```
140 OPEN "B:MYCOINS.SEQ" FOR APPEND AS #1
```

Here are the four steps necessary to append records to an existing sequential data file:

1. OPEN the file FOR APPEND.

2. Prepare your data for writing to the file.

3. Use the WRITE# instruction to write additional data records to the file.

4. CLOSE the file.

Only the first step differs from the process of creating a new file. Opening a file for APPEND readies a previously existing file to receive additional records.

If the OPEN instruction specifies a nonexistent file, the file is created just as though it was OPENed for OUTPUT.

Reading a Sequential File

You have seen how to create a database file and then how to write or append records to the file. Now you learn how to read information from a file that already exists on disk.

Obviously, a database file is not very useful unless the information can be read and processed. You may need the data for any number of reasons. For a mailing-list file, you might want to print mailing labels. Perhaps you need to read a file containing weekly sales figures to identify peak sales periods. For the coin collection, you might want to write a program to calculate the total value of all the coins.

Reading information from a sequential file involves the following steps:

1. OPEN the file FOR INPUT.

2. Use the INPUT# instruction to read data into variables.

3. Process the data.

4. CLOSE the file.

The first step introduces the third way to open a sequential data file: FOR INPUT. (Remember, you already learned how to open a file FOR OUTPUT and FOR APPEND.) By opening a file for input, you tell BASIC that you intend to *read from* the file rather than *write to* the file. When you open a file FOR INPUT, you can only read records from the file. You cannot write any records to the file. To open the file for input, simply use the phrase FOR INPUT in your OPEN instruction. For example, the following instruction opens the MYCOINS.SEQ sequential database file for input and specifies 1 to be the file number:

```
200 OPEN "B:MYCOINS.SEQ" FOR INPUT AS #1
```

Of course, when you open a file for input, that file must already exist. If BASIC cannot find your specified file, you get a File not found error.

The *INPUT#* Statement

After you open a file for input, use an INPUT# instruction to read from the file. INPUT# and WRITE# are complementary statements. Whereas WRITE# writes a data record to a file opened for output, INPUT# reads a data record from a file opened for input.

INPUT# is designed for reading sequential files created with WRITE#. An INPUT# reverses the process of a WRITE# instruction.

As you have seen, a WRITE# instruction contains a variable list whose values are written to a record in the sequential file. An INPUT# instruction also contains a variable list. INPUT# reads a data record from a sequential file and stores the data values into the variables in the variable list.

INPUT #*filenum*, *variablelist*

where *filenum* is the file number, and *variablelist* is a list of variables separated by commas.

To use INPUT#, you must know the number of fields in each record and the type of data in each field. The variables in *variablelist* should match the file data. You guarantee correct matching if the variable list in the INPUT# instruction is exactly the same as the variable list used in the WRITE# instruction that created the file record.

With INPUT#, you can read numeric data into a string variable, but you cannot read string data into a numeric variable. Of course, if you read numeric data into a string variable, you can subsequently process the data only in string form.

Even if you need only some of the information in a record, you should read all the fields of the record to make sure that BASIC keeps your place in the file correctly.

Usually, variablelist consists of the same variable names used in the complementary WRITE# instruction that created the file. Such consistency ensures that the data file is read successfully.

The Sample Program *DOVALUE.BAS*

Now let's open a data file FOR INPUT and see INPUT# in action.

What is the total value of your coin collection? You had three coins: a penny worth $70, a dime worth $47.25, and a silver dollar worth $200. The total value should be $317.25.

Let's write a program to confirm this total. The following program, called DOVALUE.BAS, opens MYCOINS.SEQ for input, reads the data with INPUT#, and calculates the total value of all the coins in the collection:

```
100 REM Program: DOVALUE.BAS (Find Total Value of Coins)
110 REM
```

Listing continues

```
120 OPEN "B:MYCOINS.SEQ" FOR INPUT AS #1
130 REM
140 TOTAL = 0!
150 WHILE NOT EOF(1)
160    INPUT #1, YEAR%, CATEGORY$, VALUE, COMMENT$
170    TOTAL = TOTAL + VALUE
180 WEND
190 REM
200 CLOSE #1
210 PRINT USING "Total Value is $$####.##"; TOTAL
220 END
```

Running this program produces the following output:

```
Total value is   $317.25
```

Your total is verified!

Note that the INPUT# instruction in line 160 reads all four fields of each record (year, category, value, comment) even though only VALUE is actually used in the calculations. This follows the practice of making the variable list of your INPUT# instruction duplicate the variable list of the WRITE# instruction that created the file. By matching the variable lists exactly, you make sure that BASIC retains the correct place in the file as you read each record.

Using the *EOF* Function

"Wait a minute," you might be saying. What is that EOF in line 150? How does the WHILE..WEND loop in lines 150 through 180 work?

EOF (*end of file*) is a BASIC function that tests whether the end of a sequential file has been reached.

EOF (*filenum*)

where *filenum* is the file number.

EOF returns a logical value: true (-1) if the end of file has been reached, or false (0) otherwise. This means that EOF can be used with IF and WHILE instructions. By using EOF, you don't have to know beforehand how many records are in your data file.

In the present case, you know that there are three records in the data file, so you could write the loop in lines 150 through 180 as follows:

```
150 FOR J% = 1 TO 3
160    INPUT #1, YEAR%, CATEGORY$, VALUE, COMMENT$
170    TOTAL = TOTAL + VALUE
180 NEXT J%
```

This method would work just fine. But suppose that you don't know before-hand how many records are in the data file. Then you wouldn't know what loop values to use in the FOR instruction.

You need some way to read all the records in a file and know when you reach the end. EOF provides this capability.

Look again at line 150 from the DOVALUE.BAS program:

```
150 WHILE NOT EOF(1)
```

The NOT ensures that you execute the loop appropriately. The EOF function returns a false value if the end of the file has *not* been reached. As a result, NOT EOF(1) is true when you *haven't* yet reached the end of file number 1. Line 150, therefore, tells BASIC to do the body of the loop if the end of the file has *not* yet been reached.

When all the records in the file have been read, the end of the file is reached. Now, EOF returns true, and the value of NOT EOF(1) becomes false. Line 150, therefore, terminates the loop, and execution continues after line 180.

Be sure that you test for EOF before you attempt to read past the end of the file. A run-time error occurs (Input past end of file) if you try to execute an INPUT# instruction when the last record has already been read.

Modifying a Sequential Data File

Suppose that you want to update some information in your data file. Let's say that some information in a database changes and you want to modify some of the records.

Updating presents a complication because you cannot open a sequential file for reading and writing at the same time. Furthermore, the OUTPUT and APPEND modes permit only adding records, not editing existing records.

There are three basic solutions to this problem:

❑ OPEN two data files simultaneously—the original file FOR INPUT and a new file FOR OUTPUT. Read each record from the old file into variables. Update the values of these variables as necessary. Then rewrite the updated record to the new file.

❏ OPEN the original file FOR INPUT. Read all the records into arrays. CLOSE the file. Update the data in the arrays as necessary. OPEN the file again, this time FOR OUTPUT. Write all the data back to the file.

❏ Use a word processor or text editor to modify the data file.

Back to the coin collection. As time passes, the values of the coins change (upward, you hope). Let's say that you want to modify MYCOINS.SEQ to update the value field of each record. The following sections show how to do this using each of the three techniques.

Opening Two Files Simultaneously

The following program uses the first technique:

```
100 REM Program: UPDATE1.BAS
105 REM (Update Coin Values into a Second File)
110 REM
120 PRINT "Update Coin Values to new file B:MYCOIN2.SEQ"
130 OPEN "B:MYCOINS.SEQ" FOR INPUT AS #1
140 OPEN "B:MYCOIN2.SEQ" FOR OUTPUT AS #2
150 REM
200 WHILE NOT EOF(1)
210    PRINT
220    INPUT #1, YEAR%, CATEGORY$, VALUE, COMMENT$
230    PRINT "    Year:"; YEAR%
240    PRINT "Category: "; CATEGORY$
250    PRINT "Comments: "; COMMENT$
260    PRINT USING "   Value:#####.##"; VALUE
270    INPUT "New Value (Hit  Enter if unchanged)"; NEWVALUE
280    IF NEWVALUE <> 0 THEN VALUE = NEWVALUE
290    WRITE #2, YEAR%, CATEGORY$, VALUE, COMMENT$
300 WEND
310 REM
320 CLOSE #1
330 CLOSE #2
340 PRINT
350 PRINT "All Done - B:MYCOIN2.SEQ created"
360 END
```

Line 130 opens MYCOINS.SEQ in preparation for reading from the file. Line 140 opens a new file MYCOIN2.SEQ that this program creates.

The main work of the program takes place in the loop from line 200 through 300. Line 220 reads the next record from MYCOINS.SEQ. Lines 230 through 260 display the values of the four fields on-screen. Then line 270 prompts you to type in the new value for the coin. (If the value remains unchanged, you can just press Enter.) If you type in a new value, line 280 updates the variable VALUE accordingly. Finally, line 290 writes the updated record to the new sequential file MYCOIN2.SEQ.

Notice that by opening two files and writing only to the new file, the original data file remains intact. This provides a measure of redundancy and safety. You always have the old data file if you make a mistake or suffer one of those "always at the worst time" power failures.

Opening Multiple Files

You can have several files open at the same time. Of course, each file must have a unique file number.

The maximum number of files you can open simultaneously depends on your hardware configuration and version of DOS. With DOS 2.0 and higher, you can use the FILES command in your *CONFIG.SYS* file to change the default maximum. Refer to your DOS documentation for more details.

Using Arrays

As shown in the following program, another way to update your data file is by using arrays:

```
100 REM Program: UPDATE2.BAS (Update Values Using Arrays)
110 REM
120 PRINT "Update Coin Values Using Arrays"
130 DIM YEAR%(100),CATEGORY$ (100),VALUE(100),COMMENT$(100)
140 OPEN "B:MYCOINS.SEQ" FOR INPUT AS #1
150 REM
200 COUNT% = 0
210 WHILE NOT EOF(1)
220     COUNT% = COUNT% + 1
230     PRINT
240     INPUT #1, YEAR%(COUNT%), CATEGORY$(COUNT%),
                VALUE(COUNT%), COMMENT$(COUNT%)'This is One line
250     PRINT "   Year:"; YEAR%(COUNT%)
260     PRINT "Category: "; CATEGORY$(COUNT%)
270     PRINT "Comments: "; COMMENT$(COUNT%)
280     PRINT USING "  Value:#####.##"; VALUE(COUNT%)
290     INPUT "New Value (Hit  Enter if unchanged)"; NEWVALUE
```

Listing continues

```
300    IF NEWVALUE <> 0 THEN VALUE(COUNT%) = NEWVALUE
310 WEND
320 CLOSE #1
330 REM
340 OPEN "B:MYCOINS.SEQ" FOR OUTPUT AS 1    'Reopen for output
350 REM
400 FOR J% = 1 TO COUNT%
410   WRITE #1,YEAR%(J%),CATEGORY$(J%),VALUE(J%),COMMENT$(J%)
420 NEXT J%
430 REM
440 CLOSE #1
450 PRINT "All done - B:MYCOINS.SEQ updated and rewritten"
460 END
```

Note: The INPUT #1... instruction in line 240 is shown on two physical lines for typographic purposes in this book. Make line 240 a single line when you type the program.

In this program, four arrays replace the four simple variables. When you use this technique, be sure to dimension your arrays sufficiently.

The WHILE..WEND loop (lines 200 through 310) reads all the data from MYCOINS.SEQ into these arrays. Note how the variable COUNT% keeps track of the total number of data records.

For each coin, the user sees the old information and can update the coin's value, just as in the previous program. Now, however, the updated information goes into the VALUE array.

The file is closed (line 320) and then immediately reopened for OUTPUT (line 340). The process of opening the file for output erases the whole file. If a program error or power failure occurs at this point, all the data information may be lost. Therefore, when you use this method, you should have a backup copy of your data file.

The FOR..NEXT loop (lines 400 through 420) writes the updated information. The value of COUNT% indicates how many records to write. The net result is a completely updated version of MYCOINS.SEQ.

Modifying the File Externally

You can modify your data file with a word processor or text editor. This is somewhat dangerous because you must be sure to preserve the file formatting. Be careful to keep the delimiters intact and make sure that your word processor does not add any extraneous control characters.

Some file modifications are easier to do externally than with a BASIC program. One example is deleting an entire record from your file. If you are familiar with a word processor that works with ASCII files, try some file modifications with your word processor.

Other Sequential File Tools

You have learned the essential tools of sequential file handling in BASIC, namely:

❏ Opening a file for `INPUT`, `OUTPUT`, or `APPEND`.

❏ Writing a record with `WRITE#`.

❏ Reading a record with `INPUT#`.

❏ Testing for the end of the file with the `EOF` function.

But there's more. BASIC offers other statements and functions for use with sequential files in special situations. We briefly review these other tools now with an emphasis on when you might need to use them.

Using the *LINE INPUT#* Statement

`LINE INPUT#` reads an entire record into a single string variable.

`LINE INPUT #`*filenum*`,` *stringvar*

where *filenum* is the file number, and *stringvar* is a string variable.

Each record is read in its entirety, including any commas or quotation marks. For example, the first record from `MYCOINS.SEQ` looks like this:

```
1910,"Lincoln Penny",70,"S mint mark, uncirculated"
```

You might read this record with the following instruction:

```
500 LINE INPUT #1, MYDATA$
```

This instruction assigns to `MYDATA$` an exact copy of the entire record, including the quotation marks and commas.

Use `LINE INPUT#` when a file has special structure or unknown structure. Perhaps the file was not created with `WRITE#` or you don't know the exact `WRITE#` instruction that was used to create the file. Another possibility is that the number of fields varies from record to record.

In such cases, the programmer has the responsibility to analyze the data in *stringvar* appropriately. Depending on the situation, your program may have to search for meaningful delimiters or otherwise break down *stringvar* into usable components.

Reading with the *INPUT$* Function

INPUT$ is a special form of the INPUT function. With INPUT$, you read only a specified number of characters from the current record.

INPUT$(*numchar*, #*filenum*)

where *numchar* is an integer expression that specifies how many characters should be read, and *filenum* is the file number.

The pound sign is optional before the file number.

For example, the following instruction reads the next 12 characters from the current record of file number 1 into the string variable NEXTDOZEN$:

```
600 NEXTDOZEN$ = INPUT$(12, #1)
```

Using the *LOF* Function

The LOF function (*length of file*) returns the number of bytes (length) of a data file. LOF is handy in certain critical disk-storage situations. One application of LOF is testing whether a file has become too large to save on disk.

LOF (*filenum*)

where *filenum* is the file number of an opened file.

As an example of LOF, the following instruction displays the length of file number 8:

```
400 PRINT "Size of file 8 is"; LOF(8)
```

Using the PRINT# and PRINT# USING Statements

In addition to WRITE#, you can write data to a sequential file with the PRINT# and PRINT# USING statements. PRINT# and PRINT# USING send data to a file in the same form that PRINT and PRINT USING send data to the screen. See Chapter 9, "Writing Text on the Video Screen," for a detailed discussion of PRINT and PRINT USING (and the required format strings).

However, PRINT# does not generally write information in a form suitable for subsequent reading by INPUT# because PRINT# does not automatically place quotation marks around strings and separate fields with commas.

So why would you ever want to use PRINT# and PRINT# USING? Actually, you wouldn't want to if you are writing to files that are later going to be read by INPUT# in another BASIC program.

But there are other reasons to create sequential files. You may want to generate a file destined to be read by people, or into a word processor, or into another application such as a spreadsheet. Such applications require files designed in specialized formats. PRINT# and PRINT# USING supply this control. Consult your BASIC documentation if you want more information.

Summary of Statements and Functions for Sequential Files

Table 10.3 summarizes the statements and functions available for sequential file processing.

Table 10.3. *Sequential file statements and functions.*

Keyword	Type	Effect
OPEN	Statement	Opens a file in specified mode
CLOSE	Statement	Closes a file
WRITE#	Statement	Writes comma-delimited information
INPUT#	Statement	Reads comma-delimited information
PRINT#	Statement	Writes space-delimited information

Table 10.3 *continues*

Table 10.3. *continued*

Keyword	Type	Effect
PRINT# USING	Statement	Writes formatted information
INPUT$	Function	Reads given number of characters
LINE INPUT#	Statement	Reads entire record
EOF	Function	Tests for end of file
LOF	Function	Returns size of file

Random-Access Files

BASIC supports a second type of data file on disk: the random-access (or simply *random*) file. Random files meet the needs of large database file applications.

If you are a beginner with BASIC, or just getting your feet wet programming disk data files, we recommend that you master sequential files before moving on to random files.

Random files require more complex programming than sequential files. We cover random files at a quicker pace than we did for sequential files. You may skip ahead to the next chapter without any loss of continuity.

Still with us? Compared to sequential files, random files offer the following significant advantages:

❏ *Two-way I/O activity.* When a random file is opened, it can be read from and written to.

❏ *Random-access.* Any record can be accessed quickly and conveniently.

❏ *Record modification.* Individual records can be modified without rewriting all other records.

As you have seen, reading a particular record of a sequential file requires reading all the previous records first. If your program wants only the information in the 75th record, for example, you must first read all the information in the initial 74 records. If your program wants the 5th record, you need to read only the initial 4 records. The further into the file the record you want to retrieve is located, the slower will be the time to access that record.

By contrast, random files are organized more like a phonograph whose needle can be lifted and replaced anywhere on an album. Random files reference individual records by number. By simply specifying a record number, you can access that record's information quickly. The access time is virtually the same for the 1st record, the 50th record, or the 2,000th record. Random files are the only practical choice for large database applications.

Furthermore, after you read a random file record, you can modify the data and rewrite the record directly—no need to close and reopen the file. Appending records is also straightforward.

By this time, you probably are thinking that random files are the cure-all for disk database programming. After all, random file records are read swiftly anywhere in the file, and the file can be opened for input and output simultaneously. Why would anyone use sequential files?

Computing, like life, is always a series of trade-offs. Here is the price you must pay to use random files:

❏ Rigid file structure. Each record of a random file must have the same configuration: the number of fields and data type for each field cannot vary from record to record.

❏ Lack of portability. You cannot easily read random files with non-BASIC programs such as word processors and spreadsheets. The TYPE command in DOS does not display random files.

❏ Increased programming effort. Programming random files is more complex than programming sequential files.

Like a sequential file, a random file is a series of records, and each record consists of data fields. Unlike a sequential file, each random file record has a predetermined size, which cannot change throughout the file.

Designing a Random-Access File

You might think of a random-access file record as something similar to a survey form—the kind of form for which you provide data in marked boxes. Such forms often provide one box for each data character (see fig. 10.2).

Note that each field in the form has its own fixed size. It is okay if the data for one field requires less than the allocated number of characters, but it is not okay to use more characters than allocated. For example, the sample form has a name field of 20 characters. You can enter a name of less than 20 characters, but you cannot use more than the 20 allotted characters.

This fixed-field size requirement is exactly the situation with random-access files. You must determine a template form for each record. The number of fields and the size of each field must remain constant throughout the file. You can make each field whatever size you want, but after you specify the size, you must stick to it.

Fig. 10.2. *A fixed-field data form.*

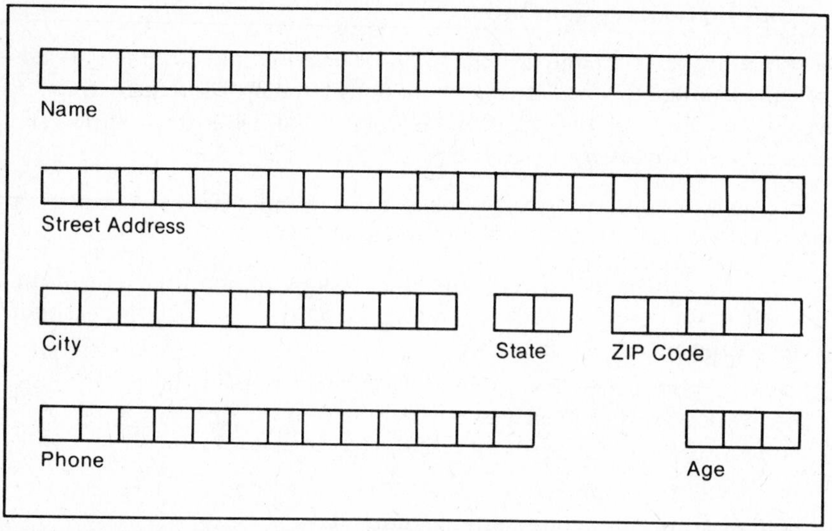

As a result, the size (number of bytes) of each record is constant in a random-access file. That's why BASIC can access any record quickly. Because the record size is constant, when a record number is given, the position of the data on the disk is readily computed. For any record in the file, the computer takes essentially the same time to determine where the data is, to find the data, and then to read the information.

Before you use a random-access file, you must design the template for each record. Decide how many fields each record will have. Then decide the size of each field. You need to treat text fields and numeric fields a little differently.

Creating Text Fields in a Random-Access File

For a text field, simply determine the maximum number of text characters allowed for that field. For each record in the file, you allocate that maximum size for the field, whether or not all the characters are actually used.

For example, you may determine that a field reserved for a customer's name should be allocated 30 characters. Whether the actual data is I. M. Sly, Ace Accordion Supply, or Rumplestiltskin Meriweather, that field always occupies 30 bytes (characters) in the data file.

Creating Numeric Fields in a Random-Access File

Random-access files save numbers in the internal binary formats that BASIC uses to store the numbers in memory. This means that for each numeric field you designate one of BASIC's three numeric types: integer, single-precision, or double-precision.

Be careful that you choose the numeric type of each field wisely. The numeric type of each field must accommodate every entry for that field. If a field contains a number with a fractional component, such as 34.67, that field must be single-precision or double-precision. Integer fields must contain whole numbers no larger than 32,767.

Because numbers are stored in their binary form, the size (in bytes) of each numeric field is determined by the numeric type (see table 10.4).

Table 10.4. *Size of numeric types.*

Number type	*Size (bytes)*
Integer	2
Single-precision	4
Double-precision	8

For example, a field reserved for a single-precision number is allocated 4 bytes. Whether the actual data is 10, 28.699, or 6.04E-28, the number is stored in 4 bytes, just as it would be in the machine's RAM memory.

A Sample Record

Suppose that you want to design a random file database for the coin collection. Each record (coin) requires four fields: Year, Category, Value, and Comment.

Year is a whole number expressed in four digits, such as 1947. Such numbers are well within the range of the integer data type, so the first field is type integer and requires 2 bytes.

Category is a text field. Twenty characters should be enough to describe each coin's category, so the second field is 20 bytes.

Value is a numeric field expressed in dollars and cents, such as 135.50. No coin will be worth more than 3000 dollars. Single-precision numbers easily satisfy this data range, so the third field is 4 bytes long.

Comment is a text field. The data for this field varies widely from coin to coin. Let's limit each comment to 50 characters, so the length of the fourth field is 50 bytes.

The Comment field typifies the squandering of disk space that sometimes occurs with random-access files. For many coins, the Comment field will be short or blank, yet a full 50 bytes is still reserved. This squandering is the price that must be paid to maintain rigid file structure. Typically, a database stored as a random file takes more room on disk than the same database stored as a sequential file.

Figure 10.3 shows the template form for each record of the coin-collection database. The total size of each record is fixed at 76 bytes.

Fig. 10.3. *The random-access record for each coin.*

Data Type	# Bytes
Integer	2
String * 20	20
Single Precision	4
String * 50	50
Total =	76

Writing a Random File Program

Use the following steps to write a program that processes a random file:

1. Open the file FOR RANDOM.

2. Establish field variables with a FIELD instruction.

3. Use GET and PUT instructions to read and write data by way of the field variables.

4. CLOSE the file.

There are some new concepts in these four steps. Let's take a look at each step.

Opening a Random-Access File

You can open a sequential file in INPUT, OUTPUT, or APPEND mode. By contrast, you always open a random file FOR RANDOM. The OPEN instruction adds a LEN clause that specifies the length of each record in the file:

OPEN *filespec* FOR RANDOM AS #*filenum* LEN = *recordlength*

where *filespec* specifies the name and path of the data file, *filenum* is the file number, and *recordlength* is an integer expression specifying—in bytes—the size of each record.

The FOR RANDOM and LEN clauses are optional, as explained in this section.

A single OPEN instruction opens a random file for any or all I/O activities—reading, writing, and appending.

Suppose that you design a random-access database file for your coin collection. Remember, the size of each record is 76 bytes (2 for the year, 20 for the category, 4 for the value, and 50 for the comments). So 76 is the value for the *recordlength* parameter in the LEN clause. Let's say that you call the file MYCOINS.RAN (we use the file extension .RAN for random files), and the file is on a disk in the B: drive. Then the following instruction opens MYCOINS.RAN as file number 1:

```
200 OPEN "B:MYCOINS.RAN" FOR RANDOM AS #1 LEN = 76
```

As you have seen, the LEN clause specifies the length, in bytes, of each random-access record. For optimal efficiency, the value in the LEN clause should precisely match the record length. Although wasteful of disk space, the value in the LEN clause can be larger than the actual record length.

The FOR RANDOM clause is optional because random-access is the default mode for the OPEN instruction. If you do not include any FOR clause, BASIC opens the file for random access. This means that you could open the file as follows:

```
200 OPEN "B:MYCOINS.RAN" AS #1 LEN = 76
```

However, we advise you to always include the FOR RANDOM clause for clarity.

The LEN clause is also optional. If you omit the LEN clause, the record length defaults to 128 bytes.

Establishing Field Variables

Data transfer between your BASIC program and the random file uses special string variables called *field variables*. You assign one field variable to each data field of your record template—that is, one field variable for each component of your database record.

The coin database, for example, has four fields (Year, Category, Value, and Comment). Any program using the coin database, therefore, must define four field variables—one field variable for each field in the database.

To define field variables, you use a FIELD instruction.

FIELD *#filenum*, *fieldwidth* AS *stringvar*,
fieldwidth AS *stringvar*, . . .

where *filenum* is the file number, *fieldwidth* is an integer expression that specifies the number of bytes (characters) allocated to the corresponding field variable, and *stringvar* declares a string variable (or specified element in a string array) to be a field variable.

The pound sign before the *filenum* parameter is optional.

FIELD associates a field variable in your program with each field of a record in your random file. Because all records of a random file have the same fields, one set of field variables is all you need for the entire file.

Field variables are a kind of two-way conduit for the data flow between your programs and the random file. When you write a record, you first store the data for each field in the appropriate field variable. (The technique for doing this is explained in the next few sections.) A PUT instruction then writes the record on the file.

Similarly, a GET instruction transfers data from a record into the appropriate field variable. Then, you decode the data from the field variables for use within your program. Later in this chapter, the section titled "Reading a Record with GET" shows you the decoding technique.

A FIELD instruction declares the name and length of each field variable. Field variables are always string variables. As you will see in the next few sections, all data, whether text or numeric, transfers with string operations.

Recall that when you design a random file, you allocate a fixed size (in bytes) for each field. The *fieldwidth* parameter designates these sizes.

One FIELD instruction defines *all* the field variables for each record of your random file. In the FIELD instruction, you repeat the *fieldwidth* AS *stringvar* clause as many times as there are fields in each record.

For example, the following FIELD instruction establishes field variables for the coin-collection database:

```
250 FIELD #1,2 AS FYEAR$,20 AS FCATEGORY$,4 AS FVALUE$,50 AS FCOMMENT$
```

Let's examine this instruction closely. The # 1 means that this FIELD instruction defines the field variables for file number 1, the same file number opened with the OPEN instruction. There are four *fieldwidth* AS *stringvar* clauses, one clause for each of the four fields in the database. The first of these clauses, 2 AS FYEAR$, defines the field variable FYEAR$ and assigns the variable a length of two bytes (characters). The next three clauses define the other three field variables and assign the appropriate length for each variable. In this instruction, you named each field variable with an "F" (for Field) followed by the name of the field. The field variables are FYEAR$, FCATEGORY$, FVALUE$, and FCOMMENT$. Note that each field variable is a string.

A given FIELD instruction can contain any number of *fieldwidth* AS *stringvar* clauses. Use as many clauses as necessary to define all the field variables for the particular file. Our coin database file has four fields per record. But another file may have only one field in each record (therefore, one clause in the FIELD instruction) or perhaps ten fields in each record (therefore, ten clauses in the FIELD instruction). You separate each clause with a comma.

Writing and Reading Records with *PUT* and *GET*

Use a PUT instruction to write a record to a random file and a GET instruction to read a record from a random file.

Writing a Record with *PUT*

Before you write a random record with PUT, you must transfer the data values for the record into the appropriate field variables. You might think of this as moving the data for each record to a loading dock. Picture having a data value for each field of the record you intend to write. You bring the data value for each field to the loading dock and then transfer each data value into the corresponding field variable. When each field variable contains the proper data, a single PUT instruction writes the entire record to the file.

But, how do you transfer data values to the field variables? BASIC provides the LSET and RSET statements for this purpose. Each LSET or RSET instruction transfers the data for one field to the appropriate field variable.

Here is the syntax for LSET and RSET:

> LSET *fieldvar* = *stringexpr*
>
> RSET *fieldvar* = *stringexpr*
>
> where *fieldvar* is a string variable previously defined as a field variable, and *stringexpr* is a string expression representing the text data to be stored in the field variable.

For each field variable, you use either an LSET or RSET instruction. The technique varies depending on whether the data field is text or numeric.

When the data field is text, the LSET or RSET instruction is straightforward. Because both the field variable and the data itself are text, the LSET or RSET instruction moves the string data directly into the field variable.

For example, *either* of the following instructions moves the data field "Midnight" into the field variable FTIME$.

```
300 LSET FTIME$ = "Midnight"

300 RSET FTIME$ = "Midnight"
```

The only difference between LSET and RSET is that, if necessary, LSET left-justifies the data string within the field variable, and RSET right-justifies. Left-over positions are padded with blank spaces. In practice, most of the time you will use LSET instructions rather than RSET.

In our example, the data field Midnight has a string length of 8 characters. Suppose that the FIELD instruction which defines the field variable FTIME$ specifies FTIME$ to have a length of 10. Then the LSET instruction assigns to FTIME$ the 10-character string consisting of Midnight followed by two blank spaces. RSET produces the 10-character string consisting of two blank spaces followed by Midnight.

If the string expression is longer than the size of the field variable, the right-most portion of the string expression is truncated as necessary. Note that the length of the field variable always remains precisely the length defined in the FIELD instruction, regardless of the length of *stringexpr*.

When a data field is numeric, things get a little more complicated. Numeric data must be converted into the proper string form before being assigned to a field variable. The following "MK$" group of string functions does this conversion.

❏ MKI$(*integerexpr*)

❏ MKS$(*numexpr*)

❏ MKD$(*numexpr*)

where *integerexpr* is a general numeric expression resolving to a value within the integer range (− 32,768 to + 32,767), and *numexpr* is any general numeric expression.

There is a separate function for each numeric data type: MKI$ for integer, MKS$ for single-precision, and MKD$ for double-precision.

The "MK$" functions convert numbers into the string forms required by the field variables. The field variables must still be assigned with LSET or RSET instructions.

For example, the coin-collection database has two numeric fields: Year and Value. Year is integer, and Value is single-precision. The following instructions use MKI$ and MKS$ to assign the numeric data in the variables YEAR% and VALUE to the corresponding field variables FYEAR$ and FVALUE$:

```
200 LSET FYEAR$  = MKI$(YEAR%)
210 LSET FVALUE$ = MKS$(VALUE)
```

Note that each "MK$" function is a string function ending with a dollar sign. MKI$ converts an integer number into the appropriate 2-character string, MKS$ converts a single-precision number into the appropriate 4-character string, and MKD$ converts a double-precision number into the appropriate 8-character string. These string lengths should match exactly with the length of the corresponding field variables. As such, you can use either an LSET or RSET instruction with these functions.

Now back to writing a record. After you assign all the field variables for a record (with LSET or RSET), use the PUT statement to actually write the random file record on disk.

PUT *#filenum, recordnum*

where *filenum* is the file number, and *recordnum* specifies the record number being written.

The pound sign is optional. Also, the *recordnum* parameter is optional. If you omit *recordnum*, BASIC uses the next higher record number from the last record written or read.

A PUT instruction always writes a complete record. When you execute a PUT instruction, BASIC assumes that you have previously assigned each field variable using LSET or RSET. The PUT instruction writes the record in the template form you established with the FIELD instruction.

The first record in a random file is considered to be record number 1. Successive records increase numerically up to a maximum record number of more than 16 million. (Yes, random files can certainly accommodate large databases!)

The *recordnum* parameter can specify any record in the file: an old record whose data is being rewritten, or a new record receiving data for the first time. Furthermore, your record numbers don't have to be continuous. For example, you can write record number 15 when only records 1 through 4 have previously been written. In this case, BASIC automatically creates records 5 through 14, although each such record would contain unknown data.

If you omit the *recordnum* parameter, the default record number is simply one more than the last record written. As a result, you can write incrementally increasing record numbers with successive PUT instructions that omit *recordnum*.

The following program, named MAKERAN.BAS, creates a random file database for the coin collection. The program prompts the user to supply the data and then writes the random file records. Compare this program with the SFCREATE.BAS program (presented earlier in this chapter), which creates a sequential data file.

```
100 REM Program: MAKERAN.BAS (Create a random-access file)
110 REM
120 PRINT "Creating Random-Access Data File: B:MYCOINS.RAN"
130 PRINT
140 OPEN "B:MYCOINS.RAN" FOR RANDOM AS #1 LEN = 76
150 FIELD #1, 2 AS FYEAR$, 20 AS FCATEGORY$,
              4 AS FVALUE$, 50 AS FCOMMENT$
160 REM ---- Begin Input Loop at Line 200 ----
170 REM
200     INPUT "Year (or  <Enter> when all done)"; YEAR%
210     IF YEAR% = 0 THEN 320            'End input loop
220     INPUT "Category of Coin"; CATEGORY$
230     INPUT "Value"; VALUE
240     LINE INPUT "Comments (if any)? "; COMMENT$
250     LSET FYEAR$ = MKI$(YEAR%)        '----------
260     LSET FCATEGORY$ = CATEGORY$      '  Transfer data to
270     LSET FVALUE$ = MKS$(VALUE)       '  field variables
280     LSET FCOMMENT$ = COMMENT$        '----------
290     PUT #1
```

Listing continues

```
300     PRINT
310     GOTO 200                        'Get data for next coin
320 CLOSE #1
330 PRINT "All done - B:MYCOINS.RAN is created"
340 END
```

Note: The FIELD#1... instruction in line 150 is shown on two physical lines for typographic purposes in this book. Make line 150 a single line when you type the program.

Line 140 opens MYCOINS.RAN as a random-access file with a file number of 1 and record lengths of 76 characters. Because this file does not previously exist, the program creates a new file. The FIELD instruction in line 150 establishes the four field variables (FYEAR$, FCATEGORY$, FVALUE$, and FCOMMENT$) and the length of each field.

The loop beginning at line 200 prompts you to supply the necessary data for each coin, just as you did in the SFCREATE.BAS program. In fact, lines 200 through 240 are identical in both programs. These lines put the raw data for each record into the variables YEAR%, CATEGORY$, VALUE, and COMMENT$.

Lines 250 through 280 assign proper values to the field variables in preparation for writing a record. An LSET instruction appears in each line. Notice lines 250 and 270 in particular. These two lines handle the numeric fields YEAR% and VALUE, respectively. The LSET instructions require the MKI$ and MKS$ functions to properly convert the numeric values into the proper string values required by the field variables.

Next, line 290 actually writes a record to the file. This instruction omits the *recordnum* parameter. So, the first time that line 290 executes, BASIC writes record number 1. The next time BASIC writes record number 2, and so on.

After you enter the data for the last record, control passes to line 320, which closes the file. The coin-collection database is now on a random-access disk file named MYCOINS.RAN.

Reading a Record with *GET*

GET and PUT are complementary statements. You write a record with PUT. You read a record with GET.

GET #*filenum*, *recordnum*

where *filenum* is the file number, and *recordnum* specifies the record number being read.

The pound sign is optional. Also, the *recordnum* parameter is optional. If you omit *recordnum*, BASIC uses the next higher record number from the last record read or written.

GET and PUT are exact opposites. PUT writes a record from data stored in the field variables. GET reads a record and places the data into the field variables. You then must decipher the string information in the field variables to finally derive the actual data in the record.

As with PUT, text fields are easy and numeric fields more complicated. After a GET, a field variable for a text field contains the actual data read from the record.

Numeric data, however, must be reconverted from the string form of the field variable back to the proper numeric format. The "CV" group of numeric functions performs this conversion. Whereas the "MK$" functions convert numbers to field variable strings, the "CV" functions convert the field variable strings back to numbers.

- ❑ CVI(*string2$*)
- ❑ CVS(*string4$*)
- ❑ CVD(*string8$*)

where *string2$* is a 2-byte string, *string4$* is a 4-byte string, and *string8$* is an 8-byte string.

You must know which numeric data type corresponds to each field variable. Then use the appropriate CV function: CVI for integer, CVS for single-precision, and CVD for double-precision.

Here is a sample program fragment that reads the third record of the coin database and transfers the data from the field variables into normal program variables. Assume that the OPEN and FIELD instructions are exactly the same as in the MAKERAN.BAS program (lines 140 and 150).

```
300 GET #1, 3           'Read record number 3
310 YEAR%     = CVI(FYEAR$)
320 CATEGORY$ = FCATEGORY$
330 VALUE     = CVS(FVALUE$)
340 COMMENT$  = FCOMMENT$
```

The GET instruction reads an entire record (four data fields in this case) and transfers the data into the four field variables FYEAR$, FCATEGORY$, FVALUE$, and FCOMMENT$. The Category and Comment fields are text data, so lines 320 and 340 can read the text fields directly from the field variables. The Year and Value fields are numeric, so lines 310 and 330 require a "CV" function when they transfer data from the field variables.

A Warning about Field Variables

Field variables have a special stature and cannot be used as normal program variables. Use only LSET and RSET instructions to assign data to field variables.

In particular, never use a field variable on the *left* side of an assignment instruction, such as

```
FCOMMENT$ = "Uncirculated"
```

or in conjunction with an INPUT instruction. Such transgressions cause the field variable to be disassociated with the file buffer and render the field variable useless for further file I/O.

Of course, field variables often appear on the *right* side of assignment statements to extract data after a GET instruction.

Closing the File

When I/O activity is finished, use a CLOSE instruction as usual.

An Example of a Random-Access File Program

Suppose that you have the coin database on a random-access file named MYCOINS.RAN. The coin market is favorable, and prices are rising. You decide to update the database file by increasing the value of each coin by 10 percent. (Earlier in this chapter, the programs UPDATE1.BAS and UPDATE2.BAS solved a similar problem for sequential files.)

The following program, named UPDATE3.BAS, modifies the random file MYCOINS.RAN to reflect the increase in values:

```
100  REM Program: UPDATE3.BAS (Increase coin values by 10%)
110  REM
120  PRINT "Updating Random-Access Data File: B:MYCOINS.RAN"
130  PRINT
140  OPEN "B:MYCOINS.RAN" FOR RANDOM AS #1 LEN = 76
150  REM
160  FIELD #1, 2 AS FYEAR$, 20 AS FCATEGORY$,
               4 AS FVALUE$, 50 AS FCOMMENT$
170  REM
200  FOR RECORD% = 1 TO 3            'File has only 3 records
210     GET #1, RECORD%
220     VALUE = CVS(FVALUE$)
230     VALUE = 1.1 * VALUE          'Increase value by 10%
240     LSET FVALUE$ = MKS$(VALUE)
250     PUT #1, RECORD%
260  NEXT RECORD%
300  CLOSE #1
310  END
```

Note: The FIELD#... instruction in line 160 is shown on two physical lines for typographic purposes in this book. Make line 160 a single line when you type the program.

MYCOINS.RAN is a small database file with only three records. The FOR...NEXT loop in lines 200 through 260 cycles through the three records using a counter variable named RECORD%.

Line 210 reads the record indicated by RECORD%. This instruction assigns a value to each of the four field variables: FYEAR$, FCATEGORY$, FVALUE$, and FCOMMENT$.

You want to modify only the data in the Value field. Line 220 extracts the data from FVALUE$ and stores the result in the single-precision variable VALUE. Line 230 increases VALUE by 10 percent. Line 240 then resets the field variable FVALUE$ with a string representing the updated VALUE.

Line 250 then writes the new record, directly replacing the old record. All four field variables are rewritten to the new record. You didn't need to LSET the field variables FYEAR$, FCATEGORY$, and FCOMMENT$ because the data for those fields remains unchanged from the old record to the new record.

This program illustrates one of the great advantages of random files over sequential files: you can read and write random files without closing and reopening the file.

Furthermore, you can read or write records in any order. For example, you could make RECORD% loop from 3 down to 1 and the program would still work fine.

Using the *LOC* Function

The LOC function returns the record number of the last record read or written:

LOC (*filenum*)

where *filenum* is the file number.

For example, consider the following program fragment.

```
400 GET #9, 2                    'Read 2nd record of file #9
410 PRINT "Last record read was"; LOC(9)
```

The output is

```
Last record read was 2
```

Using the *LOF* Function

The LOF function works for random-access files in the same manner as for sequential files. LOF returns the length of the file in bytes.

Summary of Statements and Functions for Random-Access Files

Table 10.5 summarizes the statements and functions that work with random-access files.

Table 10.5. *Random-access file statements and functions.*

Keyword	Type	Effect
OPEN	Statement	Opens a file FOR RANDOM
CLOSE	Statement	Closes a file
PUT	Statement	Writes a record
GET	Statement	Reads a record
LOF	Function	Returns size of file
LOC	Function	Returns number of last record read or written

Table 10.5 continues

Table 10.5. *continued*

Keyword	Type	Effect
FIELD	Statement	Defines field variables
LSET	Statement	Assigns data to a field variable
RSET	Statement	Assigns data to a field variable
MKI$	Function	Converts integer to field form
MKS$	Function	Converts single-precision number
MKD$	Function	Converts double-precision number
CVI	Function	Converts field variable to integer
CVS	Function	Converts to single-precision number
CVD	Function	Converts to double-precision number

Another Look at the *OPEN* Statement

As you have seen, the first step in programming with a data file is to OPEN the file. Let's review the general syntax of an OPEN instruction.

General Syntax of *OPEN*

The general syntax of an OPEN instruction is as follows:

OPEN *filespec* FOR *mode* AS *#filenum* LEN = *recordlength*

where *filespec* is a string expression that specifies the name (and optionally the path) of the data file; *mode* is one of the four terms shown in table 10.6; *filenum* is an integer expression from 1 to 255 and associates a numeric value with the opened file; and *recordlength* is an integer expression specifying the size (in bytes) of each record in a random-access file.

The *mode* parameter establishes the file type and the I/O mode (see table 10.6).

Table 10.6. *File modes.*

mode	File type	I/O activity
INPUT	Sequential	Reading from beginning of file
OUTPUT	Sequential	Writing new file
APPEND	Sequential	Writing after end of old file
RANDOM	Random-access	Reading and writing on a new or old file

The entire FOR *mode* clause is optional. If you omit the clause, BASIC opens the file as a random-access file—just as though the OPEN instruction specified FOR RANDOM.

Use the LEN = *recordlength* clause with a random file to specify the length of each record in the file. Like the FOR clause, the LEN clause is also optional. If you omit the LEN clause, the record length defaults to 128 bytes (characters).

Normally, you specify a LEN clause with any random file but omit the LEN clause with a sequential file. (With most versions of BASIC, a LEN clause with a sequential file adjusts the length of the file buffer. File buffers are managed by DOS and, generally speaking, are not something you need to concern yourself about. Consult your DOS documentation for more information about file buffers.)

As an example of OPEN, the following instruction opens the file CARDS.SEQ (on the current directory of the A: drive) as a sequential file to be read from. A file number of 18 is assigned to this file:

```
200 OPEN "A:CARDS.SEQ" FOR INPUT AS #18
```

The following instruction opens a random file named CARDS.RAN (on the current directory of the A: drive) as file number 3. The length of each file record is 93 bytes.

```
210 OPEN "A:CARDS.RAN" FOR RANDOM AS #3 LEN = 93
```

Opening Files in a Network Environment

Our discussion of OPEN's general syntax is not quite complete! OPEN accepts some optional parameters useful when you design file-handling programs for a network environment.

On a network, such as a local area network, two users running independent programs might want to open a given file at the same time. When you work in a network environment, you need control over which files can be shared and what privileges (reading and writing) you grant other users on your files.

BASIC accommodates network needs with two optional items in the OPEN instruction: the ACCESS parameter and the *lockmode* parameter. Also, the LOCK and UNLOCK statements provide additional network control.

Further discussion of network features is beyond the scope of this book. Consult your BASIC documentation for more details.

Succinct Syntax of *OPEN*

The OPEN statement has a second, more succinct syntax. This second form is like an abbreviated, stripped-down version of the general syntax.

OPEN *modestring*, *#filenum*, *filespec*, *recordlength*

where *modestring* is a string expression establishing the file type and I/O mode. The *filenum*, *filespec*, and *recordlength* parameters have the same meanings as in the original syntax.

The pound sign (#) and the *recordlength* parameter are optional.

Only the first character of *modestring* is meaningful; therefore, *modestring* is usually just a single character. Table 10.7 lists the possible values of *modestring* and their *mode* equivalents from the general syntax.

Table 10.7. *Values for* `modestring`.

modestring	Equivalent mode
"I"	INPUT
"O"	OUTPUT
"A"	APPEND
"R"	RANDOM

Here are the two previous instructions written with the succinct syntax:

```
200 OPEN "I", #18, "A:CARDS.SEQ"
210 OPEN "R", #3, "A:CARDS.RAN", 93
```

The general and succinct forms of the OPEN instruction are equivalent —just different ways of expressing the same thing. Take your pick. We think that the general syntax is easier to read in actual programs but the succinct form saves a few typing keystrokes.

More on Closing Files

As you have seen, a CLOSE instruction cancels your program's communication link with an open file. In our examples so far, each CLOSE instruction closed a single file by specifying the file number with which the file was opened.

However, a single CLOSE instruction can close two or more files. To do so, specify all the desired file numbers separated from each other with a comma. For example, the following instruction closes files numbered 2, 3, and 8.

```
150 CLOSE #2, #3, #8
```

Furthermore, CLOSE with no file-number arguments closes *all* open files. The RESET statement, which accepts no arguments, has the same effect. END and RUN statements also close all open files.

After closing a file, the file number previously associated with the file becomes available for a subsequent OPEN instruction. Similarly, after closing a file, you may reopen the file with the same or with a different file number as long as the new file number does not conflict with the file number of another opened file.

Here are some examples of instructions that close files:

```
300 CLOSE #1          'Close file number 1
310 CLOSE #2, #3      'Close files 2 and 3
320 CLOSE 2, 3        'Close files 2 and 3 (no pound signs)
330 CLOSE MYFILE%     'Close file specified by variable
CLOSE                 'Close all opened files
RESET                 'Close all opened files
```

Summary

You learned how to manage external disk files from within your programs. External files give you the power to store data separately from programs. That way, programs that regularly use data files can remain unchanged even though the data files are modified. Furthermore, one program can read or write a data file used by other programs.

A common application of disk files is the database. A database is a body of related information such as the students in a school or a hobbyist's collection of postage stamps.

When you create a disk file, you can choose between two different file types: sequential and random-access. Both kinds organize the file into a series of primary records, with each record containing one or more fields. For a stamp-collection database, each record would probably be a stamp and the fields might be the country, denomination, condition, and price of the stamp. To use either file type, you OPEN the file, read or write records as appropriate, and finally CLOSE the file.

Sequential files are easy to program. However, reading and writing records are relatively slow. For large databases, random-access files have many advantages. Any record in a random-access file can be read or written quickly. However, programming random-access files is more complicated.

BASIC has several statements that provide DOS-like file and directory management. Some of the things your programs can do are delete or rename files, and create, delete, or change subdirectories.

CHAPTER 11

Creating Graphics

```
SCREEN, CLS, WIDTH, PSET, PRESET, LINE, CIRCLE, COLOR,
PAINT, DRAW, POINT, VIEW
```

This chapter is going to be fun. (Not that you haven't been having a good time so far!) Everyone enjoys creative graphics. You will learn how to "light up" your video screen with dots, lines, circles, colors, and even animated figures.

Effective graphics can enhance almost any program by providing easy-to-see output, friendliness, animation, and just plain amusement. Fortunately, BASIC has a wealth of tools to access your PC's graphics modes and bring out the creative graphics artist inside you.

Here are some of the things you can do with graphics:

❏ Set one of several graphics modes.

❏ Use colors.

❏ Draw points, lines, and shapes.

❏ Animate your figures.

❏ Mix text and graphics.

309

Most IBM PCs and compatibles are capable of several different graphics modes. As we discuss in the following section, your particular hardware determines which modes you have available.

Standard Video Configurations

To produce graphics, your computer must have the appropriate video hardware. BASIC supports all the popular graphics hardware for the IBM PC and compatibles. Make sure that you understand your particular hardware configuration. If you are unsure, the following discussion may help.

Inside your computer is a *video display adapter*. This piece of hardware controls the type of video signals that are sent to your video screen. This adapter may be built into your computer's motherboard or be on a "card" attached to your motherboard. Table 11.1 lists the six kinds of video display adapters in popular use.

Table 11.1. *Video adapters.*

Name	Features
MDA (Monochrome Display Adapter)	Text in black and white(no graphics)
HGA (Hercules Graphics Adapter)	Text and graphics in black and white
CGA (Color/Graphics Adapter)	Text and graphics in 4 colors
EGA (Enhanced Graphics Adapter)	Text and graphics in 16 colors
MCGA (Multi-Color Graphics Array)	Text and graphics in 256 colors
VGA (Video Graphics Array)	Text and graphics in 256 colors

Video monitors, sometimes called *displays*, are the actual video screens on which you see the text and graphics. (In other words, the video adapters are hardware chips that send video signals which the monitors display.) Just as there are several types of video adapters, there are also several kinds of monitors and displays. Here are the most common types of monitors and displays:

❑ Monochrome display (for MDA and HGA adapters)

❑ RGB monitor (for CGA adapters)

❑ Composite monitor (for CGA adapters)

❑ Enhanced monitor (for EGA adapters)

❑ Analog display (for MCGA and VGA adapters)

A *monochrome display* produces sharp text but can produce only black-and-white output. (Actually, most monochrome displays produce green and black, or amber and black, but the "colors" are traditionally called black and white.)

An *RGB monitor* (the RGB stands for red, green, blue) produces color images that are generally sharper than those produced by a *composite monitor*. (Most television sets are, in effect, composite monitors.) RGB monitors and composite monitors use different technologies to produce video output. Simply stated, RGB monitors produce color signals with three different components, and the composite monitors blend color information into one signal.

An *enhanced monitor* is required to utilize the full capabilities of EGA adapters.

An *analog display* is required to utilize the full capabilities of MCGA and VGA adapters.

For the remainder of this chapter, we assume that you have the most appropriate monitor attached to your particular video adapter. Table 11.2 lists these default configurations.

Table 11.2. *Default video configurations.*

Name for Configuration	Adapter	Monitor
MDA	MDA	Monochrome
HGA	HGA	Monochrome
CGA	CGA	RGB
EGA	EGA	Enhanced
MCGA	MCGA	Analog
VGA	VGA	Analog

Other configurations are possible. For example, you can attach a monochrome monitor to an EGA adapter. But unless stated otherwise, table 11.2 shows the assumed configurations.

Introduction to Graphics Modes

With a CGA, EGA, MCGA, or VGA video adapter, your computer can produce graphics. (MDA cannot produce graphics unless special added hardware is attached to your system. HGA can produce graphics with special BASIC language extensions provided by Hercules. Consult your Hercules documentation.) The available graphics modes differ with each hardware configuration. However, there are two things that all graphics modes have in common:

☐ The video screen consists of many individual dots.

☐ You can control each of the dots.

Think of yourself as a graphics artist. Your video screen is your canvas. Your computer canvas consists of many small dots that you can turn on or off.

Each dot on the screen is called a *pixel* (picture element). You create graphics by designating a color for each pixel. When the color of the pixel is black (the background color), the dot appears to be off. The *resolution* (number of pixels per screen) and available colors for each pixel depend on the graphics mode in effect.

To get a feeling for graphics in general, and the size of one pixel in particular, try the following experiment. At the Ok prompt, type SCREEN 2:

```
Ok
SCREEN 2
```

The screen clears and the Ok prompt reappears in the upper left corner. Your computer is now in screen mode 2, one of several graphics modes. Note that the cursor (below the Ok prompt), is a small rectangle rather than the normal underline character. In any graphics mode, the cursor appears as a small rectangle.

Now type the following command:

```
Ok
PSET (320, 100)
Ok
```

Look closely at the center of your screen. Do you see the single white pixel near the center? You may have to look hard to see it. All the other pixels are black, producing a dark background. (A PSET instruction turns on a single pixel at a particular location. We examine PSET later in this chapter.)

As you can see, a single pixel is small. And you have many pixels to control. Even in the graphics mode with the crudest resolution, the screen consists of some 64,000 pixels.

Yikes! Does this mean that creating graphics is an awesome task? After all, you have to set each pixel to a particular color.

Well, yes and no. You *do* have to control many pixels, but BASIC has a variety of statements and functions that simplify the process.

To whet your appetite for graphics, try the following program, which produces the "bull's-eye" pattern shown in figure 11.1. With this one simple program, you create an interesting graphics pattern. Look at line 130. It is not hard to guess that CIRCLE instructions create circles of various sizes. We examine CIRCLE and other graphics statements throughout this chapter.

```
100 CLS
110 SCREEN 2
120 FOR J = 10 TO 200 STEP 10
130     CIRCLE (320, 100), J
140 NEXT J
```

Fig. 11.1. Concentric circles drawn with CIRCLE.

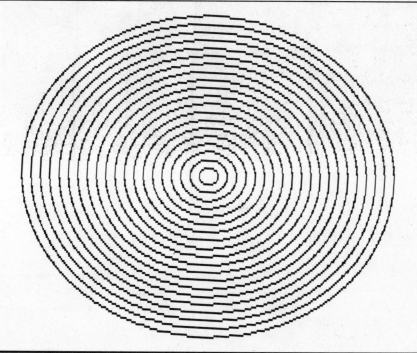

If you feel adventurous, change line 110 to `SCREEN 1` and rerun the program. This change puts the computer in a lower-resolution graphics mode. The circles appear larger, moved to the right, and too big to be fully displayed. You will understand why before the end of the chapter.

Switching Back to Text Mode

When a graphics program finishes, BASIC leaves your computer in graphics mode. From graphics mode, you can type direct-mode commands just as you would normally do from text mode. Compared to text mode, the graphics modes are a bit slower when writing information to the screen. For example, listing a program takes noticeably longer.

At the conclusion of a graphic program, you may be in a 40-column or 80-column graphics mode, depending on the most recent `SCREEN` instruction. `SCREEN 1` leaves your computer in a 40-column mode (similar to the mode produced by a `WIDTH 40` instruction from text mode). `SCREEN 2` leaves your computer in 80-column mode.

To return to normal 80-column text mode from a graphics mode, do the following:

   a. If `SCREEN 1` was the last `SCREEN` instruction:

      1. Type `SCREEN 0`. BASIC switches to 40-column text mode.

      2. Type `WIDTH 80`. BASIC switches to 80-column text mode.

   b. If `SCREEN 2` was the last `SCREEN` instruction, type `SCREEN 0`. BASIC switches to 80-column text mode.

The Available Graphics Modes—the *SCREEN* Statement

A `SCREEN` instruction initializes a graphics mode. In this chapter, we consider only the simple (one-parameter) form of the `SCREEN` instruction. (As discussed in Chapter 15, "Toward Advanced Programming," `SCREEN` accepts other optional parameters.)

SCREEN *modecode*

where *modecode* is an integer expression setting the graphics mode as shown in table 11.3.

Table 11.3. *The graphics modes.*

modecode	Adapter	# Pixels	Colors
0	HGA,CGA,EGA,MCGA,VGA	Text Mode	16
1	CGA,EGA,MCGA,VGA	320 by 200	4
2	CGA,EGA,MCGA,VGA	640 by 200	B/W
7	EGA,VGA	320 by 200	16
8	EGA,VGA	640 by 200	16
9	EGA,VGA	640 by 350	16
10	EGA,VGA	640 by 350	2

The second column of table 11.3 shows which adapters support each screen mode. An error occurs (Illegal function call) if there is a mismatch; for example, SCREEN 7 with a CGA system.

The third column shows the number of pixels associated with the particular screen mode. This column is the pixel resolution expressed as the number of horizontal pixels by the number of vertical pixels.

The last column shows the number of colors you have available for each pixel. *B/W* means that only black and white are permitted. In general, a COLOR instruction, discussed later in this chapter, selects colors.

Here is a synopsis of each graphics mode:

❏ 0—Text mode: returns the display to text mode from one of the graphics modes. If the graphics mode was 1 or 7, SCREEN 0 results in 40-column text mode; otherwise, 80-column text mode results.

❏ 1—Medium-resolution CGA graphics: sets text width to 40.

❏ 2—High-resolution CGA graphics: sets text width to 80.

❏ 7—Medium-resolution graphics on an EGA (but with more colors than CGA allows): sets text width to 40.

❏ 8—High-resolution graphics on an EGA (but with more colors than CGA allows): sets text width to 80.

❏ 9—Enhanced high-resolution EGA graphics. The 16 colors can be selected from 64 available colors. Sets text width to 80.

❏ 10—Enhanced high-resolution EGA graphics for systems with a monochrome display: sets text width to 80.

> **Note to VGA Users**
>
> BASIC does not support the special VGA video modes your system can produce.

For the remainder of this chapter, we confine our graphics discussion to CGA graphics; that is, SCREEN modes 1 and 2. These two graphics modes are available with *any* graphics video adapter (CGA, EGA, VGA, or MCGA).

If you have an EGA, VGA, or MCGA system, see Chapter 15, "Toward Advanced Programming" after you finish this chapter. In Chapter 15, we discuss the additional graphics modes and features that your system can produce.

Coordinate Systems

The location of each graphics pixel is identified by two values: an *x* (horizontal) coordinate and a *y* (vertical) coordinate. Such coordinates are often specified as an *x,y* pair and enclosed in parentheses. For example, (130, 89) identifies the pixel at x-coordinate 130 and y-coordinate 89.

Location (0, 0) identifies the pixel at the upper left corner of the screen. Note that, in graphics modes, numbering starts with 0 (not with 1, as in text mode). The x-coordinates increase moving horizontally to the right; y-coordinates increase moving vertically down.

If you are familiar with mathematical graphs, you are probably accustomed to graphs with origins in the lower left corner and *y* values increasing upward. Does it seem strange that in these graphics modes the origin is in the upper left corner and *y* values increase downward? Most likely, it does.

All we can say is that the origin in the upper left corner is a computing tradition, and traditions die hard. (However, *y* values increasing down the graph *is* similar to the way you think about row numbers increasing down a text screen.) In Chapter 15, you will learn how you can correct this "problem" by redefining the standard coordinate system.)

The coordinates of the upper left corner of the screen are (0, 0). What are the coordinates of the lower right corner of the screen?

The answer is, "It depends." The coordinates of the lower right corner depend on the SCREEN mode selected. Examples are (319, 199) for medium resolution (SCREEN 1); (639, 199) for high resolution (SCREEN 2); and (639, 349) for enhanced high resolution (SCREEN 9).

Figure 11.2 shows the layout of a high-resolution screen with the coordinates of a few pixels specified.

Fig. 11.2. Coordinate system of a high-resolution screen.

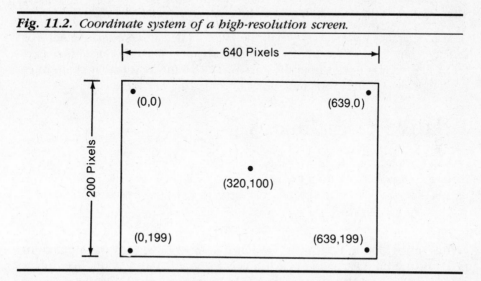

Specifying Coordinates

Most graphics statements and functions require one or more coordinate pairs as parameters. In general, there are three ways you can specify a coordinate pair:

❑ Absolute coordinates
❑ LPR (last point referenced)
❑ Relative coordinates

Absolute Coordinates

The simplest way to designate a pixel location is to specify the x- and y-coordinates explicitly.

For example, a PSET instruction (discussed shortly) plots a pixel at a specified location. Using absolute coordinates, the following instruction turns on the pixel at x-coordinate 214 and y-coordinate 89:

```
200 PSET (214, 89)
```

LPR (Last Point Referenced)

In graphics modes, BASIC keeps track of where the last point was displayed. The position of this last point is called the *LPR* (last point referenced).

Many graphics instructions accept the LPR as a default coordinate point. For example, one form of the LINE instruction accepts only a destination parameter. A line then is drawn from the current LPR to this destination point. After the line is drawn, the destination point becomes the new LPR.

Relative Coordinates

A third option, available with most graphics statements, is to specify coordinates as a displacement from the LPR. Such coordinates are called *relative*. You use the keyword STEP to identify this form. Here is a typical example:

```
300 PSET STEP (-24, 18)
```

This instruction directs BASIC to plot a point 24 pixels to the left and 18 pixels below the LPR. If the LPR happens to be at (140, 75), the new point plots at (116, 93). Note that relative coordinates can be positive or negative. Positive *x* values are to the right and negative *x* values to the left. Positive *y* values are down and negative *y* values are up.

Initializing a Graphics Mode

When you initialize a graphics mode with a SCREEN instruction, the following three things happen:

❏ The video screen clears to a black background.
❏ The default graphics color becomes white.
❏ The LPR becomes the middle of the screen.

Nothing happens, however, if a SCREEN instruction specifies the graphics mode currently in effect. In this case, the screen does not clear, and the LPR does not change. Effectively, BASIC just ignores the SCREEN instruction.

Drawing Simple Shapes in Black and White

Now let's create some graphics. The following statements produce points, lines, and circles:

- ❏ PSET, PRESET (single points)
- ❏ LINE (straight lines)
- ❏ CIRCLE (circles)

We start with the simplest forms of these statements. For now, the graphics are in black and white. Later in this chapter, you will see how to add optional parameters that produce color graphics and fancier shapes such as rectangles and pie slices.

Plotting Points—*PSET* and *PRESET*

PSET turns on a pixel at a given screen location. "Turns on" means that the pixel color changes to white from the formerly black background color.

You may specify the coordinates of the pixel in absolute or relative form:

PSET (*x-coord*, *y-coord*)   'Absolute form

PSET STEP (*x-coord*, *y-coord*) 'Relative form

where *x-coord* specifies the x-coordinate of the pixel to turn on, and *y-coord* specifies the y-coordinate.

The first form, without STEP, indicates that the coordinates are in absolute form. For example, the following instruction turns on the pixel at x-coordinate 321 and y-coordinate 103:

```
PSET (321, 103)
```

The second form, with STEP, indicates that the coordinates are in relative form. For example, the following instruction turns on the pixel 20 pixels to the right of the LPR and 18 pixels below the LPR.

```
PSET STEP (20, 18)
```

The companion statement, PRESET, turns off a pixel. Here, "turns off" means to make the pixel color black (the background color). Think of PRESET as meaning "Point RESET"—not the word PRESET. As with PSET, you can use absolute or relative coordinates.

PRESET (*x-coord, y-coord*)   'Absolute form

PRESET STEP (*x-coord, y-coord*) 'Relative form

where *x-coord* specifies the x-coordinate of the pixel to turn off, and *y-coord* specifies the y-coordinate.

Try the following experiment to get a better feel for PSET and PRESET.

At the Ok prompt, type the following commands in order to clear the screen and start SCREEN mode 1 (medium-resolution graphics).

```
CLS
SCREEN 1
```

Now type

```
PSET (250, 75)
```

This turns on a pixel at absolute coordinates (250, 75), near the right edge of the screen about two-thirds of the way down. Do you see it?

Now type

```
PSET STEP (-25, 10)
```

Another pixel goes on 25 pixels to the left and 10 pixels below the first pixel. The STEP keyword means that the coordinates are relative to the LPR, rather than absolute coordinates. The previous instruction established the LPR at absolute location (250, 75). The new pixel is at (250 −25, 75 +10) or absolute coordinates (225, 85).

Now, let's erase these two pixels. Type the following command:

```
PRESET (250, 75)
```

The first pixel turns back to black and fades into the background. The LPR is now at this location (250, 75). To erase the second pixel, type

```
PRESET STEP (-25, 10)
```

Remember, relative coordinates can be positive or negative. Positive *x* coordinates are to the right and negative *x* coordinates are to the left. Positive *y* coordinates are down and negative *y* coordinates are up.

Clearing a Graphics Screen

Just as in text mode, CLS clears a graphics screen. You can use CLS as a program instruction or as a command from direct mode.

The following program, named DRAWGRID.BAS, demonstrates PSET and PRESET with variables as parameters. First, using PSET, a grid of dots appears. Then, after you press a key, PRESET erases the grid.

```
100 REM Program: DRAWGRID.BAS (Demonstrate PSET and PRESET)
110 SCREEN 1
120 CLS                         'Clear the screen
130 FOR X% = 5 TO 315 STEP 5
140    FOR Y% = 5 TO 195 STEP 5
150        PSET (X%, Y%)         'Turn on pixel
160    NEXT Y%
170 NEXT X%
180 REM
190 WHILE INKEY$ =""            'Pause until user hits key
200 WEND
210 REM
220 FOR X% = 5 TO 315 STEP 5
230    FOR Y% = 5 TO 195 STEP 5
240        PRESET (X%, Y%)       'Turn off pixel
250    NEXT Y%
260 NEXT X%
270 END
```

The PSET and PRESET instructions in lines 150 and 240 use variables for the coordinate specifications. In general, you can use any expression for your *x* and *y* values.

The WHILE...WEND loop in lines 190 and 200 pauses the program until you press any key. The INKEY$ function returns a character typed at the keyboard. (We introduced INKEY$ in Chapter 5, "Program Flow and Decision Making," and discuss the function thoroughly in Chapter 12, "Programming Hardware Devices.")

What about Fractional Coordinates?

Because coordinates can be variables or general expressions, what happens if a coordinate value has a fractional component? Suppose, for example, that you try this:

```
200 NUMBER! = 49.33
210 PSET (NUMBER!, 2 * NUMBER!)
```

No problem. It is true that every graphics pixel is located at an integral value of *x* and *y*. However, if your coordinate expression has a fractional component, BASIC simply rounds the value to the nearest integer. This fractional rounding takes place with all graphics statements.

Drawing Straight Lines—*LINE*

The LINE statement draws a straight line. The line can be short, long, horizontal, vertical, or at any angle. You just specify the two end points, and BASIC does the rest.

LINE *startpoint* − *endpoint*

where *startpoint* is the *x,y* location of the starting point of the line, and *endpoint* is the *x,y* location of the end point of the line.

The *startpoint* parameter is optional but the hyphen and the *endpoint* parameter are mandatory. If you omit *startpoint*, the line begins at the LPR.

For example, the following instruction draws a line from the point (100, 30) to the point (210, 80).

```
LINE (100, 30) - (210, 80)
```

The following program, MOUNTAIN.BAS, shows LINE in action. The program draws the simple "mountain" shape shown in figure 11.3.

```
100 REM Program: MOUNTAIN.BAS (Demonstrate simple lines)
110 SCREEN 2
120 CLS
130 FOR XBOTTOM% = 10 TO 610 STEP 30
140     LINE (310, 20) - (XBOTTOM%, 180)
150 NEXT XBOTTOM%
```

Fig. 11.3. *The "mountain" drawn by* `MOUNTAIN.BAS`.

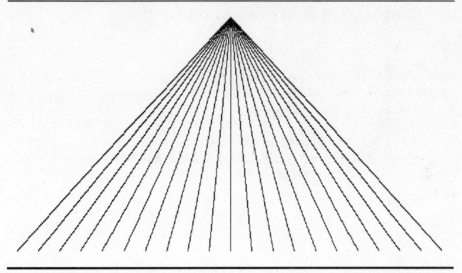

In `MOUNTAIN.BAS`, all the lines start at x-coordinate 310 and y-coordinate 20. This point is the top of the mountain. The `FOR...NEXT` loop variable `XBOTTOM%` controls the *x* coordinate at the bottom of the mountain. Note how the `XBOTTOM%` changes values to draw the various lines in the mountain.

In a `LINE` instruction, you can specify the beginning and ending points in absolute coordinates (without `STEP`), or relative coordinates (with `STEP`). As `MOUNTAIN.BAS` demonstrates, the components of *startpoint* and *endpoint* can be variables (or even expressions).

For example, the following instruction draws a line from (30, 42) to a point with an *x* coordinate given by `XVALUE` and a *y* coordinate given by the expression `YVALUE + 28`.

```
LINE (30, 42) - (XVALUE, YVALUE + 28)
```

To specify a relative coordinate, you can use `STEP` with *startpoint*, *endpoint,* or both parameters. The following sample instructions use relative coordinates:

```
LINE STEP(10, -30) - (65, 70)
```

The line begins at the point 10 pixels to the right and 30 pixels above the LPR. The line ends at the point with absolute coordinates (65, 70).

```
LINE (X%, Y%) - STEP(50, 40)
```

The line begins at the point specified by the absolute coordinates (X%, Y%). This point becomes the LPR. The line ends at the point 50 pixels to the right and 40 pixels below the newly established LPR (X%, Y%).

```
LINE STEP(-10, 20) - STEP(60, 85)
```

The line begins 10 pixels to the left and 20 pixels below the LPR. This starting point becomes the LPR. The line ends at the point 60 pixels to the right and 85 pixels below the starting point.

The last two instructions demonstrate how relative coordinates work with the *endpoint* parameter. When STEP appears with the *endpoint* parameter, the LPR for determining the end point is simply the beginning of the line.

The starting point parameter is optional in a LINE instruction. Here's an example:

```
LINE -(80, 120)
```

This instruction draws a line from the LPR to absolute location (80, 120). When you omit the startpoint parameter, the line begins at the LPR. It is just as though you specified the starting point with the parameter STEP(0, 0).

One last example:

```
LINE -STEP(60, 0)
```

This instruction draws a horizontal line beginning at the LPR and extending 60 pixels to the right.

Drawing Circles—*CIRCLE*

Use CIRCLE to draw circles. (Now that makes sense). For now, we consider only the simplest form of CIRCLE, drawing a complete circle in black and white. Later in the chapter, you will see how optional parameters produce ellipses, arcs, and pie-shaped wedges.

CIRCLE (*xcenter*, *ycenter*), *radius*   'Absolute form

CIRCLE STEP (*xcenter*, *ycenter*), *radius* 'Relative form

where *xcenter* is the x coordinate of the circle's center, *ycenter* is the y-coordinate of the circle's center, and *radius* specifies the radius of the circle.

For example, the following instruction draws a circle centered at absolute location (75, 60) with a radius of 28 pixels.

```
415 CIRCLE (75, 60), 28
```

The *xcenter* and *ycenter* parameters determine the location of the circle's center. As usual, you can use absolute coordinates (without STEP) or relative coordinates (with STEP).

A circle's radius is the distance from the center of the circle to the perimeter. With the *radius* parameter, you specify the radius length (in pixels) of the circle you want BASIC to draw.

However, drawing circles on a video screen presents a complication. Standard video monitors have a different inter-pixel spacing horizontally and vertically. To draw true-looking circles, the radius must continually adjust as the circle is drawn.

BASIC makes this adjustment automatically so that CIRCLE instructions produce accurate circles. With the *radius* parameter, you specify the pixel length *along the x axis*. If the value of *radius* is negative, an error results (Illegal function call).

The following program, named RINGS.BAS, demonstrates CIRCLE by drawing the five-circle symbol of the Olympic games. Figure 11.4 shows the result.

```
100 REM Program: RINGS.BAS (Draw the Olympic rings)
120 SCREEN 1
140 CLS
150 RADIUS% = 40
200 FOR X% = 50 TO 250 STEP 100    'Draw top 3 circles
210    CIRCLE (X%, 80), RADIUS%
220 NEXT X%
300 FOR X% = 100 TO 200 STEP 100   'Draw bottom 2 circles
310    CIRCLE (X%, 120), RADIUS%
320 NEXT X%
```

Fig. 11.4. *The "Olympic" symbol drawn by* RINGS.BAS.

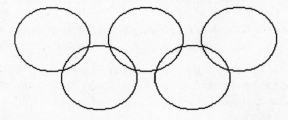

Creating Color Graphics

Enough of this drab black and white. It's time to get some color into your graphics. For starters, try the following experiment:

1. Modify line 210 of RINGS.BAS as follows (there is an added parameter at the end of the instruction):

   210 CIRCLE (X%, 80), RADIUS%, 1

2. Run the modified program. The top three circles are now cyan rather than white. (Cyan, if you have never heard of it, is a bluish-green color.)

3. Modify line 310 to look like this:

   310 CIRCLE (X%, 120), RADIUS%, 2

4. Run the program again. The bottom two circles are now magenta.

By adding a simple parameter to the CIRCLE instructions, you drew colored circles. We examine the details of this technique soon enough. But first, a little general discussion of graphics colors is in order.

CGA Color Graphics

Of the two CGA graphics modes, only SCREEN mode 1 supports color. (SCREEN mode 2 produces only black and white graphics.) In this chapter, we confine our detailed discussion of color graphics to SCREEN mode 1. In Chapter 15, "Toward Advanced Programming," we discuss color graphics in relation to the EGA modes: SCREEN modes 7 - 10.

Foreground and Background Colors

In graphics modes, just as in text mode, we speak of *foreground* colors and *background* colors. However, for graphics modes, the distinction between foreground and background is a bit vague.

After all, in graphics modes, the screen is simply a grid of pixels with each pixel having a particular color. Technically speaking, you cannot always say that one pixel is in the foreground and another pixel in the background.

Consider a quilt pattern with pixels alternating in color. Who's to say that one color is the foreground color and another color the background color? This question is similar to the old conundrum, "Is a zebra black with white stripes or white with black stripes?"

Nevertheless, we *do* speak of foreground and background colors. Practically speaking, most graphics consist of images drawn upon a uniform background. In this light, we distinguish between foreground and background colors as follows:

❏ The *foreground* color is the color of a drawn object. For example, you draw a red circle by turning each pixel of the circle into red. In this case, red is the foreground color.

❏ The *background* color, naturally enough, is the color of all the background pixels. When you initialize a graphics mode, the background is solid black.

Specifying Pixel Colors

BASIC provides two primary ways of specifying pixel colors.

1. The *color* parameter. You can add an optional color parameter to `PSET`, `PRESET`, `LINE`, and `CIRCLE` instructions. This parameter specifies the foreground color with which the pixels are drawn.

2. The `COLOR` statement. Just as in text mode, you can specify default foreground and background colors with a `COLOR` instruction.

We now discuss color in terms of each graphics mode.

Color Graphics in *SCREEN* Mode 1

As you have seen, a `SCREEN 1` instruction activates medium-resolution graphics mode. This mode is available with any video adapter (CGA, EGA, VGA, or MCGA). If you have a CGA system, this is the *only* graphics mode that supports color.

Mode 1 has the following characteristics:

❏ The screen is 320 pixels horizontally by 200 pixels vertically.

❏ Background pixels can be any of 16 possible colors.

❏ Up to four colors can be on the screen at the same time. (Black and white each count as one color.)

❏ Two different palettes are available. Each palette consists of three foreground colors preselected by BASIC and one background color that you can select.

The concept of *palette* requires some explanation. Think of yourself, the programmer, as a graphics artist. You paint from a palette that contains four cups of color. These cups are labeled numerically from 0 to 3. Whenever you draw a point, line, or circle, you choose the color by selecting one of the four cups. You indicate your choice of cup with a number from 0 to 3.

Table 11.4 shows the default colors in each cup.

Table 11.4. *Default palette colors.*

Cup Number	Color
0	Black (background color)
1	Cyan
2	Magenta
3	White

Later in this chapter, you will learn how to put any of the 16 available colors into cup 0 and also how to select an alternate palette with three different colors in cups 1 through 3. For now, let's see how to work with this default palette.

Specifying the *color* Parameter

PSET, PRESET, LINE, and CIRCLE instructions accept an optional parameter that specifies the pixel color by designating which color cup to use.

Color Graphics Instructions in Mode 1

PSET (*x-coord, y-coord*), *color*

PRESET (*x-coord, y-coord*), *color*

LINE *startpoint – endpoint, color*

CIRCLE (*xcenter, ycenter*), *radius, color*

where *color* specifies the drawing color with a value from 0 to 3.

  (The *x-coord, y-coord, startpoint, endpoint, xcenter, ycenter,* and *radius* parameters work as explained previously.)

At last, now you can understand how the modified RINGS.BAS program works. Remember, we changed line 210 and 310 as follows:

```
210     CIRCLE (X%, 80), RADIUS%, 1

310     CIRCLE (X%, 120), RADIUS%, 2
```

Line 210 specifies color cup 1 (cyan), and line 310 specifies color cup 2 (magenta).

Specifying *color* with Variables

In PSET, PRESET, LINE, and CIRCLE instructions, you can specify the *color* parameter with a variable or expression. The following short program uses a variable named CUP% for the *color* parameter.

```
100 REM Program: LINES.BAS (Draw 4 horizontal lines)
200 SCREEN 1
210 CLS
300 FOR CUP% = 0 TO 3
310    Y% = 40 * CUP%
320    LINE (20, Y%) - (200, Y%), CUP%
330 NEXT CUP%
```

In line 320, the LINE instruction specifies the *color* parameter with the variable CUP%.

LINES.BAS actually draws four horizontal lines, but you see only three! The first time through the loop, CUP% has the value of 0. Line 320 draws a horizontal line with color 0, which is black. The screen background, however, is already black. As a result, the line is invisible. The next three times through the loop, CUP% has the values of 1, 2, and 3, which result in lines of cyan, magenta, and white, respectively.

Erasing Graphic Figures

You can use color 0 to "erase" something previously drawn with another color. For example, try this:

1. In direct mode, type SCREEN 1, followed by CLS. You now have a clear graphics screen with the cursor near the upper-left corner.

2. Draw a cyan circle with the following direct mode command:

   CIRCLE (100, 90), 30, 1

3. Erase the circle with this command:

   CIRCLE (100, 90), 30, 0

That last command actually redraws the previous circle using black. The effect is to erase the circle.

This example also illustrates that direct-mode commands work fine in graphics mode. To return to normal text mode, type SCREEN 0 followed by WIDTH 80.

PSET and *PRESET* with Colors

PSET and PRESET are equivalent when you include a *color* parameter. Each instruction turns the designated pixel to the indicated color. For example, either one of the following two instructions makes the pixel at (X%, Y%) magenta.

```
300 PSET (X%, Y%), 2
300 PRESET (X%, Y%), 2
```

Illegal *color* Values

What happens if you specify a *color* parameter outside of the range from 0 to 3?

If *color* has a value from 4 to 255, BASIC acts as though the value was 3. In other words, the graphics color is white.

However, if *color* has a value less than 0, or greater than 255, the instruction is illegal. Your program terminates with the error message Illegal function call.

The *COLOR* Instruction in Mode 1

Similar to a COLOR instruction in text mode (see Chapter 9, "Writing Text on the Video Screen"), a COLOR instruction in graphics mode lets you redefine the default colors. However, graphics COLOR instructions work quite differently from text mode COLOR instructions.

The *COLOR* Instruction in Mode 1

COLOR *background, palette*

where *background* specifies the background color, and *palette* specifies one of two color palettes for foreground color selection.

Each of the parameters is optional.

With a COLOR instruction, you can do either or both of the following:

❏ Choose any one of 16 colors to be the background color—that is, the color in cup number 0.

❏ Select an alternate palette that contains green, red, and brown in color cups 1, 2, and 3, respectively. (This alternate palette replaces the default palette that contains cyan, magenta, and white in cups 1, 2, and 3.)

Note that each of the parameters is optional. You can specify 0, 1, or 2 parameters with each COLOR instruction. The parameters can be variables or numeric expressions. Here are some sample COLOR instructions:

```
410 COLOR 2, 3    'Both parameters are specified
530 COLOR HUE%    '2nd parameter retains current value
225 COLOR , 1     '1st parameter retains current value
850 COLOR         'Both parameters retain current value
```

Now let's see how both parameters (*background* and *palette*) work.

Changing the Background Color

With the *background* parameter in a COLOR instruction, you can designate cup 0 to be any of the 16 colors indicated in table 11.5. As shown in the table, each of the 16 colors has a color code value ranging from 0 to 15.

Table 11.5. *Available colors.*

Code	Color	Code	Color
0	Black	8	Gray
1	Blue	9	Light blue
2	Green	10	Light green
3	Cyan	11	Light cyan
4	Red	12	Light red
5	Magenta	13	Light magenta
6	Brown	14	Yellow
7	White	15	Bright white

By default, BASIC uses black as the background color. In other words, when you initialize graphics, cup 0 (the cup with the background color) contains color 0 (black).

To change the background color, specify the first parameter in a COLOR instruction. You can choose any of the 16 colors for the background. For example, the following instruction changes the background to blue:

```
250 COLOR 1
```

Want to see the various background colors? The following program, BACKGRND.BAS, cycles through the available colors. Just press Enter to watch the background change.

```
100 REM Program: BACKGRND.BAS (Cycle background colors)
200 SCREEN 1
210 CLS
220 FOR HUE% = 0 TO 14
230    COLOR HUE%
240    PRINT "Background color is now color"; HUE%
250    INPUT "Press Enter to see the next color", DUMMY$
260 NEXT HUE%
```

Note that line 220 makes 14, not 15, the final value of HUE%. Why? The text color is bright white. If HUE% is 15, the text color and background color are identical. The result is invisible text!

Recovering from an Invisible Screen

On occasion, you may inadvertently terminate a graphics program with identical colors for the background and foreground. This is a quandary because the screen text becomes invisible. Help!

Fortunately, BASIC provides a convenient way out. Simply press the F10 key. This key automatically issues a special SCREEN command, which returns your computer to text mode with white text on a black background. See Chapter 13, "Editing Techniques," for more information about using the F1 through F10 function keys.

Regardless of the background color, the *color* parameter in PSET, PRESET, LINE, and CIRCLE instructions draws shapes in cyan, magenta, or white (1 = cyan, 2 = magenta, 3 = white). In these instructions, however, color 0 refers to the current background color. This means that you can use color 0 to erase a previous image without having to know the current background color. For example, consider the following instructions:

```
200 CIRCLE (100, 50), 20, 1

300 CIRCLE (100, 50), 20, 0
```

Line 200 draws a cyan circle regardless of the current background color. Line 300 draws a circle in the current background color, *whatever that color happens to be*. In effect, line 300 erases the circle drawn by line 200.

A Secret about the Default Color Cups

The cyan, magenta, and white colors found in color cups 1, 2, and 3 are actually the light cyan, light magenta, and bright white colors in table 11.5. (That is, the three drawing colors correspond to codes 11, 13, and 15 rather than codes 3, 5, and 7.)

To demonstrate this, draw a cyan shape with a `CIRCLE` or `LINE` instruction. For example

```
CIRCLE (100, 50), 20, 1
```

Now change the background color. `COLOR 3` produces a cyan background, but you can still see the circle. That is because the circle is really light cyan on the cyan background. To erase the circle, use `COLOR 11` (light cyan), which makes the background the same color as the circle.

Changing the Palette

Okay, ready for more? Now we are going to change the palette. By doing so, a new set of four drawing colors becomes available.

BASIC provides two color palettes, known as the *odd* palette and the *even* palette. You can work with only one palette at a time. So far, you have worked with the odd palette, which is the default palette. This palette draws with the familiar colors of cyan, magenta, and white. By contrast, the even palette draws with green, red, and brown instead. Table 11.6 summarizes the colors in each palette.

Table 11.6. Palette colors.

Cup Number	Palette 0 (even)	Palette 1 (odd)
0	Background color	Background color
1	Green	Cyan
2	Red	Magenta
3	Brown	Bright white

To select a palette, you specify the second parameter in a `COLOR` instruction. This parameter is the *palette* parameter. When *palette* has the value of 1 (or any odd number), you select the default palette containing cyan and magenta. When *palette* is 0 (or any even number), you select the alternate palette containing green and red.

Here are some sample COLOR instructions that select a palette. Note that if you want to specify the palette but leave the background color unchanged, you use a comma between the COLOR keyword and the *palette* parameter.

```
300 COLOR 1, 0 'Background color blue, select palette 0

400 COLOR , 1  'Background color same, select palette 1
```

When you switch palettes, you instantaneously change the colors already on the screen. Images drawn with color cup 1 of the old palette switch immediately to the color in color cup 1 of the new palette. (The same holds true for color cups 2 and 3.)

Remember the LINES.BAS program that drew four horizontal lines? Let's modify the program to try the alternate palette. Here's the program with line 250 added:

```
100 REM Program: LINES.BAS (Draw 4 horizontal lines)
200 SCREEN 1
210 CLS
250 COLOR , 0
300 FOR CUP% = 0 TO 3
310    Y% = 40 * CUP%
320    LINE (20, Y%) - (200, Y%), CUP%
330 NEXT CUP%
```

Try this experiment to see how palettes work.

1. Run this modified version of LINES.BAS. Note that the horizontal lines are now green, red, and brown. The uppermost line is still invisible because it was drawn in black (the background color). Also notice that the on-screen text characters are now brown. With the even palette, brown replaces white as the default color.

2. Change the palette back to the default palette with the following direct-mode command:

   COLOR , 1

   The horizontal lines immediately change to cyan, magenta, and white.

3. Try some direct-mode COLOR commands that change the palette and/or background. Here's one to get you started:

   COLOR 9, 0

"Color" Graphics in *SCREEN* Mode 2

SCREEN 2 selects high-resolution graphics (640 pixels horizontally by 200 pixels vertically). Color graphics in this mode are simple: there aren't any!

All graphics in this mode must be in black and white (white drawing on a black background). If you try a COLOR instruction in mode 2, your program terminates with the error message: Illegal function call.

However, you don't get an error message if you specify the *color* parameter in a PSET, PRESET, LINE, or CIRCLE instruction. BASIC simply ignores this *color* parameter and always draws with white.

Color Graphics in Higher Screen Modes

Screen modes 7 through 10 work only on systems equipped with EGA, VGA, or MCGA video adapters. CGA systems cannot utilize these screen modes.

These modes support extended color capability. We discuss the modes in Chapter 15, "Toward Advanced Programming."

Painting Enclosed Areas—
the *PAINT* Statement

PAINT pours color into any enclosed region.

PAINT (*x-coord, y-coord*), *paint, bordercolor*

where *x-coord* and *y-coord* specify the x,y location where painting begins, *paint* is the paint color, and *bordercolor* designates the color of the boundary region.

The *paint* and *bordercolor* parameters are optional.

PAINT works from a single point outward. Imagine a painter with a spray gun containing the color *paint*. The painter begins at the single point given by (*x-coord, y-coord*) and sprays paint slowly in all directions. Whenever a point or area of color *bordercolor* is encountered, painting stops in that direction.

The (*x-coord, y-coord*) parameter specifies the initial painting position. This is the only mandatory parameter. As usual, these coordinates are absolute (without STEP) or relative (with STEP). For example:

```
60 PAINT (80, 50)        'Begin at absolute location (80, 50)

70 PAINT STEP (80, 50) 'Begin at relative location (80, 50)
```

paint is an integer expression that specifies the color in the spray gun. If you don't specify the *paint* parameter, BASIC uses the default value of 3. The value of *paint* corresponds to the number of the selected color cup. As such, *paint* should have a value from 0 to 3. (Values less than 0 or larger than 255 result in a run-time error: Illegal function call. BASIC treats values from 4 to 255 as the default value of 3.)

bordercolor defines the color of the boundary region. Painting stops wherever the border color is encountered. If you don't specify *bordercolor*, the default is the same color as the *paint* parameter.

Make sure that the region you want to paint is completely enclosed by a boundary of the border color. Otherwise, the paint may leak into undesired areas.

Note that the default color for *bordercolor* is the *paint* color, not color 3 (white). Suppose that you are using cyan paint in a region outlined by white. Your PAINT instruction, assuming SCREEN 1, should look something like this:

```
500 PAINT (100, 50), 1, 3   '1 = cyan paint, 3 = white border
```

Do not make the mistake of omitting the *bordercolor* parameter in such a case. The following instruction paints with cyan until a border region of cyan is reached (not until a white border is reached):

```
600 PAINT (100, 50), 1
```

This instruction causes the paint to encroach onto and through a white border.

The following program, named DOPAINT.BAS, demonstrates PAINT. Intersecting circles are drawn in white. Then regions are painted various colors. Note that the PAINT instruction in line 310 omits both the *paint* and *bordercolor* parameters. As such, BASIC uses the default value for each parameter—namely, 3. Line 310 creates white painting until the white boundary is reached.

```
100 REM Program: DOPAINT.BAS (Demonstrate PAINT statement)
110 SCREEN 1
120 '
```

```
200 CIRCLE (150, 100), 50   'Draw a white circle
210 CIRCLE (200, 100), 50   'Draw an intersecting circle
220 CIRCLE (175, 100), 100  'Draw an outer circle
230 '
300 PAINT (110, 100), 1, 3  'Paint left hemisphere cyan
310 PAINT (240, 100)        'Paint right hemisphere white
320 PAINT (170, 100), 2, 3  'Paint inside magenta
330 PAINT (100, 190), 2, 3  'Paint outside magenta
400 END
```

Drawing Boxes and Circles

The *LINE* and CIRCLE instructions accept optional parameters that permit the drawing of boxes, arcs, ellipses, and wedges.

Drawing Boxes with *LINE*

To draw a box, use the optional B parameter in a LINE instruction. With BF instead of just B, the box fills with color.

> LINE *startpoint – endpoint, color,* B
>
> or
>
> LINE *startpoint – endpoint, color,* BF
>
> where B draws an outlined box, and BF draws a box and paints the interior a solid color.
>
> The *startpoint, endpoint,* and *color* parameters have been explained previously.

When you are drawing a box (that is, a rectangle) the *startpoint* and *endpoint* parameters establish the diagonally opposite corners of the box.

You can paint the interior of the rectangle by using BF rather than B. (BF stands for *Box Filled*.) The *color* parameter determines the paint color. If you omit *color*, BASIC uses the default color cup value of 3.

The following program, SHOWLINE.BAS, demonstrates LINE with some simple line and rectangle drawing. Because it is hard to show color in a black-and-white book, the *color* parameter is not used in the LINE instructions.

```
100 REM Program: SHOWLINE.BAS (Show lines and rectangles)
110 SCREEN 1
120 CLS
130 DELTA% = 25
140 '
200 LINE (10, 20) - (35, 20)
210 LINE -STEP (DELTA%, DELTA%)
220 LINE -STEP (DELTA%, -DELTA%)
230 LINE -STEP (DELTA%, 0)          'Completes a "flying V"
240 '
300 LINE (150, 20) - (200, 45), , B       'An outlined box
310 LINE (230, 20) - STEP (50, DELTA%), , BF 'A filled box
400 END
```

Note how lines 300 and 310 use two consecutive commas to omit the *color* parameter. By omitting the *color* parameter, the value of *color* defaults to 3 in each instruction.

Figure 11.5 shows the result of SHOWLINE.BAS.

Fig. 11.5. *Lines and rectangles drawn by* SHOWLINE.BAS.

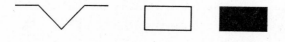

Drawing Arcs, Ellipses, and Wedges with *CIRCLE*

You can add three optional parameters (*start, end,* and *aspect*) to the end of a CIRCLE instruction. With these parameters, in addition to circles, you can draw a partial circle, partial ellipse, complete ellipse, or a pie-shaped wedge. (An ellipse is a squashed-in circle resembling the outline of a football.)

CIRCLE (*xcenter, ycenter*), *radius, color, start, end, aspect*

where *xcenter, ycenter, radius,* and *color* have been explained previously, *start* specifies the beginning point of an arc as an angle in radians, *end* specifies the ending point of an arc as an angle in radians, and *aspect* specifies the aspect ratio of the x-radius to the y-radius.

A CIRCLE instruction can contain seven parameters! That may seem impos-ing, but actually the syntax of CIRCLE is quickly learned. Remember, with CIRCLE, only the *xcenter*, *ycenter*, and *radius* parameters must be specified. The other four parameters are optional.

Use *start* and *end* to draw a partial circle (that is, an arc). The *start* and *end* parameters identify each endpoint of the arc as an angle in radians (not degrees) from the horizontal. Each angle must be in the range from -2π to $+2\pi$ (or the value is normalized into this range). The angles are located in the conventional geometric manner with 0 to the right, 0.5π straight up, π to the left, and 1.5π straight down (refer to fig. 6.2). Recall that 360 degrees equals 2π radians (see Chapter 6, "Manipulating Data").

BASIC draws each arc counterclockwise. Consider the drawing "pen" to be raised above the screen and moving in a circle with the prescribed center and radius. The pen sweeps counterclockwise. When the *start* angle is reached, the pen "drops" to the screen and begins drawing. When the *end* angle is reached, the pen "lifts" from the screen to complete the desired arc. If you specify either *start* or *end*, but not both, the absent parameter defaults to a value of zero.

If *start* or *end* is negative, BASIC draws a straight line from the respective endpoint of the arc to the center of the circle. Thus, by making both parame-ters negative, you generate a pie-shaped wedge. To locate an arc, the minus sign is stripped from the parameter to form a positive number (that is, the absolute value of the parameter determines the location angle).

By adjusting *aspect*, you create an ellipse (or partial arc of an ellipse) rather than a true circle. When *CIRCLE* draws an ellipse, the *radius* parameter spe-cifies the length of the major (larger) axis of the ellipse. When *aspect* is less than 1, *radius* is the x-radius, and the ellipse has a larger x-radius than y-radius. When *aspect* is greater than 1, *radius* is the y-radius, and the ellipse has a larger y-radius than x-radius. If *aspect* is negative, the results are unpredictable, but no fatal error occurs. You have to experiment with your particular hardware to determine appropriate values of aspect for your desired circles and ellipses.

When a complete circle or ellipse is drawn, the LPR becomes the center of the circle or ellipse. When an arc is drawn, the LPR becomes the center that the circle or ellipse would have if the arc were completed.

The following program, called DOCIRCLE.BAS, demonstrates many features of CIRCLE:

```
100 REM Program: DOCIRCLE.BAS (Demonstrate CIRCLE statement)
110 SCREEN 2                 'Select high-resolution graphics
120 CLS
130 PI = 4 * ATN(1)          'Calculates the value of Pi
200 CIRCLE (100, 30), 30               'Shape A
```

Listing continues

Listing continued

```
210 CIRCLE (200, 30), 30, , PI / 10, PI / 2      'Shape B
220 CIRCLE (300, 30), 30, , PI / 2, PI / 10      'Shape C
230 CIRCLE (100, 140), 30, , -PI / 10, -PI / 2   'Shape D
240 CIRCLE (200, 140), 30, , , , .2              'Shape E
250 CIRCLE (300, 140), 30, , , , 2               'Shape F
300 LOCATE 8, 13:PRINT "A"; TAB(26); "B"; TAB(38); "C"
310 LOCATE 23, 13:PRINT "D"; TAB(26); "E"; TAB(38); "F"
400 END
```

Figure 11.6 shows the results of DOCIRCLE.BAS. The screen image contains six shapes, in two rows of three. Shapes A through C are in the top row, and shapes D through F are in the bottom row.

Fig. 11.6. *Output from the* DOCIRCLE.BAS *program.*

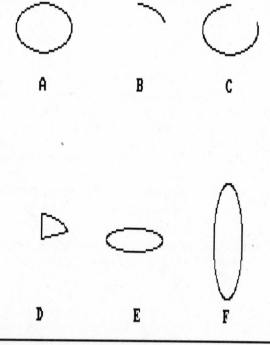

Shape A is a complete circle. Shapes B and C are partial circles that demonstrate the flip-flopping of the *start* and *end* parameters. Shape D is a pie-shaped wedge created with negative values for *start* and *end*. Shapes E and F demonstrate how changing *aspect* creates different ellipses.

Note that the LOCATE and PRINT instructions in lines 300 and 310 work fine in graphics mode. One nice feature of BASIC's graphics modes is that you can freely mix text and graphics on the same screen.

A Graphics Language— the *DRAW* Statement

As you can see, BASIC certainly has an impressive repertoire of graphics statements. With PSET, LINE, COLOR, and PAINT, you can readily create a variety of graphic images.

But there's more. You can also describe graphic images with DRAW instructions. A DRAW instruction consists of the keyword DRAW followed by a string expression. The string expression expresses graphic images according to a special graphics language.

DRAW *strexpr*

where *strexpr* is a string expression conforming to the conventions of the graphics language.

The DRAW language contains strings that can do the following:

❏ Produce lines.
❏ Set colors.
❏ Paint areas.
❏ Rotate images.
❏ Scale shapes.

As such, DRAW can do some things, such as image rotation and scaling, that are difficult with BASIC's "regular" graphics statements. On the other hand, DRAW cannot easily produce certain shapes, especially circles and arcs.

Fortunately, DRAW works easily in conjunction with the other BASIC graphics statements. The result is a powerful, integrated graphics capability.

Each DRAW string expression contains one or more fundamental *command strings*. The fundamental DRAW command strings consist of a one- or two-letter abbreviation followed, in most cases, by an optional numeric argument. Table 11.7 shows the fundamental DRAW commands.

Table 11.7. *Fundamental* DRAW *commands.*

Command	Action
U*n*	Move up
D*n*	Move down
L*n*	Move left
R*n*	Move right
E*n*	Move diagonally up and right
F*n*	Move diagonally down and right
G*n*	Move diagonally down and left
H*n*	Move diagonally up and left
M*x,y*	Move to point *x,y*
B	Raise pen (move without plotting)
N	Move, but return to original LPR when done
A*n*	Set rotation angle
TA*n*	Set turn angle
C*n*	Set color
S*n*	Set scale factor
P	Paint area
X	Execute substring

Before you use DRAW, you must put your computer in one of BASIC's graphics modes with a SCREEN instruction.

Movement Commands

The M command draws a line from the LPR to the point specified by *x,y*. For example, the following instruction draws a line from the LPR to the point (85, 99):

```
800 DRAW "M 85,99"
```

This has the same effect as the instruction

```
800 LINE -(85, 99)
```

Movement can be expressed in relative coordinates by preceding the *x* destination with a plus (+) or minus (−) sign. Such a sign designator establishes both the *x* and *y* coordinates as relative. Here are some examples:

```
500 DRAW "M  23, 48" 'Move  to absolute coordinate (23,48)
510 DRAW "M +23, 48" 'Move 23 pixels right, 48 down from LPR
```

```
520 DRAW "M +23,-48" 'Move 23 pixels right, 48 up from LPR
530 DRAW "M -23, 48" 'Move 23 pixels left, 48 down from LPR
540 DRAW "M -23,-48" 'Move 23 pixels left, 48 up from LPR
```

Relative Movement

For relative moves, you can move in any of the eight basic compass directions (see fig. 11.7).

Fig. 11.7. *The eight movement directions.*

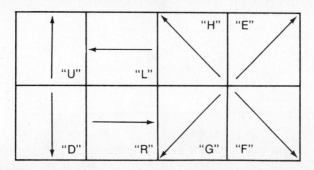

Each of the eight relative movement commands takes an integer argument that specifies how many pixels to move. If you omit the argument, a single pixel is drawn in the specified direction. If the argument is negative, movement occurs in the opposite (180 degree) direction. Here are some examples:

```
600 DRAW "R16"      'Draw 16-pixel line from LPR to the right
610 DRAW "E"        'Draw 1 pixel "northeast" from LPR
620 DRAW "U8"       'Draw 8-pixel line from LPR upward
630 DRAW "U-8"      'Draw 8-pixel line from LPR downward
```

After any movement command, the LPR is set to the destination point.

Movement Prefixes

Two prefixes are available to modify a movement command.

❏ B   Move without plotting, for example, DRAW "BD14"

❏ N   Move without updating LPR—for example,
         DRAW "NM8,29"

Use B to adjust the LPR without drawing any line. Use N to draw a line without updating the LPR.

Forming Command Strings

The fundamental command strings can be, and usually are, grouped together to form one string expression. For example, the following program produces the kite shown in figure 11.8. Note how the individual command strings are joined into one string literal.

```
100 SCREEN 1        'Must be in graphics mode to use DRAW
200 DRAW "H25 E25 F25 G25 D10 NL5 NR5 D10"      'Draw Kite
```

Fig. 11.8. *A kite produced by* DRAW.

In DRAW strings, blank spaces are not significant between the fundamental command strings. You may use spaces to separate commands for readability but such spaces are not required. Also semicolons are optional delimiters. Upper- and lowercase are interchangeable for the command letters. For example, the kite command could be written as follows:

```
200 DRAW "H25 e25f25G 25; D10 N L5; Nr5d10"
```

It surely is harder to read that way, but it's legal.

Angle Commands

The A*n* command causes all subsequent images to be rotated at the angle (*n* ∗ 90) degrees where *n* can be 0, 1, 2, or 3. For example, DRAW "A2" rotates subsequent images 180 degrees.

The TA*n* command (Turn Angle) sets the rotation angle to *n* where *n* can range from −360 to +360 degrees. Negative *n* causes clockwise rotations, and positive *n* causes counterclockwise rotations.

Note that these commands specify angles in degrees. This is a departure from the usual BASIC standard of angles measured in radians.

Figure 11.9 shows the kite rotated clockwise 30 degrees. In line 120, we added a TA command to cause the rotation.

```
100 SCREEN 1
150 DRAW "TA-30"                       'Set 30-degree rotation
200 DRAW "H25 E25 F25 G25 D10 NL5 NR5 D10"      'Draw Kite
```

Fig. 11.9. The kite is rotated 30 degrees.

Scaling an Image

S*n* makes subsequent images larger or smaller. The parameter *n* sets the scale factor to *n*/4. Thus "S12" creates images three times larger, and "S2" halves the size. *n* can range from 1 to 255. The default for *n* is 4, which sets the scaling to unity (that is, no scaling).

To see the scaling effect, try adding a DRAW "S8" instruction just after line 100 in either kite-drawing program. The kite becomes twice (8/4) the original size.

Colorizing and Painting

You can adjust the foreground (drawing) color with the C*n* command. Here, as usual, *n* can assume any value consistent with the current SCREEN mode and your system's video hardware.

Try adding the following instruction in either kite program:

```
110 DRAW "C2"
```

You will see a magenta kite.

One use of the C command is to erase all or parts of already drawn figures. Just set the drawing color to the background color (usually black). Then redraw the figure. Bingo, it's gone.

Use the P command to paint the interior of any enclosed shape.

> P *paintcolor, bordercolor*
>
> where *paintcolor* specifies the color to use for painting. The entire area is painted until a boundary of the color *bordercolor* is reached. Painting begins at the current LPR.

To illustrate the P and C commands, the following program draws the kite in magenta with the interior painted cyan:

```
100 SCREEN 1
110 DRAW "C2"                            'Set color to magenta
200 DRAW "H25 E25 F25 G25 D10 NL5 NR5 D10" 'Draw Kite
250 DRAW "BU25"                          'Move LPR inside kite
300 DRAW "P1, 2"                         'Paint interior cyan
```

Using Variables with *DRAW*

So far, all our example DRAW strings and numeric arguments have been literals, but you can use variables also.

For numeric variables as parameters, the syntax requires the following components in order:

1. The command letter.

2. An equal sign.

3. The name of the numeric variable.

4. A semicolon.

Don't forget that semicolon.

Table 11.8 shows some DRAW instructions written with numeric literals and the equivalent instructions using numeric variables.

Table 11.8. Using numeric variables with DRAW.

Instruction	Equivalent Form with Numeric Variables
50 DRAW "R65"	50 SPAN% = 65: DRAW "R = SPAN%;"
50 DRAW "P1,2"	50 C% = 1: B% = 2: DRAW "P = C%;, = B%;"
50 DRAW "U3 L6"	50 X% = 3: Y% = 6 DRAW "U = X%; L = Y%;"

> ## Use String Variables for DRAW Arguments
>
> DRAW arguments can be any string expressions, including string variables. You can assign an entire command string to a string variable and then DRAW the variable directly. For example, here's an alternative way to draw the diamond part of the kite:
>
> ```
> 200 DIAMOND$ = "H25 E25 F25 G25"
>
> 210 DRAW DIAMOND$
> ```
>
> Take advantage of string variables to store frequently used command strings. Then you can "draw" the strings with simple string variables rather than lengthy string literals.

Using Substrings

The X subcommand specifies that a secondary string variable be executed from within the primary string. This is something like a GOSUB. The primary string makes a "call" to a secondary string command.

The syntax of the X subcommand requires the following components in order:

1. The command letter X.

2. The string variable name (which contains graphics strings).

3. A semicolon.

Again, don't forget that semicolon.

For example, the following program draws two enlarged, cyan diamonds.

```
100 SCREEN 1
120 DIAMOND$ = "H25 E25 F25 G25" 'Define the diamond shape
140 DRAW "S8 C1 XDIAMOND$; BR15 XDIAMOND$;"
```

You can duplicate the effect of the X command by concatenating direct strings. To illustrate, here's an alternative line 140 that draws the same two diamonds:

```
140 DRAW "S8 C1" + DIAMOND$ + "BR15"  + DIAMOND$
```

The *POINT* Function

The POINT function returns information about a given pixel. There are two distinct forms of POINT: the color form and the coordinate form.

The Color Form of the *POINT* Function

POINT(*xycoordinates*)

where *xycoordinates* specify an *x* and *y* position.

In this form, POINT returns the color of the pixel at the specified location. The returned value is the color cup number from 0 to 3. If *xycoordinates* specify a location off the screen, POINT returns a value of −1.

For example, the following instruction assigns to HUE% the color of the pixel at location (65, 30):

```
700 HUE% = POINT(65, 30)
```

You can use POINT to specify the *color* parameter in various graphing instructions. For example, the following instruction turns the pixel at location (233, 108) into the same color as the pixel at (44, 21):

```
830 PSET(233, 108), POINT(44, 21)
```

The Coordinate Form of the *POINT* Function

In the second form of the POINT function, only one parameter appears. The parameter can have the value of 0 or 1. POINT returns LPR information as shown in table 11.9.

Table 11.9. POINT *function options.*

Function	Meaning
POINT(0)	Returns X coordinate of LPR
POINT(1)	Returns Y coordinate of LPR

Clipping

What happens if you try to graph outside the normal screen boundary? For example, suppose that you specify `LINE` coordinates above the upper edge of the screen. Is this an error?

No. Most graphics instructions, such as `LINE` and `CIRCLE`, permit graphics coordinates outside the screen boundaries. The instructions draw only the portion of the image lying inside the screen boundaries.

This process of suppressing out-of-bounds graphics is called *clipping*. To understand clipping, think of your video screen lying inside a much larger imaginary canvas. This large canvas permits coordinates extending past those of your video screen.

`LINE` and other graphics instructions work on this canvas. Whenever part of the image comes into your screen area, the graphics become visible. Anything solely on the imaginary canvas is clipped.

The following program demonstrates the clipping of a circle and a box. Note that the center of the circle lies above the upper edge of the video screen. Line 120 draws a rectangle with one side lying to the left of the screen boundary.

```
100 SCREEN 2
110 CIRCLE (300, -50), 200
120 LINE (-90, 50)-(150, 150), , , B
```

Adjusting the Viewport—*VIEW*

With a `VIEW` instruction, you confine graphics to a specified rectangular area of the screen. This area is called a *viewport*. Anything drawn outside the viewport is clipped

`VIEW` has two forms, with and without the `SCREEN` keyword.

`VIEW` (*upleftxy*)-(*lowrightxy*), *viewcolor*, *bordercolor*

or

`VIEW SCREEN` (*upleftxy*)-(*lowrightxy*), *viewcolor*, *bordercolor*

where *upleftxy* specifies the upper left corner of the viewport in absolute coordinates, *lowrightxy* specifies the lower right corner of the viewport in absolute coordinates, *viewcolor* specifies the color to paint the viewport, and *bordercolor* specifies a border color to draw around the viewport.

The *viewcolor* and *bordercolor* parameters are optional.

When you establish a viewport, PSET, PRESET, LINE, CIRCLE, and DRAW work only within the viewport. However, text printing and related functions, such as LOCATE, still operate on the full screen.

If *viewcolor* is present, the entire rectangular area of the viewport is painted the specified color. If *bordercolor* is present and if there is screen space available, a one-pixel wide border is drawn around the viewport in the specified color.

When you omit the SCREEN keyword, subsequent coordinate references are relative to the upper left corner of the viewport. Graphic images thus are translated (displaced) into the viewport. When you include SCREEN, coordinate references remain relative to the upper left corner of the video screen. In either case, graphics outside the viewport are clipped.

You can activate only a single viewport at any one time. A second VIEW instruction redefines the viewport.

VIEW without any arguments restores the entire screen as the viewport. Using the SCREEN statement to change video modes also cancels any previous viewport setting.

upleftxy and *lowrightxy* can actually designate any two diagonally opposite corners, not necessarily the upper left and lower right corners.

The following program, named VIEWPORT.BAS, demonstrates the use of viewports with and without the SCREEN keyword. Note that the LOCATE instructions position text relative to the whole screen. The output of this program is shown in figure 11.10.

```
100 REM Program: VIEWPORT.BAS (Show viewports and clipping)
110 SCREEN 1
120 CLS
200 VIEW (20, 20) - (300, 180), , 1      'Cyan border
210     CIRCLE (140, 80), 120            'x,y relative to viewport
220     LOCATE 4, 14
230     PRINT "Outer Viewport"
300 VIEW SCREEN (50, 45) - (270, 155), 0, 2 'Magenta border
310     CIRCLE (160, 100), 80            'x,y relative to screen
320     LOCATE 12, 14
330     PRINT "Inner Viewport"
400 END
```

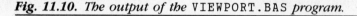

Fig. 11.10. *The output of the* VIEWPORT.BAS *program.*

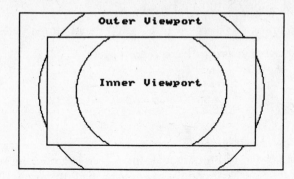

Mixing Text and Graphics

As you have seen throughout this chapter, you can freely mix text with graphics. The normal text statements, such as PRINT and LOCATE, work correctly in the graphics modes. You can superimpose text onto graphics images and graphics images onto text.

Scrolling text (by printing on the bottom line with a carriage return), causes the entire screen to scroll. Graphics and text scroll upward together.

A WIDTH instruction can toggle the screen mode. A WIDTH 80 instruction issued from SCREEN mode 1 causes the graphics mode to switch to mode 2—just as though you issued a SCREEN 2 instruction. Similarly, a WIDTH 40 instruction from SCREEN mode 2 acts just as though you had issued a SCREEN 1 instruction.

Advanced Graphics

We have covered much material in this chapter, but we have barely scratched the surface. Wait a minute, that's not true—we certainly have "scratched the surface." However, believe it or not, BASIC provides many graphics features that we have not yet mentioned.

In Chapter 15, "Toward Advanced Programming," we introduce the following advanced graphics topics:

❏ Drawing stylized lines.

❏ Filling areas with patterned tiles.

❑ Animating graphic images.

❑ Customizing the coordinate system.

❑ Graphing options available with EGA, VGA, and MCGA video adapters.

❑ Storing images on alternative screen "pages."

Summary

BASIC has extensive graphics capability. You initialize graphics with a SCREEN instruction. In graphics modes, the screen is a rectangular grid of tiny dots called *pixels*. You have control over each pixel. By turning the pixels on or off (white or black), or making them various colors, you can create exciting visual screens.

Of course, to use graphics, your computer must have the appropriate hardware. BASIC supports CGA (medium and high-resolution graphics), EGA, VGA, and MCGA video adapters. With a color monitor, BASIC can produce color graphics.

A number of special instructions aid you in drawing images. LINE draws straight lines and rectangles. CIRCLE draws circles, ellipses, and arcs. PSET and PRESET turn on any individual pixel. Each of these instructions works with color as well as with black and white.

Speaking of color, the COLOR instruction adjusts the default colors. In medium-resolution graphics (mode 1), you can make the background any one of 16 colors. A COLOR instruction also selects one of two color palettes; each palette has 3 predefined colors for drawing objects.

High-resolution graphics (mode 2) does not support color. Only black and white graphics are possible. Because the screen has twice as many pixels, however, you can create finer detailed drawings than with mode 1.

DRAW provides a separate facility for specifying graphic images. With DRAW instructions, you specify graphic parameters using special string expressions. DRAW can scale and rotate images.

Graphics modes blend readily with text. The various text mode statements such as PRINT and LOCATE work smoothly in graphics modes. You can freely integrate text and graphics with text superimposed directly onto graphic images.

CHAPTER 12

Programming Hardware Devices

```
LPRINT, LPRINT USING, WIDTH LPRINT, LPOS, LLIST, INPUT,
LINE INPUT, INKEY$, KEY, BEEP, SOUND, PLAY, DATE$,
TIME$, TIMER
```

The preceding three chapters attest to the considerable control you have over the video screen and the disk drives. But BASIC also supports other hardware on your computer system. This chapter shows you how to control the following devices:

- ❏ The line printer
- ❏ The keyboard
- ❏ The speaker
- ❏ The DOS date and time

Using the Printer

Your computer system probably includes a line printer—perhaps a dot-matrix, daisy wheel, or laser printer. You can control your printer from your BASIC programs or generate program listings from BASIC's direct mode.

Of course, your printer must be on before you can produce any printed output. You cannot turn your printer on or off directly from BASIC. You have to flip your printer's power switch (or press your printer button) the old-fashioned way—by hand.

Sending Output to the Printer

Often you want to produce printed output. Some programs produce financial or inventory reports, for example. You can easily direct your output to the printer rather than to the video screen. BASIC has two statements that direct output to the printer.

LPRINT *exprlist*

LPRINT USING *formatstr*; *exprlist*

where *exprlist* is a list of expressions separated by commas and semicolons, and *formatstr* is a string expression containing formatting instructions.

LPRINT and LPRINT USING send data to your printer in the same way that PRINT and PRINT USING send data to your video screen:

❑ Comma separators in the expression list delineate multiple expressions into print zones.

❑ A trailing semicolon in the expression list suppresses the carriage return/line feed.

❑ The simple instruction LPRINT (without an expression list) prints a blank line on the printer.

❑ LPRINT USING works with format strings just the way PRINT USING does.

❑ The TAB and SPC functions work within LPRINT and LPRINT USING instructions.

The essential point is that just as any PRINT instruction creates output on the video screen, the equivalent LPRINT instruction produces the same output on the line printer. Similarly, LPRINT USING duplicates on your printer what PRINT USING produces on your video screen.

> ### What Does the *L* Stand for?
> You can think of the *LP* in LPRINT as an abbreviation for *line printer*.

See Chapter 9, "Writing Text on the Video Screen," for a complete discussion of PRINT, PRINT USING, TAB, and SPC.

Adjusting the Printer Width

BASIC assumes that your printer has a width of 80 characters. This means that you cannot normally print past column 80. After printing in column 80, BASIC "tells" the printer to do a carriage return and line feed.

The WIDTH LPRINT statement, however, lets you adjust the printer width. (*Note:* Some versions of BASIC do not support the WIDTH LPRINT statement.)

> WIDTH LPRINT *width*
>
> where *width* specifies the default width for the line printer. The *width* parameter should have a value from 1 to 255.

You may want to make *width* larger or smaller than 80. If you have a wide-carriage printer, you can set *width* to 136 (or whatever your actual printer width is) to enable wide-carriage printing. For printer emulation of 40-column screen mode, set *width* to 40.

The following program, PRNWIDTH.BAS demonstrates the effect of adjusting the printer width:

```
100 REM Program: PRNWIDTH.BAS (Adjust printer default width)
110 MOTTO$ = "A stitch in time saves nine."
120 WIDTH LPRINT 80     'Set printer width to 80
130 LPRINT MOTTO$
140 LPRINT              'Print a blank line
200 REM
```

```
210 WIDTH LPRINT 20       'Set printer width to 20
220 LPRINT MOTTO$
230 LPRINT
300 REM
310 WIDTH LPRINT 10       'Set printer width to 10
320 LPRINT MOTTO$
400 END
```

The output of PRNWIDTH.BAS looks like this on your printer:

```
A stitch in time saves nine.

A stitch in time sav
es nine.

A stitch i
n time sav
es nine.
```

The *LPOS* Function

Use the LPOS function to determine the horizontal (column) position of the print head. LPOS does for the printer what POS does for the screen.

LPOS(*printernum*)

where *printernum* specifies the printer number. For single-printer systems, the value of *printernum* is (usually) 1.

The value of *printernum* specifies the DOS line printer designation. Most single-printer systems configure the line printer as device LPT1:. Systems with two or three printers have LPT2: and/or LPT3: as well. A value of 0 or 1 for *printernum* refers to LPT1:, 2 refers to LPT2:, and 3 refers to LPT3:.

The vast majority of computer systems have a single printer (which is almost always configured as LPT1:). If your system is in this large group, use 0 or 1 as the value for *printernum*.

Note: some versions of BASIC treat *printernum* as a dummy argument. With these versions, LPOS can reference only a single line printer. No matter what value you use for *printernum*, LPOS refers to the single printer (LPT1:).

LPOS is handy when you print multiple items on a single line. At a given point in your program, you might need to know whether there is enough room on the current printer line to print the next item. If there is enough room, you want to print the item. If not, you want to issue a carriage return before you print the item.

As an example, the following program fragment checks that there is sufficient room on the current line of an 80-column printer to print the value of ITEM$. If not, the program issues a carriage return (that is, an LPRINT) before printing.

```
730 IF (LPOS(1) + LEN(ITEM$)) > 80 THEN LPRINT
740 LPRINT ITEM$
```

LPOS and TAB Don't Mix

Be aware that LPOS does not work correctly if you use the TAB function in your LPRINT instructions. TAB characters are not recognized correctly by LPOS. Avoid TAB if you intend to use LPOS.

Generating Printed Program Listings

Chapter 3, "A Hands-On Introduction to Programming," discussed the LIST command, which lists your program on the screen. The companion command, LLIST, also lists your program, but this time on your printer.

Although you can use LLIST as a program instruction, you normally will issue LLIST commands while editing in direct mode.

LLIST works exactly like LIST. You can print all or part of your program. Table 12.1 shows some sample LLIST commands.

Table 12.1. Sample LLIST commands.

Command	Effect
LLIST	Prints all lines of your program
LLIST 200-550	Prints all lines numbered from 200 to 550
LLIST 300-	Prints all lines numbered 300 or higher
LLIST -780	Prints all lines numbered from 0 to 780

Using the Keyboard

Now turn your attention to an extremely important part of your computer—the keyboard. We examine the following ways that you can control this device with which your fingers are so familiar:

❏ Accept input from the user while the program is running.

❏ Detect a user keystroke.

❏ Redefine the function keys to produce specified strings.

❏ Manipulate the Function Key Display on the bottom of your screen.

Obtaining User Input

Frequently, you want a user to supply information while your program is running. You are already familiar with the two statements BASIC provides to request and accept input data:

❏ INPUT prompts the user for numeric or string data (or both). We introduced INPUT in Chapter 3, "A Hands-On Introduction to Programming," and have used INPUT frequently in our program examples.

❏ LINE INPUT stores an entire line typed by the user into a single string variable. We introduced LINE INPUT in conjunction with disk files in Chapter 10, "Using Disk Files."

Here, we condense what you have learned about INPUT and LINE INPUT as well as present some additional details.

The *INPUT* Statement

INPUT has several forms.

In INPUT instructions, punctuation has the following meanings:

❏ A semicolon after the keyword INPUT makes the cursor stay on the same line after the user presses Enter.

❏ No semicolon (or other punctuation character) after the keyword INPUT causes the cursor to move down to the next line after the user presses Enter.

❏ A semicolon after *promptstr* displays a question mark at the end of *promptstr*.

❏ A comma after *promptstr* means that no question mark is displayed at the end of *promptstr*.

INPUT ; "*promptstr*"; *varlist*

where *promptstr* is a string literal displayed on-screen to prompt the user for input, and *varlist* is a comma-delimited list of variables to which the user's input is assigned.

The semicolon after INPUT is optional. The semicolon after *promptstr* can be replaced by a comma. Different punctuation causes different effects.

The entire "*promptstr*" clause can be omitted, yielding this simpler form of INPUT:

INPUT *varlist*

When you don't include a prompt string with INPUT, only a question mark (no message) prompts the user. Here is an example of the simplest form of the INPUT instruction:

400 INPUT USERNUMBER!

The results of this instruction are as follows:

1. A question mark displays on the screen.

2. The program pauses for the user to supply a number. After typing the number, the user must press Enter.

3. The number typed by the user is assigned to the variable USERNUMBER!

4. The program continues.

By including *promptstr*, INPUT prompts the user with a customized message. Here's an example:

400 INPUT "Please enter a number"; USERNUMBER!

Now the message Please enter a number? prompts the user to enter a number. Note the question mark at the end of the message. If line 400 has a comma rather than a semicolon after *promptstr*, no question mark appears.

You can prompt for multiple values by using additional variables in the variable list. The user must separate each typed-in value with a comma. The following program, AREARECT.BAS, is an example of prompting for two input values:

```
100 REM Program: AREARECT.BAS (INPUT with 2 variables)
110 PRINT "Area of a rectangle given two connecting sides."
120 INPUT "Enter the lengths of the sides"; SIDE1, SIDE2
130 AREA = SIDE1 * SIDE2
140 PRINT "The area is"; AREA
```

Here is sample output from this program:

```
Area of a rectangle given two connecting sides.
Enter the lengths of the sides? 10.6, 3.9
The area is 41.34
```

Variables in *varlist* can be string variables as well as numeric variables. For example, the following instruction requests the user's name:

```
800 INPUT "Please type your name"; USERNAME$
```

When you type string input, you don't have to enclose your response in double quotation marks. However, just as with numeric input, a comma has a special meaning. The comma separates distinct data values. By using double quotation marks around a string, a single input string can contain embedded commas. See the upcoming discussion of LINE INPUT for an example of input containing a comma.

Leading blanks and tab characters are ignored in the typed input unless double quotation marks are used around string data.

In addition to simple string or numeric variables, *varlist* may also include array elements.

When you respond to an INPUT prompt, your input must match *varlist* in number and type. That is, the number of input responses you give and their type (string or numeric) must correspond exactly to the number and type of variables in the variable list. If there is any discrepancy, BASIC displays the following message:

```
Redo from start
```

You must then reenter the entire line of data.

The *LINE INPUT* Statement

LINE INPUT is similar to INPUT.

LINE INPUT ; *"promptstr"*; *strvar*

where *promptstr* is a string literal displayed on-screen to prompt the user for input, and *strvar* is a string variable to which the user's input is assigned.

The semicolon after LINE INPUT is optional.

The entire *"promptstr"* clause can be omitted, yielding this simpler form of LINE INPUT:

LINE INPUT *varlist*

If included, the semicolon after LINE INPUT causes the cursor to stay on the same line after the user presses Enter.

LINE INPUT differs from INPUT in the following ways:

❏ Data input from the keyboard can be assigned to only one variable, which must be a string variable.

❏ No question mark prints automatically. To get a question mark, you must explicitly include one as part of your *promptstr*.

❏ Delimiters (such as commas) in the user's input have no special meaning. Everything the user types (up to 255 characters) before pressing Enter is stored as a single string value in *strvar*.

Use LINE INPUT when commas may be required as part of the input. Consider these two instructions:

```
200 INPUT "What is your full name"; FULLNAME$
300 LINE INPUT "What is your full name? "; FULLNAME$
```

Either instruction works fine if the input is John Wesley Harding. But suppose that the input is Harding, John Wesley. Now line 300 works okay (the comma is accepted), but line 200 fails because the comma after Harding separates the input into two values (when only one value was expected).

Detecting a Keystroke

Suppose, in a particular program, that you need to display two screens full of information. You want the first screen to remain visible until the user is ready to read the next screen. One solution is to print a message with the first screen that tells the user to hit a key in order to see the second screen.

That's fine, but how do you pause your program's execution and detect when the user hits a key? Well, we wouldn't ask this question if BASIC didn't provide a way, would we?

The INKEY$ function not only detects whether a key has been pressed but also indicates the particular key that was pressed. INKEY$ has no parameters, so the syntax is simple.

```
INKEY$
```

The INKEY$ function examines the keyboard buffer to see whether a key has been pressed. Only the first keystroke is recognized, even if multiple characters are waiting in the buffer. INKEY$ returns a zero-, one-, or two-character string interpreted as follows:

- ❏ *Null string.* No character is in the keyboard buffer. That is, no character has yet been pressed.

- ❏ *One-character string.* The string contains the actual character read from the keyboard buffer. For example, if the user pressed the *g* key, INKEY$ returns "g"; if the user pressed Shift-g, INKEY$ returns "G".

- ❏ *Two-character string:* This indicates that a special key was pressed such as one of the special function keys (F1 through F10, Home, or Del, for example) or a key combination (Ctrl-Q, for example). A two-character string is called an *extended key code*. The first character always has an ASCII value of 0. See Appendix C, "Keyboard Codes," for a list of the extended codes.

The Keyboard Is Buffered

Whenever you press a key, whether or not you are in BASIC, DOS records the keystroke in the *keyboard buffer*. This buffer is simply an area of memory that retains the values of the most recent keystrokes. (As your application "reads" your keystrokes, they are removed from the buffer, leaving room for as many as 16 new keystrokes to be recorded. This process usually happens so fast that you never notice any delay.)

While a program is running, keystrokes are not normally removed from the buffer (except by INPUT and other specialized instructions). Any keys you press build up in the buffer.

INKEY\$, unlike INPUT, does not wait for the user to press a key. INKEY\$ simply removes the first keystroke found in the keyboard buffer, if the buffer contains any keystrokes at all. Try the following short demonstration program to see the effect of keyboard buffering and INKEY\$:

```
100 FOR J = 1 TO 10000: NEXT J     'Waste time
200 PRINT INKEY$
```

The loop in line 100 wastes time, about five seconds on an AT-class machine. During this wait, you can press a key to store a keystroke in the buffer.

For starters, run the program. (Type RUN and press Enter.) Don't press any key after you press Enter. This is what you should see:

```
RUN

Ok
```

Note the time delay (from line 100) from when you press Enter until you finally see Ok. The blank line between RUN and Ok is the result of line 200. Because you didn't press any keys while the program was running, INKEY\$ returns a null string that displays as the blank line.

Now, run the program again but quickly press the *h* key (the unshifted letter H) before the Ok prompt appears. You see the following:

```
RUN
h
Ok
```

Note how the h keystroke remains in the buffer while waiting for the loop in line 100 to terminate. The INKEY\$ then "pulls" this keystroke from the buffer, and line 200 dutifully displays it.

Now for the big finish. Run the program one last time. Quickly press the *h, j,* and *k* keys in rapid succession, before the Ok prompt appears. The result:

```
RUN
h
Ok
jk
```

The *h, j,* and *k* keystrokes were all stored in the buffer. The INKEY\$ in line 200 pulls out the *h*. After the program concludes, BASIC detects keys remaining in the buffer (*j* and *k*) and displays them as normal direct-mode keystrokes.

The most frequent use of INKEY$ is, undoubtedly, to pause program execution until the user presses a key. Remember the problem we posed of displaying two screens of information and waiting for the user to press a key?

One solution is to place the following program fragment between the code sections that display each screen.

```
700 PRINT "Press a key to see the next screen."
710 WHILE INKEY$ = ""     'Test INKEY$ for null string
720 WEND
```

Lines 710 and 720 form a simple WHILE...WEND loop that executes until the user presses any key. As long as the user doesn't press a key, INKEY$ continually returns the null string and the loop keeps going.

As soon as the user presses a key, INKEY$ returns *some* character, and the condition in line 710 fails. The loop terminates and the program continues with the next line after 720.

As this program demonstrates, INKEY$ is most useful in some sort of loop.

Defining the Function Keys

One exotic keyboard technique at your disposal is to redefine the F1 through F10 function keys. You can associate your own string (up to 15 characters long) with any of the function keys. That way, when the user presses a function key, out pops the string you have preassigned. You will feel like an honest-to-goodness programming wizard.

The KEY statement does the trick.

KEY *funckeynum*, *strexpr*

where *funckeynum* is a numeric expression with a value from 1 to 10, and *strexpr* is any string expression.

Values of 1 through 10 for *funckeynum* correspond to the function keys F1 through F10.

KEY assigns the value of *strexpr* to the designated function key. When the function key is pressed during program execution, the effect is just as though *strexpr* were typed instead. *strexpr* can be as much as 15 characters. Characters beyond 15 are ignored.

Use KEY when specific strings or substrings are repeated frequently during user input. For example, suppose that you are writing a program that prints invitations and seating cards for a dinner dance. The user must type in a list of the attendees. (INPUT instructions prompt the user for the names.) Consider the benefits of adding these lines to the program:

```
400 KEY 1, "Dr. "
410 KEY 2, "Mr. "
420 KEY 3, "Mrs. "
430 KEY 4, "Ms. "
440 KEY 5, "Mr. and Mrs. "
```

Now, for example, instead of typing Mr. and Mrs. John Hannan, only F5 followed by John Hannan is necessary. Quite a time-saver.

Here's a short program that reassigns the F1 key:

```
100 KEY 1, "The honorable " 'Blank space before final quote
110 INPUT "Who are you anyway"; PERSON$
120 PRINT
130 PRINT "You are: "; PERSON$
```

Try the program. It's fun. When you are prompted for input, press F1 before typing your name. Kind of neat, isn't it?

Key Trapping

Imagine this: a program interrupts itself to perform a special task whenever the user presses a particular key. For example, a program might display a help screen whenever the user presses F1.

This capability of instant response to a keystroke is called *key trapping*. In effect, you set a trap for a particular key. If the user "falls into" the trap by pressing the "hotkey," the program responds appropriately.

We discuss how to key-trap in Chapter 15, "Toward Advanced Programming."

Manipulating the Function Key Display

BASIC pre-assigns a particular string to each of the F1 through F10 function keys. These strings are frequently used BASIC commands such as "LIST" and

"RUN". We explain editing with the function keys in Chapter 13, "Editing Techniques."

For now, we want to clarify how the Function Key Display works. As you know, when you first start BASIC, you see the Function Key Display on the bottom line of your screen.

Three special forms of the KEY statement allow you to display the key strings on-screen (see table 12.2). Usually, you use these commands in direct mode, but you can use them as program instructions also. Many programmers place a KEY OFF instruction near the beginning of their programs (in order to turn off the Function Key Display).

Table 12.2. *Alternate forms of the* KEY *statement.*

Command	Meaning
KEY OFF	Removes the Function Key Display.
KEY ON	Turns the Display on (if it was off). The Display consists of the first six characters of the strings assigned to each function key.
KEY LIST	Displays the complete string value of each function key in a vertical list.

Want to see the Function Key Display change right in front of your eyes?

Let's reassign a function key in direct mode. For example, type the following: (Be sure that your Function Key Display is on. If not, type KEY ON.)

```
Ok
KEY 5, "WOW"
```

Watch the middle of the Display as you press Enter. "WOW" instantly appears as the definition for F5.

Using the Speaker

The sound capability of IBM personal computers is rather modest. The speaker is limited to one voice in a single timbre. Furthermore, you cannot adjust the volume. Even so, the speaker can produce music and various sound effects.

Creating Sound Effects with *BEEP* and *SOUND*

As you have seen (heard?), BEEP creates a short (about a quarter-second) tone. The statement accepts no arguments, so the syntax is straightforward.

```
BEEP
```

Use BEEP to get the user's attention. Typical uses are when you request input and when you display an error message. Here's an example:

```
640 PRINT "Sorry, your checkbook is out of balance."
650 BEEP
```

SOUND instructions generate more sophisticated sound effects.

SOUND *frequency, duration*

where *frequency* specifies the pitch of the sound in Hz (cycles per second), and *duration* specifies the length of time (in "clock ticks") to play the tone.

frequency can range from 37 to 32,767. In practice, you should avoid frequencies above 7,000 because frequencies in the high range cause poor response in most speakers. Above 7,000, the tones tend to dwindle in volume until they become inaudible around 12,000 Hz.

duration is measured in clock ticks. There are approximately 18.2 clock ticks per second. The following instruction plays, for five seconds, a tone of 440 Hz (which, for you music aficionados, is an A note):

```
400 SOUND 440, 91
```

The SOUND instruction does not suspend program execution until the tone completes. Instead, the tone begins, and execution proceeds immediately with the subsequent instruction. The tone continues for the prescribed duration while other instructions execute simultaneously.

If a second SOUND instruction occurs while a tone is still playing and the second SOUND instruction has a duration of zero, the speaker is turned off (canceling all sounds). If the duration is greater than zero, the first tone completes before the new SOUND begins.

SOUND can create special audio effects. Here's a program that produces a sound effect something like a bouncing ball:

```
100 REM Makes "bouncing ball" sound
110 FOR J% = 20 TO 0 STEP -1
120     FOR K% = 500 TO 700 STEP 10
130         SOUND K%, .1
140     NEXT K%
150     SOUND 32000, J% * .3
160 NEXT J%
```

This program uses a trick. The SOUND instruction in line 150 specifies a frequency of 32,000. As we mentioned, a frequency this high is inaudible. As a result, the effect of line 250 is a short pause between sounds generated by the SOUND instruction in line 130.

The NOISES.BAS program from Chapter 7, "Modular Programming with Subroutines," produces a variety of sound effects with SOUND.

Playing Music with the *PLAY* Statement

Although SOUND can generate music, BASIC provides a much more flexible mechanism for playing tunes. With the PLAY statement, you can define musical passages with specialized string expressions and then play the music through the speaker.

If you know how to read sheet music, you are in business. You can transcribe music directly into your programs.

PLAY *strexpr*

where *strexpr* is a string expression conforming to the conventions of BASIC's music language.

PLAY uses a special string language in much the same way that DRAW creates graphics with its special string language.

There are 84 available notes spanning seven octaves. The lowest note, note 1, is the C note three octaves below middle C. Note 37 is middle C. The highest note, note 84, is the B note on the seventh octave.

Notes can be specified by number or by letter. For example, the following line:

```
200 PLAY "N37"
```

plays note 37. The following instruction plays the same note (the C in octave 3):

```
210 PLAY "O3 C"
```

With the PLAY language, you can do the following:

❑ Play individual notes.

❑ Play rests (musical pauses).

❑ Adjust the tempo.

Fundamental PLAY strings consist of a one- or two-letter mnemonic followed, in some cases, by a numeric argument. Table 12.3 lists the PLAY commands.

Multiple commands can be placed in a single string literal. For example, PLAY "T150 O4 CDE" plays three notes (C, D, and E) at a specified tempo. Within strings, spaces are irrelevant. Use spaces to clarify the components of your command strings.

Upper- and lowercase letters can be used interchangeably in the command strings.

Setting the Octave

There are seven octaves numbered from zero to six. Each octave ranges from a C note to the higher B note. Middle C is the beginning of octave three.

The O*n* (the letter O) command sets the current octave with *n* ranging from zero to six. Setting the octave establishes the default octave for all notes to follow. Unless otherwise specified, each subsequent note plays from the current octave.

The greater-than sign (>) increases the current octave by one; the less-than sign (<) decreases the current octave by one. However, you cannot set the octave less than zero or greater than six. The default octave is four.

Table 12.3. PLAY *commands.*

Command	Action
O*n*	Set the current octave.
>	Increase the octave by 1.
<	Decrease the octave by 1.
N*n*	Play note number *n*.
A	Play the A note in the current octave.
B	Play the B note in the current octave.
C	Play the C note in the current octave.
D	Play the D note in the current octave.
E	Play the E note in the current octave.
F	Play the F note in the current octave.
G	Play the G note in the current octave.
L*n*	Set the duration of each subsequent note.
MS	Set "Music Staccato."
MN	Set "Music Normal."
ML	Set "Music Legato."
P*n*	Pause for specified number of beats.
T*n*	Set the music tempo.
MF	Play music in foreground.
MB	Play music in background.
X	Execute substring.
+	Suffix to indicate a sharp.
#	Suffix to indicate a sharp (same effect as +).
−	Suffix to indicate a flat.
.	Suffix to increase note duration by 50 percent.

Playing an Individual Note

A letter from A to G specifies which note to play in the current octave. By adding a pound (#) or plus (+) symbol after the note, you change the note to a sharp. By adding a minus (−) symbol, you create a flat. The following instruction plays the entire 12-note sequence of octave 5:

```
600 PLAY "O5 C C# D D+ E F F# G A- A B- B"
```

Instead of specifying letters, you can specify notes by number with the N*n* command. Here, *n* is a number from 0 to 84 specifying which note to play. If *n* is 0, a rest (or pause) plays instead of a tone.

Adjusting the Length of Each Note

The L*n* command sets the length for all notes to follow. The note length is 1/*n*. For example, L1 is a whole note, and L4 is a quarter note. *n* can range from 1 to 64. The default for *n* is 4 (a quarter note).

A numeric length argument can follow a particular note to change the length of only that note. For example, the following instruction plays a B flat eighth note, an E eighth note, an F half note, and a C eighth note.

```
330 PLAY "L8 B-EF2C"
```

A period after an individual note plays a dotted note. This means that the length of the note is multiplied by 3/2. More than one dot may appear after each note, each dot specifying another 3/2 multiplier to the total length. For example, PLAY "L4 C.." plays a C that is 9/4 as long as a quarter note. Dots can appear after a note even if a numeric length designator appears (for example, PLAY "A8.").

Use the P*n* command to specify a pause or rest. *n* can range from 1 to 64. The length of the pause is determined by *n*, using the same scale as for the L command. Dots may be used after a P command to extend the pause length.

Although the L command specifies the time for each note, the note actually plays only a percentage of this time. The three commands MS, MN, and ML specify this percentage. MS plays each subsequent note 3/4 of the time specified by L. The remaining 1/4 time is silent. With MN, each note is on 7/8 of the time and off 1/8. ML plays each note the full period specified by L (no delay between notes). The MS, MN, and ML abbreviations stand for the musical terms "music staccato" (quick), "music normal," and "music legato" (slow).

Adjusting the Tempo

The T*n* command adjusts the tempo for the subsequent music. This command sets *n* to the number of quarter notes per minute. The value of *n* may range from 32 to 255. The default is 120 (a quarter note plays for half a second).

Setting Foreground and Background Music

Music generally plays in the foreground. This means that a PLAY instruction must conclude before any subsequent instruction (PLAY or otherwise) executes.

You can also specify background music. In this mode, a PLAY instruction places the music into a buffer. The following program instructions execute while the music *simultaneously* plays from the buffer. The buffer can accept as many as 32 notes at a time. If more than 32 notes stack up, music plays in the foreground until the number drops to 32.

Use MB to initialize background music. The MF command resets music to the foreground.

Using Variables with *PLAY*

So far, all the example PLAY strings and numeric arguments have been literals. But you can use variables instead.

Numeric variables can be used as parameters. The syntax, however, requires the command letter to be followed by an equal sign and then a numeric variable name. Also, you must place a semicolon after the variable name. Don't forget the semicolon!

Table 12.4 shows some PLAY instructions written with numeric literals and the equivalent instructions written with numeric variables.

Table 12.4. *Using numeric variables with* PLAY.

Instruction	Equivalent Form with Numeric Variables
50 PLAY "N45"	50 NOTE% = 45: PLAY "N=NOTE%;"
75 PLAY "O5 L8"	75 X% = 5: Y% = 8
	80 PLAY "O=X%; L=Y%;"

You can assign an entire command string to a string variable and then PLAY the string variable. For example, the natural notes from C to B can be played as follows:

```
200 SCALE$ = "CDEFGAB": PLAY SCALE$
```

Using Substrings

The X subcommand specifies that a secondary string variable be executed from within the primary string. The subcommand consists of X immediately followed by the string variable name and a trailing semicolon. Again, don't forget the semicolon.

For example, the following instruction plays the natural-note scale at two different tempos (assuming that SCALE$ is defined as in the previous example):

```
300 PLAY "T50 XSCALE$; T200 XSCALE$;"
```

The X subcommand is a bit awkward. You can get the same effect by directly concatenating the strings. For example, the following instruction plays the same two musical scales as does the previous instruction:

```
310 PLAY "T50" + SCALE$ + "T200" + SCALE$
```

Sample Music

Let's put it all together. As an example of a complete tune, the program PLAYTUNE.BAS plays the classic melody from *The Beautiful Blue Danube*, by Johann Strauss, Jr., in the key of D. Run the program, sit back, and enjoy!

```
100 REM Program: PLAYTUNE.BAS (Play the Blue Danube Waltz)
110 REM
200 TUNEPART$ = "DF#AL2 O4 D L4 O5 DDP4"
210 PLAY "T180 DF#A L2 AL4 O4 AAP4F#F#P4 O3 D"
220 PLAY "DF#A L2 A L4 O4 AAP4GGP4 O3 C+"
230 PLAY "C#EB L2 B L4 O4 BBP4GGP4 O3 C+"
240 PLAY "C#EB L2 B L4 O4 BBP4F+F+P4 O3 D"
250 PLAY TUNEPART$
260 PLAY "O4 AAP4 O3 D"
270 PLAY TUNEPART$
280 PLAY "O4 BBP4EEG L8 BP8 ML B1 L4 MN G+A ML L2 O5 F#1"
290 PLAY "L4 MN D O4 F# ML L2 F+ MN L4 E ML L2 B MN L4 A"
300 PLAY "DP8D8D4"
400 END
```

> ### Music Trapping
>
> As we mentioned, you can play background music while your program does other things. The background music buffer holds as many as 32 notes. Suppose that you want to continuously play a 60-note tune in the background. Is this possible?
>
> Yes. The technique is known as *music trapping* because you set a trap for the background music buffer. When the number of notes in the buffer becomes small, the program automatically interrupts whatever it's doing to refill the buffer with more notes.
>
> We show you how to trap music in Chapter 15, "Toward Advanced Programming."

Using Dates and Times

Manipulating the date and time is often important. You might have a program that prints inventory reports. You want to print the current date on the report but don't want to have to type the date each time you run the program.

You can get the current date with a simple BASIC function. BASIC includes several statements and functions that make dealing with dates and times quite convenient. You can do the following:

❏ Set or retrieve the current calendar date.
❏ Set or retrieve the current time of day.
❏ Measure elapsed time.

Manipulating the Date with *DATE$*

DOS maintains the current date. On newer computers, this date is generated by a clock-calendar chip. When you start your computer, this chip sends the current date to DOS. On older computers, you must explicitly provide the date when you boot your system.

Retrieving the Current Date

```
DATE$
```

The DATE$ function, which has no arguments, returns the current date as a 10-character string. This string has the following form:

mm-dd-yyyy

where *mm* is the month from 01 to 12, *dd* is the day of the month from 01 to 31, and *yyyy* is the year from 1980 to 2099.

For example, on the Fourth of July in 1991, the instruction PRINT DATE$ displays the following output:

```
07-04-1991
```

Setting the Current Date

The DATE$ statement changes the date maintained by DOS.

DATE$ = *datestr*

where *datestr* is a string expression specifying the date.

You can format *datestr* in any of the following four ways:

mm-dd-yy
mm/dd/yy
mm-dd-yyyy
mm/dd/yyyy

Four-character year values must be within the range from 1980 to 2099. Two-character year values must range from 80 to 99—representing the years from 1980 to 1999.

The instruction DATE$ = "12-25-90" sets the system date to Christmas Day of 1990.

The following program fragment asks the user to input the current date and then displays the date for confirmation:

```
400 INPUT "Type today's date in form MM-DD-YY"; NEWDATE$
410 DATE$ = NEWDATE$
420 PRINT "Today's date is "; DATE$
```

Manipulating the Current Time of Day

DOS also maintains the time of day. You can retrieve and set this time in a manner similar to that used for the date.

Retrieving the Current Time

```
TIME$
```

The `TIME$` function, which has no arguments, returns the current time of day as an eight-character string. This string has the following form:

hh:mm:ss

where *hh* is the hour from 00 to 23, *mm* is minutes from 00 to 59, and *ss* is seconds from 00 to 59.

For example, at 10 seconds before 2 o'clock in the afternoon, the instruction `PRINT TIME$` displays the following output:

```
13:59:50
```

Note the use of military time (hours from 00 to 23).

Setting the Current Time

The `TIME$` statement resets the current time maintained by DOS.

```
TIME$ = timestr
```

where *timestr* is a string expression specifying the time.

You can format *timestr* in any of the following three ways:

hh
hh:mm
hh:mm:ss

If you omit minutes or seconds, the values of the missing parameters become 0. Again, because military time is used, hours past noon are greater than 12.

The instruction `TIME$ = "17:30:15"` sets the time of day to 15 seconds after 5:30 p.m.

Measuring Elapsed Time with the *TIMER* Function

```
TIMER
```

The `TIMER` function returns the number of seconds elapsed since midnight (or since the computer was booted if the time of day was not set with the DOS TIME command or with BASIC's `TIME$` statement).

The instruction `PRINT TIMER` displays the elapsed time. Here's a sample in direct mode:

```
Ok
PRINT TIMER
 39601.11
Ok
```

That's a lot of seconds, and it's only about 11 o'clock in the morning! (How many seconds are there in a day? Believe it or not, exactly 86,400.)

How Accurate Is TIMER?

`PRINT TIMER` displays a single-precision number (usually expressed with two decimal digits). Because the IBM PC's internal clock is updated approximately 18.2 times a second (actually every 0.0549255 seconds), the `TIMER` function is accurate to a little better than one-tenth of a second.

Timing Program Execution

Sometimes, you need to know the elapsed time between two points in a program. For example, in an educational testing program, you might want to know how long the user takes to make responses.

The TIMER function does the job. Here are the required steps to measure the elapsed time between two points in a program.

1. Assign the value of TIMER to a variable; for example, STARTTIME! = TIMER.

2. Execute the part of the program to be measured.

3. Immediately assign the current value of TIMER to a second variable; for example, ENDTIME! = TIMER.

4. Subtract the values of the two variables to determine the elapsed time.

As an example, the following program shows the time required to calculate the square roots of the numbers from 1 to 3000:

```
100 REM Program: ELAPTIME.BAS (Measure computing time)
110 REM
120 STARTTIME! = TIMER
130 FOR INDEX% = 1 TO 3000          'Loop to be timed
140    MYVAL! = SQR(INDEX%)
150 NEXT INDEX%
160 ENDTIME! = TIMER
170 PRINT "Elapsed time (seconds) ="; ENDTIME! - STARTTIME!
```

Here is the output of ELAPTIME.BAS on our particular IBM AT-compatible computer. (Is your computer faster or slower?)

```
Elapsed time (seconds) = 4.729981
```

The precision of this output is deceptive. Because the TIMER function is accurate to one-tenth of a second, the accuracy of this output must be considered the same, namely, 4.7 seconds.

How fast can you type? HOWFAST.BAS asks you to type the alphabet and then times your typing speed.

```
100 REM Program: HOWFAST.BAS (Measure typing time)
110 REM
120 STARTTIME! = TIMER
130 PRINT "Type the letters from A to Z as fast as you can"
140 INPUT STUFF$
150 ENDTIME! = TIMER
160 PRINT "You took"; ENDTIME! - STARTTIME!; "seconds"
```

Here's what one of the nimble-fingered authors produced:

```
RUN
Type the letters from A to Z as fast as you can"
? abcdefghijklmnopqrstuvwxyz
You took 6.859986 seconds
Ok
```

How about you?

Pausing Execution for a Specified Time Period

You may want a program to pause for a specified time period. Let's say that you are programming a "slide show" that displays several consecutive screens of text and graphics. In order for the viewer to absorb each screen, you need the program to pause about 10 seconds between displays of each screen.

Time delays are another use for TIMER. One technique consists of invoking TIMER inside a WHILE...WEND loop until the specified time period elapses.

Suppose, for example, that you want to produce two speaker beeps spaced five seconds apart. The following program does just that:

```
100 REM Program: TWOBEEPS.BAS (Pause 5 between beeps)
110 '
120 WAITTIME! = 5        'Length of pause time (in seconds)
130 STARTTIME! = TIMER 'Store the starting time
140 BEEP                'First beep
150 '
200 WHILE (TIMER - STARTTIME!) < WAITTIME!
210 WEND                'Loop for WAITTIME! seconds
220 '
300 BEEP                'Second beep
400 END
```

The critical component is the WHILE...WEND loop in lines 200-210. Line 200 continually invokes TIMER until the total elapsed time is greater than or equal to the value of WAITTIME!. This technique has the benefit of working correctly on a computer with any CPU chip (8088, 8086, 80286, or 80386) and at any clock speed.

The Midnight Problem

If you intend to time long events (several hours) or you work in the wee hours, you should become familiar with the "midnight problem."

TIMER, as you know, returns the number of seconds since midnight. There are 86,400 seconds in a day. So, close to midnight, TIMER returns values around 86,000. But as soon as midnight passes, TIMER suddenly returns very small numbers.

As a result, if midnight occurs while you are timing an event, the loop in lines 200-210 of TWOBEEPS.BAS no longer works. The dramatic decrease in the values returned by TIMER causes the test condition to automatically be satisfied. The loop perpetuates too long.

To get around this problem, you need a fancier WHILE...WEND loop that checks for the bewitching hour. Here is such a loop: (If you are so inclined, you can substitute this loop for lines 200 through 220 of TWOBEEPS.BAS.)

```
200 NOW! = STARTTIME!
210 WHILE (NOW! - STARTTIME!) < WAITTIME!
220   OLDTIME! = NOW!
230   NOW! = TIMER
240   IF (NOW! < OLDTIME!) THEN NOW! = NOW! + 86400!
250 WEND
```

Line 240 checks for midnight and updates the value of NOW! if necessary.

Summary

BASIC certainly gives you extensive control over your computer hardware. In previous chapters, you learned how to program your disk drives and fill your video screen with text and graphics. Here, you learned how to program the rest of your computer hardware: the printer, keyboard, speaker, and the internally maintained date and time.

With your printer, you can write programs that *print* the output (rather than display the output on the screen). You can also print program listings. This way, you can permanently save important results and view them at your leisure.

The keyboard is more intriguing than you might first imagine. Of course, you can have the user type information when he or she is prompted by your program. But you can also assign string values to function keys and detect whenever the user presses a key.

Although the speaker is a simple piece of hardware, it is a gold mine for creative programmers. You can create sound effects and musical melodies. With PLAY, you can perform real music—your own compositions or popular favorites.

BASIC can manipulate the date and time maintained by DOS. You can print the current date and time as part of a sales report. In an educational testing program, you might time how long the user takes to provide particular answers.

Part IV

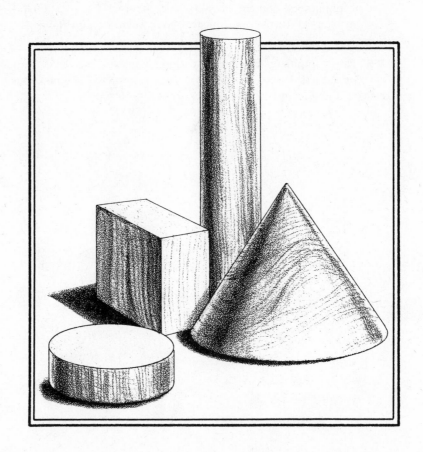

Odds and Ends

By now, you have a solid foundation in BASIC programming. In fact, with only your present knowledge, you can write successful programs for most of your day-to-day programming tasks.

But BASIC is a rich language with a wealth of additional features. Part IV presents an eclectic mix of more advanced programming topics.

The following topics are among the subjects covered in Part IV:

❏ Defining your own functions
❏ Trapping events and errors
❏ Animating graphics
❏ Editing with powerful techniques that facilitate program manipulation
❏ Debugging and testing: what to do when things go wrong

CHAPTER 13

Editing Techniques

```
KEY, EDIT, DELETE, AUTO, RENUM, MERGE, SAVE
```

Editing is a simple reality of programming life. After all, you are editing whenever you type a program into memory or whenever you make corrections to an existing program.

So far, we have only touched on the available editing methods. This chapter fills the gap by introducing techniques such as the following:

❏ Full screen editing
❏ Insert mode
❏ Special shortcut keys
❏ Direct mode commands (EDIT, DELETE, AUTO, RENUM)

We suggest that you experiment with the techniques described in this chapter. Many of the techniques provide alternate ways of doing similar things. It takes practice to determine what works best for you. Find out.

Line Editing

While typing a line of a program (or a command in direct mode), you may notice a typing error before you press Enter. If so, BASIC provides several special keys to assist you in editing the line. Remember, you must press Enter to "officially" send the typed line to BASIC. As such, you can edit the line before pressing Enter.

In chapter 3, we discussed line editing with the left and right arrow keys and with the Backspace key. Recall that you can move the cursor left and right with the arrow keys. With the cursor in the middle of a line, any character you type replaces the old character.

Backspace deletes the character to the immediate left of the cursor. If you've just typed a character, Backspace deletes that character.

However, Backspace and the arrow keys are just the beginning of line editing. There are many other special keys. Table 13.1 summarizes the special line-editing keys. In the table, "Left" and "Right" denote the left arrow and right arrow keys, respectively.

Notice that each special key has an alternate form involving a Ctrl key combination. The two forms do exactly the same thing. For example, Backspace and Ctrl-H each delete the character to the left of the cursor.

Line Editing Notes

Table 13.1 introduces some new features. Here are a few details:

Enter
: You do not have to move the cursor to the end of a line before pressing Enter; the cursor can be anywhere on the line. Regardless of the cursor position, pressing Enter sends the *entire* line to BASIC (including the characters to the right of the cursor). The cursor can even be at the beginning of the line.

Insert mode
: This mode allows you to insert characters in the middle of a line. To use Insert, first move the cursor to the location where you want to insert new characters. Then press Ins. To indicate insert mode, the cursor changes to a small rectangle. Characters you type now are inserted at the cursor position. Characters to the right of the cursor move right to accommodate the newly typed text. Pressing Ins a

Table 13.1. *Special keys for line editing.*

Key	Alternate Key	Effect
Left	Ctrl-]	Moves the cursor one position to the left.
Right	Ctrl-\	Moves the cursor one position to the right.
Backspace	Ctrl-H	Deletes one character to the left of the cursor. All characters to the right of the cursor move one space to the left.
Del	Ctrl-Backspace	Deletes the character at the cursor. All characters to the right of the cursor move one space to the left.
Ins	Ctrl-R	Turns insert mode on or off.
Ctrl-Left	Ctrl-B	Moves the cursor to the beginning of the previous word.
Ctrl-Right	Ctrl-F	Moves the cursor to the beginning of the following word.
End	Ctrl-N	Moves the cursor to the end of the line.
Tab	Ctrl-I	Moves the cursor one tab stop to the right. Tab stops occur every eight columns.
Esc	Ctrl-[	Erases the entire line. The cursor moves to column one.
Ctrl-End	Ctrl-E	Erases all text from the cursor to the end of the line.

second time turns off insert mode. Also, you automatically turn off insert mode by pressing any cursor-movement key or the Enter key.

Word movement   While you press the Ctrl key, you can move the cursor from word to word by pressing the left- or right-arrow key. In this context, a "word" begins with the first letter or digit following a blank space or other punctuation. Word movement provides a quick way to move the cursor along lengthy lines.

Deleting
Del and Backspace are similar but not identical. Del deletes the character at the cursor, and Backspace deletes the character to the left of the cursor. Note that, with the cursor at the end of a line, Backspace deletes the last character but Del does not.

A Hands-On Example

Here is a short exercise to acquaint you with some of the line-editing features.

1. Type NEW to erase any program in memory.

2. Type the following line but don't press Enter:

```
50 IF MYAGE = 35 THEN PRINT "Who cares?"
```

3. While you hold down the Ctrl key, experiment with the left- and right-arrow keys. Watch the cursor move from word to word. Release the Ctrl key.

4. Press End to move the cursor quickly to the end of the line.

5. Move the cursor back to the M in MYAGE.

6. Press Del twice. MYAGE changes to AGE.

7. Move the cursor to the c in cares.

8. Press Ins to start insert mode. Type the heck followed by a blank space. The new text is inserted into the old text. Press Ins again to turn off insert mode.

9. Press Enter. This step sends the entire line to BASIC. Type LIST for confirmation. You should see the following:

```
Ok
LIST
50 IF AGE = 35 THEN PRINT "Who the heck cares?"
Ok
```

Full Screen Editing

Editing is not confined to the current line. The whole screen is your canvas. You can edit any program line (or direct mode command) that you see on the screen. The ability to move the cursor and edit anywhere is known as *full screen editing*.

To move the cursor vertically off the current line, use the up- or down-arrow key. We refer to these keys as "Up" and "Down" respectively. As you no doubt surmise, Up moves the cursor up, and Down moves the cursor down.

Note, however, that you cannot scroll through your program by attempting to move the cursor off the screen. Nothing happens if you press Up with the cursor on the top line (or Down with the cursor on the bottom line).

To edit any line, move the cursor to that line and make your changes. Then press Enter to send the newly edited line to BASIC. The effect is just as though you had freshly typed the *entire* line and pressed Enter.

That last point deserves reiteration. You must press Enter to have BASIC record your modified line. The cursor can be anywhere on the line but you must press Enter. If you edit a line but then press Up or Down before pressing Enter, the edited line is *not* sent for processing.

Table 13.2 shows special keys for use with full screen editing.

Table 13.2. Special keys for full screen editing.

Key	Alternate Key	Effect
Enter	Ctrl-M	Sends the line containing the cursor to BASIC for processing. The cursor moves down to the first column of the next line.
Ctrl-Break	Ctrl-C	Aborts editing on the current line. The cursor moves down to the first column of the next line. The old line is not sent to BASIC for processing.
Up	Ctrl-6	Moves the cursor up one line.
Down	Ctrl-−	Moves the cursor down one line.
Home	Ctrl-K	Moves the cursor to the upper left corner of the screen.
Ctrl-Home	Ctrl-L	Clears (blanks) the screen and moves the cursor to the upper left corner. This keystroke does not erase any program lines in memory but simply clears the screen for further typing.

Using *LIST*

To edit your current program, take advantage of LIST in conjunction with full screen editing. Here's how:

1. Use the LIST command to display the line (or lines) you want to edit. Remember, you can list only a portion of your program by specifying the desired line-number range as part of a LIST command. See Chapter 3, "A Hands-On Introduction to Programming," if you need to brush up on using LIST.

2. Move the cursor to each line you want to edit. Make your changes and then press Enter.

A Hands-On Example

Here's another short exercise. This one familiarizes you with full screen editing.

1. Erase any program in memory with NEW.

2. Enter the following short program.

```
10 FOR J = 1 TO 5
20    PRINT J
30 NEXT J
```

3. Move the cursor to line 20. Edit the line to read as follows:

```
20    PRINT SIN(J)
```

4. Press Enter. This step sends the edited line to BASIC.

5. Move the cursor to line 10. Edit the line to read as follows:

```
10 FOR K = 3 TO 4
```

Do not press Enter after editing this line.

6. Move the cursor to a line below the program. Type LIST. You should see the following:

```
LIST
10 FOR J = 1 TO 5
20    PRINT SIN(J)
30 NEXT J
Ok
```

Note that line 10 did not change because you moved off the line before pressing Enter. Line 20 *did* change because you pressed Enter after making the modifications.

Some Editing Shortcuts

You can take advantage of the full screen editor to quickly enter repetitive instructions. Suppose, for example, that you are entering a program which will contain several occurrences of the instruction `FOR INDEX% = MINVAL% TO MAXVAL%`. Each time, of course, the line number is different. Let's say that your program will contain this instruction in lines 140, 210, 315, 420, and 550.

Here's a shortcut. Type the instruction once using line number 140. Press Enter. Now move the cursor back up over the 1 in 140. Type `210`, the next line number containing that instruction. Immediately press Enter. You have just entered the line a second time. BASIC still has a record of line 140. You can repeat this with line numbers 315, 420, and 550. The result: you have swiftly entered the five program lines.

Another shortcut: you can reissue any direct mode command that appears on your screen. Move the cursor anywhere on the line containing the desired command. Then, press Enter and you immediately issue the command. For example, you might see `SAVE "MYPROGRAM.BAS"` from a previous file save. You have made a few program changes since issuing that `SAVE` command. Move the cursor to the `SAVE` line and press Enter. The file is resaved.

Saving Keystrokes with the Function Keys

With your computer's function keys (F1 through F10), you can save keystrokes when you type frequently used keywords. Each function key is preset to produce one of BASIC's keywords. You can reset these preassignments to customize the key assignments for your own application. This is a powerful technique that can save many keystrokes and reduce typing errors.

Using the Preassigned Function Keys

Try this. With a program in memory, move the cursor to a blank line on the screen. Press F1. `LIST` jumps out on-screen; just as though you typed `LIST` instead of pressing F1. Press Enter and you will list your program.

Now press F2. This step runs your program! Do you see RUN on-screen at the point where you pressed F2? Pressing F2 is equivalent to typing RUN followed by Enter. Hmmm, there's something to these function keys after all.

Table 13.3 shows the keystrokes preassigned to the function keys. Pressing a function key produces the keystrokes shown in the second column. In this table, the "less than" symbol (<) represents Enter. For example, pressing F2 corresponds to typing RUN followed by Enter.

Table 13.3. Function key preassignments.

Key	Keystrokes	Meaning
F1	LIST	Lists your program. You must press Enter after pressing F1.
F2	RUN<	Runs your program.
F3	LOAD"	Loads a program. You must type the file name and the closing quotation mark.
F4	SAVE"	Saves a program. Again, you must type the file name and the closing parentheses.
F5	CONT<	Continues a program after pausing. See Chapter 14, "Debugging and Testing."
F6	,"LPT1"<	The designation for the printer.
F7	TRON<	Turns on tracing. See Chapter 14, "Debugging and Testing."
F8	TROFF<	Turns off tracing. See Chapter 14, "Debugging and Testing."
F9	KEY	The KEY command is discussed in the following section.
F10	SCREEN 0,0,0<	Returns the screen to normal text mode from a graphics mode. See Chapter 11, "Creating Graphics," and Chapter 15, "Toward Advanced Programming."

Reassigning the Function Keys

Now we get really fancy. You can reassign the text string associated with any of the function keys. Use the direct mode KEY command:

KEY *keynum*, *strexpr*

where *keynum* is the number of the function key to be reassigned, and *strexpr* is the string expression to assign.

For example, the following command assigns the string SQR(ANGLE!) to the F5 key:

KEY 5, "SQR(ANGLE!)"

Now, when you enter a program, whenever you press F5 the editor types SQR(ANGLE!) for you.

Note that you enclose the string expression with quotation marks. The *strexpr* parameter must be a string. Surround a text literal with quotes.

One restriction: the length of *strexpr* is limited to 15 characters.

A Time-saving Tip

Before you enter a lengthy program, you can reassign the function keys with the names of frequently appearing variables. Then you can quickly "type" any of these variable names by simply pressing the associated function key.

Listing the Function Key Assignments

On the bottom line of your screen, the Function Key Display shows the first six characters assigned to each function key. When you reassign a function key, you see the key's value change on the Display.

In Chapter 3, "A Hands-On Introduction to Programming," you learned how to turn the Display on or off with special forms of the KEY command. You can list the *complete* text assigned to each function key with a KEY LIST command.

Table 13.4 summarizes these special forms of the KEY command.

Table 13.4. Special KEY commands.

Command	Effect
KEY OFF	Turns off the Function Key Display
KEY ON	Turns on the Function Key Display
KEY LIST	Lists the complete text assigned to each function key

Using the Alt-Key Shortcuts

We are not done yet! BASIC has yet another set of editing shortcut keys. The Alt key in combination with a letter key produces a preset keyword beginning with that letter.

For example, press Alt-C and watch your screen. Out comes COLOR. Table 13.5 lists these Alt keystrokes. To use one, press the indicated letter while simultaneously pressing Alt.

As for these Alt keystrokes being significant time-savers, we think that the jury is still out. Experiment. You may find them helpful. Pressing Alt-P for PRINT is fairly handy.

Table 13.5. The Alt-key abbreviations.

Alt-letter	Keyword	Alt-letter	Keyword
A	AUTO	N	NEXT
B	BSAVE	O	OPEN
C	COLOR	P	PRINT
D	DELETE	Q	-----
E	ELSE	R	RUN
F	FOR	S	SCREEN
G	GOTO	T	THEN
H	HEX$	U	USING
I	INPUT	V	VAL
J	-----	W	WIDTH
K	KEY	X	XOR
L	LOCATE	Y	-----
M	MOTOR	Z	-----

Using the Direct-Mode Editing Commands

BASIC features a number of direct-mode commands to facilitate your program editing:

❏ EDIT displays a line for editing.

❏ DELETE deletes a range of line numbers.

❏ AUTO automatically generates line numbers.

❏ RENUM renumbers program lines.

We discuss each of these commands in the following section.

Displaying a Line for Editing—*EDIT*

EDIT displays a line in preparation for your editing. The command has two forms.

EDIT *linenumber*

or

EDIT .

where *linenumber* is the line number of the line to be edited.

The command EDIT 300, for example, does the following:

1. Displays line 300 on screen.

2. Moves the cursor to the first character on the line (that is, the first digit of the line number—3, in this case).

3. Lets you edit the line normally. When you are done, you press Enter to submit the line for processing.

In the second form of EDIT, the period denotes the current line. The effect is as though you specified the current line number.

What line does BASIC consider to be the current line? Whenever you type a new program line, that line becomes the current line. Also, BASIC updates the current line to be the last line referenced by an EDIT command, a LIST command, or an error message.

Deleting a Range of Lines—*DELETE*

As you know, you can delete a line from your program by just typing the line number and pressing Enter. What about deleting an entire range of line numbers? No problem. The DELETE command does the job.

DELETE *startlinenum - endlinenum*

where *startlinenum* is the first line number of a range of lines to be deleted, and *endlinenum* is the last line number of the range.

You specify the line-number range in much the same manner as with the LIST command (see Chapter 3, "A Hands-On Introduction to Programming"). Table 13.6 shows some example commands.

Table 13.6. Sample DELETE commands.

Command	Effect
DELETE 200	Deletes line 200.
DELETE 200-300	Deletes lines 200 through 300.
DELETE 200-	Deletes all lines numbered 200 and higher.
DELETE -200	Deletes all lines from the lowest line number up to and including line 200.
DELETE	Deletes the entire program with some versions of BASIC. Causes an Illegal function call error with other versions of BASIC. Be careful.
DELETE .-300	Deletes all lines from the current line up to and including line 300.

Note that the last example in table 13.6 uses the period to denote the current line. In DELETE commands, you can use the period as the *startlinenum* or *endlinenum* parameter.

Using a Period with LIST Commands

Just as with EDIT and DELETE commands, the period can be used with LIST commands to denote the current line. Here are a few examples:

```
LIST .    'Lists the current line

LIST .-400'Lists from the current line up to line 400

LIST -.    'Lists all lines up to the current line
```

Automatically Generating Line Numbers—*AUTO*

When you enter a program, you can have BASIC automatically generate your line numbers! Use the AUTO command.

AUTO *linenumber*, *increment*

where *linenumber* is the first line number, and *increment* is the amount to increase each successive line number.

To see how AUTO works, try this experiment:

1. Erase any current program with NEW.

2. Type **AUTO 100, 20** (followed by Enter). You see the following:

```
AUTO 100, 20
100
```

The cursor remains to the right of 100. Now you can type any BASIC instruction, press Enter, and you have entered line 100 of a new program. To continue this example, type **FOR J = 1 TO 5** and press Enter.

3. BASIC accepts your line 100 and prompts you with 120 to type in line 120. Type **PRINT J** and press Enter.

4. You are now prompted for line 140. Note how each line number increases by 20. That's because you typed 20 for the second (*increment*) parameter in the AUTO command. Type **NEXT J** and press Enter.

5. The test program is complete. However, BASIC is prompting you for line 160. To stop the AUTO command, press Ctrl-Break or Ctrl-C. Try pressing Ctrl-Break now. You get the Ok prompt, and BASIC returns to direct mode.

6. Type LIST to confirm that your program is entered. Your screen should like this:

```
Ok
NEW
Ok
AUTO 100, 20
100 FOR J = 1 TO 5
```

Listing continues

```
120 PRINT J
140 NEXT J
160
Ok
LIST
100 FOR J = 1 TO 5
120 PRINT J
140 NEXT J
Ok
```

In an AUTO command, you can explicitly specify the line-number parameter, the increment parameter, both parameters, or neither parameter. The default value for each parameter is 10. Table 13.7 shows various examples of AUTO commands.

Also, you can substitute a period (.) for the line-number parameter. This step tells BASIC to start with the current line number.

If you follow the line-number parameter with a comma but do not specify the *increment* parameter, BASIC assumes that the last increment specified in a previous AUTO command (or 10 otherwise).

Table 13.7. Sample AUTO commands.

Command	Starting Line Number	Increment
AUTO	10	10
AUTO 250, 35	250	35
AUTO 100	100	10
AUTO , 25	10	25
AUTO 150,	150	Last increment
AUTO ., 20	Current line number	20
AUTO .	Current line number	10

You can use AUTO to add new lines to an existing program. If AUTO generates a line number that already exists, an asterisk appears after the number as a warning. For example:

```
Ok
NEW
Ok
200 REM This is a test
AUTO 150, 50
150 REM Hey look, AUTO generated the line number
200*
```

In this example, the cursor is just to the right of the asterisk. You can now type a new instruction (that replaces the old line 200) or press Enter to maintain the old line 200 and make AUTO generate the next line number.

Renumbering Program Lines—*RENUM*

Sometimes, when you edit a program, you get caught in a line number logjam. This usually happens when you want to do something such as add 15 new lines between lines 140 and 150, for example. Help!

The RENUM command is your way out of this kind of mess. RENUM renumbers all (or optionally some) of your program lines.

RENUM *newnumber, oldnumber, increment*

where *newnumber* is the first line number for the new sequence, *oldnumber* is the line number from the existing program in which renumbering should begin, and *increment* is the increment for the new sequence of line numbers.

The beauty of RENUM is that the command also changes the line-number references inside your program. That is, RENUM automatically corrects the line numbers that follow GOTO, GOSUB, THEN, ELSE, and other similar commands. These internal references are brought up to date with the new line numbers.

You can explicitly specify any combination of the three parameters. The default values are 10 for *newnumber*, the first program line for *oldnumber*, and 10 for *increment*.

Table 13.8 shows some sample RENUM commands.

Here's a short experiment that demonstrates RENUM.

```
NEW
Ok
300 PRINT "I'm stuck in an endless loop"
302 GOTO 300
620 REM No way to get here
RENUM
Ok
LIST
10 PRINT "I'm stuck in an endless loop"
20 GOTO 10
30 REM No way to get here
Ok
```

Table 13.8. Sample RENUM *commands.*

Command	Effect
RENUM	Renumbers the whole program. The new first line number is 10, and successive lines increment by 10.
RENUM 200, , 50	Renumbers the entire program. The new first line number is 200, and successive lines increment by 50.
RENUM 200, 100, 50	Renumbers only the lines from 100 upward. The old line 100 becomes line 200, and successive lines increment by 50.
RENUM 200, 100	Same as previous command except that successive lines increment by 10 (the default value).
RENUM , , 5	Renumbers the entire program. The new first line number is 10, and successive lines increment by 5.
RENUM 100	Renumbers the entire program. The new first line number is 100, and successive lines increment by 10.

The RENUM command renumbered the program lines as 10, 20, and 30. In line 20, note how the reference to old line 300 was corrected automatically to now refer to line 10. (This program still causes an endless loop, but at least the line numbers now look better!)

Working with ASCII Program Files

Normally, when you save program files on disk with the SAVE command, BASIC saves the file in a special format known as *compressed binary* format. The details of this format are not too important. What's relevant is that such files cannot be easily read outside of BASIC.

Why would you want to use a program outside of BASIC? There are a few occasions. For example, you might want to load a program into your word processor. Or, from DOS, you might want to list the program with DOS's TYPE command. If you try a compressed binary file is these situations, the results are gibberish.

Instead, you can save a program file in ASCII format. This format means that each character in the file is saved according to its ASCII code value. There are two main advantages to saving a file in ASCII format:

❏ The program file will be "portable" to other applications such as your word processor.

❏ The program file can be merged with another program already in memory.

The disadvantage is that, on disk, an ASCII file requires a little more disk space than does a compressed binary file.

Saving Files in ASCII Format

To save a program file in ASCII format, use the optional A parameter with the SAVE command.

SAVE *filename*, A

where *filename* is a string expression that specifies the name (and path) of the file to save.

For example, the following command saves your program in ASCII format with the name MYPROG.BAS:

SAVE "MYPROG", A

(Recall that BASIC automatically adds the extension .BAS if you do not specify any extension. See Chapter 3, "A Hands-On Introduction to Programming," for more details on saving disk files and the SAVE command.)

Whether or not you use the A parameter when you save a file, the LOAD command successfully loads the program from disk. LOAD automatically determines under which format the file was saved and successfully reads the file in either case. You don't need any special parameter with LOAD to read an ASCII file.

Merging Files

You can merge a file saved on disk into the current program in memory. Use the MERGE command.

MERGE *filename*

where *filename* is a string expression that specifies the name (and path) of the disk file to merge.

For example, the following command merges a file named MYPROG.BAS with whatever program is already in memory (again, the extension .BAS is assumed if no extension is specified):

MERGE "MYPROG"

To merge a file from disk, the file must have been saved with ASCII format. If not, the merge is unsuccessful and you get an error message: Bad file mode.

Merging combines the line numbers from the disk file with the program already in memory. If any line numbers in the file duplicate line numbers already in memory, the lines from the file replace the corresponding lines in memory.

Use MERGE for Frequently Used Subroutines

You may develop subroutines that you use in program after program. One trick is to save each of these subroutines as a separate ASCII file. Then, when you need one of the subroutines in your current program, you can merge the subroutine into your program with MERGE.

However, you must avoid line number conflicts. You can avoid conflicts by saving each subroutine with a distinct range of (large) line numbers that you reserve exclusively for that subroutine.

Summary

BASIC provides a wealth of editing tools. For example, you can move the cursor over the full screen to edit any visible line. Special shortcut keys save numerous keystrokes. And you can manipulate your program's line numbering with direct mode commands such as `AUTO`, `DELETE`, and `RENUM`.

Editing is a skill—almost a craft. Some editing techniques are simple, others are more complex. There is more than one way to accomplish many editing tasks.

We suggest that you experiment with the various techniques shown in this chapter. Develop your own comfortable editing style. Find out what works best for you.

CHAPTER 14

Debugging and Testing

STOP, CONT, TRON, TROFF

Beginning programmers are often surprised when they learn that most programs don't work correctly the first time, at least programs longer than the tiny five-line-or-less variety. Some beginners get frustrated and lose confidence in the mistaken belief that no one makes as many errors as they do. It is often comforting to know that even expert programmers frequently make programming mistakes.

In fact, you can gauge a programmer's experience by his or her attitude toward testing and debugging. Experienced programmers realize that, in order to assume that any program is working properly, thorough testing is essential.

Some programmers detest testing and debugging. They would rather spend endless hours in the design and planning stages. By the time they type in their programs, they are positive that no bugs could have crept in.

Programmers at the other extreme say to themselves, "Let me just type anything halfway close. I'll fix the errors later." These programmers tend to produce sloppy, jumbled code that is needlessly difficult to debug.

405

A middle ground between these two extremes, of course, is preferable.

The sloppy-program trap is easy to fall into! BASIC's interactive nature and debugging tools may lead you to thinking that you can readily debug your way out of any mess. Here are some debugging techniques that you can utilize when you troubleshoot:

- ❏ Display the values of variables or expressions after you stop your program (direct mode PRINT).
- ❏ Determine the location of nonspecific error messages (ON ERROR GOTO).
- ❏ Repeatedly suspend and resume execution (STOP, CONT).
- ❏ Trace your program's logic flow by displaying each line number as the line executes (TRON, TROFF).

By design, our example programs are short and contain conspicuous errors. We recognize that your difficult problem-solving tasks will occur in larger programs in which the errors are not so apparent. In this chapter, our main concerns are showing errors and demonstrating debugging techniques. We believe that short, to-the-point examples are the best teaching method.

A Debugging Philosophy

To write successful programs, you must perform the interrelated actions of testing and debugging.

- ❏ *Testing* refers to the actions that determine whether a program runs correctly.
- ❏ *Debugging* is the subsequent activity of finding and removing the errors or bugs.

Some programmers lump both activities together under just one name —either testing or debugging—but we think that the distinction is important.

Sometimes a test run shows clearly that a program has errors. The testing part can be easy, but the debugging process may be much more difficult. In a sense, testing and debugging never end. Every time you run a program, you are testing.

Programmers (cautious programmers, anyway) often say that every non-trivial program has a bug waiting to be found. And when the bug is found and fixed, another still remains. Figure 14.1 depicts the process of programming a project from beginning to end. As the figure lightheartedly demonstrates, you never really reach the end.

Where Did That "Bug" Come from?

"Bug" and "debug" are accepted terms from programming jargon. A *bug* is an error or problem in a program. When a program doesn't work correctly, we say that the program has a "bug." The process of finding and correcting the bug is called *debugging the program*, or simply, *debugging*.

Undoubtedly, you have heard "bug" and "debug" in reference to programming problems. Did you ever wonder where these colorful terms came from?

The story goes that, when computers were in their infancy, some computer operators were having hardware problems. The setting was the late 1940s at an East Coast naval installation. The computers, which were less powerful than the one on your desk, were vacuum tube devices that required warehouse-sized rooms.

To get back to the story, a computer was malfunctioning and the operators went to take a look. They found a dead moth lodged in one of the electric circuits. The moth was apparently killed from the heat of the vacuum tubes or from contact with one of the exposed circuits. When they removed the moth, the computer worked again. By eliminating the "bug," the operators solved the problem. The earliest "bug" was just that: a real insect.

This first "debugging" was actually the correction of a hardware problem. But somehow, over the years, debugging has come to mean the elimination of programming (software) errors.

Here are some principles of a sound debugging philosophy:

❑ *Assume that your program has errors.* No one is perfect, and no one writes perfect programs all the time. Expect to find errors. Exposing the errors—all of them—is your purpose in testing and debugging. Enjoy the detective work.

❑ *No single test run can prove a program to be bug-free.* Plan to run many test cases and to use a variety of test data. A program running to completion and producing expected output is a good sign but that is only the beginning of testing.

❑ *Try to make your programs fail during testing.* Do not rely on "friendly" data when you test. If the program is destined to be used by other users who must supply data, try all kinds of unreasonable values.

Fig. 14.1. The programming process.

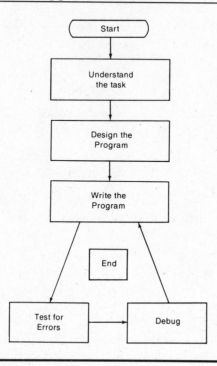

Your users may type almost anything when they are prompted for input. Your goal should be a "bulletproof" program—one that cannot "crash" (encounter a BASIC error message condition) or produce an incorrect result no matter what users try.

❑ *Write modular programs.* Follow the procedures outlined in Chapter 7, "Modular Programming with Subroutines." Make liberal use of functions and subroutines. Several smaller components are easier to program, test, and debug than one larger component. Divide and conquer.

Types of Errors

Programming errors can be classified in the following three categories:

❑ *Syntax errors.* When you run a BASIC program, the editor points out many types of typing, spelling, and punctuation errors by displaying the familiar Syntax error in nnnn message, where nnnn is the line number of the erroneous line. A syntax error means that BASIC just doesn't understand one of your typed instructions. Usually you can quickly correct syntax errors by looking for a misspelled keyword, a missing quotation mark, or some such oversight. Chapter 3, "A Hands-On Introduction to Programming," shows an example of a syntax error and BASIC's response of displaying the line so that you can make corrections. Chapter 13 discusses editing techniques.

❏ *Execution errors*. This kind of error occurs when BASIC can't perform a program instruction. The syntax of the instruction is fine, but the action requested by the instruction is impossible. When an execution error occurs, BASIC displays an informative error message. Generally the error message quickly points you to the problem, although sometimes the cause of the error is not very obvious. Here is a simple example of an execution error:

```
100 B = 35
110 GOTO 105
```

When you run this program, the program stops and BASIC displays the following error message:

```
Undefined line number in 110
```

The error message leads you to line 110. You see that the GOTO instruction tries branching to a nonexisting line. Note that nothing is wrong with the syntax of line 110. BASIC just cannot perform the requested action.

Appendix D lists all of BASIC's error messages. Along with each error message, the appendix contains a short explanation of the error. Also, the appendix discusses the probable causes of many of the errors.

❏ *Logic errors*. These errors usually are the hardest errors to debug. Your program runs to completion, but the results are incorrect. All your instructions have legal syntax, and BASIC executes all of them. As far as BASIC is concerned, everything went fine. However, the program just doesn't work correctly. Often a logic error results in program output that is clearly wrong. BASIC's debugging facilities are helpful with these types of errors. In this chapter, we provide some tips to narrow down where your program went astray. Look at the following short program, which contains a simple logic error:

```
100 ITEMS% = 50
110 UNITCOST = 2.25
120 PRINT "Total cost ="; UNITCOST * ITEMS
```

Here's the output:

```
Total cost = 0
```

That can't be right. Do you see the problem? Line 120 contains the variable ITEMS when ITEMS% was intended. When line 120 executes, BASIC uses the default value of 0 for ITEMS because no other line assigned any other value to ITEMS. So line 120 displays the product of UNITCOST (2.25) and ITEMS (0), which produces the result of zero.

The program has no syntax errors or execution errors, only a logic error.

General Debugging Tips

Here are some general tips for debugging the trickier types of errors—the execution errors and logic errors that don't have evident causes.

❏ *Start by looking for the obvious.* Most errors result from obvious, not subtle, causes. Look for simple mistakes, such as careless typing errors. Here are a few common errors:

1. Interchanging the colon and semicolon characters.

2. Improperly nesting parentheses in an expression.

3. Typing a capital I or a lowercase letter l when you mean to type the number 1.

4. Interchanging the less than (<) and greater than (>) signs.

❏ Obvious errors often are the hardest ones to find because you cannot believe that you could make such a stupid mistake. Take heart, all programmers make them.

❏ *Reasonable-looking output often is wrong.* Usually, incorrect output is so wrong that it leaps out at you and screams, "I'm wrong!" But beware of reasonable-looking output. The worst kind of error causes slightly incorrect results, which may lead you to carelessly assume that everything is working correctly. Be suspicious. For example, suppose that you want to see the fraction 1/7 displayed with full double precision accuracy (16 digits). You might try the following direct-mode command:

```
PRINT CDBL(1/7)
```

The CDBL function converts the argument to double-precision (see Chapter 6, "Manipulating Data"). BASIC displays the very precise-looking result of

```
.1428571492433548
```

Unfortunately, only the first eight digits are correct. The last eight are garbage! The reason is that, inside the parentheses, 1/7 produces only a single-precision result. CDBL converts the argument to 16 digits, but the final 8 digits are not accurate. Try PRINT CDBL(1#=7#) to see the fully accurate 16-digit result.

❏ *Verify that built-in statements and functions work as you expect.* You may have an incorrect assumption about how a BASIC statement or function works. LOG, for example, works with natural, not common, logarithms. Use this book and your BASIC manual for confirmation.

❏ *Make sure that your algorithms are correct.* An *algorithm* is simply a step-by-step procedure for solving a problem. If you use algorithms from books and magazines, be skeptical of what you read. Printed algorithms and program listings contain errors more often than you might guess. Look for a second source, if possible. Goodness knows, in spite of our painstaking efforts, a programming error could be lurking somewhere in this book.

❏ *Learn BASIC's debugging features and techniques.* They are the subjects of the rest of this chapter.

Debugging Execution Errors

So what can you do when you receive a BASIC error message, but you can't figure out what is wrong? This question has many answers, depending on what the error message is and what the program line contains. Here are some things to try, and tips about a few of the more common error messages:

❏ *Look again for typing errors.* We cannot stress this enough: Look *carefully* for simple errors first, and the most common simple errors are typing errors.

❏ PRINT *the current values of your main variables.* When your program aborts with an error message, you can use BASIC's direct mode to print the values of variables. We discuss this technique later in this chapter.

Watch for These Typing Errors

Here are some characters that are most frequently typed incorrectly—either omitted or interchanged with other characters listed:

```
Alphabetic   I  l  O  S
Numeric      1  0
Special      .  ,  :  ;  (  [  )  ]  <  >  '  "  /  \  $
```

Are you one of those people accustomed to typing the lowercase letter *l* rather than the number *1*? If so, beware. The two characters look almost identical when you type them, but BASIC treats them very differently. However, because BASIC converts variable names to uppercase when you LIST a program, you should spot the difference easily. Typing the letter *O* rather than the number *0* is a little harder to see until you get used to the slash that is displayed in the zero.

❏ *Split up multi-instruction program lines.* If you get the Subscript out of range error message for a line containing half a dozen subscript references, you do not know which instruction is the culprit. Put each instruction on a separate program line. If necessary, use RENUM to provide room for more line numbers.

❏ *Look in other parts of the program that manipulate the same variables.* If BASIC says that a program line is doing something illegal, the problem often stems from a previous line that erroneously computed the variable. The following error messages are frequently caused by incorrect manipulation of a variable elsewhere in the program:

```
Illegal function call
Subscript out of range
Division by zero
```

❏ *Add an* ON ERROR GOTO *instruction.* This technique lets you call a special subroutine whenever an error occurs. This is an advanced topic that we defer to Chapter 15, "Toward Advanced Programming."

❏ Out of DATA in nnnn *error.* Even though this error message always refers to a line with a READ instruction, the problem is most likely either in your DATA instructions or in a loop around the READ instruction. In either case, your program tried to read more data elements than remained in your data list. Often the cause is simply a mistyped comma in a DATA instruction. Look at this program example:

```
100 SUM = 0
110 FOR J% = 1 TO 8
120    READ QTY
130    SUM = SUM + QTY
140 NEXT
150 PRINT "The sum is"; SUM
160 PRINT "The average is"; SUM / 8
170 END
180 DATA 68.5, 71, 66, 67.5, 70. 67, 69, 72
```

The program tries reading the eight data values in line 180. But the program aborts with the error message Out of DATA in 120. Count the data values in line 180. Are there eight? Yes. Does the loop in lines 110 through 140 read eight data values? Yes. Well, then, what's wrong? How can the program be "out of data" when it reads eight data values and we provide eight? To find the answer, insert the following line:

```
125 PRINT QTY;
```

Run the program again. Before encountering the error, the program displays each QTY value immediately after reading it. You see the following output:

```
68.5  71  66  67.5  70.67  69  72
```

Compare these seven numbers with the numbers in line 180. Where did that fifth number come from? BASIC interprets the fifth number as 70.67 when we wanted 70, followed by 67 as the sixth number. The problem is that we typed a period, not a comma, after the 70 in line 180. BASIC interprets this period to be a decimal point, not a separator between different numbers.

Debugging with Direct Mode

One of the big advantages of BASIC's interactive environment is that, after your program stops with an error message, you can do detective work directly from direct mode. Most important, you can print the values of important variables to help determine what went wrong.

When a program stops, whether normally or due to an error condition, BASIC retains the current values of all the variables. With direct mode PRINT commands, you can display the value of any variable or array element.

For example, suppose that your program aborts with the following error message:

```
Illegal function call in 780
```

You list line 780, which reads:

```
780 LENGTH! = SQR(AREA!)
```

Apparently something is wrong with the value of AREA!. To find out, all you have to do is issue the direct mode command PRINT AREA!, and BASIC shows you the current value of AREA!.

You probably will discover that AREA! has a negative value. If so, that is the problem because BASIC's SQR function works only with positive arguments (or zero). Your work session might look like this:

```
RUN
Illegal function call in 780
LIST 780
780 LENGTH! = SQR(AREA!)
Ok
PRINT AREA!
-43.29451
Ok
```

Yep, AREA! is negative, just as you suspected. Of course, this discovery is only the beginning of the whole solution. Now you must find how AREA! was calculated. If AREA! was manipulated several times before line 780, you need to backtrack to determine how AREA! erroneously became negative. More PRINT commands should narrow down the problem.

Interrupting a Program—Ctrl-Break

While your program is running, you can suspend execution at any time by pressing Ctrl-Break. BASIC displays the following messages:

```
^C
Break in 2150
Ok
```

The ^C is BASIC's shorthand notation for Ctrl-Break. That simply means that you pressed Ctrl-Break. The next message tells you what line number BASIC was executing when you pressed Ctrl-Break. Here, the 2150 is just an example. The Ok indicates that you are now in direct mode.

Resuming a Program—*CONT*

From direct mode, you can issue commands such as `LIST` or `PRINT`. But here's the kicker. You can resume execution of your program from the point at which it was interrupted. All you have to do is type the direct mode command `CONT`. (`CONT` is short for CONTinue.)

```
CONT
```

Think about that. You can interrupt a program, display variable values, and then resume the program from wherever the interruption occurred. That's an impressive debugging capability.

An Example of Ctrl-Break and *CONT*

Ctrl-Break is handy when a program seems to be executing for an unduly long time. Usually, the problem is an inadvertent endless loop.

For example, suppose that you write a program which computes the sum of all the odd integers from 1 to 99. Here's your program:

```
100 INCREMENT% = 2
110 SUM% = 0
120 FOR J% = 1 TO 99 STEP INCREMENT
130    SUM% = SUM% + J%
140 NEXT J%
150 PRINT SUM%
```

This seems reasonable. The counter variable J% in the `FOR...NEXT` loop assumes all odd integer values from 1 to 99. Line 130 computes the desired sum. But when you run the program, a strange thing happens. The program "hangs." No answer is displayed, and no error message occurs.

You press Ctrl-Break. BASIC interrupts the program in line 140. You display the value of `SUM%` with a `PRINT SUM%` command. BASIC displays a large number that seems plausible. Next, you display the value of J% with `PRINT J%`. Lo and behold, the value of J% is 1. That's funny, the loop doesn't seem to be getting anywhere.

Now you type `CONT`. The program resumes execution but still hangs. So you press Ctrl-Break again. You now redisplay `SUM%` and J%, to see whether the values change. SUM% has a larger value but J% is still 1. Apparently the counter variable is not increasing.

Then you see it. In line 120, you forgot the percent sign suffix on INCREMENT. You type PRINT INCREMENT in direct mode, which confirms that INCREMENT is zero. Your typing error (INCREMENT rather than INCREMENT%) creates an endless loop with J% always having a value of 1. (If you examine the program, you will see that the value of SUM% actually indicates how many times the loop has executed).

You edit line 120 to add the percent suffix onto INCREMENT. The program now runs fine.

You Cannot Continue If You Edit Your Program

After you interrupt your program with Ctrl-Break, you can issue direct mode commands and then resume execution with the CONT command. However, CONT does not work if you edit any lines in your program.

After you make any program modifications, you must rerun your program from the beginning. The CONT command produces the Can't continue error message.

Debugging Logic Errors

Okay, let's say that you have written a program, cleaned up all the syntax errors, and eliminated all execution errors, but the program doesn't do what you intended. You have *logic errors*. Now what?

❏ Look *again* for typing errors.

❏ Display the contents of variables after the program ends.

❏ Insert PRINT and STOP instructions to isolate where the program begins to misbehave, then use direct mode CONT commands to continue the program.

❏ Use TRON and TROFF instructions to trace the logic flow of the program.

❏ Examine your variable usage. Look for reusing the same name accidentally, and look for unmatched or omitted suffixes on a variable name.

❏ Verify that BASIC's statements and functions work the way you think.

❏ Redesign troublesome parts of the program. Rewrite sections in smaller modules.

Stopping a Program—*STOP*

A STOP instruction is one of a debugger's best friends. STOP is something like Ctrl-Break inserted directly into your program.

```
STOP
```

A STOP instruction interrupts your program and returns to direct mode. From there, you can print variable values or issue other direct mode commands. Then, you can resume execution with a CONT command.

When encountering a STOP instruction, BASIC displays the message Break in *nnnn*, where *nnnn* is the line number containing the STOP instruction.

A Debugging Example with *STOP*

As an example of STOP and CONT, suppose that you are testing a subroutine which finds the minimum value in a single-precision array named MYARRAY. The number of array elements is given by the variable NUMVALUES%. The subroutine stores the minimum value in a variable named MINVAL. Here's your test subroutine:

```
1000 REM Subroutine that finds smallest value in MYARRAY
1010 MINVAL = MYARRAY(1)
1020 FOR J% = 1 TO NUMVALUES%
1030    IF MYARRAY(J%) < MINVAL THEN MINVAL = MYARRAY(J%)
1040 NEXT J%
1050 RETURN
```

Line 1010 assigns to MINVAL the value of the first array element. Then the loop in lines 1020 through 1040 examines all the array elements. Line 1030 tests each array element and updates the value of MINVAL when a new lowest value is found.

You decide to test this subroutine with a program that reads a few data values into MYARRAY. To provide a simple first test, your program dimensions MYARRAY to a modest three values. The three data values are 35.2, 42.1, and 28.6. The subroutine should find the smallest of these three values. Then the program displays the result. Here's your complete program:

```
100 NUMVALUES% = 3
105 DIM MYARRAY(NUMVALUES%)
110 FOR INDEX% = 1 TO NUMVALUES%
120    READ MYARRAY(INDEX%)
130 NEXT INDEX%
140 DATA 35.2, 42,1, 28.6
200 GOSUB 1000    'Call sub that finds smallest array value
300 PRINT "Minimum value ="; MINVAL
900 END
1000 REM Subroutine that finds smallest value in MYARRAY
1010 MINVAL = MYARRAY(1)
1020 FOR J% = 1 TO NUMVALUES%
1030    IF MYARRAY(J%) < MINVAL THEN MINVAL = MYARRAY(J%)
1040 NEXT J%
1050 RETURN
```

When you run the program, this is the result:

```
RUN
Minimum value = 1
Ok
```

Hmmm, that answer isn't right. What went wrong with the subroutine? You add a STOP instruction in line 150 to see whether the data is read correctly. Here's your debugging session:

```
Ok
150 STOP
RUN
Break in 150
Ok
FOR Q = 1 TO 3: PRINT MYARRAY(Q): NEXT Q
 35.2
 42
 1
Ok
MYARRAY(2) = 42.1
Ok
MYARRAY(3) = 28.6
Ok
CONT
Minimum value = 28.6
Ok
```

Let's examine this session step-by-step.

1. You add line 150 (a STOP instruction) and run the program.

2. The program pauses when BASIC encounters the STOP instruction. BASIC displays the message: Break in 150. You are now in direct mode.

3. You display the values for the three array elements. Note how a multi-instruction loop can be issued on a single command line. The variable Q is a new variable that acts only as a counter variable for the loop. In order to put the loop on a single direct-mode line, a colon separates each individual instruction. This command is the direct mode equivalent of a multiple-instruction program line.

4. BASIC displays the three array values as 35.2, 42, and 1. Well now, these are suspicious. You were expecting 35.2, 42.1, and 28.6. Then you see the problem. The DATA instruction in line 140 contains a comma (rather than a period) after the value 42. So the error is in the DATA instruction, not in the subroutine.

5. You take advantage of direct mode to assign the correct values to the erroneous array elements. Note that an assignment instruction works fine in direct mode. You can actually change the value of any variable directly.

6. With the array elements now properly assigned, you resume the program with CONT. The final answer is now correct.

Before you run the program again, you should edit line 140 to remedy the DATA instruction.

Using *STOP*

STOP lets you place "breakpoints" at critical places in a program. When you test a complicated program that's not working correctly, you might place several STOP instructions throughout the program. You can then run the program and check the values of important variables when the program breaks. After each break, you can resume the program.

STOP is particularly useful in the following two situations:

❏ You are not sure which part of your program is generating which output.

❏ Your program clears the screen before you have a chance to see some output that would help you figure out what is wrong.

Tracing Program Execution—*TRON* and *TROFF*

TRON and TROFF provide a convenient way to display the logic flow of a program. TRON and TROFF stand for TRace ON and TRace OFF.

```
TRON

TROFF
```

TRON turns on the trace feature of BASIC. In trace mode, BASIC displays each line number in square brackets as the line executes. TROFF turns off the trace feature. TRON and TROFF are suitable as direct-mode commands as well as instructions within programs.

Sometimes a program is so long and complex that inserting numerous PRINT and STOP instructions would just take too long. Many times you will find it easier to simply trace the program.

The following program demonstrates TRON and TROFF as program instructions:

```
100 PRINT "Here comes a trace"
110 TRON
120 FOR J = 1 TO 2
130     PRINT J
140 NEXT J
150 PRINT "The loop is done"
160 TROFF
170 PRINT "Trace is now off"
180 END
```

The results of this program show how the traced line numbers intermix with the output produced by the PRINT instructions:

```
Here comes a trace
[120][130] 1
[140][130] 2
[140][150]The loop is done
[160]Trace is now off
```

Notice that lines 100 and 110 are not shown in square brackets by the trace, because TRON doesn't turn on tracing until after line 110 executes. Tracing displays a line number only when TRON occurs before the line number executes. In this example, because the trace is not yet active when line 110 begins to execute, line 110 is not shown in brackets.

Near the end of the program, trace *does* display line number 160, because the trace is not turned off until after line 160 executes. Of course, trace doesn't display line numbers 170 and 180 because TROFF turned off the trace back in line 160.

Notice that line number 120 only displays the first time the loop executes, not every time the FOR...NEXT loop logically loops back to the FOR instruction. Suppose that we change our program example, and put a second instruction on line 120 after the FOR instruction. Will the trace display line number 120 now that the line contains a new executable instruction? Here is the modified program:

```
100 PRINT "Here comes a trace"
110 TRON
120 FOR J = 1 TO 2: PRINT "This is the FOR line"
130    PRINT J
140 NEXT J
150 PRINT "The loop is done"
160 TROFF
170 PRINT "Trace is now off"
180 END
```

And here is the output:

```
Here comes a trace
[120]This is the FOR line
[130] 1
[140]This is the FOR line
[130] 2
[140][150]The loop is done
[160]Trace is now off
```

No, the trace does not display line number 120 a second time even though line 120 displays output with PRINT. The guiding rule is that trace displays a line number only when the beginning of the line executes.

Here is one more example of trace output. The same program is modified again, to include a subroutine that executes from within a FOR...NEXT loop.

```
100 PRINT "Here comes a trace"
110 TRON
120 FOR J = 1 TO 2
130     GOSUB 200: PRINT "This is the GOSUB line"
140 NEXT J
150 PRINT "The loop is done"
160 TROFF
170 PRINT "Trace is now off"
180 END
200 PRINT "Here's a subroutine"
210 RETURN

[120][130][200]Here's a subroutine
[210]This is the GOSUB line
[140][130][200]Here's a subroutine
[210]This is the GOSUB line
[140][150]The loop is done
[160]Trace is now off
```

As expected, trace displays the line numbers of the subroutine ([200] and
[210]) after line 130 executes. However, trace does not redisplay [130]
immediately after the subroutine finishes.

These examples are short for ease of understanding. But you can imagine
how useful TRON and TROFF can be in a large, complex program filled with
many loops, IF instructions, and subroutines.

Don't forget that you can turn on tracing from direct mode. Just type TRON
and press Enter. Now, BASIC traces any program you subsequently run. (You
don't need a TRON instruction in your program.) You can turn off tracing from
direct mode with TROFF.

Avoid Screen Disruption with LPRINT

If your program produces carefully formatted screen output, you will
mess up your screen displays by debugging with PRINT, STOP/CONT, or
TRON. Instead, you can insert LPRINT instructions to route your debugging messages to the printer. Another possibility is to insert differently
pitched SOUND instructions (not recommended for tone-deaf programmers).

Looking for Variable Conflicts

BASIC makes it easy to create new variables, but this convenience sometimes fosters program bugs. Here are the two variable conflicts most likely to introduce logic errors into your programs:

❑ Accidentally using a not-quite-the-same variable name

❑ Reusing a temporary variable that is still in use

We have already presented examples of the first type of conflict. Here's one more example:

```
100 FOR J% = 1 TO 5
110    PRINT J%, SQR(J%), J * J%
120 NEXT
```

This program attempts to produce a little table of the square roots and squares of the integers from one to five. But it doesn't work quite right. Here is the output:

```
1              1              0
2              1.414214       0
3              1.732051       0
4              2              0
5              2.236068       0
```

The first two columns correctly show each number and its square root, but the third column should contain the squares—the numbers 1, 4, 9, 16, and 25. Can you find the bug?

The problem is in line 110. The current number is given by the variable named J% (including the percent sign). The last expression in line 110 reads J * J% when it should read J% * J% instead. BASIC obediently creates a new variable for J and sets the value to zero. The result is zero times the number J%, which equals zero regardless of the value of J%.

The other type of variable conflict comes up when a variable erroneously serves double-duty. Suppose that a variable occurs in one part of a program. Another part of the program subsequently re-uses the variable during an independent calculation. However, the first part of the program regains control and needs the old value of the variable. In reusing the variable name, the programmer either assumed that the variable was freely available or simply forgot that the variable was still needed by the first part of the program.

This kind of error often occurs in subroutine calls. Take a look at the following program:

```
100 PRINT "Number", "SQUARE", "SUM"
110 FOR J% = 1 TO 5
120     SQUARE% = J% * J%
130     GOSUB 900
140 PRINT J%, SQUARE%, SUM%
150 NEXT J%
700 END
900 SUM% = 0
910 FOR J% = 1 TO SQUARE%
920     SUM% = SUM% + J%
930 NEXT J%
940 RETURN
```

Here's what the programmer intended. The subroutine in lines 900 through 940 calculates the sum of all the integers from 1 to the value of SQUARE%. This sum is stored in the variable SUM% for use by the calling program. The subroutine is correct and works properly.

The main program loops over the values from 1 to 5 (line 110). For each value of J%, the program calculates the square of J% and temporarily stores that square in the variable SQUARE%. With SQUARE% calculated, the program calls the subroutine to find the value of SUM%. In line 130, the program displays each value from 1 to 5, along with the associated values of SQUARE% and SUM%. The logic of the main program is also correct. But here's the output when the program executes.

```
RUN
Number         SQUARE         SUM
  2              1             1
 10              9            45
Ok
```

What happened? The table has only two lines (we expected five lines with the first column varying from 1 to 5). Furthermore, the values in the table don't look correct.

Do you see the problem? Of course. The same loop variable J% occurs in the main program *and* in the subroutine. The problem is that J% is still active in the main program when the subroutine gets called. To correct the problem, either the main program or the subroutine must use a different counter variable.

Here's the program modified to use K% as the subroutine's counter variable:

```
100 PRINT "Number", "SQUARE", "SUM"
110 FOR J% = 1 TO 5
120    SQUARE% = J% * J%
130    GOSUB 900
140 PRINT J%, SQUARE%, SUM%
150 NEXT J%
700 END
900 SUM% = 0
910 FOR K% = 1 TO SQUARE%
920    SUM% = SUM% + K%
930 NEXT K%
940 RETURN
```

Now everything works fine:

```
RUN
Number          SQUARE          SUM
  1               1             1
  2               4             10
  3               9             45
  4               16            136
  5               25            325
Ok
```

Summary

Experienced programmers realize that testing and debugging are a necessary part of successful programming. As a general rule, nontrivial programs contain bugs that must be found and eliminated. Many programmers dislike testing and debugging. But actually, testing and debugging can be kind of fun. Much depends on your state of mind. After all, most people like solving puzzles and being "detectives."

Three kinds of errors crop up in programs: *syntax* errors, which are incorrectly worded instructions that seem like gibberish to BASIC; *execution* errors, which cause diagnostic messages as the result of (correctly worded) instructions that BASIC just cannot perform; and *logic* errors, which occur when your program runs to completion but the results are wrong.

Fortunately, BASIC provides several debugging techniques. You can pause a program with Ctrl-Break or STOP and then print the current values of variables in direct mode. After pausing, you can resume the program with CONT. TRON and TROFF provide program tracing. With ON ERROR GOTO (discussed in-depth in Chapter 15, "Toward Advanced Programming"), you can intercept program errors and branch to a designated subroutine.

Most programming errors stem from simple mistakes rather than obscure bugs. Look for the obvious before the subtle. By far, the most likely source of any error is a simple typing mistake. When errors occur, double- and triple-check your typing.

Occasionally, you can get stuck tracking down an elusive bug. We advise you to walk away for a while! Do something relaxing such as watch TV, take a walk, play ping-pong, or just take a nap. It is amazing how some nagging bugs are swiftly found after a rejuvenating break.

15

Toward Advanced Programming

```
DEF FN, DEFINT, DEFSNG, DEFDBL, DEFSTR, ON ERROR GOTO,
RESUME, ERR, ERL, ERDEV, ERDEV$, ERROR, ON event GOSUB,
RETURN, HEX$, DEF SEG, PEEK, POKE, LINE, GET, PUT, PAL-
ETTE, SCREEN, PCOPY, WINDOW
```

By now, you have a sound understanding of BASIC programming. As you have no doubt concluded from the previous chapters, BASIC is a rich language with many statements, functions, and features. If you have mastered the material in those chapters, you should be able to successfully program almost any task.

But BASIC has even more to offer. The language has a number of more advanced features for specialized situations. This chapter introduces many of these advanced features.

We present here a potpourri of topics. We cover some topics in-depth, others quickly. We do not cover *every* advanced BASIC programming topic—that would be a little too imposing.

Feel free to pick and choose the subjects that interest you. You may just want to browse and explore some new topics. Perhaps a published program in a book or magazine uses a BASIC feature with which you are not familiar. You may find the feature in this chapter.

At any rate, it is a good sign that you are reading this chapter. You have the programming confidence to strive toward the limits of BASIC. Congratulations.

Here are some of the topics covered in this chapter:

❏ Defining your own functions
❏ Error trapping
❏ Event trapping
❏ Referencing individual memory locations
❏ Advanced graphing

Defining Your Own Functions

As you have learned in the previous chapters, BASIC provides a host of built-in functions. Occasionally, however, these functions are not enough. With DEF FN, you can create your own customized functions. A user-defined function, just like a built-in function, always returns a single value. The value can be numeric or string depending on the data type of the function.

After your function is defined, you can call it repeatedly throughout your program. Just as with the built-in functions, the value of the calling arguments can change each time you invoke the function.

DEF FN*funcname*(*paramlist*) = *expression*

where *funcname* preceded by FN constitutes the name of the function, *paramlist* is a comma-delimited list of the formal parameters, and *expression* is a general expression that defines the value of the function.

A Sample User-Defined Function

To see how DEF FN works, let's jump right into an example.

BASIC provides the SQR function to calculate the square root of a number. Suppose that you want a function which computes the square of a number.

(The square of a number is simply the number times itself.) Here's a short program that defines a function named FNSQUARE. The program uses FNSQUARE to produce a short table of squares and square roots.

```
100 DEF FNSQUARE(VALUE) = VALUE * VALUE
150 PRINT "Number", "Square", "Square root"
200 FOR NUMBER = 1 TO 5
210    PRINT NUMBER, FNSQUARE(NUMBER), SQR(NUMBER)
220 NEXT NUMBER
```

Here's the output:

```
Number        Square        Square root
  1             1           1
  2             4           1.414214
  3             9           1.732051
  4            16           2
  5            25           2.236068
```

Line 100 defines the FNSQUARE function. All user-defined function names begin with FN followed by a name of your choosing. (By the way, you now see why variable names cannot begin with FN.)

In line 100, the argument VALUE is a dummy argument, also known as a *formal parameter*. A formal parameter name has no relation to a possible variable of the same name found elsewhere in the program. The formal parameter name merely serves to define the function. (This program *could* contain a regular variable named VALUE that would exist entirely independently of the function.)

The expression on the right side of a DEF FN instruction defines the value of the function in terms of the formal parameters. In this case, FNSQUARE returns the value of the argument multiplied by itself.

To invoke a user-defined function, you simply use the function name in exactly the same manner as you would use one of BASIC's built-in functions. Remember, each user-defined function name begins with FN. Of course, before invoking your function, your program must have defined the function with a DEF FN instruction.

In our example, line 100 defines FNSQUARE and line 210 uses the function. Note how line 210 uses FNSQUARE as well as the built-in function SQR.

As you can see, you invoke the function with *actual parameters* in the argument list. To compute the value for the function, BASIC uses the value of the actual parameter everywhere the formal parameter appears in the definition (see fig. 15.1).

Fig. 15.1. *Formal and actual parameters.*

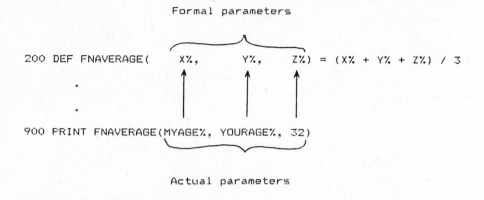

Multiple Parameters

A user-defined function can have more than one parameter. For example, the following function, named FNAVERAGE, calculates the average (mean) of three arguments.

```
150 DEF FNAVERAGE(X, Y, Z) = (X + Y + Z) / 3
```

With this function definition, the following instruction assigns to the variable NORMSCORE the average value of the variables MYSCORE, YOURSCORE, and 78.

```
300 NORMSCORE = FNAVERAGE(MYSCORE, YOURSCORE, 78)
```

Note that X, Y, and Z are three separate formal parameters. Each time you invoke the function, you use three actual parameters. FNAVERAGE then computes the average value of your three actual parameters.

Whenever you invoke a user-defined function, the number of actual parameters must match the number of formal parameters. If not, your program terminates with an error message (Syntax error).

For example, with FNAVERAGE defined as in line 150, the following instructions are in error:

```
400 MEAN = FNAVERAGE(1, 2, 3, 4)
```

```
450 MEAN = FNAVERAGE(MYNUM, YOURNUM)
```

In line 400, the function call to *FN AVERAGE* specifies too many formal parameters. By contrast, the function call in line 450 does not specify enough formal parameters.

Types of Function Expressions

The expression on the right side of a DEF FN can be quite general. The expression can call other functions and include variable names that occur elsewhere in the program.

For example, the following function, named FNHYPOTENUSE, computes the hypotenuse of a right triangle given the lengths of the two sides. The expression for FNHYPOTENUSE contains the SQR function.

```
150 DEF FNHYPOTENUSE(X, Y) = SQR( (X * X) + (Y * Y) )
```

You can even use another user-defined function in your expression! Here's how to redefine FNHYPOTENUSE in terms of the FNSQUARE function.

```
100 DEF FNSQUARE(VALUE) = VALUE * VALUE
150 DEF FNHYPOTENUSE(X, Y) = SQR( FNSQUARE(X) + FNSQUARE(X) )
```

When a variable name (or array element) appears in the defining expression, BASIC uses the current value of that variable (or array element).

For example, consider the following function definition:

```
300 DEF FNTAX(PRICE) = TAXRATE * PRICE
```

This function computes the tax of an item given its price. The function definition contains the variable TAXRATE. When the program invokes FNTAX, BASIC uses the current value of TAXRATE to compute the function. If the value of TAXRATE changes during the program, BASIC uses the current value whenever FNTAX is called.

"No Argument" Functions

You can create functions that have no arguments. That's right—it is legal (and often worthwhile) to create no-argument functions. Usually, your defining expression uses variables that change between function calls. For example, consider the following function definition:

```
300 DEF FNVOLUME = LENGTH * DEPTH * HEIGHT
```

You invoke this function without any arguments. Simply use the name FNVOLUME (for example, PRINT FNVOLUME). FNVOLUME computes the product of the current values of the variables LENGTH, DEPTH, and HEIGHT.

Numeric and String Functions

User-defined functions can have any data type, including string. Furthermore, each formal parameter can have any data type. The data-type suffixes (%, !, #, and $) are valid for function names and parameters.

In our examples so far, the functions and parameters have been single-precision. Here's the "averaging" function written as an integer function:

```
200 DEF FNAVERAGE%(A, B, C) = (A + B + C) / 3
```

Note that the function is integer but the arguments are single-precision. When you invoke FNAVERAGE%, BASIC adds the three arguments and divides by three. Then, if necessary, BASIC rounds the result to the nearest integer to produce the final answer.

Compare the following version of FNAVERAGE% with the previous version:

```
250 DEF FNAVERAGE%(A%, B%, C%) = (A% + B% + C%) / 3
```

Now, if necessary, each argument is converted to integer before the summation.

String functions are possible also. Just use the dollar-sign suffix to identify the string data type. Here's an example:

```
100 DEF FNEXTREME$(A$) = LEFT$(A$, 1) + RIGHT$(A$, 1)
200 TEST$ = "Make time to ski"
300 PRINT FNEXTREME$("Drop in" + "Anytime you want to")
400 PRINT FNEXTREME$("Riverdale")
500 PRINT FNEXTREME$(TEST$)
```

FNEXTREME$ returns a two-character string consisting of the first and last characters of the string argument. Here's the output from this program:

```
Do
Re
Mi
```

The following function definition contains both string and numeric arguments:

```
500 DEF FNPERCENT!(NUMSTR$, FRAC!) = FRAC! * VAL("NUMSTR")
```

Some Restrictions

Here are a few things you cannot do with user-defined functions:

❑ Invoke a function with a numeric argument when the formal parameter is a string (or vice versa). The data type (string or numeric) of each actual parameter must correspond to the data type of the formal parameter. Otherwise, BASIC terminates your program with the error message `Type mismatch`.

❑ Use the name of the function in the expression that defines the function. That is, a user-defined function cannot call itself.

❑ Use `DEF FN` in direct mode.

Wholesale Variable Typing—DEF*type*

By default, BASIC treats any variable without a type-declaration suffix as single-precision. With a DEF*type* instruction, you can change this default to one of the other data types.

The four DEF*type* instructions have a similar form:

```
DEFINT letterranges

DEFSNG letterranges

DEFDBL letterranges

DEFSTR letterranges
```

where *letterranges* specifies a range of letters.

Each DEF*type* instruction corresponds to a particular data type (see table 15.1).

Table 15.1. *Data types of the* DEF*type statements.*

Statement	Data Type
DEFINT	Integer
DEFSNG	Single-precision
DEFDBL	Double-precision
DEFSTR	String

A DEF*type* instruction changes the default data type for all subsequent (non-suffixed) variables that begin with a letter included in the *letterranges* parameter. DEF*type* instructions also affect array names and user-defined FN function names.

For example, the following instruction declares that all variables beginning with the letter *C* are of type integer.

```
150 DEFINT C
```

The *letterranges* parameter is either an individual letter from A to Z or a letter range indicated by two letters separated with a dash. You can specify multiple ranges in a single instruction. To do so, separate ranges with commas.

Here are some more examples of DEF*type* instructions:

```
200 DEFDBL A, Q-T

300 DEFSTR A-Z

400 DEFINT C-F, R, T, W-Z
```

Because single-precision is the initial default, you need DEFSNG only when you want to undo the effect of one of the other DEF*type* instructions.

DEF*type* instructions affect only variables whose names have no trailing type character (%, !, #, or $). A type-declaration suffix on a variable takes precedence over any defaults established with DEF. For example, consider the following program fragment:

```
200 DEFINT N
210 NUMBER = 2
220 NUMBER$ = "Few"
```

There is no conflict in the two variables. Line 200 causes the first variable, NUMBER, to be treated as an integer variable. The second variable, NUMBER$, is a different variable and is of string type due to the explicit dollar-sign suffix. (Although this program fragment works, to maximize program clarity, you should avoid multiple variables with the same root name.)

Tips on Using DEF*type*

We have some straightforward advice on using DEF*type* instructions: Don't!

We recommend that you use explicit data type suffixes on all your variable names (or let nonsuffixed variables always default to single-precision). This approach avoids possible ambiguities and errors resulting from certain typos. Many programmers balk at this advice, complaining of the extra cumbersome keystrokes needed for the suffix characters. Our counterargument is simply that the extra keystrokes become easy and natural once you acquire the habit. And you can acquire the habit with just a few programs. Try it.

Because we recommend using the suffixes, as a general rule, we recommend against using DEF*type* instructions. There is too much danger of programming mistakes due to confusion about which default data type is in effect at a certain point in the program.

Of course, we really shouldn't say "never." In the following two programming situations, DEF*type* instructions make sense:

1) A relatively short program with few variables. Here, it is easy to keep track of every variable name.

2) A program in which *every* variable has the same data type, usually integer. A single DEFINT A - Z instruction takes care of all the variables.

Error Handling and Error Trapping

Normally, a run-time error terminates your program. BASIC displays a pertinent error message and unceremoniously dumps you into direct mode.

However, there is an alternative for dealing with run-time errors. You can activate error trapping. *Error trapping* lets your program intercept an error and pass control to an error-handling routine. That is, when an error occurs, instead of terminating your program, program control passes to the first line of an error handler. An *error handler* is a user-written group of program lines, something like a subroutine, to which execution branches when an error occurs.

With error trapping, you can do the following:

❏ Pass control to an error handler when an error occurs.

❏ Determine what line caused the error.

❏ Determine what error occurred.

❏ Correct the problem or prompt the user for information.

❏ Resume execution anywhere in your program.

Using Error Trapping

Error trapping is most valuable in the following situations:

❏ You anticipate that certain errors may occur during a program, especially when you know what you want the program to do should the errors materialize.

❏ An error-producing bug has you baffled. With error trapping as a debugging tool, you can trap the error and branch to a special routine that (hopefully) diagnoses the problem.

❏ You write programs that request others to input data. Your users may occasionally type bad data that causes program errors. (This situation is common with coworkers in a job environment.) Error trapping lets you intercept possible program errors. In the error handler, you can correct the problem and continue the program. Often, such remedial action involves prompting the user for new (or corrected) input data.

If nothing else, an error handler provides graceful program termination. If you cannot fix the problem, at least you can display informative messages before you cancel the run.

Table 15.2 shows the keywords involved with error trapping.

Table 15.2. *Error-handling statements and functions.*

Keyword	Action
ON ERROR GOTO	Enables error trapping and designates the first line of the error handler
RESUME	Branches to a designated line when the error handler finishes
ERR	Returns an error code for execution errors
ERL	Returns the line causing the error
ERDEV	Returns an error code for device errors
ERDEV$	Returns the device causing the error
ERROR	Simulates or creates an error

Enabling Error Trapping

The heart of BASIC's error trapping is the ON ERROR GOTO statement.

ON ERROR GOTO *linenum*

where *linenum* is the line number on which the error handler begins.

ON ERROR GOTO does two things:

❑ It enables error trapping; no error trap occurs until an ON ERROR GOTO instruction executes.

❑ It specifies which line gets control when an error occurs.

The following program shows the "bare bones" technique of using an error handler:

```
100 REM World's simplest error handler program
200 REM ON ERROR GOTO 900    'Remove REM to try error handler
210 '
300 GOTO 500                 'This line branches nowhere
310 PRINT "No way to get here"
400 END
410 '
900 REM Error handler begins here
910    PRINT "I think you made a boo-boo"
920    END
```

Note that line 200 is inactive because the line begins with REM.

When you run this program, line 300 causes a run-time error because there is no line number 500 for the program to "go to." BASIC aborts the program and displays the following error message:

```
Undefined line number in 300
```

Now, remove the REM at the beginning of line 200. This line now activates the error-handling routine that begins at line 900. Should a program error occur, control branches directly to line 900.

Try running the program. The output of the program is

```
I think you made a boo-boo
```

Do you understand what happened? You don't get any error message this time. When line 300 attempts to execute, BASIC intercepts the impending error and branches directly to line 900. Line 910 displays the "boo-boo" message. Finally, line 920 ends the program.

You can have multiple error handlers and multiple ON ERROR GOTO instructions in one program. The most recently executed ON ERROR GOTO designates the active error handler. Only one error handler, of course, can be active at any one time. An ON ERROR GOTO instruction can appear anywhere in the flow of execution, even inside a subroutine.

However, you cannot place an error handler at line number 0 because the instruction ON ERROR GOTO 0 has special significance. The effect depends on where the instruction occurs:

❏ If ON ERROR GOTO 0 occurs outside the error handler, the instruction turns off error trapping. A subsequent error then halts the program in the usual way. In other words, use the instruction ON ERROR GOTO 0 to turn off error trapping that has been turned on previously.

❏ If ON ERROR GOTO 0 occurs inside an error handler, BASIC displays the regular error message for the current error, and the program terminates. In other words, BASIC acts as though the error occurred without an error trap.

An error handler is simply a group of lines placed somewhere in your program. As with subroutines, you usually place error handlers at the highest line numbers in your program, but that is not a requirement.

Returning from an Error Handler

An error handler should include one or more RESUME instructions. RESUME passes control from the error handler back to the main program in much the same way as RETURN passes control back from a subroutine. There are three different forms of RESUME instructions:

```
RESUME linenum          'Line number form
RESUME NEXT             'NEXT form
RESUME                  'Basic form
where linenum is a line number in the program.
```

The form of a RESUME instruction determines where execution resumes (see table 15.3).

Table 15.3. *Forms of the* RESUME *instruction.*

Instruction	Return Location
RESUME	At the line that caused the error
RESUME 0	At the line that caused the error (same as RESUME)
RESUME NEXT	At the instruction immediately following the one that caused the error
RESUME *linenum*	At the line designated by *linenum*

RESUME instructions are valid only in error-handling routines. A run-time error (RESUME without error) occurs if you execute a RESUME instruction outside of an error handler. Furthermore, your program cannot simply run out of instructions in a RESUME-less error handler. This mistake causes a run-time error (No RESUME).

Writing an Error Handler

Inside the error handler, you generally want to accomplish the following:

❏ Determine the error and what line caused it.
❏ Display diagnostic messages.
❏ Correct the problem.
❏ Resume execution if feasible.

The built-in functions ERR, ERL, ERDEV, and ERDEV$ often provide useful information for your error handler.

Using the *ERR* and *ERL* Functions

```
ERR
ERL
```

`ERR` returns the code of the error that invoked the error handler. Appendix D, "Error Messages," lists the errors and the associated error codes. `ERL` returns the line number in which the error occurred.

Debugging `Overflow` and `Division by Zero` Errors

Unlike most BASIC errors, `Overflow` and `Division by zero` errors do not terminate your program. When either error occurs, BASIC displays a warning message that does not indicate the offending line number.

However, if you have `ON ERROR GOTO` active, your error-handling routine can examine `ERR` and `ERL` to determine which line caused the error. `ERR` returns 6 for an `Overflow` error and 11 for a `Division by zero` error (see Appendix D, "Error Messages"). `ERL` returns the number of the line that caused the error.

Using the *ERDEV* and *ERDEV$* Functions

`ERDEV` and `ERDEV$` provide information about errors generated by hardware devices (such as the line printer or disk drive).

```
ERDEV

ERDEV$
```

`ERDEV$` returns the name of the device that produced the most recent error. `ERDEV` returns a code number that indicates the type of error which occurred.

The information returned by `ERDEV$` and `ERDEV` is quite technical and beyond the scope of this book. If you are interested in writing error handlers that use `ERDEV$` and `ERDEV`, refer to another of our Que books, *Using Quick-BASIC 4.*

Philosophy of Error Handlers

An error-handler can be simple or complex. Especially in workplace environments, use error handlers to anticipate possible problems and recover smoothly.

In polished programs, most errors come from simple user mistakes. The likely culprits are faulty data supplied by users and silly mistakes with equipment, such as placing the wrong data disk in a disk drive or not turning on the printer.

User-supplied numeric data often is a source of errors. Bad data typed by users can lead to errors such as division by zero. You might write an error handler that checks for division by zero (among other possibilities). If that is the problem, you can redisplay a user's input and ask whether the information is correct. If the information is incorrect, branch back to where the data was entered and start over.

Disk drive errors are common when users must place a disk into a drive and type in the name of a desired file saved on the disk. Users may forget to place the disk in the drive, use the wrong disk, the wrong drive, or supply an invalid file name. You can check for all these errors and recover without causing the program to "bomb."

Error handlers often have a series of IF instructions. The handler checks for various errors by using ERR, ERL, and ERDEV and executes individualized instructions that recover from each error found.

At the least, you may write an error handler that displays diagnostic information and solicits the user to notify you. For example:

```
800 REM My Error Handler
810     PRINT "Program error has occurred"
820     PRINT
830     PRINT "Please report the following information to"
840     PRINT "Joe Programmer, Bldg. Q8, Extension 389"
850     PRINT
860     PRINT "Error number"; ERR; "in line"; ERL
870     PRINT "Device name and problem are", ERDEV$, ERDEV
880     PRINT "     - Thank you"
890 END
```

Simulating Errors

Use an ERROR instruction to simulate errors or create user-defined error codes.

ERROR *errorcode*

where *errorcode* is an integer expression in the range from 0 to 255 that specifies an error code.

If *errorcode* is one of the error codes defined by BASIC (see Appendix D, "Error Messages"), ERROR causes your program to behave as though the error occurred. Control passes to your error handler, and the ERR function returns the value of *errorcode*. If you have no error handler, BASIC displays the associated error message and terminates your program.

With ERROR, you can induce different errors while testing your program. You can find out whether your error handler recovers suitably.

To define your own error code, use an *errorcode* value not defined by BASIC. An ERROR instruction passes control to the error handler. Inside the error handler, you can use ERR to test for the value of *errorcode* and take appropriate action.

If your program has no error handler, an ERROR instruction that has an invalid *errorcode* halts your program and displays the message

```
Unprintable error
```

User-defined error codes provide a way to test for special conditions or dangerous data. You can intercept potential errors and handle the problem in an error handler. For example, here is the skeleton form of a program that asks the user to type in a password. If the user types the proper password ("Swordfish"), the program displays confidential information. If the typed password is invalid, program control passes to an error handler.

```
200 ON ERROR GOTO 600
    .
    .
    .
400 INPUT "What is the authorizing password"; PASSWORD$
410 IF PASSWORD$ <> "Swordfish" THEN ERROR 254
420 PRINT "Strategic Plan Briefing"
    .
    .
    .
500 END
590 '
600 REM Error handler begins here
    .
    .
    .
650    IF ERR <> 254 THEN 800
660        PRINT "Unauthorized request"
670        REM If possible, correct the problem here
    .
    .
700        RESUME NEXT
800 REM Check for other errors here
    .
    .
    .
900 REM End of error handler
```

Event Trapping

Event trapping is error trapping's kissing cousin. An error trap intercepts a run-time error, but an *event trap* monitors a selected peripheral device for a certain event. BASIC checks for the event between execution of each program instruction. When the event occurs, BASIC executes a specified subroutine before continuing the program.

For example, you can trap the pressing of a particular key, say, the F1 key. Once the trap is set, the program continues executing normally. However, should the user press F1 *at any time*, the program interrupts whatever it is doing and branches immediately to your designated subroutine. (Among other things, the subroutine might display help information or request certain input.) When the subroutine concludes, the program continues from the point of interruption.

You can trap the following events:

❑ Pressing a certain key (or key combination).

❑ Depleting the background-music buffer.

❑ Allowing a specific time period to elapse.

❑ Receiving data at a serial communications port.

❑ Activating the light pen.

❑ Pressing a joystick trigger.

To trap an event, you must do the following three things:

1. Write a subroutine, called an event handler, to which control branches when the event occurs.

2. Execute an ON *event* GOSUB instruction that associates the event handler with the desired event.

3. Execute an *event* ON instruction that activates the event trap.

Specifying an Event Trap

ON *event* GOSUB specifies the event to trap and the location of the associated event handler.

ON *event* GOSUB *linenum*

where *event* is the event to trap, and *linenum* is the line number of the first instruction in the event-handler subroutine.

Table 15.4 shows the possible values for *event*.

Table 15.4. *"Trappable" events.*

event	Trapped event
KEY(*keynum*)	Designated keystroke
PLAY(*noteminimum*)	Depletion of background-music buffer
TIMER(*numseconds*)	Elapsing of a given time interval
COM(*serialport*)	Data at a serial port
PEN	Light-pen activity
STRIG(*button*)	Pressing a joystick button

You can enable, disable, or suspend each event trap.

---

event ON

event OFF

event STOP

where *event* is the event to enable, disable, or suspend (see table 15.4).

ON enables the event trap.

OFF disables an event trap previously turned on. Should the event take place, BASIC ignores the event and does not branch to the event-trap subroutine.

STOP suspends the event trap. Should the event take place, no GOSUB occurs. However, BASIC "remembers" the event. A subsequent *event* ON instruction causes an immediate trap.

We now discuss the trapping of TIMER, KEY, and PLAY events.

Trapping a *TIMER* Event

TIMER keeps track of passing time and causes an event trap whenever a designated time period elapses.

```
ON TIMER(numseconds) GOSUB linenum

TIMER ON
TIMER OFF
TIMER STOP
```

where *numseconds* specifies the number of seconds to elapse, and *linenum* identifies the first line of the event-handler subroutine.

The *numseconds* parameter must have a value from 1 to 86,400. The maximum value, 86,400, is the number of seconds in 24 hours.

Here's a sample timer trap. The following program, PROMPTER.BAS turns on a timer trap while waiting for the user to reply Yes or No to a question. If the user does not respond within 15 seconds, the program beeps and displays a not-so-gentle reminder.

```
100 REM Program: PROMPTER.BAS (Demonstrate TIMER trap)
110 ON TIMER (15) GOSUB 900  'Prepare trap on 15-sec. interval
200 PRINT "Do you want instructions (Y or N)?"
210 '
300 TIMER ON                 'Turn on trap while waiting for reply
310 REPLY$ = ""
320 WHILE REPLY$ = ""
330    REPLY$ = INKEY$
340 WEND
350 TIMER OFF                'Turn off trap once reply is made
360 '
400 REM Now test value of REPLY$ and continue with program
410 REM
800 END
900 REM The event handler subroutine begins here
910    BEEP
920    PRINT "Please reply immediately!"
930    RETURN
```

Line 110 prepares the trap. This line does two things:

1. Designates the time period interval as 15 seconds.

2. Specifies line 900 as the beginning of the event trap subroutine.

Note that line 110 does not actually activate the trap. That's the purpose of line 300. You must execute a TIMER ON instruction before BASIC starts checking for a timer event.

Lines 310 through 340 continuously loop until the user presses a key. When the user presses a key, the key value is stored in the variable REPLY$.

However, if the user does not press a key within 15 seconds, the event trap occurs. BASIC immediately "GOSUB"s to the subroutine at line 900. Here, the program beeps and displays a reminder. The RETURN in line 930 closes the subroutine and returns control back into the loop at lines 320 through 340.

When the user does press a key, line 350 turns off the event trap. Now the program no longer checks for the elapsing of 15-second intervals.

Try PROMPTER.BAS a few times. First, press a key when prompted. The program "falls into" line 400 and terminates at line 800. Next, don't press any key when prompted. After every 15 seconds, the program beeps and displays the message in line 920.

Trapping a *KEY* Event

With KEY, you can trap the pressing of any key or keystroke combination.

ON KEY(*keynum*) GOSUB *linenum*

KEY (*keynum*) ON
KEY (*keynum*) OFF
KEY (*keynum*) STOP

where *keynum* identifies the key you want to trap (see table 15.5), and *linenum* identifies the first line of the event-handler subroutine.

Table 15.5. *Trapped keys.*

keynum	Key
1 to 10	Function keys F1 through F10
11	Direction key—up arrow
12	Direction key—left arrow
13	Direction key—right arrow
14	Direction key—down arrow
15 to 20	User-defined keys

The following program fragment demonstrates how multiple events can share event handlers:

```
200 ON KEY(11) GOSUB 800        'Up-arrow key
210 ON KEY(14) GOSUB 800        'Down-arrow key
220 ON KEY(12) GOSUB 900        'Left-arrow key
230 ON KEY(13) GOSUB 900        'Right-arrow key
250 KEY(11) ON
260 KEY(12) ON
270 KEY(13) ON
280 KEY(14) ON
 .
 .
 .
800 REM Subroutine to handle trapping of "vertical" keys
810     PRINT "You pressed the up- or down-arrow key."
820     RETURN
900 REM Subroutine to handle trapping of "horizontal" keys
910     PRINT "You pressed the left- or right-arrow key."
920     RETURN
```

In table 15.5, note that key numbers from 15 to 20 identify user-defined keys. This means that you can trap any key or keystroke combination. You can assign any or all the key numbers from 15 to 20 to individual keys (or keystroke combinations). You can trap, for example, the space bar, Shift-Q, and Ctrl-Alt-Esc, to name a few.

Trapping user-defined keys requires the following three instructions:

❑ KEY *userkeynum*, CHR$(*shiftcode*) + CHR$(*scancode*)

❑ ON KEY(*userkeynum*) GOSUB linenum

❑ KEY(*userkeynum*) ON

where *userkeynum* is a user-defined key number ranging from 15 to 20; *shiftcode* identifies the special keys, if any, that are being trapped; *scancode* identifies the primary key to be trapped; and *linenum* identifies the beginning of the event-handler subroutine.

Note that the first KEY instruction is new; you use this instruction only when trapping keys not found in table 15.5. This KEY instruction accomplishes two things:

❑ Uses *shiftcode* and *scancode* to identify the key or keystroke combination to trap.

❑ Associates that key or keystroke combination with *userkeynum* (a number from 15 to 20).

You can determine the proper value for *shiftcode* and *scancode* in the following manner:

❑ If the trap is any single key (even a special key such as Esc or Num Lock), *shiftcode* is 0; *scancode* can be found in Appendix C, "Keyboard Codes."

❑ If the trap is a keystroke combination (such as Ctrl-Alt-K), consider the combination to have a primary key (K in this example) and secondary special keys (Ctrl and Alt). Use table 15.6 to determine the *shiftcode* contribution for each secondary key. Add these contributions to determine the final value of *shiftcode*. Look up *scancode* for the primary key in Appendix C.

Table 15.6. *shiftcode values for keystroke combinations.*

Key	Value of shiftcode
Right Shift	1
Left Shift	2
Ctrl	4
Alt	8
Num Lock	32
Caps Lock	64
Extended Key (Enhanced Keyboard)	128

Here are some examples:

```
200 KEY 15, CHR$(0) + CHR$(57)      '/ Traps the space bar
210 ON KEY(15) GOSUB 2000           '|  - 57 is scan code
220 KEY(15) ON                      '\  - User key number 15
200 KEY MYKEYNUM%, CHR$(3) + CHR$(57)      'Shift-space bar
200 KEY MYKEYNUM%, CHR$(0) + CHR$(1)       'Esc key
200 KEY MYKEYNUM%, CHR$(12) + CHR$(83)     'Ctrl-Alt-Del
```

The last example traps Ctrl-Alt-Del. By trapping this combination, you can disable rebooting should the user press Ctrl-Alt-Del while your program is running.

Trapping a *PLAY* Event

ON PLAY(*noteminimum*) GOSUB *linenum*

PLAY ON
PLAY OFF
PLAY STOP

where *noteminimum* specifies the minimum number of notes in the background music buffer with a value from 1 to 32, and *linenum* identifies the first line of the event-handler subroutine.

PLAY works only for music playing in background mode. When music plays in the background, BASIC maintains a buffer that holds the remaining notes to play.

PLAY ON causes an event trap when the number of notes in the music buffer first decreases to *noteminimum*. No trap occurs if you execute PLAY ON when the buffer already has fewer notes than *noteminimum*. Note that ON PLAY uses the *noteminimum* argument, but PLAY ON does not.

The following program, PLAYMORE.BAS, demonstrates music trapping. The program continuously plays an up-and-down musical scale in the background while the screen fills with 5000 random graphic dots.

```
100 REM Program: PLAYMORE.BAS (Play music continually)
110 '
200 ON PLAY(5) GOSUB 900        'Trap when 5 notes left
210 PLAY ON                     'Try PLAY OFF to see the effect
220 '
300 PLAY "MB"                   'Turn on background music
310 GOSUB 900                   'Invoke event handler to play notes
320 '
400 SCREEN 1                    'Low resolution graphics
410 FOR COUNTER% = 1 TO 5000
420     X = RND * 320
430     Y = RND * 200
440     PSET (X, Y)             'Draw random point on the screen
450 NEXT COUNTER%
500 END
510 '
900 REM Event handler subroutine
910     PLAY "O2 C D E F G A B A G F E D"
920     RETURN
```

Event Trapping inside the Handler

BASIC executes an implied *event* STOP instruction when an event trap occurs and control passes to the handler subroutine. When a RETURN instruction closes the handler, BASIC executes an implied *event* ON instruction to reactivate trapping of the event. Without this safeguard, the handler could get in an infinite loop or incorrectly process multiple events.

BASIC "remembers" an event that occurs while the handler executes. The implied *event* STOP only suspends the trap. After the handler closes, an immediate trap takes place.

> **Returning from an Event-Handler Subroutine**
>
> An event handler is an ordinary subroutine that relinquishes control with a RETURN instruction. In many cases, you want control to resume at a specific instruction rather than immediately after the instruction that initiated the event trap.
>
> A special form of the RETURN instruction permits a subroutine to return to *any* line number in the main program:
>
> RETURN *linenum*
>
> where *linenum* is any line number in your program.
>
> For example, the following instruction returns control to line number 430:
>
> 980 RETURN 430
>
> You can use this technique with your regular subroutines also.

Comparing Event Trapping to Error Trapping

Event trapping and error trapping are similar, but not identical. The following list compares the two techniques:

❑ An event handler is a regular BASIC subroutine. The event handler, therefore, relinquishes control with a RETURN instruction. An error handler is a specialized routine that relinquishes control with a RESUME instruction.

❏ An event trap requires an `ON` *event* `GOSUB` instruction to define the handler and an *event* `ON` instruction to activate the trap. To define and activate an error trap, you need only a single `ON ERROR GOTO` instruction.

❏ You "`GOSUB`" to an event handler. You "`GOTO`" an error handler.

❏ You can trap multiple events simultaneously. Each event can have its own event handler, or multiple events can share the same event handler. On the other hand, error trapping is either on or off. Only one error handler can be active at any moment.

Using Alternate Numbering Systems—Binary and Hexadecimal

You have probably heard of binary numbers. In *binary*, you represent integer numbers with only the digits 0 and 1. Counting from 0, the first few binary numbers are 0, 1, 10, 11, 100, 101, which represent the decimal numbers 0, 1, 2, 3, 4, and 5, respectively.

Compared with our familiar decimal notation, representing a number in binary notation generally requires many more digits. There must be a tradeoff. Why ever use binary numbers? As it turns out, binary numbers are quite natural in computer applications. Why? Because a binary digit has only two states (0 or 1) and can be easily represented by an electric circuit being either off or on.

Hexadecimal is another popular computer numbering system. Each hexadecimal digit represents four binary digits. Because a binary digit has 2 states (on or off), 4 binary digits represent 2^4 or 16 values. It follows that hexadecimal is a base 16 numbering system. This means that there are 16 hexadecimal digits. By convention, these digits are the numerals 0 through 9 followed by the letters A through F.

In other words, to count from 0 in hexadecimal, you count up to 9 as usual. However, the decimal number 10 is simply the single hexadecimal digit A. The next hexadecimal number is B. The hexadecimal digit F is the decimal number 15. At this point, you run out of hexadecimal digits and must go to two-digit numbers. The hexadecimal number 10 is decimal 16. Table 15.7 shows the binary and hexadecimal conversion of the decimal numbers from 0 to 16.

Table 15.7. *Conversion of decimal numbers to binary and hexadecimal.*

Decimal	Binary	Hexadecimal
0	0	0
1	1	1
2	10	2
3	11	3
4	100	4
5	101	5
6	110	6
7	111	7
8	1000	8
9	1001	9
10	1010	A
11	1011	B
12	1100	C
13	1101	D
14	1110	E
15	1111	F
16	10000	10

In BASIC, you can specify integer values with hexadecimal notation. Just use the prefix &H before the hexadecimal value. For example, the literal &H10 refers to the hexadecimal number 10, which is 16 in decimal.

Because each hexadecimal digit directly corresponds to four binary bits, hexadecimal notation is convenient when you work with bit patterns or memory addresses. For example, the literal &H3B evaluates to the bit pattern 0011 1011, which in turn evaluates to the decimal integer 59.

The range for hexadecimal literals is from &H0 to &HFFFF. Table 15.8 gives some examples. (BASIC uses a special scheme for negative numbers. The literals from &H0 to &H7FFF correspond to the decimal numbers from 0 to 32,767. However, the literals &H8000 to &HFFFF correspond to the negative decimal numbers from −32,768 to −1.)

Table 15.8. *Examples of hexadecimal literals.*

Hex Literal	Binary Bit Pattern	Decimal Value
&H4ACE	0100 1010 1100 1110	19150
&H2	0000 0000 0000 0010	2
&H7FFF	0111 1111 1111 1111	32767
&H8000	1000 0000 0000 0000	−32768
&H8001	1000 0000 0000 0001	−32767
&HFFFF	1111 1111 1111 1111	−1

The BASIC function `HEX$` converts a decimal number into the corresponding hexadecimal string.

`HEX$(numexpr)`

where *numexpr* has a numeric value from −32,768 to 32,767. If necessary, BASIC rounds the value of *numexpr* to the nearest integer.

The following program, `HEX.BAS`, displays a short table of decimal numbers and their hexadecimal equivalents:

```
100 REM PROGRAM: HEX.BAS (Show hexadecimal conversion)
110 PRINT "Decimal", "Hexadecimal"
120 FOR NUM% = 100 TO 500 STEP 100
130    PRINT NUM%, HEX$(NUM%)
140 NEXT NUM%
```

Here is the output of `HEX.BAS`:

```
Decimal      Hexadecimal
 100         64
 200         C8
 300         12C
 400         190
 500         1F4
```

Referencing Memory Locations

As a BASIC programmer, you generally write programs with nary a thought about memory management. BASIC automatically supervises memory to handle variable storage, array allocation, and string management.

Occasionally, you need to exert explicit control over memory resources. BASIC provides the following functions and statements with which you can examine or change the contents of specific memory locations:

❑ The `PEEK` function, which examines a memory location

❑ The `POKE` statement, which changes the contents in a memory location

❑ The `DEF SEG` statement, which sets the memory segment within which `PEEK` and `POKE` operate

The syntax of PEEK and POKE specifies only the *offset* portion of a memory address, and DEF SEG specifies only a *segment* address. To understand what these terms mean and how memory addresses are used, we need to delve into a little background about your computer's memory-addressing scheme.

Memory Architecture of the IBM PC

Here is a whirlwind tour of memory architecture in the IBM PC computer family. Be warned, your first exposure to these concepts may be a little confusing. Until you feel comfortable with the computer's memory methodology, we recommend that you don't play around with PEEK and POKE.

Memory Bytes

Memory is a collection of 8-bit units called *bytes*. At a given instant, each bit is either on or off (1 or 0). Therefore, at any moment, each byte is in one of 2^8 (or 256) possible configurations.

You can consider any given byte configuration to be a number ranging from 0 (all bits off) to 255 (all bits on). For example, figure 15.2 depicts some sample byte configurations and the number that each configuration represents.

***Fig. 15.2.** Some sample memory bytes.*

Binary	Hex	Decimal
0 0 0 0 0 0 0 0	0 0	0
0 0 0 0 0 1 0 0	0 4	4
0 0 1 0 1 1 0 0	2 C	4 4
1 0 0 1 1 0 0 1	9 9	1 5 3
1 1 1 1 1 1 1 1	F F	2 5 5

Physically, each memory byte is one of the following two types:

❏ RAM (random-access memory)
❏ ROM (read-only memory)

RAM memory can be written to and read from—that is, the configuration of a RAM byte can change. When your computer's processor is given the proper instructions, it can alter the value of any RAM byte. BASIC stores the values of variables in RAM because such values frequently change during the execution of a program.

ROM memory, on the other hand, is "hard-wired." Each byte of ROM has an unchangeable configuration set at the factory. The processor can read the value of a ROM byte but cannot change the bit configuration. As you might suppose, ROM memory stores essential information that must not vary, such as much of your computer's operating system.

Memory Addresses

Each byte, whether RAM or ROM, has a unique *address*. The address is the memory location of that particular byte.

Early IBM PC models, and competitors' "clone" models, are built around the Intel 8088 (or 8086) microprocessor. The hardware design of these computers allots 20 signal lines to specify an address value. Like a bit, each signal line can have a value of 1 or 0. Quick arithmetic shows that the number of possible addresses is 2^{20}, which is 1,048,576 (1 megabyte). The actual address values range from 0 to 1,048,575.

When programmers discuss memory addresses, hexadecimal number notation is more convenient than decimal. Because a hex digit has 1 of 16 possible values (from 0 to 9 and A to F), each 20-bit address value can be expressed with a 5-digit hex number ($16^5 = 2^{20}$). In hex notation, memory addresses range from 00000 to FFFFF.

For convenience, you can consider the 1-megabyte address space divided into 16 blocks of 64 kilobytes each. The first block has addresses from 00000 to 0FFFF, the second block from 10000 to 1FFFF, the last block from F0000 to FFFFF. The first hex digit identifies the block in which that address appears. Figure 15.3 shows the organization of this memory.

All would be relatively simple if not for the fact that the 8088 is a 16-bit microprocessor and cannot work directly with numbers larger than 16 bits. With 16 bits, you get only 2^{16} or 65,536 (64K) possible values.

Fig. 15.3. *Memory block structure.*

F 0 0 0 0	Permanent System ROM
E 0 0 0 0	Other Use (Cartridge ROM)
D 0 0 0 0	Other Use (Cartridge ROM)
C 0 0 0 0	ROM Expansion
B 0 0 0 0	Standard Video Memory
A 0 0 0 0	Extended Video Memory (EGA)
9 0 0 0 0	Working RAM, up to 640K
8 0 0 0 0	Working RAM, up to 576K
7 0 0 0 0	Working RAM, up to 512K
6 0 0 0 0	Working RAM, up to 448K
5 0 0 0 0	Working RAM, up to 384K
4 0 0 0 0	Working RAM, up to 320K
3 0 0 0 0	Working RAM, up to 256K
2 0 0 0 0	Working RAM, up to 192K
1 0 0 0 0	Working RAM, up to 128K
0 0 0 0 0	Working RAM, up to 64K

What Is a *K* and a Kilobyte?

K is short for *kilo*, which in computing terminology stands for 1024, the closest power of 2 to 1000. So, 64K means 64 times 1024, which is 65,536.

In computer literature, 64K bytes (64 kilobytes) is often abbreviated 64KB, and sometimes just 64K. It is dangerous, however, to use "K" to mean "kilobytes." Why? Because K is often used to mean 1024 of something other than bytes, such as bits, memory locations, or memory configurations. Here, we use "K" to mean 1024. When we refer to bytes, we just say "64 kilobytes" rather than "64K."

This creates a dilemma. The processor uses 16-bit numbers (four hex digits) but the addressing system accommodates 20-bit numbers (5 hex digits). The solution is an addressing scheme involving *segmented addresses*.

Segmented Addresses

A segmented address specifies a memory location with two 16-bit numbers: a *segment* and an *offset*.

Each segment begins at a memory location evenly divisible by 16. As a result, the last hex digit of each segment's first location is 0. For example, each of the following addresses specifies the beginning of a segment: 00010, FEDC0, 382A0, FFFF0. Note that because the last digit is always 0, you can identify each segment by just specifying the first 4 digits.

Well, four hex digits is a 16-bit number, and you are halfway home.

To complete an address, the offset specifies the relative location from the beginning of the segment. Each offset address is also a 16-bit number (4 hex digits). Therefore, each offset is within 64 kilobytes of the beginning of the segment.

So you use two 16-bit numbers to specify an address: a segment and an offset. Each number is usually represented by four hex digits. In conventional notation, you place a colon between the two values. For example, the address 38CE:A22B means that the segment address is 38CE0 and the offset from this segment is A22B (remember that the segment has an implied 0 at the end). To find the absolute address, you must add the two values together (see fig. 15.4).

Fig. 15.4. Calculating an absolute address.

Segmented Address	38CE:A22B
Segment (Add 0)	38CE0
Offset	+ A22B
Absolute Address	42F0B

Note that you can specify a particular memory location with several different segmented addresses. Because a segment begins every 16 bytes and an offset ranges up to 64K bytes, there is considerable overlap in the 64K address space of each segment.

Given a particular segmented address, you can specify the same location by decreasing the segment part and increasing the offset part or vice versa. For each unit decrease in the segment, you must raise the offset value by 16. For example, the following segmented addresses all refer to the identical memory location: 2345:8F23, 2344:8F33, 2335:9023, 3C37:0003.

The IBM PC AT and the high-numbered models of the PS/2 line of micro-computers use advanced central processor chips: namely, the 80286, 80386, or 80486. These newer chips have additional address-signal lines and can address more memory than the 8088. But from BASIC's point of view through DOS, all these IBM PC-compatible computers use addressing limited to 1 megabyte, using the same segment and offset architecture.

Using *DEF SEG*, *PEEK*, and *POKE*

Now with some understanding of memory addressing under your belt, you are ready to try DEF SEG, PEEK, and POKE.

Setting the Segment Address: *DEF SEG*

When you first start BASIC, the default segment address is set to some value that you do not know. The exact memory address of this segment depends on your computer configuration, the size of DOS, and any resident programs.

What if you want to use PEEK or POKE to work with memory locations outside the default segment's 64-kilobyte chunk of memory? The answer is to use DEF SEG to tell BASIC which segment you want.

DEF SEG = *segaddress*

or simply

DEF SEG

where *segaddress* specifies the new default segment address.

For example, the following instruction sets the default segment address to the upper 64-kilobyte memory area (the F block):

880 DEF SEG = &HF000

If the *segaddress* parameter is present in a DEF SEG instruction, the parameter must resolve to a whole number in the range from 0 to 65,535 (&H0 to &HFFFF). DEF SEG with no argument restores the current default segment to the original value when BASIC started.

Segment values are commonly specified as hexadecimal literals because hexadecimal is a natural notation for memory addresses. The hex values from &H0 to &HFFFF map directly into decimal memory addresses from 0 to 65,535.

When you issue a DEF SEG instruction, the current segment pointer stays in effect until you issue another DEF SEG instruction. Be sure to leave a blank space between DEF and SEG. The following instruction refers to a variable named DEFSEG, not to the DEF SEG statement:

```
420 DEFSEG = &HB800
```

The following discussion of PEEK and POKE contains examples of DEF SEG instructions.

Examining What Is in Memory: *PEEK*

Use the PEEK function to examine the contents of any memory location.

PEEK(*offset*)

where *offset* specifies an offset address.

The ROM memory byte at address F000:FFFE contains a value that indicates the computer model. Not surprisingly, this memory location is known as the *model identification byte*.

Here's a short program that examines and displays this model identification byte:

```
100 DEF SEG = &HF000
110 ID% = PEEK(&HFFFE)
120 PRINT "The model ID byte is"; ID%
```

In decimal, this ID byte is 255 for the original IBM PC, 254 for an IBM XT (251 for late models), 252 for an IBM AT, XT-286, or PS/2 with an 80286 processor, 250 for PS/2s with an 8086 processor, 249 for the PC Convertible, and 248 for PS/2s with an 80386 processor. IBM has not been completely consistent in the numbers used, but this byte is generally reliable. Most makers of compatible computers use the same values for corresponding computers.

The *offset* parameter used with PEEK is a general numeric expression specifying an offset address. The offset does not have to be a hex constant. Variables, expressions, and decimal literals are fine too. The offset value must be in the range from 0 to 65,535 (&H0 to &HFFFF).

PEEK returns an integer value in the range from 0 to 255. This value represents the 8-bit memory byte at the designated address.

Changing What Is in Memory: *POKE*

The POKE statement is the complement to the PEEK function. Whereas PEEK examines a memory byte, POKE writes a value into a memory location.

POKE *offset*, *databyte*

where *offset* specifies an offset address, and *databyte* specifies the value to be written.

The following program uses POKE to write directly into video memory. The program displays a character on the screen.

```
100 SCREEN 0
110 DEF SEG = &HB800      'Beginning of CGA/EGA/VGA video RAM
120 POKE 2000, 3          'Displays ASCII 3 (heart character)
```

The result is a single heart symbol in the approximate center of the screen. The POKE instruction in line 120 writes at offset 2000 (decimal), which maps into the character position where the heart displays. The 3 represents the ASCII character to display—a heart symbol. Appendix B, "ASCII Character Set," lists these numbers and characters.

POKE's first argument is an offset value—a general numeric expression from 0 to 65,536 specifying an offset address. The second argument is the value to write into memory and must be a general numeric expression in the range from 0 to 255.

Use DEF SEG to specify the segment address of the referenced memory location. In the example, DEF SEG points to the start of the RAM area used for the video display. (*Note:* This program will not work on a computer using the monochrome display adapter, which maps its video into the RAM area starting at segment &HB000.)

You must be careful when you use POKE. Be sure that you correctly specify the address. Because POKE has access to any RAM location, you can accidentally "step on" part of DOS, BASIC, or some other sensitive location. Crashing your system is possible, meaning that you might have to turn the power off and back on again to restart. Be sure to SAVE any program that uses POKE before you RUN it!

Using Advanced Graphics

In Chapter 11, "Creating Graphics," we discussed graphics in some depth. Now we are going to pick up where we left off. Here, we discuss the following advanced graphics features:

❏ Drawing stylized lines
❏ Filling areas with patterned tiles
❏ Animating graphic images
❏ Graphing options available with EGA, VGA, and MCGA video adapters
❏ Storing images on alternate screen "pages"
❏ Customizing your coordinate system

Styling and Tiling

Straight lines and painted areas do not have to be solid. You may want a dashed line or a patterned fill. BASIC has instructions to let you design and customize such features.

The *style* of a line consists of the sequence of pixels that are on and off. By default, BASIC draws a solid line (all pixels in the specified color). But you may desire a dotted or dashed line—in a mathematical graph, for example.

A *tile* is the two-dimensional equivalent of a line style. Normally, painted areas are filled with a solid color. But you may want to fill an enclosed area with a pattern. You can design your own tiles. Each tile has a specified pattern of pixels that are on and off. These tiles can be laid to fill the desired area.

Styles and tiles occur in these situations:

❏ You specify a line style in a LINE instruction.
❏ You specify a tile in a PAINT instruction.

Constructing a Line Style

Consider a line fragment of 16 consecutive pixels. You can construct a line style by establishing a pattern for which of these 16 pixels are on and which are off.

BASIC uses your line style when drawing a line. The 16-pixel pattern repeats as necessary for the entire length of the line. You specify a style with a 4-digit hexadecimal number that represents your custom pixel pattern.

Let's say that you want a line style with two dashes followed by two dots. The 16-pixel sequence consists of 3 on, 2 off, 3 on, 2 off, 1 on, 2 off, 1 on, and 2 off. Figure 15.5 shows the process of determining the hexadecimal number corresponding to this line. The following four steps are involved:

1. Represent the 16-pixel pattern visually.

2. Create a 16-bit binary number. A 1 represents each on-pixel, and a 0 represents each off-pixel.

3. Divide the 16 binary bits into four sets of four bits. Each set of four bits becomes a hexadecimal digit. Table 15.7 shows the conversion between 4-bit groups and hexadecimal digits.

4. Prefix the four-digit hexadecimal number with &H in standard BASIC notation.

Fig. 15.5. *Creating a line style.*

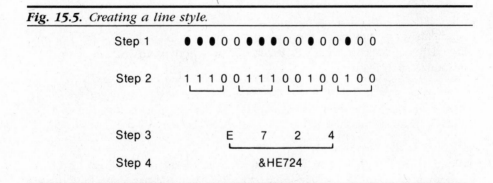

The resulting hexadecimal number is suitable for the *pattern* argument (the last parameter) in a LINE instruction. The complete syntax of a line instruction includes the *pattern* argument.

LINE *startpoint − endpoint, color*, B, *pattern*

where *pattern* specifies the dot pattern for the line or box. The *startpoint, endpoint, color*, and B parameters have been previously explained in Chapter 11, "Creating Graphics."

To illustrate, the following program produces the stylized boxes shown in figure 15.6. The outer box is styled with our sample pattern.

```
100 SCREEN 1
110 CLS
200 LINE (10, 10) - (290, 190), , B, &HE724
210 LINE (30, 30) - (270, 170), , B, &H1111
220 LINE (50, 50) - (250, 150), , B, &HF0F0
230 LINE (70, 70) - (230, 130), , B, &HFFCC
```

Fig. 15.6. *Four line styles.*

Constructing a Tile

Unlike a line style, you specify a tile with a string. This string becomes the *paint* parameter in a PAINT instruction. (See Chapter 11, "Creating Graphics," for a general discussion of the PAINT statement.)

The technique for constructing tiles depends on the SCREEN mode. We now explain high-resolution and medium-resolution tiles.

High-Resolution Tiles—*SCREEN* Mode 2

A tile consists of a rectangular grid of pixels—8 pixels horizontally and 1 to 64 pixels vertically. Consider each row of 8 pixels to be a binary number. An on pixel is represented by a 1, and an off pixel is represented by 0. Every row corresponds to an 8-bit binary number of zeroes and ones. Each binary number reduces to a decimal number from 0 to 255.

You form the tile string by concatenating these numbers with the CHR$ function. Figure 15.7 shows this process for an 8 × 6 tile containing a triangle design.

Fig. 15.7. *Constructing a high-resolution tile.*

Tile Pattern	Convert to Binary	Convert to Decimal	Tile$ = Resulting BASIC Instruction
0 0 0 0 0 0 0 0	0 0 0 0 0 0 0 0	0	CHR$ (0)
0 0 0 ● 0 0 0 0	0 0 0 1 0 0 0 0	16	+ CHR$ (16)
0 0 0 ● ● 0 0 0	0 0 0 1 1 0 0 0	24	+ CHR$ (24)
0 0 0 ● ● ● 0 0	0 0 0 1 1 1 0 0	28	+ CHR$ (28)
0 0 0 ● ● ● ● 0	0 0 0 1 1 1 1 0	30	+ CHR$ (30)
0 0 0 ● ● ● ● ●	0 0 0 1 1 1 1 1	31	+ CHR$ (31)

The following program uses these tiles to fill the inside of a circle. The result is shown in figure 15.8.

```
100 REM Tile a circle with a triangle pattern
110 SCREEN 2
120 CLS
200 TILE$ = CHR$(0) + CHR$(16) + CHR$(24)
210 TILE$ = TILE$ + CHR$(28) + CHR$(30) + CHR$(31)
300 CIRCLE (300, 100), 150
310 PAINT (300, 100), TILE$
```

Fig. 15.8. *An example of high-resolution tiles.*

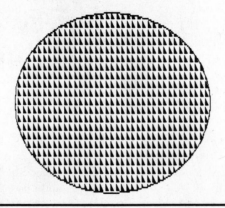

Medium-Resolution Tiles—*SCREEN* Mode 1

The situation is similar to that of high-resolution tiles, but now colors are involved. A tile is 4 pixels wide and from 1 to 64 pixels high. In a given 4-pixel row, each pixel can be assigned one of the four color values from 0 to 3. Thus, each row is represented by a 4-digit number, each digit being 0, 1, 2, or 3.

To construct the appropriate tile string, convert each digit to a 2-bit binary number (0 is 00, 1 is 01, 2 is 10, and 3 is 11). Then concatenate the bits to form an 8-bit binary number for each row. Next convert each binary number to a decimal number (from 0 to 255). Finally, you form the tile string by concatenating these numbers with CHR$, just as in high-resolution tiling.

Figure 15.9 shows a 4-row tile created by this technique. Try the following program, which fills a circle with these tiles:

```
100 REM Example of medium-resolution tiling
110 SCREEN 1
120 CLS
200 TILE$ = CHR$(24) + CHR$(36) + CHR$(130) + CHR$(130)
300 CIRCLE (150, 100), 100
310 PAINT (100, 100), TILE$
```

Fig. 15.9. *Constructing a medium-resolution tile.*

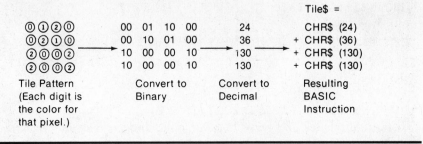

Animation with *GET* and *PUT*

Animating graphic images is easy with BASIC's GET and PUT statements. GET takes a snapshot of any rectangular screen area and saves the snapshot into a numeric array. PUT reproduces the snapshot anywhere on the screen. You can create multiple copies of an image or smoothly move an image along the screen.

GET (*upleftxy*) − (*lowrightxy*), *arrayname*

where *upleftxy* is the *x,y* location of the upper left corner of the rectangular area to save, *lowrightxy* is the *x,y* location of the lower right corner of the rectangular area to save, and *arrayname* is the name of the numeric array in which to store the snapshot image.

PUT (*upleftxy*), *arrayname*, *drawoption*

where *upleftxy* is the *x,y* location of the upper left corner of the rectangular area to receive the stored image, *arrayname* is the name of the numeric array holding the image, and *drawoption* specifies how the information in *arrayname* is drawn on the screen.

The *drawoption* parameter is optional.

With GET, *upleftxy* and *lowrightxy* can, in fact, be any two diagonally opposite corners. For most applications, *upleftxy* is actually the upper left corner for consistency with subsequent PUT instructions.

You can define the location of the snapshot area with absolute or relative coordinates. For example, the following instruction takes a snapshot of the rectangular area defined by the diagonally opposite corners (45, 18) and (125, 78):

```
300 GET (45, 18) - (125, 78), IMAGE%
```

Here are a few examples of relative coordinates:

```
400 GET (45,18)-STEP(80,60),IMAGE%        'Same effect as line 300

420 GET STEP(20,42)-STEP(10,10),IMAGE% 'Both corners relative

440 PUT STEP(38,-12),IMAGE%               'Top left corner relative
```

In these examples, the array IMAGE% holds the graphics information. You can use any numeric array with GET as long as the array has been previously dimensioned with a DIM instruction.

Don't Confuse Graphic GET and PUT with File GET and PUT

BASIC has two entirely different sets of GET and PUT statements. The graphic GET and PUT statements, discussed in this chapter, are entirely different from the file-access GET and PUT statements discussed in Chapter 10, "Using Disk Files."

Determining the Array Size

The numeric array, *arrayname*, can be any numeric type but must be dimensioned large enough to hold the graphics information. The minimum acceptable dimensioning depends on the size of the snapshot area, the SCREEN mode, and the numeric data type of *arrayname*.

We recommend that you use integer arrays to hold your image snapshots. As a rule of thumb, a snapshot of the entire screen in modes 1 or 2 requires an integer array of approximately 8,000 elements. You can proportion the dimension size downward based on the size of your image.

In a program using GET, BASIC generates an Illegal function call error if you don't dimension *arrayname* sufficiently large. You may have to find the necessary array size by trial and error.

A Test Case—Stick Figures

Let's try an example. The following program draws the stick figure depicted in figure 15.10:

```
200 SCREEN 1
210 CLS
300 CIRCLE (20, 20), 6
310 PAINT (20, 20)
320 DRAW "D16 NE8 NH8 D4 NF8 NG8"
```

Fig. 15.10. *A simple stick figure.*

Now, suppose that you want to store the stick figure and reproduce the image at various screen locations.

First, you must save the stick figure into an array. A box with diagonally opposite corners at (8, 8) and (31, 51) surrounds the stick figure. You can verify this by adding the following instruction to the end of the program:

```
350 LINE (8, 8) - (31, 55), , B
```

This box is the snapshot area that you will save into the array.

How large must the array be? Our image occupies a small percentage of the screen. An integer array dimensioned to 150 should be sufficient. We will call the storage array IMAGE%.

Before you try actual animation, let's have PUT produce multiple copies of the stick figure. The program now looks like this:

```
150 DIM IMAGE%(150)                    'Dimension the storage array
200 SCREEN 1
210 CLS
220 '
300 CIRCLE (20, 20), 6
310 PAINT (20, 20)
320 DRAW "D16 NE8 NH8 D4 NF8 NG8"
330 GET (8, 8) - (31, 55), IMAGE% 'Store the snapshot IMAGE%
400 CLS
410 '
420 FOR X% = 50 TO 250 STEP 50
430    FOR Y% = 50 TO 150 STEP 50
440       PUT (X%, Y%), IMAGE%      'Draw a copy
450    NEXT Y%
460 NEXT X%
```

This program draws 15 new stick figures in 3 rows of 5 each.

Adding Animation

Now, let's try true animation. We will move a single stick figure across a complex background. After the image is stored and the background drawn, animation requires the following steps:

1. PUT the image on the screen.

2. Calculate the next position of the image.

3. PUT the image on the screen at the old location (this step removes the original image).

4. Go back to step 1, using the new position.

This technique uses a process called XOR animation. (XOR, and the other *drawoption* alternatives of the PUT statement, are discussed in the following section.)

XOR animation has the remarkable property that when an image is PUT a second time at the same location, the original background is restored, including all colors. PUT uses XOR animation by default if you omit the *drawoption* parameter.

The ANIMATE.BAS program demonstrates XOR animation. A stick figure "walks" across a background consisting of various colored squares.

```
100 REM Program: ANIMATE.BAS (Demonstrate XOR Animation)
150 DIM IMAGE%(150)
200 SCREEN 1
210 CLS
220 '
300 CIRCLE (20, 20), 6
310 PAINT (20, 20)
320 DRAW "D16 NE8 NH8 D4 NF8 NG8"
330 GET (8, 8) - (31, 55), IMAGE%
400 CLS
410 '
500 LINE (100, 60) - STEP(20, 20), 1, BF  'Draw a
510 LINE (150, 60) - STEP(20, 20), 3, BF  'background of
520 LINE (100, 90) - STEP(20, 20), 3, B   'various colored
530 LINE (150, 90) - STEP(20, 20), 2, BF  'boxes
540 '
600 FOR X% = 20 TO 200 STEP 2
610     PUT (X%, 60), IMAGE%, XOR       'Draw stick figure
620         NOW! = TIMER
630         WHILE (TIMER - NOW!) < .15 'Pause program for
640         WEND                       '.15 seconds
650     PUT (X%, 60), IMAGE%, XOR       'Erase stick figure
660 NEXT X%
700 END
```

The first PUT instruction (line 610) draws the stick figure at the updated X% position.

The second PUT instruction (line 650) erases the stick figure and restores the original background.

Note the delay loop (lines 620 through 640) between the two PUT instructions. You need a delay loop to reduce screen flicker and to let your eye adjust to the just drawn image. In general, you want a short delay between the drawing and erasing of the image. However, you want the shortest possible time between the erasure and the redrawing of the next image.

Other *drawoption* Values

The optional PUT parameter, *drawoption*, defines how the image interacts with the background over which the PUT takes place. There are five possible values of drawoption: PSET, PRESET, AND, OR, and XOR. Table 15.9 shows the resulting effects.

Table 15.9. The effects of the drawoption parameter.

drawoption	Effect
PSET	Places the image in all cases
PRESET	Places the complementary image in all cases
AND	Places image only if background exists
OR	Superimposes the image on the background
XOR	Reverses image only if background exists

The PSET option simply draws the stored image, obliterating any background. PRESET does the same thing, but the stored image is drawn with inverted colors (black for white, cyan for magenta, in SCREEN 1).

To understand the effect of one of the logical operators (AND, OR, XOR), you must calculate the result of each interaction between an image pixel and the corresponding background pixel.

Try adding various *drawoption* parameters to either or both PUT instructions in the ANIMATE.BAS program. Experiment with the different effects. The following change to the first PUT instruction is interesting:

```
610    PUT (X%, 60), IMAGE%, OR    'Draw stick figure
```

EGA, MCGA, and VGA Considerations

If your computer system has an EGA, VGA, or MCGA video adapter, you have more graphics options than discussed in Chapter 11, "Creating Graphics." SCREEN modes 7, 8, 9, and 10 become available. Also, you can utilize more colors and options in SCREEN modes 1 and 2.

EGA Colors

Altogether, you can access 64 colors, identified with the numbers from 0 to 63. The following program, EGACOLOR.BAS, cycles through the various colors. Each color number displays below the corresponding color box. The colors change every five seconds.

```
100 REM Program: EGACOLOR.BAS (Cycle the 64 EGA colors)
110 SCREEN 9: CLS
120 PRINT "EGA Colors"
130 FOR J% = 1 TO 9
```

```
140    LINE (J% * 63, 50) -STEP(40, 70), J%, BF
150 NEXT J%
160 '
200 FOR PAGE% = 0 TO 6
210    FOR BOX% = 1 TO 9
220       VALUE% = PAGE% * 9 + BOX%
230       LOCATE 11, BOX% * 8 + 1
240       PRINT VALUE%
250       PALETTE BOX%, VALUE%       'Change colors
260    NEXT BOX%
270       NOW! = TIMER
280       WHILE (TIMER - NOW!) < 5    'Pause for 5 seconds
290       WEND
300 NEXT PAGE%
310 END
```

The *PALETTE* Statement

In line 250, EGACOLOR.BAS uses a PALETTE instruction to change colors. PALETTE is valid only with an EGA, MCGA, or VGA adapter.

If you recall from Chapter 11, "Creating Graphics," the colors available in any SCREEN mode were predetermined. For example, only two colors (black and white) were available in mode 2, and four colors (black, cyan, magenta, and white) were available in SCREEN mode 1. (Though in SCREEN mode 1, a COLOR instruction can toggle the palette to provide a different set of four colors.)

With your EGA hardware (from now on, *EGA* means EGA, VGA or MCGA) and PALETTE, you can extend the color capabilities of your graphing. A PALETTE instruction reorganizes the numeric color values. Previously, a *color* parameter in a graphics instruction specified a particular color. Now, think of such a parameter as an *attribute*.

For example, consider the following instruction:

```
200 PSET (50, 30), 2
```

Think of this instruction as giving attribute 2, not color 2, to the pixel at (50, 30). With a PALETTE instruction, you can assign whatever color you choose to attribute 2.

The situation is analogous to an artist painting from a palette of different colors. The artist's palette has a fixed number of slots. He or she can choose any color to fill each slot.

Depending on the SCREEN mode, you have a certain number of slots in your palette. These are the attributes. By default, BASIC assigns a particular color (in the range from 0 to 15) to each slot. But with a PALETTE instruction, you can put any of 64 colors into each slot.

PALETTE *attribute, color*

or simply

PALETTE

where *attribute* specifies which attribute number to change, and *color* specifies which color to assign to *attribute*.

For screen modes 7 through 9, the value of *color* can range from 0 to 63.

A PALETTE instruction affects text and graphics already on the screen as well as subsequent text and graphics. Images drawn with *attribute* instantly change to the new color specified by *color*.

The ranges of attribute and color depend on the screen mode and video adapter (see table 15.10).

Table 15.10. *Attribute and color ranges on EGA systems.*

SCREEN *mode*	*attribute range*	*color range*
0	0 − 15	0 − 63
1	0 − 3	0 − 15
2	0 − 1	0 − 15
7	0 − 15	0 − 15
8	0 − 15	0 − 15
9	0 − 15	0 − 63
10	0 − 3	0 − 8

Note that text mode (SCREEN 0) supports PALETTE. For example, in mode 0 the following instruction assigns color 38 to attribute 3:

```
530 PALETTE 3, 38
```

In mode 2, *attribute* can only be 0 or 1, corresponding to the background and foreground. The following instruction assigns color 27 to the foreground:

```
600 PALETTE 1, 27
```

Modes 7, 8, and 9 restrict the *attribute* range from 0 to 3 if your EGA has only 64K bytes of memory.

In mode 10, for monochrome monitors, each attribute can be assigned a "color" from 0 to 8 interpreted as follows: 0 is black, 4 is white, 8 is high-intensity white, and the other values produce various blinking effects.

A PALETTE instruction with no arguments simply reassigns the default colors.

You might want to run the EGACOLOR.BAS program to see the actual color associated with each of the 64 values of the *color* parameter.

The following program demonstrates adding color to SCREEN mode 2. When you are prompted for a color, give a number from 0 to 15 to see what color fills the circle. Note how the text color changes as well as the paint color.

```
100 REM Demonstrate colors in screen mode 2
110 SCREEN 2
120 CLS
200 CIRCLE (300, 100), 150
300 HUE% = 1
310 WHILE HUE% <> 0
320     LOCATE 23, 5
330     INPUT "Paint color (0 - 15, 0 = quit)"; HUE%
340     PALETTE 1, HUE%
350     PAINT (300, 100), 1
360 WEND
370 PALETTE                'Restore default palette
```

You can use PALETTE to instantly display images. First, assign one or more *attribute* values to the background color. Then draw a complex screen with text and graphics. Images drawn with the background color are temporarily invisible. Such images immediately pop into view when a PALETTE instruction reassigns *attribute* to a new color.

The *SCREEN* Statement Revisited— Graphics Pages

Until now, each SCREEN instruction contained only one parameter (the graphics mode). However, the full syntax of the SCREEN instruction includes three optional parameters.

SCREEN *modecode, colorswitch, activepage, visualpage*

where *modecode* sets the screen mode, *colorswitch* is a numeric expression enabling or disabling color, *activepage* specifies the working page, and *visualpage* specifies the page in view.

---

modecode is the only mandatory parameter; its use has been discussed at length in Chapter 11, "Creating Graphics."

colorswitch has meaning only for composite monitors (including TV sets) used in SCREEN modes 0 and 1. This parameter controls whether a color signal is sent to the monitor. Because composite monitors are rarely used today, we will not discuss *colorswitch* in detail.

A *page* is a screen image stored in RAM. The number of available pages depends on your hardware and the screen mode. The *active* page is the page with which text and graphic instructions are currently working. This page may or may not be visible.

The *visual* page is the page currently visible on the screen. By utilizing pages, you can build images on one page in memory while viewing another page on your screen. Then, with a SCREEN instruction, you can make a new page instantly visible. This allows animation and other effects.

Pages are designated with integer numbers from zero upward. The number of active pages depends on the screen mode and your hardware.

CGA systems reserve 16 kilobytes of RAM for paged memory. Text mode (SCREEN mode 0) supports multiple pages. SCREEN modes 1 and 2 do not support multiple pages.

EGA systems can have 64, 128, or 256 kilobytes of memory on the EGA card. This EGA memory can store page images. SCREEN modes 7 to 10 support multiple pages.

Table 15.11 shows the available pages as a function of screen mode and hardware configuration.

Table 15.11. *Memory pages.*

Mode	Resolution	EGA Memory	Page Size	Page Range
0	WIDTH 40	— —	2K	0 – 7
0	WIDTH 80	— —	4K	0 – 3
1	320 x 200	— —	16K	0
2	640 x 200	— —	16K	0
7	320 x 200	64K	32K	0 – 1
7	320 x 200	128K	32K	0 – 3
7	320 x 200	256K	32K	0 – 7
8	640 x 200	64K	64K	0
8	640 x 200	128K	64K	0 – 1
8	640 x 200	256K	64K	0 – 3
9	640 x 350	64K	64K	0
9	640 x 350	128K	128K	0
9	640 x 350	256K	128K	0 – 1
10	640 x 350	128K	128K	0
10	640 x 350	256K	128K	0 – 1

The last column, Page Range, shows the range of values that *activepage* and *visualpage* can assume.

Copying Screen Pages

A PCOPY instruction copies a specified screen page to another screen page.

> PCOPY *sourcepage, targetpage*
>
> where *sourcepage* specifies the page to be copied, and *targetpage* specifies the page to receive the copy.

For example, the following instruction copies the contents of page 2 to page 3:

```
400 PCOPY 2, 3
```

The value of *sourcepage* and *targetpage* must each be within the appropriate range for the SCREEN mode and video configuration. These ranges are shown in the rightmost column of table 15.11.

Redefining Coordinate Systems—*WINDOW*

Let's face it. The coordinate systems used in the various SCREEN modes are somewhat arbitrary and unnatural. You may have a preferred coordinate system for certain applications. As a simple example, you may like to think of Y values increasing as you move up the screen rather than down the screen.

WINDOW maps the default screen coordinates into a coordinate system of your own choosing. For example, you can define the lower left corner of the screen to be location (0, 0) and the upper right corner of the screen (1, 1). Then you can reference all pixels with an X and a Y value between 0 and 1. X values increase toward the right, and Y values increase upward. With this system, the center of the screen is always (0.5, 0.5), regardless of the SCREEN mode.

WINDOW has two forms, with and without the SCREEN keyword.

WINDOW (*leftxy*) − (*rightxy*)

WINDOW SCREEN (*leftxy*) − (*rightxy*)

where *leftxy* specifies the x,y location of either the upper left corner or the lower left corner, and *rightxy* specifies the x,y location of either the upper right corner or the lowxer right corner.

When you include SCREEN, *leftxy* refers to the upper left corner of the screen, and *rightxy* refers to the lower right corner. Y values increase down the screen in the normal way. When you omit SCREEN, *leftxy* refers to the lower left corner of the screen, and *rightxy* refers to the upper right corner. Y values increase moving up the screen.

You specify *leftxy* and *rightxy* as pairs of single-precision numbers. This gives you great range in designing a coordinate system. (*Note:* If your coordinate system permits *leftxy* and *rightxy* to be integer numbers, objects will subsequently draw significantly faster than if *leftxy* and *rightxy* are single-precision numbers.)

Consider the following instruction:

```
340 WINDOW (-30000, -.2) - (30000, .2)
```

Line 340 causes the entire screen to map into a numeric range from −30,000 to +30,000 in the X direction but only from −0.2 to +0.2 in the Y direction.

Note that subsequent coordinate references can be single-precision numbers in order to specify exact points in the Y direction. For example, assuming that line 340 is in effect, the following instruction plots a point centered horizontally but 7/8 of the way up the screen.

```
500 PSET (0, .15)
```

To illustrate WINDOW and the effect of SCREEN, figures 15.11, 15.12, and 15.13 compare the default coordinate system with two WINDOW-created coordinate systems. High resolution (SCREEN 2) is assumed.

Fig. 15.11. *The default coordinate system.*

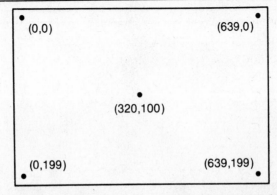

Fig. 15.12. *Coordinates after* WINDOW (-100, -1)-(100, 1).

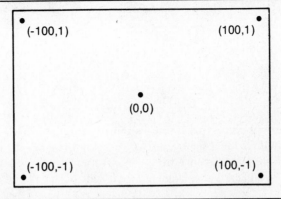

Fig. 15.13. Coordinates after `WINDOW SCREEN (-100, -1)-(100, 1)`.

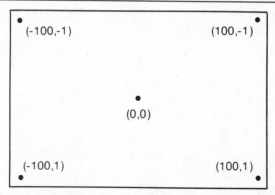

User-Defined Coordinate Systems

You may discover many applications for user-defined coordinate systems. Here are two common applications:

❑ Converting graphics from one `SCREEN` mode to another.

❑ Creating natural coordinate systems for mathematical graphs.

Suppose that you have a program which does graphics in `SCREEN` mode 1. The program is full of absolute coordinate references in the standard (320-by-200) coordinate system. You upgrade your hardware to an EGA, and you want to convert your program to the enhanced resolution (640-by-350) available in `SCREEN` mode 9. Instead of changing every coordinate reference, all you need is a `WINDOW (0, 0)-(319, 199)` instruction after the initial `SCREEN 9` instruction. Quite a time-saver!

Beyond BASIC

We think you will agree that BASIC is quite a language. Full of features and easy to learn, BASIC is ideal for beginning programmers. What's more, you can develop sophisticated applications that will serve you well as you become more accomplished. If you learn the language, you will be happy with BASIC for a long, long time.

But (there's always a "but"), BASIC is not perfect. The language does have some limitations that crop up when you develop long programs, especially if you merge program pieces from different sources. If you become a dedicated programmer, perhaps even a professional programmer, you may encounter occasional frustrations. Here are BASIC's main limitations:

❏ *Variables are global to the entire program.* You may inadvertently reuse variable names in different parts of the same program. Moving a portion of a program from one program to another requires careful avoidance of variable-naming clashes.

❏ *Block structures are restricted.* IF...THEN, DEF FN, and other structures are limited to a single line. This situation cramps clarity.

❏ *Each line must have a line number.* To merge program components from different sources, you must resolve the amalgamated line numbers.

❏ *Program size is limited to (approximately) 60 kilobytes.*

❏ *You cannot create an executable file.* You cannot create a .EXE version of your program that runs directly from DOS. For other people to run your program, they must have BASIC and load your program into BASIC.

So, what can you do about these limitations? Fortunately, a ready solution exists. With one of the modern BASIC compilers, these problems are corrected. We recommend that you take a look at QuickBASIC, a software product developed by Microsoft, the same company that developed BASIC.

The beauty of QuickBASIC is that you already know 80 percent of it. In most cases, QuickBASIC can run your BASIC programs without a hitch.

QuickBASIC is kind of a super-BASIC. QuickBASIC offers upward compatibility with BASIC and adds several new language features plus a sleek user interface. Also, your programs will execute faster. It's worth a look.

Summary

Sometimes the list of BASIC's features seems to go on indefinitely. Indeed, BASIC offers a wealth of programming tools and features. In the course of this book we have not mentioned every BASIC feature, but we have covered most of the language.

This chapter offers a grab-bag collection of advanced BASIC programming topics. You learned how to define your own functions, trap execution errors and hardware events, work with specific memory locations, and use many advanced graphing features.

Explore this chapter as your time permits and your programming needs demand. Try some of the short programs. Your confidence and programming expertise will grow rapidly.

Best wishes for successful BASIC programming.

Part V

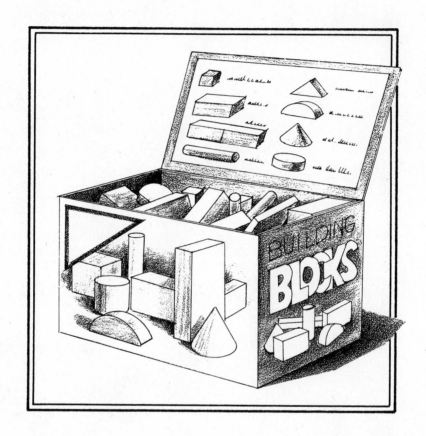

Instant Reference

This section is an instant reference dictionary of every BASIC keyword. This information puts at your fingertips the answers to simple questions that might arise during programming: "Is SQR or SQRT the function to calculate square roots? With what statement or function is the USING keyword associated? Do I need quotation marks around the file parameter in an OPEN instruction?"

These reference descriptions are meant to be brief but informative. They are not designed to teach new concepts or subtleties. Refer to the main text for detailed explanations.

No harm is done, of course, if you skim this material during your idle moments. As your confidence and ability with BASIC grow, such browsing may introduce you to new capabilities of the language.

Keyword Reference

This quick reference section presents an alphabetic, dictionary-like description of every BASIC keyword. Most entries consist of the name, type, and purpose of the keyword plus a short example of an instruction that uses the keyword.

Descriptions

Each keyword's description consists of the following items:

❑ Name (the keyword is listed in all caps)

❑ Type (the category to which the keyword belongs)

❑ Purpose (what the keyword does)

❑ Example (a sample instruction or command using the keyword)

The Name, Page Reference, and Purpose categories are self-explanatory, but some further discussion of Type and Example is in order.

Types of Keywords

Each keyword is placed into one of the following categories:

❏ Statement
❏ Command
❏ Function
❏ Operator
❏ Embedded keyword

A *statement* is a BASIC verb such as PRINT or DRAW; every BASIC instruction begins with a statement. A *command* is a BASIC verb usually used in direct mode; LIST or RENUM, for example. (Some commands double as statements also.) A *function* returns a value and usually is called with one or more arguments; examples of functions are SIN and LEFT$. An *operator* connects one or more operands to form expressions; examples of operators are OR and MOD. An *embedded keyword* is a keyword used in conjunction with a statement to form an instruction; examples of embedded keywords include STEP (used with the FOR statement) and THEN (used with the IF statement).

Functions are further subdivided into the categories shown in table R.1.

Table R.1. *BASIC functions.*

Function Category	Usage
Numeric	Manipulates numbers
String	Manipulates strings
Screen	Controls video text or graphics
Conversion	Manipulates data types
Memory	Manages memory resources
File	Controls file I/O
Error handling	Processes run-time errors
Device	Controls hardware peripherals
Formatting	Controls printed output

Operators are placed into one of two categories as shown in table R.2.

Table R.2. *BASIC keyword operators.*

Operator Category	Usage
Logical	Creates Boolean expressions
Arithmetic	Creates numeric expressions

Examples Using Each Keyword

For each statement, we provide an example instruction that uses the statement. The instruction does not necessarily contain all the possible optional clauses. However, the instruction *does* demonstrate a typical use of the statement. We arbitrarily give each sample instruction a line number of 10.

For each command, we give a direct mode usage example. No line number appears in these examples. Note, however, that some commands can also appear as statements inside programs. For example, the RUN command can appear as a program statement.

Alphabetic List of BASIC Keywords

ABS　　　　　　Numeric function

Purpose: Returns the absolute value of a numeric expression.

Example: `10 MYVALUE! = ABS(NUMBER1 * NUMBER2!)`

AND　　　　　　Logical operator

Purpose: Creates the logical (Boolean) result of ANDing two quantities together.

Example: `10 IF (BIG > 20) AND (SMALL < 5) THEN PRINT "Voila"`

APPEND   Embedded keyword

Purpose: Prepares a sequential file for appending as part of the OPEN
statement.

Example: `10 OPEN "B:MYFILE" FOR APPEND AS #1 LEN = 512`

AS   Embedded keyword

Purpose: The AS keyword has several uses:

❑ Specifies fields as part of the FIELD statement.

❑ Specifies a file number as part of the OPEN statement.

❑ Renames a file as part of the NAME statement.

ASC   Numeric function

Purpose: Returns the ASCII code value of the first character of a string
expression.

Example: `10 FIRSTCHAR% = ASC(TITLE$)`

ATN   Numeric function

Purpose: Returns the arctangent of a numeric expression.

Example: `MYVALUE! = ATN(NUMBER1 #* NUMBER2#)`

AUTO   Command

Purpose: Displays a program line in preparation for editing

Example: `AUTO 100, 300, 20`

BASE   Embedded keyword

Purpose: Adjusts the allowable range of array subscripts as part of the `OPTION BASE` statement.

Example: `10 OPTION BASE 1`

BEEP   Statement

Purpose: Sounds the PC's internal speaker.

Example: `10 BEEP`

BLOAD   Statement

Purpose: Loads into memory a file previously saved with `BSAVE`.

Example: `10 BLOAD "IMAGE.CGA", OFFSET%`

BSAVE   Statement

Purpose: Saves a portion of memory onto a disk file.

Example: `10 BSAVE "IMAGE.CGA", 0, LENGTH%`

CALL   Statement

Purpose: Invokes an assembly language subroutine.

Example: `10 CALL UPDATE(COST%, ITEM$)`

CDBL   Numeric function

Purpose: Converts a numeric expression into double-precision format.

Example: `10 MYVALUE# = CDBL(TERMA% + TERMB%) / TERMC%`

CHAIN   Statement

Purpose: Transfers control to another program.

Example: `10 CHAIN "A:NEWPROG.BAS"`

CHDIR   Statement

Purpose: Changes the current directory on a particular drive.

Example: `10 CHDIR "B:\HOMES\SALES"`

CHR$ String function

Purpose: Converts a numerical ASCII code into the equivalent string character.

Example: `10 CHARACTER$ = CHR$(65)`

CINT   Numeric function

Purpose: Converts, by rounding, a numeric expression into integer format.

Example: `10 MYVALUE% = CINT(TERMA# * TERMB!)`

CIRCLE   Statement

Purpose: Draws a circle, ellipse, pie wedge, or part of one.

Example: `10 CIRCLE STEP (MYX%, MYY%), 30, 8, , , MYASPECT!`

CLEAR   Command

Purpose: Sets numeric variables to zero and string variables to null, closes all files, and reinitializes the stack.

Example: `CLEAR , , 1000`

CLOSE   Statement

Purpose: Ceases I/O operations (close and flush) on specified files or devices.

Example: `10 CLOSE 2, #6`

CLS   Statement

Purpose: Clears the screen.

Example: `10 CLS`

COLOR   Statement

Purpose: Selects colors for the video display (both text and graphics).

Text Mode (SCREEN 0)—
Example: `10 COLOR FORE%, BACK%, BORDER%`

Graphics Modes (SCREEN 1 - SCREEN 10)—
Example: `10 COLOR Hue%, 1`

COM   Statement

Purpose: Controls event trapping at a serial communications port.

Example: `10 COM(1) ON`

COMMON   Statement

Purpose: Declares a block of global variables for sharing between modules or for passing to a chained program.

Example: `10 MYSTRING$, MYARRAY!(), PRICE!`

CONT   Command

Purpose: Resumes program execution after a break.

Example: `CONT`

COS   Numeric function

Purpose: Returns the trigonometric cosine of an angle.

Example: `10 MYVALUE! = COS(ANGLE!)`

CSNG   Numeric function

Purpose: Converts a numeric expression into single-precision format.

Example: `10 MYVALUE! = CSNG(TERMA%) * TERMB%`

CSRLIN   Screen function

Purpose: Returns the cursor's vertical position (row).

Example: `10 CURSORROW% = CSRLIN`

CVD   Conversion function

Purpose: Converts an eight-byte string read from a random-access file into a double-precision value.

Example: `10 MYVALUE# = CVD(MYSTRING$)`

CVI   Conversion function

Purpose: Converts a two-byte string read from a random-access file into an integer value.

Example: `10 MYVALUE% = CVI(MYSTRING$)`

CVS   Conversion function

Purpose: Converts a four-byte string read from a random-access file into a single-precision value.

Example: `10 MYVALUE! = CVS(MYSTRING$)`

DATA   Statement

Purpose: Stores numeric and string literals for `READ` statements.

Example: `10 DATA Wade Boggs, 0.373, Reggie Jackson, 0.228`

DATE$ Statement

Purpose: Sets the current date.

Example: `10 DATE$ = "9/15/90"`

DATE$ String function

Purpose: Retrieves the current date.

Example: `10 TODAY$ = DATE$`

DEF FN   Statement

Purpose: Names and defines a user-created function.

Example: `10 DEF FNAVERAGE# (A#, B#, C#) = (A# + B# + C#) / 3#`

DEFDBL   Statement

Purpose: Makes double-precision the default type for variables and functions that begin with specified letters.

Example: `10 DEFDBL A, C, M-T`

DEFINT   Statement

Purpose: Makes integer the default type for variables and functions that begin with specified letters.

Example: `10 DEFINT B-E, I-N`

DEFSNG   Statement

Purpose: Makes single-precision the default type for variables and functions that begin with specified letters.

Example: `10 DEFSNG A-R, Y`

DEFSTR   Statement

Purpose: Makes string the default type for variables and functions that begin with specified letters.

Example: `10 DEFSTR B, S-U, Z`

DEF SEG   Statement

Purpose: Assigns the default segment address for a subsequent BLOAD, BSAVE, PEEK, or POKE.

Example: `10 DEG SEG = &HB800`

DEF USR   Statement

Purpose: Specifies the starting address of an assembly language subroutine.

Example: `10 DEF USR4 = 23000`

DELETE   Command

Purpose: Deletes a range of program lines from memory.

Example: `DELETE 300 - 750`

DIM   Statement

Purpose: Declares and dimensions arrays.

Example: `10 DIM ARRAYA$(100), GRID!(20, 35)`

DRAW   Statement

Purpose: Draws graphics figures specified with a special string definition language.

Example: `10 DRAW "USRSDSLS"`

EDIT   Command

Purpose: Displays a program line in preparation for editing.

Example: `EDIT 850`

ELSE   Embedded keyword

Purpose: Forms conditional tests as part of the `IF` statement.

Example: `10 IF TERMA% <= TERMB% THEN PRINT "Yes" ELSE PRINT "No"`

END   Statement

Purpose: Terminates program execution.

Example: 10 END

ENVIRON   Statement

Purpose: Modifies the DOS-environment table before executing a child process with the SHELL statement.

Example: 10 ENVIRON "PATH = A:\CLIENTS"

ENVIRON$ Memory function

Purpose: Returns a parameter from the DOS-environment table.

String-Parameter Form—
Example: 10 MYPATH$ = ENVIRON$("PATH")

Numeric-Parameter Form—
Example: 10 MY3ENVIRON$ = ENVIRON$(3)

EOF   File function

Purpose: Tests whether the end of a sequential or communication (hardware device) file has been reached.

Example: 10 IF EOF(3) THEN PRINT "End of file"

EQV   Logical operator

Purpose: Creates the logical result of the equivalence operator on two quantities (opposite of XOR).

Example: `10 IF (MY$ = "M") EQV (YOUR$ = "Y") THEN PRINT "OK"`

ERASE   Statement

Purpose: Erases arrays from a program.

Example: `10 ERASE MYARRAY#, GRID%`

ERDEV   Error-handling function

Purpose: Returns the integer error code when a device error occurs.

Example: `10 ERRORCODE% = ERDEV`

ERDEV$ Error-handling function

Purpose: Returns the (string) name of the device causing a device error.

Example: `10 PRINT "Error detected on device: "; ERDEV$`

ERL   Error-handling function

Purpose: Returns the line number of the instruction causing the most
recent error.

Example: `10 PRINT "Error occurred at (or after) line number"; ERL`

ERR   Error-handling function

Purpose: Returns the error code of the most recent error.

Example: `10 IF ERR = 11 THEN PRINT "You can't divide by zero."`

ERROR   Statement

Purpose: Simulates a run-time error or creates a user-defined error code.

Example: `10 ERROR 64`

EXP   Numeric function

Purpose: Returns the exponential of a number x (that is, e raised to the
power x).

Example: `10 PRINT "The value of e is"; EXP(1)`

FIELD   Statement

Purpose: Allocates string variables as field variables in a random-access file
               buffer.

Example:
```
10 FIELD #1, 8 AS DOUBPREC$, 20 AS LAST$, 2 AS BADGENUM$
```

FILES   Statement

Purpose: Displays the file names contained in a specified directory.

Example: `10 FILES "B:\HOMES\*.SLD"`

FIX   Numeric function

Purpose: Converts, by truncation, a numeric expression into integer
               format.

Example: `10 MYVALUE% = FIX(NUMBER#)`

FN   Embedded keyword

Purpose: Names and defines a user-created function as part of the DEF FN
               statement.

Example: `10 DEF FNAVERAGE# (A#, B#, C#) = (A# + B# + C#) / 3#`

FOR   Statement

Purpose: Defines a loop containing instructions to be executed a specified number of times.

Example:
```
10 FOR ITEMNUMBER% = 1 TO LASTITEM%
20    SUM# = SUM# + PRICE(ITEMNUMBER%)
30     PRINT ITEMNUMBER%, PRICE(ITEMNUMBER%), SUM#
40 NEXT ITEMNUMBER%
```

FRE   Memory function

Purpose: Returns the available number of RAM bytes left in BASIC's work space.

Example:
```
10 ARRAYMEM = FRE(0)
```

GET   Statement (files)

Purpose: Reads data from a random-access file into a buffer.

Example:
```
10 GET 3, MYRECORD%
```

GET   Statement (graphics)

Purpose: Stores a graphics image from the screen into an array.

Example:
```
10 GET (10, 15)-(36, 45), MYARRAY%
```

GOSUB Statement

Purpose: Branches to a subroutine.

Example: `10 GOSUB 2000`

GOTO Statement

Purpose: Branches to a specified statement.

Example: `10 GOTO 320`

HEX$ Conversion function

Purpose: Converts a numeric quantity into the equivalent hexadecimal string.

Example: `10 MYSTRING$ = HEX$(32767)`

IF Statement

Purpose: Conditionally executes specified statements depending on the evaluation of an expression.

Example:

`10 IF TERMA% >= TERMB% THEN PRINT "Yes" ELSE PRINT "No"`

IMP   Logical operator

Purpose: Creates the logical result of the implication operator on two quantities.

Example:
```
10 IF (ANGLE > 1.5) IMP (DIAM > 14) THEN PRINT "Circle"
```

INKEY$ Device function

Purpose: Returns a character read from the keyboard.

Example: `10 MYKEY$ = INKEY$`

INP   Device function

Purpose: Returns a byte read from a specified I/O port.

Example: `10 MYDATA% = INP(68)`

INPUT   Statement

Purpose: Reads input from the keyboard and prompts the user to provide the desired input.

Example:
```
10 INPUT "What is your name and age"; FULLNAME$, AGE%
```

INPUT#   Statement

Purpose: Reads data from a sequential file or device into specified variables.

Example: `10 INPUT #6, ITEM$, PRICE!, HUE%, SUPPLIER$`

INPUT$ Device function

Purpose: Reads a string of a specified number of characters from the keyboard or from a file.

Example: `10 NEXT8BYTES$ = INPUT$(8, #1)`

INSTR   String function

Purpose: Searches a string for a specified substring and returns the position where the substring is found.

Example: `10 POSITION% = INSTR(FULLNAME$, "Phil")`

INT   Numeric function

Purpose: Calculates the largest whole number less than or equal to a specified numeric expression.

Example: `10 MYVAL% = INT(3.1415 * LENGTH#)`

IOCTL   Statement

Purpose: Transmits string data to a device driver.

Example: `10 IOCTL #43, "PL44"`

IOCTL$ Device function

Purpose: Reads a control data string from a device driver.

Example: `10 CONTROLSTRING$ = IOCTL$(#43)`

KEY   Statement (function-key display)

Purpose: Assigns or displays strings associated with the function keys.

Assignment Form—
Example: `10 KEY 1, "HELP"`

Display Form—
Example: `10 KEY ON`

KEY   Statement (key trapping)

Purpose: Assigns key trap values and enables or disables key trapping.

Assignment Form—
Example: `10 KEY 15, CHR$(&H12) + CHR$(&H22)`

Trapping Form—
Example: `10 KEY(8) OFF`

KILL   Statement

Purpose: Deletes a file or files from a specified directory.

Example: `10 KILL "C:\SALARY\*.BAK"`

LEFT$ String function

Purpose: Returns the specified number of leftmost characters from a given string.

Example: `10 PRINT LEFT$("My dog has fleas", 6)`

LEN   String function

Purpose: Returns the number of characters in a string or the number of bytes required by a variable or record.

Example: `10 LENGTH% = LEN(MYSTRING$)`

LET   Statement

Purpose: Assigns a value to a given variable.

Example: `10 LET MYARRAY%(18) = 322`

LINE   Statement

Purpose: Draws a line or rectangle on the screen.

Example: `10 LINE (5,12)-(75, 44), 6, B`

LINE INPUT   Statement

Purpose: Reads a line typed at the keyboard (ignoring delimiters) into a
string variable.

Example:
    `10 LINE INPUT "What are your lucky numbers?"; LUCKYNUMS$`

LINE INPUT #   Statement

Purpose: Reads a line from a sequential file (ignoring delimiters) into a
string variable.

Example: `10 LINE INPUT #12, NEXTLINE$`

LIST   Command

Purpose: Displays program lines on screen.

Example: `LIST 200-500`

LIST   Embedded keyword

Purpose: Displays function-key assignments as part of the KEY statement.

Example: `10 KEY LIST`

LLIST   Command

Purpose: Lists a program on the printer

Example: `LLIST 300-600`

LOAD   Command

Purpose: Loads a program file from disk into memory.

Example: `LOAD "MYPROG.BAS"`

LOC   File function

Purpose: Returns the current position within a specified file.

Example: `10 PRINT "The file 3 pointer is at"; LOC(3)`

LOCATE   Statement

Purpose: Moves the cursor to a specified position and/or changes the cursor's physical attributes.

Example: `10 LOCATE 10, 40, 1, 4, 7`

LOCK   Statement

Purpose: Establishes the permissible access to an opened file in a network environment.

Example: `10 LOCK #5, 6 TO 18`

LOF   File function

Purpose: Returns the number of bytes (length) of a specified file.

Example: `10 FILELENGTH% = LOF(8)`

LOG   Numeric function

Purpose: Returns the natural logarithm (base e) of a given numeric expression.

Example: `10 PRINT "The natural log of 16 is"; LOG(16)`

LPOS   Device function

Purpose: Returns the column position of the specified line printer's print head within the printer buffer.

Example: `10 PRINT "LPT1: is positioned at column"; LPOS(1)`

LPRINT   Statement

Purpose: Prints data on the line printer (LPT1:).

Example: `10 LPRINT COMPANYNAME$, ADDRESS$, SALES!`

LPRINT USING   Statement

Purpose: Prints data on the line printer (LPT1:) under format control of a formatting string.

Example: `10 LPRINT USING "$$###.##"; COST!, TOTALSALE!, 442`

LSET   Statement

Purpose 1: Moves left-justified string data into a file buffer in preparation for writing to a random-access file.

Purpose 2: Left-justifies a string expression within a string variable.

Example: `10 LSET MYSTRING$ = "Inventory List"`

MERGE   Command

Purpose: To merge an ASCII program file on disk into a program in memory.

Example: `MERGE "MYPROG.BAS"`

MID$ Statement

Purpose: Replaces a portion of a given string with another specified string.

Example: `10 MID$(MYSTRING, 8) = "08=02=89"`

MID$ String function

Purpose: Returns a length-specified substring from a given string expression.

Example: `10 PRINT "Characters 10-15 are:"; MID$(MYSTRING$, 10, 6)`

MKDIR   Statement

Purpose: Creates a subdirectory.

Example: `10 MKDIR "C:\ERRORLOG"`

MKD$ Conversion function

Purpose: Converts a double-precision quantity to the proper eight-byte string before writing to a random-access file.

Example: `10 DOUBSTRING$ = MKD$(DOUBNUMBER#)`

MKI$ Conversion function

Purpose: Converts an integer quantity to the proper two-byte string before writing to a random-access file.

Example: `10 INTSTRING$ = MKI$(MYINTEGER%)`

MKS$ Conversion function

Purpose: Converts a single-precision quantity to the proper four-byte string before writing to a random-access file.

Example: `10 SINGSTRING$ = MKS$(SINGNUM!)`

MOD   Arithmetic operator

Purpose: Calculates the modulo of one integer expression with respect to a second integer expression.

Example: `10 PRINT "Remainder of 89 divided by 7 is"; 89 MOD 7`

MOTOR   Statement

Purpose: Turns the cassette player on and off

Example: `10 MOTOR 1`

NAME   Statement

Purpose: Renames a specified disk file.

Example: `10 NAME "ROSTER89.DTA" AS "ROSTER90.DTA"`

NEXT   Statement

Purpose: Defines the terminus of loops created with the FOR statement.

Example: `10 NEXT INDEX%`

NEW   Command

Purpose: Deletes the program in memory and clears all variables.

Example: `NEW`

NOT   Logical operator

Purpose: Creates the logical (Boolean) negation of a quantity.

Example:
```
10 IF NOT (MYCOLOR$ = "Red") THEN PRINT "It's not red"
```

OCT$ Conversion function

Purpose: Converts a numeric quantity into the equivalent octal (base 8) string.

Example:
```
10 MYSTRING$ = OCT$(32767)
```

OFF   Embedded keyword

Purpose: Disables event trapping of a particular device as part of the COM, KEY, PEN, PLAY, STRIG, or TIMER statement.

Example:
```
10 PEN OFF
```

ON   Embedded keyword

Purpose: Enables event trapping of a particular device as part of the COM, KEY, PEN, PLAY, STRIG, or TIMER statement.

Example:
```
10 PEN ON
```

ON COM GOSUB   Statement

Purpose: Designates the subroutine to be invoked when a serial communication port event is trapped.

Example: `10 ON COM(1) GOSUB 2500`

ON ERROR GOTO   Statement

Purpose: Enables run-time error trapping and designates the line to branch to when an error occurs.

Example: `10 ON ERROR GOTO 4000`

ON GOSUB   Statement

Purpose: Invokes one of a designated list of subroutines according to the value of a numeric expression.

Example: `10 ON SIBLINGS% GOSUB 1000, 2000, 3000`

ON GOTO   Statement

Purpose: Branches to one of a specified set of lines according to the value of a numeric expression.

Example: `10 ON STROKES% GOTO 500, 600, 700, 350, 1000`

ON KEY GOSUB   Statement

Purpose: Specifies the first line of a trap subroutine to be invoked if a particular key is pressed.

Example: 10 ON KEY(6) GOSUB 5000

ON PEN GOSUB   Statement

Purpose: Specifies the first line of a trap subroutine to be invoked if the light pen is activated.

Example: 10 ON PEN GOSUB 3500

ON PLAY GOSUB   Statement

Purpose: Specifies the first line of a trap subroutine to be invoked when the music buffer has less than a certain number of notes.

Example: 10 ON PLAY(15) GOSUB 2350

ON STRIG GOSUB   Statement

Purpose: Specifies the first line of a trap subroutine to be invoked when a certain joystick button is activated.

Example: 10 ON STRIG(2) GOSUB 4900

ON TIMER GOSUB   Statement

Purpose: Specifies the first line of a trap subroutine to be invoked at a given time interval.

Example: `10 ON TIMER(60) GOSUB 2100`

OPEN   Statement

Purpose: Initializes a file or device for I/O activity.

Verbose Form—
Example: `10 OPEN "A:MYFILE.DTA" FOR INPUT AS #4`

Succinct Form—
Example: `10 OPEN "I", #4, "A:MYFILE.DTA"`

OPEN COM   Statement

Purpose: Opens and initializes a serial communications port.

Example: `10 OPEN "COM2: 1200, , 8, , LF" FOR RANDOM AS #2`

OPTION BASE   Statement

Purpose: Declares, for subsequent `DIM` statements, the default minimum value for array subscripts.

Example: `10 OPTION BASE 1`

OR   Logical operator

Purpose: Creates the logical (Boolean) result of ORing two quantities together.

Example:
```
10 IF (DEBT! < 0) OR (ORDERS% > 50) THEN PRINT "Success"
```

OUT   Statement

Purpose: Transmits a data byte to an I/O port.

Example: `10 OUT PORT%, 127`

OUTPUT   Embedded keyword

Purpose: Initializes a file or device to be written to as part of the OPEN statement.

Example: `10 OPEN "A:MYFILE.DTA" FOR OUTPUT AS #4`

PAINT   Statement

Purpose: Fills a graphics region on the screen with a specified color or pattern.

Example: `10 PAINT (60,35), COLORCODE%, 1`

PALETTE   Statement

Purpose: Changes a color in the palette used for EGA graphics.

Example: `10 PALETTE 1, 14`

PALETTE USING   Statement

Purpose: Redefines the 16 colors used in the palette for EGA graphics.

Example: `10 PALETTE USING EGACOLORS%(4)`

PCOPY   Statement

Purpose: Copies a specified screen page to another screen page.

Example: `10 PCOPY 2, 3`

PEEK   Memory function

Purpose: Returns the value of the data byte stored at a specified memory location.

Example: `10 PRINT PEEK(79)`

PEN   Statement

Purpose: Enables or disables the trapping of light-pen activity.

Example: `10 PEN ON`

PEN   Device function

Purpose: Returns the status of light-pen activity.

Example: `10 IF PEN(0) THEN PRINT "Light pen is activated."`

PLAY   Statement

Purpose: Plays music specified with a special string definition language, or enables or disables music trapping.

Music Playing Form—
Example: `10 PLAY "O2L4CC#DEFGAB-B"`

Trapping Form—
Example: `10 PLAY ON`

PLAY   Device function

Purpose: Returns the number of unplayed notes in the background music buffer.

Example: `10 IF PLAY(1) < 10 THEN PRINT "Almost done"`

PMAP   Screen function

Purpose: Translates a physical coordinate into the proper world coordinate or vice versa.

Example: `10 LINE -(PMAP(XVALUE%, 0), PMAP(YVALUE%, 1))`

POINT   Screen function

Purpose: Returns the color of a screen pixel or returns the x or y
coordinate of a screen pixel.

Color Form—
Example: `10 IF POINT(20,25) = 12 THEN PRINT "Light red"`

Coordinate Form—
Example: `10 PRINT "Physical y coordinate is"; POINT(1)`

POKE   Statement

Purpose: Writes a specified byte into a given memory location.

Example: `10 POKE &H1FFF, 255`

POS   Device function

Purpose: Returns the current horizontal position of the cursor.

Example: `10 PRINT "The cursor is at column number"; POS(DUMMY)`

PRESET   Statement

Purpose: Draws a point at a specified position on the graphics screen.

Example: `10 PRESET (230, 55), 4`

PRINT   Statement

Purpose: Writes data on the video screen.

Example: `10 PRINT "The values of A% and B$ are", A%, B$`

PRINT #   Statement

Purpose: Writes data to a specified file.

Example: `10 PRINT #7, "03/04/91", NUMORDERS%, SALES!`

PRINT USING   Statement

Purpose: Writes data on the video screen under formatting control.

Example: `10 PRINT USING "$$####.##"; BALANCE!, AMOUNT!`

PRINT # USING   Statement

Purpose: Writes data to a specified file under formatting control.

Example: `10 PRINT #5, USING "$$####.##"; BALANCE!, AMOUNT!`

PSET   Statement

Purpose: Draws a point at a specified position on the graphics screen.

Example: `10 PSET (230, 55), 4`

PUT   Statement (files)

Purpose: Writes a record from a random-access buffer or a variable to a random-access file.

Example: `10 PUT #3, MYRECORD%`

PUT   Statement (graphics)

Purpose: Draws on the video screen a graphics image stored in a specified array.

Example: `10 PUT (300, 106), MYIMAGE%, AND`

RANDOM   Embedded keyword

Purpose: Opens random-access files as part of the OPEN statement.

Example: `10 OPEN "MYFILE.DTA" FOR RANDOM AS #12`

RANDOMIZE   Statement

Purpose: Reseeds the random-number generator.

Example: `10 RANDOMIZE TIMER`

READ   Statement

Purpose: Assigns to a variable or variables data values read from DATA statement(s).

Example: `10 READ CLUBNAME$, MEMBERS%, MEETINGNIGHT$`

REM   Statement

Purpose: Declares the rest of a program line to be explanatory remarks (and thus not source code for compilation).

Example: `10 REM This program computes your biorhythms.`

RENUM   Command

Purpose: Renumbers program lines.

Example: `RENUM 300, , 20`

RESET   Statement

Purpose: Ceases I/O operations (close and flush) on all opened files and devices.

Example: `10 RESET`

RESTORE   Statement

Purpose: Resets the DATA statement pointer to a specified line for a subsequent READ statement.

Example: 10 RESTORE 200

RESUME   Statement

Purpose: Resumes program execution at a specified location after control is passed to an error-handling routine.

Example: 10 RESUME NEXT

RETURN   Statement

Purpose: Terminates a subroutine and resumes execution at a specified location.

Example: RETURN

RIGHT$ String function

Purpose: Returns the specified number of rightmost characters from a given string.

Example: 10 PRINT RIGHT$("I don't think you are right", 13)

RMDIR   Statement

Purpose: Removes (deletes) an existing disk directory.

Example: 10 RMDIR "A:\OLDFILES"

RND   Numeric function

Purpose: Returns a pseudorandom number between 0 and 1.

Example: 10 IF RND > .5 THEN PRINT "Coin toss is heads"

RSET   Statement

Purpose 1: Moves right-justified string data into a file buffer in preparation for writing to a random-access file.

Purpose 2: Right-justifies a string expression within a string variable.

Example: 10 RSET MYSTRING$ = "Inventory List"

RUN   Statement

Purpose: Restarts the current program or begins execution of another (specified) program.

Example: 10 RUN "C:\DEMOS\BIRTHDAY.EXE"

SAVE   Command

Purpose: Saves a program file on disk.

Example: `SAVE "B": MYPROG.BAS"`

SCREEN   Statement

Purpose: Sets the screen display mode.

Example: `10 SCREEN 7, , 2`

SCREEN   Screen function

Purpose: Returns the character or the character's color (attribute) at a specified row and column of the screen.

Example:
`10 PRINT "Upper left character in ASCII is"; SCREEN(1,1)`

SEG   Embedded keyword

Purpose: Assigns the default segment address as part of the DEF SEG statement.

Example: `10 DEF SEG = 12000`

SGN   Numeric function

Purpose: Returns the sign of a numeric expression.

Example: `10 IF SGN(OURSCORE - THEIRSCORE) = 1 THEN PRINT "We won"`

SHELL   Statement

Purpose: Executes another program or DOS shell while retaining BASIC in memory.

Example: `10 SHELL "CHKDSK A:"`

SIN   Numeric function

Purpose: Returns the trigonometric sine of an angle.

Example: `10 MYVALUE = SIN(ANGLE)`

SOUND   Statement

Purpose: Sounds a tone from the internal speaker.

Example: `10 SOUND 4000, 100`

SPACE$ String function

Purpose: Returns a string comprised of a specified number of spaces (blank characters).

Example: `10 HEADER$ = "1" + SPACE$(7) + "9"`

SPC   Formatting function

Purpose: Generates a specified number of spaces within a `PRINT` or `LPRINT` statement.

Example: `10 PRINT FIRSTNAME$; SPC(25); SECONDNAME$`

SQR   Numeric function

Purpose: Returns the square root of a numeric expression.

Example:
`10 HYPOTENUSE! = SQR(SIDEA! * SIDEAA! + SIDEB! * SIDEB!)`

STEP   Embedded keyword

Purpose: Specifies the increment to advance the counter variable as part of the `FOR` statement; also specifies relative (not absolute) coordinates as part of the `CIRCLE`, `GET`, `LINE`, `PAINT`, `PRESET`, `PSET`, and `PUT` statements.

Example: `10 FOR INDEX% = 10 TO 200 STEP 5`

STICK   Device function

Purpose: Returns the x or y coordinate of the specified joystick.

Example: `10 PRINT "X value of Joystick B is"; STICK(2)`

STOP   Statement

Purpose: Terminates program execution.

Example: `10 STOP`

STOP   Embedded keyword

Purpose: Suspends event trapping of a particular device as part of the `COM`, `KEY`, `PEN`, `STRIG`, or `TIMER` statement.

Example: `10 PEN STOP`

STR$ Conversion function

Purpose: Converts the value of a numeric expression into the equivalent string representation.

Example: `10 EQUATION$ = "Pi = " + STR$(4 * ATN(1))`

STRIG   Statement

Purpose: Enables or disables joystick-button trapping.

Example: `10 STRIG(2) OFF`

STRIG   Device function

Purpose: Returns joystick-button activity.

Example: `10 IF STRIG(1) THEN PRINT "Joystick A button is down"`

STRING$ String function

Purpose: Returns a string consisting of a specified number of identical characters.

Example: `10 DOZENDASH$ = STRING$(12, "-")`

SWAP   Statement

Purpose: Exchanges the values of two variables or array elements.

Example: `10 SWAP MYAGE%, YOURAGE%`

SYSTEM   Statement

Purpose: Terminates program execution.

Example: `10 SYSTEM`

TAB — Formatting function

Purpose: Advances to a specified column position within a PRINT or LPRINT statement.

Example:
```
10 PRINT TAB(5); CLIENT$; TAB(25); ZIP$; TAB(50); PHONE$
```

TAN — Numeric function

Purpose: Returns the trigonometric tangent of an angle.

Example:
```
10 MYVALUE = TAN(ANGLE)
```

THEN — Embedded keyword

Purpose: Forms conditional tests as part of the IF statement.

Example:
```
10 IF TERMA% >= TERMB% THEN PRINT "Yes" ELSE PRINT "No"
```

TIME$ — Statement

Purpose: Sets the current time.

Example:
```
10 TIME$ = "14:08:35"
```

TIME$ String function

Purpose: Returns the current time.

Example: `10 PRINT "The time is now"; TIME$`

TIMER   Statement

Purpose: Enables or disables the trapping of timer activity.

Example: `10 TIMER OFF`

TIMER   Device function

Purpose: Returns the elapsed time (in seconds) since midnight.

Example: `10 NUMMINUTES! = TIMER / 60`

TO   Embedded keyword

Purpose: Defines loops as part of the `FOR` statement, specifies screen rows to display as part of the `VIEW PRINT` statement, or specifies a range of records as part of the `LOCK` and `UNLOCK` statements.

TROFF   Command

Purpose: Turns off the tracing of program statements.

Example: `TROFF`

TRON   Command

Purpose: Turns on the tracing of program statements.

Example: `TRON`

UNLOCK   Statement

Purpose: Reestablishes full access to an access-restricted file in a network environment.

Example: `10 UNLOCK #5, 6 TO 18`

USING   Embedded keyword

Purpose: Prints data under formatting control as part of the `PRINT` (video screen) or `LPRINT` (line printer) statement, or changes palette colors as part of the `PALETTE USING` statement.

Example: `10 PRINT USING "$$####.##"; BALANCE!, AMOUNT!`

USR   Embedded keyword

Purpose: Specifies the address of an assembly language subroutine as part of the `DEF USR` statement.

Example: `10 DEF USR4 = 24000`

VAL   Conversion function

Purpose: Returns the numeric value of a string expression.

Example: `10 ZIPCODE = VAL(ZIPCODE$)`

VARPTR   Memory function

Purpose: Returns the offset address of a given variable.

Example: `10 PRINT "The offset of INDEX% is"; VARPTR(INDEX%)`

VARPTR$ Memory function

Purpose: Returns the address of a variable in string form.

Example: `10 PLAY "AB-CX" + VARPTR$(REFRAIN$)`

VIEW   Statement

Purpose: Sets the rectangular area on the screen where future graphics
may be displayed.

Example: `10 VIEW SCREEN (40,20)-(200,100), 4, 2`

VIEW PRINT   Statement

Purpose: Sets the upper and lower row on the screen where text may be displayed.

Example: `10 VIEW PRINT 10 TO 22`

WAIT   Statement

Purpose: Pauses program execution until a specified input port presents a given byte pattern.

Example: `10 WAIT &H20, 4`

WEND   Statement

Purpose: Terminates loops created with the `WHILE` statement.

Example:
```
10 WHILE TERMX% < 100
20 SUM% = SUM% + TERMX%
30 PRINT TERMX%, SUM%
40 WEND
```

WHILE   Statement

Purpose: Creates loops with a testing expression at the beginning.

Example:
```
10 WHILE TERMX% < 100
20 SUM% = SUM% + TERMX%
30 PRINT TERMX%, SUM%
40 WEND
```

WIDTH   Statement

Purpose: Sets the default line width on a given device or file, or changes the screen-display text mode.

Device and File Form—
Example: `10 WIDTH "LPT1:", 255`

Screen-Display Form—
Example: `10 WIDTH , 43`

WINDOW   Statement

Purpose: Redefines the graphics coordinate system.

Example: `10 WINDOW SCREEN (-100, -100)-(100, 100)`

WRITE   Statement

Purpose: Writes data on the screen with commas between items, quotes around strings, and no space before numbers.

Example: `10 WRITE "A stitch in time saves", 9`

WRITE #   Statement

Purpose: Writes data to a specified sequential file using the same formatting as the `WRITE` statement.

Example: `10 WRITE #7, "03/04/89", NUMORDERS%, SALES!`

XOR   **Logical operator**

Purpose: Creates the logical (Boolean) result of exclusive ORing two quantities together.

Example:

```
10 IF (MYAGE > 21) XOR (YOURAGE > 21) THEN PRINT "Same"
```

Reserved Words

The following list shows BASIC's reserved words (keywords). You should not use any of these words as a variable name.

```
ABS
AND
APPEND
AS
ASC
ATN
AUTO
BASE
BEEP
BLOAD
BSAVE
CALL
CDBL
CHAIN
CHDIR
CHR$
CINT
CIRCLE
CLEAR
CLOSE
```

```
CLS
COLOR
COM
COMMON
CONT
COS
CSNG
CSRLIN
CVD
CVI
CVS
DATA
DATE$
DEF
DEFDBL
DEFINT
DEFSNG
DEFSTR
DELETE
DIM
DRAW
EDIT
ELSE
END
ENVIRON
ENVIRON$
EOF
EQV
ERASE
ERDEV
ERDEV$
ERL
ERR
ERROR
EXP
FIELD
FILES
FIX
FN...
FOR
FRE
GET
GOSUB
GOTO
```

```
HEX$
IF
IMP
INKEY$
INP
INPUT
INPUT#
INPUT$
INSTR
INT
IOCTL
IOCTL$
KEY
KILL
LEFT$
LEN
LET
LINE
LIST
LLIST
LOAD
LOC
LOCATE
LOCK
LOF
LOG
LPOS
LPRINT
LSET
MERGE
MID$
MKD$
MKDIR
MKI$
MKS$
MOD
MOTOR
NAME
NEW
NEXT
NOT
OCT$
OFF
ON
```

```
OPEN
OPTION
OR
OUT
OUTPUT
PAINT
PALETTE
PCOPY
PEEK
PEN
PLAY
PMAP
POINT
POKE
POS
PRESET
PRINT
PRINT#
PSET
PUT
RANDOM
RANDOMIZE
READ
REM
RENUM
RESET
RESTORE
RESUME
RETURN
RIGHT$
RMDIR
RND
RSET
RUN
SAVE
SCREEN
SEG
SGN
SHELL
SIN
SOUND
SPACE$
SPC
SQR
```

```
STEP
STICK
STOP
STR$
STRIG
STRING$
SWAP
SYSTEM
TAB
TAN
THEN
TIME$
TIMER
TO
TROFF
TRON
UNLOCK
USING
USR...
VAL
VARPTR
VARPTR$
VIEW
WAIT
WEND
WHILE
WIDTH
WINDOW
WRITE
WRITE#
XOR
```

ASCII Character Set

Hex	Dec	Screen	Ctrl	Key
00h	0		NUL	^@
01h	1	☺	SOH	^A
02h	2	●	STX	^B
03h	3	♥	ETX	^C
04h	4	♦	EOT	^D
05h	5	♣	ENQ	^E
06h	6	♠	ACK	^F
07h	7	•	BEL	^G
08h	8	◘	BS	^H
09h	9	○	HT	^I
0Ah	10	◙	LF	^J
0Bh	11	♂	VT	^K
0Ch	12	♀	FF	^L
0Dh	13	♪	CR	^M
0Eh	14	♫	SO	^N
0Fh	15	☼	SI	^O
10h	16	►	DLE	^P
11h	17	◄	DC1	^Q
12h	18	↕	DC2	^R
13h	19	‼	DC3	^S
14h	20	¶	DC4	^T
15h	21	§	NAK	^U
16h	22	▬	SYN	^V
17h	23	↨	ETB	^W
18h	24	↑	CAN	^X
19h	25	↓	EM	^Y

Hex	Dec	Screen	Ctrl	Key
1Ah	26	→	SUB	^Z
1Bh	27	←	ESC	^[
1Ch	28	∟	FS	^\
1Dh	29	↔	GS	^]
1Eh	30	▲	RS	^^
1Fh	31	▼	US	^_
20h	32			
21h	33	!		
22h	34	"		
23h	35	#		
24h	36	$		
25h	37	%		
26h	38	&		
27h	39	'		
28h	40	(		
29h	41	)		
2Ah	42	*		
2Bh	43	+		
2Ch	44	,		
2Dh	45	–		
2Eh	46	.		
2Fh	47	/		
30h	48	0		
31h	49	1		
32h	50	2		
33h	51	3		

Hex	Dec	Screen	Hex	Dec	Screen	Hex	Dec	Screen
34h	52	4	62h	98	b	90h	144	É
35h	53	5	63h	99	c	91h	145	æ
36h	54	6	64h	100	d	92h	146	Æ
37h	55	7	65h	101	e	93h	147	ô
38h	56	8	66h	102	f	94h	148	ö
39h	57	9	67h	103	g	95h	149	ò
3Ah	58	:	68h	104	h	96h	150	û
3Bh	59	;	69h	105	i	97h	151	ù
3Ch	60	<	6Ah	106	j	98h	152	ÿ
3Dh	61	=	6Bh	107	k	99h	153	Ö
3Eh	62	>	6Ch	108	l	9Ah	154	Ü
3Fh	63	?	6Dh	109	m	9Bh	155	¢
40h	64	@	6Eh	110	n	9Ch	156	£
41h	65	A	6Fh	111	o	9Dh	157	¥
42h	66	B	70h	112	p	9Eh	158	₧
43h	67	C	71h	113	q	9Fh	159	ƒ
44h	68	D	72h	114	r	A0h	160	á
45h	69	E	73h	115	s	A1h	161	í
46h	70	F	74h	116	t	A2h	162	ó
47h	71	G	75h	117	u	A3h	163	ú
48h	72	H	76h	118	v	A4h	164	ñ
49h	73	I	77h	119	w	A5h	165	Ñ
4Ah	74	J	78h	120	x	A6h	166	a
4Bh	75	K	79h	121	y	A7h	167	o
4Ch	76	L	7Ah	122	z	A8h	168	¿
4Dh	77	M	7Bh	123	{	A9h	169	⌐
4Eh	78	N	7Ch	124	|	AAh	170	¬
4Fh	79	O	7Dh	125	}	ABh	171	½
50h	80	P	7Eh	126	~	ACh	172	¼
51h	81	Q	7Fh	127	∆	ADh	173	¡
52h	82	R	80h	128	Ç	AEh	174	«
53h	83	S	81h	129	ü	AFh	175	»
54h	84	T	82h	130	é	B0h	176	▒
55h	85	U	83h	131	â	B1h	177	▓
56h	86	V	84h	132	ä	B2h	178	█
57h	87	W	85h	133	à	B3h	179	│
58h	88	X	86h	134	å	B4h	180	┤
59h	89	Y	87h	135	ç	B5h	181	╡
5Ah	90	Z	88h	136	ê	B6h	182	╢
5Bh	91	[	89h	137	ë	B7h	183	╖
5Ch	92	\	8Ah	138	è	B8h	184	╕
5Dh	93	]	8Bh	139	ï	B9h	185	╣
5Eh	94	^	8Ch	140	î	BAh	186	║
5Fh	95	_	8Dh	141	ì	BBh	187	╗
60h	96	`	8Eh	142	Ä	BCh	188	╝
61h	97	a	8Fh	143	Å	BDh	189	╜

Hex	Dec	Screen		Hex	Dec	Screen		Hex	Dec	Screen
BEh	190	⌐		D4h	212	╘		EAh	234	Ω
BFh	191	┐		D5h	213	╒		EBh	235	δ
C0h	192	└		D6h	214	╓		ECh	236	∞
C1h	193	┴		D7h	215	╫		EDh	237	φ
C2h	194	┬		D8h	216	╪		EEh	238	∈
C3h	195	├		D9h	217	┘		EFh	239	∩
C4h	196	─		DAh	218	┌		F0h	240	≡
C5h	197	┼		DBh	219	█		F1h	241	±
C6h	198	╞		DCh	220	▄		F2h	242	≥
C7h	199	╟		DDh	221	▌		F3h	243	≤
C8h	200	╚		DEh	222	▐		F4h	244	⌠
C9h	201	╔		DFh	223	▀		F5h	245	⌡
CAh	202	╩		E0h	224	α		F6h	246	÷
CBh	203	╦		E1h	225	β		F7h	247	≈
CCh	204	╠		E2h	226	Γ		F8h	248	°
CDh	205	═		E3h	227	π		F9h	249	•
CEh	206	╬		E4h	228	Σ		FAh	250	·
CFh	207	╧		E5h	229	σ		FBh	251	√
D0h	208	╨		E6h	230	μ		FCh	252	n
D1h	209	╤		E7h	231	τ		FDh	253	²
D2h	210	╥		E8h	232	Φ		FEh	254	■
D3h	211	╙		E9h	233	θ		FFh	255	

Keyboard Codes

T he following table presents code values to use with the INKEY$ function and the KEY statement (key trapping).

The first column designates a physical key on the keyboard.

The second column is the scan code used when you key trap with the KEY statement.

The remaining columns represent ASCII values returned by the INKEY$ function for various keystrokes. The INKEY$ function returns a one- or two-character string for each recognized keystroke.

When INKEY$ returns a single character, that character's ASCII value is shown with a single number in the appropriate column. For example, pressing the Q key causes INKEY$ to return a one-character string whose ASCII value is 113. Pressing Shift-Q returns 81.

When INKEY$ returns a two-character string, the first character is always a null (ASCII value 0). The second character has an ASCII value greater than 0. For example, pressing Alt-Q causes INKEY$ to return a two-character string. The first character is NUL (ASCII value 0); the second character has the ASCII value 16.

All numbers in the table are decimal.

Key	Scan Code	INKEY$ Key	INKEY$ Shift-Key	INKEY$ Ctrl-Key	INKEY$ Alt-Key
Esc	1	27	27	27	27
1 or !	2	49	33		NUL-120
2 or @	3	50	64	NUL-3	NUL-121
3 or #	4	51	35		NUL-122
4 or $	5	52	36		NUL-123
5 or %	6	53	37		NUL-124
6 or ^	7	54	94	30	NUL-125
7 or &	8	55	38		NUL-126
8 or *	9	56	42		NUL-127
9 or (	10	57	40		NUL-128
0 or)	11	48	41		NUL-129
- or _	12	45	95	31	NUL-130
= or +	13	61	43		NUL-131
BKSP	14	8	8	127	
Tab	15	9	NUL-15		
Q	16	113	81	17	NUL-16
W	17	119	87	23	NUL-17
E	18	101	69	5	NUL-18
R	19	114	82	18	NUL-19
T	20	116	84	20	NUL-20
Y	21	121	89	25	NUL-21
U	22	117	85	21	NUL-22
I	23	105	73	9	NUL-23
O	24	111	79	15	NUL-24
P	25	112	80	16	NUL-25
[or {	26	91	123	27	
] or }	27	93	125	29	
Enter	28	13	13	10	
Ctrl	29				
A	30	97	65	1	NUL-30
S	31	115	83	19	NUL-31
D	32	100	68	4	NUL-32
F	33	102	70	6	NUL-33
G	34	103	71	7	NUL-34
H	35	104	72	8	NUL-35
J	36	106	74	10	NUL-36
K	37	107	75	11	NUL-37
L	38	108	76	12	NUL-38

Key	Scan Code	INKEY$ Key	INKEY$ Shift-Key	INKEY$ Ctrl-Key	INKEY$ Alt-Key
; or :	39	59	58		
' or "	40	39	34		
` or ~	41	96	126		
LeftShift	42				
\ or |	43	92	124	28	
Z	44	122	90	26	NUL-44
X	45	120	88	24	NUL-45
C	46	99	67	3	NUL-46
V	47	118	86	22	NUL-47
B	48	98	66	2	NUL-48
N	49	110	78	14	NUL-49
M	50	109	77	13	NUL-50
, or <	51	44	60		
. or >	52	46	62		
/ or ?	53	47	63		
RightShift	54				
PrtSc•	55	42	(Print)	16	
Alt	56				
Space bar	57	32	32	32	32
CapsLock	58				
F1	59	NUL-59	NUL-84	NUL-94	NUL-104
F2	60	NUL-60	NUL-85	NUL-95	NUL-105
F3	61	NUL-61	NUL-86	NUL-96	NUL-106
F4	62	NUL-62	NUL-87	NUL-97	NUL-107
F5	63	NUL-63	NUL-88	NUL-98	NUL-108
F6	64	NUL-64	NUL-89	NUL-99	NUL-109
F7	65	NUL-65	NUL-90	NUL-100	NUL-110
F8	66	NUL-66	NUL-91	NUL-101	NUL-111
F9	67	NUL-67	NUL-92	NUL-102	NUL-112
F10	68	NUL-68	NUL-93	NUL-103	NUL-113
F11	133	NUL-133	NUL-135	NUL-137	NUL-139
F12	134	NUL-134	NUL-136	NUL-138	NUL-140
NumLock	69				
ScrollLock	70				
Home	71	NUL-71	55	119	
Up	72	NUL-72	56		
PgUp	73	NUL-73	57	NUL-132	
Grey-	74	45	45		
Left	75	NUL-75	52	NUL-115	

Key	Scan Code	INKEY$ Key	INKEY$ Shift-Key	INKEY$ Ctrl-Key	INKEY$ Alt-Key
Center	76		53		
Right	77	NUL-77	54	NUL-116	
Grey +	78	43	43		
End	79	NUL-79	49	NUL-117	
Down	80	NUL-80	50		
PgDn	81	NUL-81	51	NUL-118	
Ins	82	NUL-82	48		
Del	83	NUL-83	46		

Error Messages

This appendix lists BASIC's error messages. The error number is the value returned by the ERR function (see Chapter 15, "Toward Advanced Programming.")

For each error, the comments indicate the most likely cause or causes. If your program generates an error message, this information should help you track down the problem.

Error number 1: NEXT without FOR

A NEXT instruction occurs when no FOR instruction is active. Look for unmatched variable names on the FOR and NEXT instructions, or two different NEXT instructions trying to match the same FOR instruction (each FOR instruction must correspond with a single NEXT instruction).

Error number 2: Syntax error

An instruction has a punctuation error, a misspelled keyword, unbalanced parentheses, or some similar violation of BASIC's syntax rules. BASIC enters edit mode and displays the erroneous line for editing.

Error number 3: `RETURN without GOSUB`

No `GOSUB` instruction is active when a `RETURN` instruction executes. Look for "falling into" a subroutine or using a `GOTO` rather than a `GOSUB` to invoke the subroutine.

Error number 4: `Out of DATA`

No `DATA` values remain to be read by the `READ` instruction. Look for punctuation errors in the `DATA` instructions, such as using periods rather than commas, or for miscounting how many times the program executes the `READ`.

Error number 5: `Illegal function call`

The program attempts to call a function with an illegal argument. Examples: taking the `SQR` of a negative number; taking the `LOG` of zero or a negative number; using a negative subscript in an array reference; and using an impossible number (usually negative or zero) in many of the string functions, such as `LEFT$`, `MID$`, `RIGHT$`, and `STRING$`.

Error number 6: `Overflow`

A numeric variable or literal is larger than BASIC's maximum value. For single- and double-precision variables, BASIC displays the error message (without providing the offending line number), substitutes its largest data value (slightly greater than $1.7E+38$), and *continues executing*. Chapter 15, "Toward Advanced Programming," shows how `ON ERROR GOTO` can help you figure out which program line caused the error. For integer variables, BASIC stops the program and displays the line number causing the error.

Error number 7: `Out of memory`

The program tries to use more memory than BASIC permits. Likely causes: The program is too big for the approximately 60,000 bytes that BASIC allows; arrays are `DIM`med too large; `GOSUB` instructions are repeatedly executed but never terminated by `RETURN`; `FOR...NEXT` loops or `GOSUB`s are nested too deeply. Try `PRINT FRE(0)` at various places (such as before and after `DIM` instructions) to monitor how much memory remains.

Error number 8: `Undefined line number`

The program line references a line number that does not exist. For example, `GOTO 350` when line 350 does not exist anywhere in the program.

Error number 9: Subscript out of range

An array subscript is larger than the size of the array. If you have no DIM instruction for an array, the maximum allowable subscript is 10. Also look for a misspelled function name: if you type TAG(20) when you mean TAB(20), BASIC assumes that you are referring to a TAG array, not to the TAB function.

Error number 10: Duplicate Definition

An array is defined for a second time, either because there are two DIM instructions (or one DIM instruction that is executed twice), or because an array is implicitly dimensioned by usage of an array variable name and then a subsequent DIM instruction tries to redimension the array.

Error number 11: Division by zero

The program attempts to divide a number by zero, which is mathematically impossible. BASIC makes the result of the division the highest number it can represent, and *continues executing*. Chapter 15, "Toward Advanced Programming," shows how ON ERROR GOTO can trap this error and determine the instruction causing the error.

Error number 12: Illegal direct

The direct mode command is allowed only as a program instruction (DEF FN, for example).

Error number 13: Type mismatch

A conflict occurs between string and numeric data types. Either an assignment instruction tries to assign a string value to a numeric variable (or vice versa), or a function tries to operate on the wrong type of data (such as trying to use SQR on a string).

Error number 14: Out of string space

The program tries to use more memory for string data than BASIC has available. Use PRINT FRE("") at a few points in the program to monitor the remaining string space.

Error number 15: String too long

The instruction tries to create a string longer than 255 bytes.

Error number 16: `String formula too complex`

A string expression is too complex for BASIC to interpret. Break up the expression into two or more simpler expressions.

Error number 17: `Can't continue`

A direct-mode `CONT` command attempts to resume a program after a break, but the program has changed. Changing variable values is legal before continuing; but adding, deleting, or changing program lines is not.

Error number 18: `Undefined user function`

BASIC cannot execute the `USR` function because no `DEF USR` instruction previously defined the assembly language subroutine.

Error number 19: `No RESUME`

The program ran out of instructions in an error-handling routine. (You should place a `RESUME` instruction in every error handler.)

Error number 20: `RESUME without error`

A `RESUME` instruction occurs when no error is trapped. Either `RESUME` occurs outside an error-handler or an error-handler has control without trapping an active error.

Error number 22: `Missing operand`

An operator (such as an equal sign or a plus sign) is not followed by a required operand (such as a variable name or literal).

Error number 23: `Line buffer overflow`

The program line is longer than BASIC allows. Break up the line into two or more separate lines.

Error number 24: `Device timeout`

An input/output device has not responded within a set time period.

Error number 25: `Device fault`

An input/output device reports that a hardware error occurred, or an expected device reply does not occur within a prescribed time period.

Error number 26: FOR without NEXT

A FOR instruction has no matching NEXT instruction.

Error number 27: Out of paper

The printer is out of paper, or is not powered on, or is not cabled to the computer correctly.

Error number 29: WHILE without WEND

A WHILE instruction has no matching WEND instruction.

Error number 30: WEND without WHILE

No WHILE instruction is active when a WEND instruction executes.

Error number 50: FIELD overflow

A FIELD instruction specifies more data bytes than the record length given in the OPEN instruction.

Error number 51: Internal error

Something has gone wrong inside BASIC itself. Probable causes: a bug may exist in BASIC itself; your disk copy of BASIC may be damaged; or an error in your program (especially if your program uses POKE or USR) may result in the mistaken modification of a BASIC memory location.

Error number 52: Bad file number

An instruction uses a file number of an unopen file, or the file number is outside the legal range of file numbers.

Error number 53: File not found

The file name does not exist. Look for a misspelled file name, and make sure that the entire filespec is correct, including disk drive and subdirectory.

Error number 54: Bad file mode

The instruction attempts an operation that conflicts with the file specification. PUT and GET require files opened as random-access, not sequential. When OPEN is using a string expression for the file mode, OPEN requires that the mode be A, I, O, or R.

Error number 55: `File already open`

The file is already open. Either this is an attempt to `OPEN` a file for the second time, or the program tries to `KILL` an open file.

Error number 57: `Device I/O error`

An input/output error occurs from which DOS cannot recover.

Error number 58: `File already exists`

NAME tries to rename a file with a name that already exists in the same directory.

Error number 61: `Disk full`

No more disk space exists on the referenced disk.

Error number 62: `Input past end`

`INPUT` tries to read past the end of the file. Use the `EOF` function to be sure that the program does not attempt to read more data than the file contains. Also, be sure that the file is open for input, not for output or append.

Error number 63: `Bad record number`

The record number is outside the legal range of 1 through 16,777,215.

Error number 64: `Bad filename`

The file name does not follow the rules for a legal file name.

Error number 66: `Direct statement in file`

`LOAD` or `CHAIN` loads a program file that contains an instruction in direct mode format (without a line number).

Error number 67: `Too many files`

No disk space remains for more file directory entries, or a file's specifications are illegal.

Error number 68: `Device unavailable`

No such device exists for the file specified. The device has been disabled or has not been installed.

Error number 69: Communication buffer overflow

No more room exists in the communication buffer area. Either process the input characters faster, create a larger communication buffer (use /C when you start BASIC), slow down the speed of arriving characters, or change communications protocols so that your program can tell the other computer to stop sending data until your program can catch up.

Error number 70: Permission denied

The program is not allowed to read or write to the file. Either the program attempts to write on a write-protected floppy disk (that is, one using tape to cover the notch), or the UNLOCK range does not match the previous LOCK, or in a network environment another program already has exclusive control of the file.

Error number 71: Disk not ready

A floppy disk drive's door is open, or no floppy disk is in the drive. An ON ERROR GOTO routine can recover from this condition.

Error number 72: Disk media error

An error occurs on a disk, probably due to a damaged floppy disk. Try recovering whatever data you can by copying to a new floppy disk. Then use the DOS FORMAT command to reformat the bad disk or discard the bad disk.

Error number 73: Advanced feature

The instruction uses a reserved word that is not implemented in your version of BASIC.

Error number 74: Rename across disks

A file being renamed must remain on the same disk. The new name cannot specify a different disk drive.

Error number 75: Path/File access error

A path or file name specifies an inaccessible file. Probable causes: the file name is really a directory name or volume label, or your program tries writing to a file marked with the read-only attribute.

Error number 76: `Path not found`

The path does not exist. Probable causes: you misspelled a directory name, you specified the wrong disk drive, or you have the wrong floppy disk in the disk drive.

INDEX

D

E

G

H

L

Q

R

T